The New Racial Regime

'An extraordinary theoretical and methodological engagement with Cedric Robinson's indispensable conceptualisation of "racial regimes." Simultaneously an intellectual tribute and expansive explication, *The New Racial Regime* works from an archival foundation of Black and Indigenous, liberationist and anti-colonialist thinkers, honing analytical tools that make sense of the ongoing racial reconstructionist moment.'
—Dylan Rodríguez, author of *White Reconstruction: Domestic Warfare and the Logics of Genocide*

'A vital and well-written analysis of the regimes of racial capitalism that have reinvented themselves within the past decade. Lentin's analysis of white supremacy's dynamism and durability is incisive and she offers readers terrific suggestions about how to organise for change in a world where evil sometimes feels insurmountable.'
—Steven Salaita, author of *An Honest Living: A Memoir of Peculiar Itineraries*

'Thinking through and with Cedric Robinson's framework of "racial regime", Alana Lentin offers a powerful reminder that, without an emphatic rejection of colonialism and imperialism, white supremacy, Zionism, and antiblack racial oppression will endure in our intellectual and political projects. Accessible, rigorous, and unequivocal, *The New Racial Regime* is the principled treatise we sorely need in this "time of monsters".'
—Charisse Burden-Stelly, author of *Black Scare/Red Scare: Theorizing Capitalist Racism in the United States*

'A crucial theorisation of the new "racial regime", where fervent support for genocide, and the rejection of racial equality have become components of a new common sense. From the war on critical race theory, through to the legitimation of genocide through a discourse of "decolonization", Lentin's book offers deep insights into just how deep the new racial regime characterises our new social landscape. Social problems of our time need to be theorised, and Lentin's book provides us with the vital theorisation we need in order to fight back.'
—Ali Meghji, Associate Professor in Social Inequalities, University of Cambridge

The New Racial Regime

Recalibrations of White Supremacy

Alana Lentin

Foreword by
Elizabeth Peters Robinson

PLUTO PRESS

First published 2025 by Pluto Press
New Wing, Somerset House, Strand, London WC2R 1LA
and Pluto Press, Inc.
1930 Village Center Circle, 3-834, Las Vegas, NV 89134

www.plutobooks.com

Copyright © Alana Lentin 2025

The right of Alana Lentin to be identified as the author of this work has been asserted in accordance with the Copyright, Designs and Patents Act 1988.

British Library Cataloguing in Publication Data
A catalogue record for this book is available from the British Library

ISBN 978 0 7453 4796 7   Paperback
ISBN 978 0 7453 5119 3   PDF
ISBN 978 0 7453 4797 4   EPUB

This book is printed on paper suitable for recycling and made from fully managed and sustained forest sources. Logging, pulping and manufacturing processes are expected to conform to the environmental standards of the country of origin.

Typeset by Stanford DTP Services, Northampton, England

Simultaneously printed in the United Kingdom and United States of America

EU GPSR Authorised Representative
LOGOS EUROPE, 9 rue Nicolas Poussin, 17000, LA ROCHELLE, France
Email: Contact@logoseurope.eu

For Noam and Partho

Contents

Foreword by Elizabeth Peters Robinson   viii
Prologue and Acknowledgements   xii

Introduction: Stitching the New Racial Regime   1
1. 'A Drop of Poison': What the War on Critical Race Theory Tells Us about the New Racial Regime   35
2. On History and the Technologies of White Forgetting   77
3. Institutionalising Dissent in a Time of Genocide   124
4. Capturing Indigeneity, Colonising Decolonisation   173
5. Against Definitions   219

Index   263

Foreword

Elizabeth Peters Robinson

Even as Alana Lentin's manuscript, *The New Racial Regime: Recalibrations of White Supremacy* wends its way through the publication process, yet another racial regime is being constructed and embraced with enthusiasm in many quarters. From national government corridors, to local ones, to corporate boardrooms, to the blogosphere, to bumper stickers we are being advised that much is amiss. We are warned that sweeping reforms must erase 'DEI', various efforts towards social equity including gender, environmental prescriptions, public health programs and much more. Absolutely, the 'T' must be dropped from 'LGBQ'. All we need do is step aside. Of course, some are complying while others are not, and among the latter is Alana Lentin who assures us that this is just another iteration of white supremacist fantasy.

While I did not know Alana's work when I was asked to write a foreword for this manuscript, I was told that she engages in depth with *Forgeries of Memory and Meaning* ... and with some of the work Cedric Robinson and I had done together. I soon found that she had studied not only *Forgeries* but also *Black Marxism* and other of his works. Moreover, her writing and argument draw on the work of scholars, theorists and activists who preceded Cedric or were contemporaries (e.g. C.L.R. James, W.E.B. Du Bois, Sylvia Wynter, A. Sivanandan, Oliver Cox, Amílcar Cabral), many of his contemporaries (Angela Davis, Ruth Wilson Gilmore), many who studied with him (e.g. Robin Kelley, H.L.T. Quan, Damien Sojoyner, Tiffany Willoughby-Herard), and still more who have engaged with his work after his demise. This extended family gave me courage to take on this task with the caveat that I am neither a scholar nor a theorist. Thus my words should not be confused or conflated with Cedric's considerable written record. However, media have been my home and Cedric my partner and at this historical moment, I think *Forgeries* is instructive, particularly in Lentin's hands. Cedric's intentions and mine have always been internationalist and liberationist, and, I think, we both understood that media could be used against us collectively or in our service. Alana Lentin's work seems similarly based and she surely moves beyond the terrain with which we were most familiar.

Cedric and I and many of our kindred often noted that every few years another paternalistic often racist initiative, a new theory of race etc., would emerge, something else to assure us that we needn't worry about constructing a historical record that included the many, not just the few. Frequently those constructs have fallen within the bounds of science, especially physical sciences. Others have abandoned any scientific premises, opting for and/or feeling comfortable with bald efforts to regain ill-gotten ground or bury yet again histories that expand Western versions to include so many more of us, and that have had to be excavated repeatedly. European and American histories are riddled with examples, but I will mention only a couple as illustrative drawn from shared experiences.

While a graduate student in social and political anthropology at a Research 1 (doctoral) university, I attended a lecture by a physical anthropologist who was examining cranial remains of Africans to establish the routes of Bantu migrations from parts of West and Central Africa to southern Africa. He explained that he was documenting these routes based on the presence or absence of a small congenital hole in skulls found in a morgue in South Africa. I don't remember the frequency with which he found this evidence, but I do remember the period – the mid to late 1970s. At that time South Africa's apartheid regime was experiencing increasing challenges from within and without as a United Nations resolution calling for divestment from South Africa had been launched and was growing. I also recall that the cranial samples had been gathered from a South African morgue that held unclaimed and unidentified deceased individuals. And I recall that the professor was South African and classified as white by the South African regime. Certainly at issue at the time was whether Europeans or Black Africans were the original settlers in South Africa with the white settler population claiming to have come to an unpopulated land. Ah, the serendipitous discovery! On the occasion of the lecture the nature of the South African regime was never mentioned, nor was the professor's possible stake in the game. And what of the frequency with which individuals ended in paupers' morgues unclaimed despite rather robust kinship systems. None of this was queried in the event.

While this is simply a sketch drawn from my own recollections, there are innumerable documented instances from which one might draw a critique. Consider the work of early anthropologists like E.E. Evans-Pritchard who went to Sudan at the behest of the Anglo-Egyptian government to study the Nuer. He recounted their hostility, their refusal to carry his considerable belongings another half mile to a shady area. He apparently failed to see his presence as part of an occupying colonial entity. For a more critical perspective, see Stephen J. Gould's *The Mismeasure of Man* or Robert V. Guthrie's *Even the Rat Was White*. Gould was specifically debunking some of the specious arguments put forth in Cyril Burt's research on I.Q. which were substantially based on fabricated data. Burt's 'science' earned him a British knighthood and would later be used to 'prove' racial inferiority in the hands of the likes of Arthur Jensen and Charles Murray. Beyond the academy, we are witnessing on a daily basis the claim that the oft-repeated lie becomes truth. And we are living in a moment of controlled media where the test is frequently engaged.

If we are paying attention, as Alana Lentin encourages, we can follow this new racial regime as it is constructed before our very eyes. Just now in the US and elsewhere, we are apprised of the fragility of our access to knowledge through what has been known as the 'world wide web'. Overnight, websites we considered open have been disappeared, access to sites and the information found in them is seemingly 'missing' or unavailable. The very notion of open access seems to have been compromised and whole categories are being expunged along very specific subject lines with attempts to erase references to race, gender, ethnicity, etc. A private internet archive, 'The Wayback Machine', with a mission to document such web material estimates that hundreds of thousands of sites have been expunged in a matter of days.

If this sounds alarmist or defeatist, we must consider, as Cedric and Alana advise us, that these regimes are fragile, unstable and subject to rejection and resistance. There is refusal to be found on the streets, from legal institutions, and internationally. 'Push back' is real and powerful.

Finally, it is important that we recognize social conditions that suggest ways forward and here I make a deep bow to Alana Lentin. One inescapable reality as sure as attempts at repression is that while racism and racial regimes move and change sometimes with alacrity, so too do new struggles and new alliances. In reading *The New Racial Regime,* I have encountered struggles that I know little of but that have had and will have repercussions globally. Of course, she is situated in Australia and thus is attuned to Aboriginal rights and history and the significance there and globally of struggles for Indigenous rights to land and other rights of full personhood. For me, her call evoked 'Land Back' movements that most often are imagined as improbable if not impossible. For both of us, it demands taking up Palestine. The last piece that Cedric and I wrote focused on Ferguson, Missouri and the killing of Michael Brown at the hands of Ferguson police. Regardless of the exact circumstances of Brown's death, death of Black people through official violence was and is a near daily occurrence. Palestinians who expressed solidarity with the Black community in Ferguson did so out of a sense of solidarity even before genocide began to unfold in Gaza and beyond. This gift of caring, of common cause must be engaged and engaged quickly.

March 2025

Prologue and Acknowledgements

> You want to be an intellectual? Then you must resist. Otherwise, you and your education are useless.
>
> Bassel al-Araj

In the final paragraph of *Black Marxism: The Making of the Black Radical Tradition* by Cedric J. Robinson, published in 1983, he observed the 'threat of physical annihilation' faced by Black people in the face of capitalist-produced famines and the 'near genocidal proportions' of 'mass unemployment and conditions of housing and health'. These terrors were compounded by the 'systematic attack on radical Black polities, and the manipulation of venal political puppets [which] are now routine occurrences'.[1] Over 40 years later, these systematic attacks are still routine. Understanding them is not helped by an unwillingness in many quarters to contend with the fact that fascism, as the Black revolutionary George Jackson remarked in *Blood in My Eye*, 'is still a developing movement'.[2] Because fascism is a response to class struggle within the constraints imposed by capitalism,[3] it has neither been resolved nor, in the current conjuncture, could it be.

A decade after the publication of *Black Marxism*, in the 1990s, Robinson wrote of the 'current controversy' of 'anti(post) modernist multiculturalism'[4] which resulted in a 'campaign of deterrence and containment against the democratization and radicalization of

---

1 Cedric J. Robinson, *Black Marxism: The Making of the Black Radical Tradition* (Chapel Hill, N.C.: University of North Carolina Press, 2000), p. 318.
2 George Jackson, *Blood in My Eye* (Baltimore, MD: Black Classic Press, 1972), p. 135. The poverty of many analyses of fascism is their failure to recognise this and to dwell instead on the question of analogy with the Italian and German regimes of the mid-twentieth century. Alberto Toscano, *Late Fascism: Race, Capitalism and the Politics of Crisis* (Brooklyn, NY: Verso, 2023).
3 Jackson, *Blood in My Eye*.
4 Cedric J. Robinson, 'Ota Benga's Flight through Geronimo's Eyes: Tales of Science and Multiculturalism', in *Cedric Robinson: On Racial Capitalism, Black*

knowledge'.[5] His aim, however, was not to appeal for the rescuing of academic multiculturalism, but to trace the role played by pre-modernist 'discourses in alterity' in consecrating 'the West as *the* civilisation, and the European white as *the* conscious agency of humanity's development'.[6] Although the Black and anticolonial studies movements had succeeded in puncturing this dominant mode of thought, Robinson warns that the 'racial fabulists' who had developed it 'remain eminent, powerful and committed'. He thus concluded that any success will be 'momentary' in the face of those determined to 'preserve their systems of knowledge for as long as the social order they "legitimate" endures'.[7]

For this reason, and due to the lessons gleaned from my engagement with Cedric Robinson's work, I laughed wryly when I was told some years ago, upon proposing to write what was initially to be a book about the war on critical race theory, that by the time it would be published 'all that' would have blown over. It was clear to me then that the battle declared on the 'poison' of CRT, woke, and diversity, equity and inclusion was just another front opened to combat the knowledge developed by Black, Indigenous and colonised peoples as a weapon of resistance against the barbarism of western civilisation. Donald Trump's inaugurating action to 'abolish all discriminatory diversity, equity, and inclusion nonsense' in January 2025 was thus no surprise.[8] Even aviation collisions, he claimed, are due to a 'diversity push' in air traffic controller recruitment![9] Just as Robinson warned decades previously, such assaults

---

Internationalism, and Cultures of Resistance, ed. H.L.T. Quan (London: Pluto Press, 2019), p. 111.
5 H.L.T. Quan, 'Emancipatory Social Inquiry: Democratic Anarchism and the Robinsonian Method', *African Identities* 11, no. 2 (May 1, 2013), p. 122.
6 Robinson, 'Ota Benga's Flight through Geronimo's Eyes: Tales of Science and Multiculturalism', p. 111.
7 Ibid., 122.
8 Donald J. Trump, 'Remarks by President Trump at the World Economic Forum', *The White House*, January 23, 2025, https://tinyurl.com/4zm6dbb3 (last accessed February 2025).
9 Jake Horton and Lucy Gilder, 'Fact-Checking Trump's Claims about Diversity Schemes and the Washington Plane Crash', *BBC News*, January 31, 2025, https://tinyurl.com/4p6kt7tb (last accessed February 2025).

are the 'form assumed by anti-democracy for the moment'.[10] They are thus not apropos antifascism writ large. Consequently, this time must be seized, not in the attempt to gather and store the crumbs dropped by liberal institutions to pacify insurgent thinkers and activists but, as the Black radical scholar Momodou Taal put it, 'to demand more'.

I am honoured that David Shulman at Pluto Press saw beyond the blinkered belief that the problem I wished to interrogate was a flash in the pan. He allowed me the freedom to move far beyond the proposal I initially pitched to write what would become *The New Racial Regime*, a more consequent engagement with the analytical and methodological horizons opened by Cedric Robinson's idea of racial regimes.

Throughout the research and writing of this book, I have been so incredibly lucky to have been supported in what I hope is a somewhat successful journey of intellectual expansion by many people. My developing understanding of Cedric Robinson's thinking, particularly on racial capitalism, owes so much to Kieron Turner and the many conversations we have had over the last years. Joshua Myers' contribution, not only to knowledge on Robinson, but also to making us see his project within that of Black study and struggle, and what 'ultimately mattered ... "the work"', has been invaluable to me.[11] I was honoured to have been able to share space and learn from Myers and Robin D.G. Kelley at an event organised by James Renton of the International Centre on Racism at Edge Hill University to mark the 40th anniversary of the publication of *Black Marxism*. I was also fortunate to attend the 'Archives Unbound' conference held to inaugurate the Cedric J. Robinson and Elizabeth P. Robinson archives at University of California Santa Barbara in May 2024 and to hear many students and comrades of the Robinsons share their knowledge. *Millennials are Killing Capitalism*, the podcast hosted by Jared Ware and Joshua Briond, continues to be a port of call for deepening my understanding. I am particularly grateful to the participants of the *Black*

---

10   Robinson, 'Ota Benga's Flight through Geronimo's Eyes', p. 123.
11   Joshua Myers, *Cedric Robinson: The Time of the Black Radical Tradition*, Black Lives (Cambridge, UK ; Medford, MA: Polity Press, 2021), p. 241.

Marxism, Counterinsurgency Field Manual, and *Blood in My Eye* readings groups led by Jared, and for the many incisive conversations with Palestinian scholars and activists held on their platform since October 2023 for helping hone many of the ideas in these pages. I have also been fortunate to have been invited to have nourishing conversations on many of the subjects broached in the book with Chantelle Lewis, Momodou Taal, and Khadijah Diskin on the podcasts *Surviving Society* and *The Malcolm Effect*.

Radical scholarship on race generally goes unbacked. A key avenue of support was the crowdsourced research I reached out for among the global community of antiracist scholars. Penny Rabiger helped me populate my spreadsheet with all sorts of titbits from the UK outrage orbit. Many others gave their time generously to advise me on key aspects of the book as it developed. They are Kian Aspinall, Debbie Bargallie, Joshua Briond, Alex Charnley, Souheir Edelbi, Jairo Fúnez-Flores, Ali Meghji, Lin, Michael Richmond, Tom Six, Keiran Stewart-Assheton, and Anna Younes. I also enjoyed conversations with P.M. Irvin, Noah Tesfaye, Jasmine Kelekay, and Alexandra Gessesse during my trips to Northern California including a visit to the Freedom Archives in Berkeley. In 2023, I benefited from discussing some of the ideas in the book at a seminar organised by Bridget Byrne, with support from Sudip Sen, at the Centre on the Dynamics of Ethnicity at the University of Manchester. Joining the Founding Collective of the Institute for the Critical Study of Zionism in 2023 has been a particular honour. I am grateful to the insights offered by Rabab Abdulhadi, Emmaia Gelman, Christine Hong, Amira Jarmakani, Sean Malloy, and Dylan Rodríguez regarding Zionist attacks on ethnic studies and the insidiousness of 'hate' and 'safety' as approaches to purported antiracism.

'The circle', the group chat I formed to share knowledge, bemoan the state of the world, and bind bonds of solidarity has been a rock to which to cling throughout. No words can adequately express the horror of these times. Rising to the measure demanded of the moment, Marilena Indelicato galvanised us to do what matters, as Cedric said, to provide what we can to families in Gaza standing steadfast on their land and tending to the future generation of Palestinians. A special mention goes, as always, to Ronit Lentin, my radical intellectual guide and razor-sharp editor.

For all who struggle collectively for the liberation of the oppressed, I hope my book can clarify some things. It can do little more. In writing it, I was guided by the lines with which Cedric Robinson ended *Black Marxism*:

> 'It is not the province of one people to be the solution or the problem. But a civilization maddened by its own perverse assumptions and contradictions is loose in the world. A Black radical tradition formed in opposition to that civilization and conscious of itself is one part of the solution. Whether the other oppositions generated from within Western society and without will mature remains problematical. But for now we must be as one.'[12]

---

12 Cedric J. Robinson, *Black Marxism*, p. 318.

Introduction:
Stitching the New Racial Regime

[As] we have recounted, there were no historical grounds for the dream that a permanent, stable racial regime could be instituted. Notwithstanding, the new fabulists in the industries of motion pictures gave it their best shot.[1]

... anti-wokeness is the perfect example of the functioning of the racial regime.[2]

The 'racial reckoning' of 2020 sought to 'neutralise' the 'Black rage' which followed the state killing of George Floyd on 25 May of that year.[3] Almost as soon as the Speaker of the US House of Representatives Nancy Pelosi had hung up her kente cloth scarf, as the British Labour Party leader Keir Starmer had got up off his bended knee, and as institutions had mandated unconscious bias trainings, the first shots of the 'war on critical race theory' were fired, followed rapidly by 'the war on woke'. The warriors sought to claw back any accommodation made to quell the movement that demanded an end to the racial state's killing of Black people. Moving rapidly beyond its USian source, 'le wokesime' dovetailed with concomitant panics about 'Indigenisme' and 'Islamoleftism' to send French elites into a tailspin of 'violent clampdowns' tar-

---

1 Cedric James Robinson, *Forgeries of Memory and Meaning: Blacks and the Regimes of Race in American Theater and Film before World War II* (Chapel Hill, NC: University of North Carolina Press, 2007), p. 81.
2 Robin D.G. Kelley and Jordan T. Camp, 'Against Pessimism', *Conjuncture Series 2*, 2022, www.youtube.com/watch?v=euoC8k3iB3o (last accessed October 2022).
3 Too Black, 'Laundering Black Rage', *Black Agenda Report*, 2022, https://tinyurl.com/afethehz (last accessed July 2022).

geting their critics with repressive laws and aggressive policing.[4] A movement of cantankerous right-wing historians rose up to 'reclaim history', publishing blog posts on 'the constructive and beneficent role of the British in India'[5] and on how 'rather than excoriate him as a racist, we should praise Churchill for resisting the tides of a less tolerant era with eloquence and courage'.[6] Raging on into 2024, amid this phase of Israel's genocide of the Palestinian people in Gaza, the liberal Israeli press bemoaned the 'woke threat' provoking pro-Palestine group-think among western youth.

Nothing about these attempts to stifle antiracist resistance is new. There is nothing particular to the sociology of 'anti-wokeism' that cannot be summarised simply as the white supremacist negation of radical Black, Indigenous and anticolonial consciousness and its potential to sow the seeds for revolutionary action, and thus the necessity to bring it to heel. Instead, they are a window onto what the Black radical political scientist, Cedric J. Robinson called racial regimes. The Black radical historian Robin D.G. Kelley, a student of Robinson, remarked in a 2022 interview that 'anti-wokeness is the perfect example of the functioning of the racial regime'.[7] *The New Racial Regime* starts with the war on critical race theory, expanding from there to interrogate a wider question: How is a racial common sense produced and reproduced today? Why does race remain a central mechanism for organising the material and structural relations between groups of people who are constituted as wholly different from each other? How is this fundamentally fictive process of differentiation represented to us through a variety of media? How do these representations change, often contradicting each other? In short, how do we weave a way through what Robinson insisted was the intrinsically chaotic nature of race's manufacture?

---

4   Harrison Stetler, 'Emmanuel Macron's Government Is Gagging Its Critics', *Jacobin*, 2023, https://tinyurl.com/yc7und2b (last accessed January 2025).
5   Rohan P. Fernando, 'Indian Commemorations of British Legacies – History Reclaimed', 2023, https://tinyurl.com/yk7bkpt6 (last accessed February 2023).
6   Richard M. Langworth, 'Churchill and Language: Hearsay Doesn't Count: The Truth about Churchill's "Racist" Epithets – History Reclaimed', 2022, https://tinyurl.com/bdfn4vch (last accessed August 2024).
7   Kelley and Camp, 'Against Pessimism'.

INTRODUCTION: STITCHING THE NEW RACIAL REGIME

The only way to stand firm in the face of the chaos sown by race is to try to keep track of the interactions between ostensibly disparate locations and the interconnected dynamics they produce. For example, towards the tail-end of the 'postracial era' in 2014, Cedric and Elizabeth Robinson noted that the killing of Michael Brown, which fired Black rebellion in Ferguson, Missouri, spreading across the US with global reverberations, had been preceded by 'horrific civilian deaths in Gaza'. It looped back to Ferguson via the 'militarised police force'[8] which 'trained with Israeli police and military units' and murdered that young man and so many others.[9] They wrote, 'in the past racial oppression had been overt' but 'it is now submerged in a "post-racial" nation' which reverses 'the freedom movement's achievements' while concealing its operations 'in race projects like the war on drugs'. 'Once you have feasted on WMDs in Iraq', they remarked, 'it is no stretch really to seriously entertain the notion that the immigrant children from Central America are a terrorist threat.'[10]

The Robinsons drew attention to the fact that race is never one thing and discourse is a trickster. Racial oppression was once more overt, to be sure, but it was never secure; it was never inevitably going to work. The levels of discursive sophistication increased as a function of how hard racial mechanisms had to work while concealing their operations and fending off resistance at the same time. The rise of insurgent movements on the ground in Ferguson, in Gaza, at Standing Rock, and on the streets of towns and cities across racial states, exploding in the summer of 2020, made those operations more difficult to conceal, easier to call out and trip up. The response from the side of power was an attempt to re-seed confusion.

As I write, the genocide enacted on the people of Gaza by the Zionist colony in Palestine enters a new phase as US President Donald Trump pledges to 'take over' the strip, 'own it' and 'develop

---
8   Cedric J. Robinson and Elisabeth Robinson, 'The Killing in Ferguson', in *Cedric Robinson: On Racial Capitalism, Black Internationalism, and Cultures of Resistance*, ed. H.L.T. Quan (London: Pluto Press, 2019), pp. 354–55, p. 354.
9   TeamEbony, 'The Ferguson/Palestine Connection', *Ebony*, 2014, https://tinyurl.com/494efy6h (last accessed August 2024).
10 Robinson and Robinson, 'The Killing in Ferguson', p. 355.

it'.[11] A movement galvanised by the Palestinian resistance in which millions have protested, organised, boycotted and occupied in the streets, squares and university lawns, faces *both* the overt oppression of the carceral state and the soft power of electoralism. Fascism which, as the imprisoned intellectual George Jackson claimed, can be defined as 'reform',[12] and thus invariably appearing in myriad forms, including what the former New York Black Panther Party leader Dhoruba bin-Wahad calls 'democratic fascism',[13] is always here, influencing the masses and institutions through elites.[14] The resources to oppose it are under attack from multiple directions. Attempts to blunt the 'weapon of theory' without which 'no one as yet has successfully practiced revolution' abound.[15] They come from without but also from inside movements that profess the radical transformation of the conditions of oppression created under racial capitalism, but often cede to reformism and anti-intellectualism. However, resistance and critique endure. As Robinson wrote of the protagonists of the Black radical tradition, their purpose 'became the overthrow of the whole race-based structure'.[16] Their thought and action help us to see the mechanisms powering that structure and to attack the racial regime.

The new racial regime is not new, but renewed, restitched from old cloth, recalibrated and recursive. In this introductory chapter, I explore the racial regime as an analytic and a methodology for tracing the ideological constructs that prop up racial capitalism conceived by Cedric Robinson in his 2007 book, *Forgeries of*

---

11   Kevin Liptak, 'Trump Says US Will "Take over" Gaza Strip and Doesn't Rule out Using American Troops', *CNN*, (4 February 2025), https://tinyurl.com/ywe6s5be (last accessed February 2025).
12   George Jackson, *Blood in My Eye* (Baltimore, MD: Black Classic Press, 1972), p. 58.
13   Dhoruba bin-Wahad, 'Rise of Militarized Policing in Response to Black Dissent', *Black Agenda Report*, 2024, https://tinyurl.com/nhkaky5k (last accessed August 2024).
14   Jackson, *Blood in My Eye*, p. 5.
15   Amilcár Cabral, 'The Weapon of Theory', in *Address Delivered to the First Tricontinental Conference of the Peoples of Asia, Africa and Latin America Held in Havana in January, 1966* (Havana, 1966), p. 129.
16   Cedric J. Robinson, *Black Marxism. The Making of the Black Radical Tradition*, First edition (London: Zed Books, 1983), p. 32.

INTRODUCTION: STITCHING THE NEW RACIAL REGIME

Memory and Meaning: Blacks and the Regimes of Race in American Theater and Film before World War II.[17] The analytic of the racial regime places 'questions of culture and representation, of cultural productions, and of aesthetics, politics, and power' which are, Stuart Hall reminds us, 'of absolute centrality' for conceptualising 'the question of race itself'.[18] Robinson helps us connect this to the material demands of the state and capital.[19]

The racial regime is made up of representational mythologies that tend to throw us off course, because it is their function to do so. These mythologies are constantly recalibrated in response to attack from below, when as Robin Kelley puts it, 'you're running for your life you're trying to create a mythology ... to make it seem like, you know, the emperor actually does have clothes, when really he doesn't'.[20] The work is grounded in that of Black radical thinkers active during the interregnum of the 1930s who demonstrated how emergent European fascist movements were creating the conditions for bourgeois capital to expand 'its domination and expropriation to the Third World', thus making fascism central rather than aberrant to the nation-state and colonialism.[21] This purview, developed by thinkers such as C.L.R. James, W.E.B. Du Bois and George Padmore, to name some of the most prominent among them, sets out the terms elaborated by Robinson for seeing how the various factions of capital have always struggled with each other, some appearing in more liberal and others in more fascist forms.[22] These Black radical thinkers provide the basis for understanding why it should be of no surprise that neoliberal elites profess commitments to antiracism while deepening and

---

17   Robinson, *Forgeries of Memory and Meaning*.
18   Ibid., p. 330.
19   Although it came out too late to be included in my discussion, the interview series on *Forgeries of Memory and Meaning* with Mtume Gant by Millennials Are Killing Capitalism Live is recommended as a guide. Mtume Gant and Jared Ware, 'Discussing Cedric Robinson's *Forgeries of Memory & Meaning* (Part 1)', 2025, https://tinyurl.com/2bnxd8h6 (last accessed January 2025).
20   Kelley and Camp, 'Against Pessimism'.
21   Cedric J. Robinson, *Black Marxism: The Making of the Black Radical Tradition*, Second edition (Chapel Hill, NC: University of North Carolina Press, 2000), p. 28.
22   Kelley and Camp, 'Against Pessimism'.

widening 'organised abandonment' at the same time.[23] *The New Racial Regime* builds on this work to examine our current conjuncture. How does race continue to confuse us? An answer, I suggest, is the existence of overlapping, sometimes contradictory, and in all cases power-building racial regimes.

A RACIAL REGIME ANALYTIC

> The racial regime is this nimble force that continuously recapitulates the idea that Africans have to be controlled, maintained, have to be disciplined through representation.[24]

With some exceptions,[25] most of the existing work that refers to Robinson's conception of racial regimes tends to cite the clearest definition provided in the preface to *Forgeries*:

> Racial regimes are constructed social systems in which race is proposed as a justification for relations of power. While necessarily articulated with accruals of power, the covering conceit of a racial regime is a makeshift patchwork masquerading as memory and the immutable.[26]

---

23 Ruth Wilson Gilmore, *Abolition Geography: Essays towards Liberation*, ed. Brenna Bhandar and Alberto Toscano (London; New York: Verso, 2022).
24 Joshua Myers and Adam McNeil, 'Cedric Robinson: The Time of the Black Radical Tradition', *New Books in African American Studies*, 2022, https://tinyurl.com/3jc7f9dm (last accessed August 2024).
25 Cf. Brenna. Bhandar, *Colonial Lives of Property: Law, Land, and Racial Regimes of Ownership* (Durham, NC: Duke University Press, 2018); César 'Che' Rodríguez, Jared Ware, and Joshua Briond, '"Record the Noise" – César 'Che' Rodríguez on Racial Regimes and Blues Epistemology in the Lead-up to the Oscar Grant Moment', 2023, https://tinyurl.com/4fmz4c5u (last accessed August 2024); H.L.T. Quan, 'Emancipatory Social Inquiry: Democratic Anarchism and the Robinsonian Method', *African Identities* 11, no. 2 (1 May 2013): 117–32; Jordan T. Camp, '"We Know This Place": Neoliberal Racial Regimes and the Katrina Circumstance', *American Quarterly* 61 (2009): 693–717; Brian Williams, '"The Fabric of Our Lives"?: Cotton, Pesticides, and Agrarian Racial Regimes in the U.S. South', *Annals of the American Association of Geographers* 111, no. 2 (23 February 2021): 422–39.
26 Robinson, *Forgeries of Memory and Meaning*, p. xii

The use of the term 'social system' implies that racial regimes are structures or institutions in themselves. But the idea is much less rigid, more deceptive and tractable. Racial regimes are composed of a myriad of histories, theories, hypotheses, studies, representations and lies. As César 'Che' Rodríguez explains, racial regimes are historically and geographically specific. Thus 'the racial regime in Oakland is different from say the racial regime organised around the spectre of the Mara in El Salvador or the Muslim in Northern India'. While there are comparable factors between them, 'there are different discourses being produced and different political economic practices that are being justified as a result of them'.[27] As Yousuf Al-Bulushi summarises, racial regimes are best understood as 'conjuncturally specific and fluid formations that must constantly adapt in the face of a Black radical tradition' than as 'unilateral structural determinants'.[28]

Crucially, racial regimes are made to appear natural – just the way things are – existing outside of any traceable history. In theorising the 'racial regime of ownership' at work in settler colonialism, Brenna Bhandar describes racial regimes as the 'conceptual apparatus' which bind the justification of private property to a racialised vision of who is human.[29] We can see this most clearly in the abiding idea, used to nullify Indigenous life, that to consider land as property is to be fully human. Racism too is naturalised as observable in the common notion that all peoples have always been, and are always bound to be, racist. However, as Robinson insists, 'racial regimes do possess history, that is discernible origins and mechanisms of assembly'.[30] They are successful because they intrinsically hide their histories and social relations. Hence, we are tasked with the role of aggressively exposing them. Ongoing expositions due to oppressive contexts revealing themselves, becoming unliveable and tipping over into protest, in turn

---

27 Rodríguez et al., 'Record the Noise'.
28 Yousuf Al-Bulushi, 'Thinking Racial Capitalism and Black Radicalism from Africa: An Intellectual Geography of Cedric Robinson's World-System', *Geoforum* 132 (2022): 252–62, p. 260.
29 Bhandar, *Colonial Lives of Property*, p. 14.
30 Ibid.

trigger adjustments to the racial regime. It is this recursive process that *The New Racial Regime* attends to.

To trace the production of racial regimes historically and situate them within their social context, then, 'threatens their authority and ... saps their vitality', undermining 'their founding myths'.[31] As I shall return to through the course of this book, racial regimes are ultimately 'unstable truth systems' that 'may "collapse" under the weight of their own artifices, practices and apparatuses'.[32] They therefore 'tend to wear thin over time', requiring considerable effort by 'interested cultural and social powers' to ensure their invention, dissemination and maintenance'.[33] Since so much effort is required to keep alive what are obvious fictions, when stripped back, rarely are racial regimes completely reinvented. Rather, 'regime maintenance takes precedence over wholesale reconstruction'.[34] Robinson focuses on the racial regime which was central to the building of US American national identity around 'a new whiteness'. The ways in which whiteness is partially detached from actual white bodies and integrated into a politics and a consequent individual consciousness beyond the 'west' signals the adaptive nature of the racial regime. This whiteness, which always already implies supremacism, is recalibrated in various ways over time, eventually becoming attached to what Dylan Rodríguez calls 'multiculturalist white supremacy'.[35] The capacity for recalibration inherent to white supremacy demonstrates that, despite appearances to the contrary, the world has not exited a racial regime where whiteness, reproduced through capitalism and ongoing forms of imperialism, has been superseded.

Racial regimes are composed of conflicting ideas including ostensibly antiracist ones, as Chapters 3 and 4 discuss in different ways. Many public institutions and corporations may appear to challenge racism superficially but can actually be upholding racialist structures. The same is true for scholarship. As I show in Chapter 3, some

---

31 Robinson, *Forgeries of Memory and Meaning*, p. xiii.
32 Ibid., p. xii.
33 Ibid.
34 Ibid., p. xiv.
35 Dylan Rodríguez, *Domestic Warfare and the Logics of Genocide*, First edition (New York: Fordham University Press, 2021).

ideas that either stem from critical race theory itself or emerge from derivations or popular interpretations of some of its tenets, by eliding questions of colonialism and imperialism may create the conditions in which race as a system of global rule is reproduced. The translation of the demand to end the state killing of Black people into more representation in media, politics and workplaces ultimately maintains the racial regime under the guise of challenging it.[36] Likewise, the lauding of any form of political representation by Black, Indigenous or people of colour no matter their political standpoint neglects the important reminder that racialised diversity is entirely consistent with racial capitalism,[37] and mainly serves the empowerment of those whom Dhoruba bin-Wahad calls 'misleaders' and 'the classes that they come from'.[38] These discussions are variably taken up in Chapters 3 and 4.

As long as race remains a useful idea for organising and managing societies, then it will continue to be prioritised. However, this is also the weak point of racial regimes, because in being recycled, they are easier to expose as repeating old tropes and repurposing them for new times. It bears repeating that racial regimes must be so frequently recalibrated because they are constantly challenged by those who they play a role in subjugating. Those who are made to appear as just naturally inferior, irredeemably different, nefariously threatening or enduringly exotic – whatever the script might be – are the people who pick over the bones of racial regimes, leaving them bare and desperate for new flesh.

THE RACIAL REGIME METHODOLOGY

Forgeries of Memory and Meaning is a book about the racialisation of Black people in and through the US American film industry. The

---

36 Too Black, 'Laundering Black Rage'; Alana Lentin, 'Against Representation', *Sydney Review of Books*, 2022, https://tinyurl.com/373s9myf (last accessed July 2022).
37 Gargi Bhattacharyya, *Rethinking Racial Capitalism: Questions of Reproduction and Survival* (Lanham, MD: Rowman & Littlefield International, 2018).
38 Dhoruba bin-Wahad, Jared Ware, and Joshua Briond, 'The Last of the Loud' – Dhoruba bin Wahad, *Philosopher of the Whirlwind*, 2022, https://tinyurl.com/smt6asaj (last accessed September 2024).

book uses film and capitalism as filters for writing Black history. Put another way, it employs a 'black analytics'[39] to show 'how the needs of finance capital, the dominant centre of American commerce in the late nineteenth and early twentieth centuries, determined the construction of successive racial regimes publicised by motion pictures'.[40] The book traces a 'fractious' and 'contested' racial regime which emerges at the end of the nineteenth century with the development of finance capital to determine the shape of race in the twentieth century. The defining feature of this racial regime is that it manifests in reactionary and liberal forms which are both derived from the same transformation of capitalism and are still with us today. The construction of a divide between the two is a mystification that serves to conceal the imbrication of liberalism in a fascism that is always racial.

Robinson traces the representation of Black people, beginning with the Elizabethan period in England,[41] through the birth of American film and into the 'oppositional cinema'[42] of Black directors such as Oscar Micheaux in the late 1930s who 'pushed race movies into explicit political critiques of the American national myth'.[43] Robinson shows the importance of film for the construction of 'a new racial regime' at the end of the nineteenth century, pointing towards the ramifications this still has in the present.[44]

As an art form, film had the capacity to offer 'an otherwise explanation for the conditions and experiences of the Black community'.[45] However, any attempt to use the medium to counter the harmful representations of Black people and present their own counter-narratives was opposed by an adjustment to the racial regime in the form of an amping up of racist representations

---

39 Barnor Hesse, 'Racism's Alterity: The After-Life of Black Sociology', in *Racism and Sociology*, ed. Wulf D. Hund and Alana Lentin, Racism Analysis – Series B: Yearbooks (Berlin: Lit Verlag, 2014).
40 Robinson, *Forgeries of Memory and Meaning*, p. xv
41 Joshua Myers, *Cedric Robinson: The Time of the Black Radical Tradition*, Black Lives (Cambridge: Polity Press, 2021), p. 185.
42 Ibid.
43 Robinson, *Forgeries of Memory and Meaning*, p. xvii.
44 Ibid., p. xiv
45 Myers, *Cedric Robinson*, p. 179.

served by the Golden Age of Hollywood. This cycle of attack and repair can be observed in present-day media representations in which the reactionary and the progressive comingle to crowd out more radical interpretations, using the conjoined efforts of bans or censorship and liberal repackaging to do so. Robinson's mode of analysis causes us to see what happens when there is opposition to dominant narratives, what forces kick into action, and how these narratives often seem to contradict each other in the aim of 'regime maintenance'.[46]

Take the example of *Washington Times* journalist Cheryl K. Chumley's objection to the Walt Disney Company's introduction of 'racially-segregated "affinity groups"' for its staff: '[T]he company of fairy tales and childhood fantasies has "elevated the ideology of critical race theory into a new corporate dogma – and bombarded employees with trainings on "systemic racism," "white privilege," "white fragility," "white saviors" …'. 'Is nothing sacred anymore?' Chumley asks, worried that the fairyland of American childhood dreams will go up in a puff of smoke if Disney workers have to 'fill out a "privilege checklist" that will help guide them to stop engaging in "white dominant culture"'.[47] She ignores Disney's long history of worker exploitation.[48] A documentary made by Abigail Disney, granddaughter of Walt Disney Company co-founder Roy Disney, exposes how checking their privilege is probably the least of these workers' worries. In *The American Dream and Other Fairytales*, Disney employees are shown to be living beneath the poverty line, many sleeping in their cars or going without medical care: 'A custodian would have to work for 2,000 years to make what [Disney CEO] Bob Iger makes in one.'[49] Nothing is sacred, indeed; least of all justice for workers.

---

46 Robinson, *Forgeries of Memory and Meaning*, p. xiv.
47 Cheryl K. Chumley, 'Walt Disney Catches Critical Race Theory Craze – Washington Times', 2021, https://tinyurl.com/3mv6fw6f (last accessed September 2022).
48 Peter Dreier, 'Disney Is Not the Greatest Place on Earth to Work', 2020, https://tinyurl.com/4s4avn3e (last accessed September 2024).
49 Abigail Disney, 'The American Dream and Other Fairy Tales – Official Trailer', *YouTube*, 2022, www.youtube.com/watch?v=rxb2Fol5INI (last accessed October 2022).

The role played by Disney in constructing the spectacles that accompanied and propagated 'race discourse' in the twentieth century is well established.[50] Most concerns lie in Disney's racist representations of Black, Indigenous and other racialised peoples in its classic movies. In recognition of this, while the Global North was having its 'racial reckoning' in 2020, Disney added content warnings to many of its movies, such as *Dumbo* (1941), *Peter Pan* (1953) or *The Jungle Book* (1967). The warning reads, 'These stereotypes were wrong then and they are now. Instead of removing this content, we want to recognize its harmful impact, learn from it, and generate conversations to create a more inclusive future together.'[51]

Disney has tried to address racist representation, not only with content warnings but with the advent of more characters who are not the standard white nor the stereotypically racist, such as *Moana* from Maui and *Coco*, the story of Día de los Muertos, or the Colombian tale, *Encanto*. Outrage at the diversification of Disney characters reached boiling point with the 2023 live action remake of *The Little Mermaid*, starring Black performer, Halle Bailey. One racist commentator on the epidermalisation of fish apparently believes that 'from a scientific perspective, it doesn't make a lot of sense to have someone with darker skin who lives deep in the ocean'.[52] It should not need repeating that mermaids are fictitious beings. Nevertheless, the issue caused unfortunate lines to be written such as: 'Not all sea creatures are white. Rainbow fish are not white. Orcas are not (all) white. Even white fish are mostly black, brown and green.'[53]

---

50   Robinson, *Forgeries of Memory and Meaning*, p. 80.
51   BBC News, 'Disney Updates Content Warning for Racism in Classic Films', *BBC News*, 2020, https://tinyurl.com/mrcpkz34 (last accessed October 2022).
52   David Pescovitz, 'Far-Right Commentator Matt Walsh Explains the "Science" of Why Mermaids Can't Be Black', *Boing Boing*, 2022, https://tinyurl.com/mrtwfy76 (last accessed September 2022).
53   James Felton, 'Racists Are Trying and Failing to Prove That Mermaids Can't Be Black Using "Science"', *Business Insider*, 2022, https://tinyurl.com/36r8pcy8 (last accessed October 2022).

The right's attack on Disney as 'the wokest place on earth'[54] could well have made an appearance in *Forgeries of Memory and Meaning*. Robinson's mode of analysis is apt for linking seemingly diverse problematics to each other. A picture of Disney's 'woke capitalism' would emerge that considered it in relation to the company's long-standing worker exploitation and its founder's appreciation for fascism, as well as the racist representations that pepper its classic productions. As another film aficionado, the Black radical historian Gerald Horne shows, the Communist Party became a powerful force in Hollywood in the mid-twentieth century because 'the labor policies of studios – like Disney – were so draconian and their profits were so significant'.[55] And it was not merely that Disney's creation of racist representations was 'of its time', to use the language of racism apologists today. Walt Disney was a fascist admirer who 'visited Italy and was entertained by Mussolini himself in his private villa' during the making of *Snow White* as well as wining and dining Nazi filmmaker Leni Riefenstahl during her US tour.[56] This was not anomalous. As Robinson reveals, Hollywood was virulently anti-communist and for that reason many of its bosses admired Mussolini, seeing fascism as the adversary of the communism championed by 'international labor'.[57] The success of the Russian Revolution inspired movements across the world, especially in the colonised regions of the South and East, igniting 'the inevitable native insurrections'.[58] It is against this backdrop that Hollywood ventured into the 'jungle film genre', leading on from the earlier 'plantation genre'.

---

54 Christopher Rufo, 'Racial Politics at Disney', *City Journal*, 2021, https://tinyurl.com/4avvmbec (last accessed January 2025).
55 Gerald Horne, *Class Struggle in Hollywood, 1930–1950: Moguls, Mobsters, Stars, Reds, & Trade Unionists*, First edition (Austin, TX: University of Texas Press, 2001), p. 13.
56 Ibid., p. 250. The company's support for fascism continues today with Disney pledging $2 million to Israeli NGOs following the Palestinian uprising of 7 October 2023. Middle East Monitor, 'Disney Donates $2m to Israeli Relief', *Middle East Monitor*, 2023, https://tinyurl.com/yxuz8an9 (last accessed October 2024).
57 Robinson, *Forgeries of Memory and Meaning*, p. 294.
58 Ibid., p. 296.

Robinson relates how jungle films rationalised a vision of a 'greater America' to build on 'domestic colonisation [which had] settled down to a mundane protocol of exploitation'.[59] Colonial ambitions were declared from the early days of the post-revolutionary United States. Just over a century later, military or economic domination over territories from Hawai'i to Haiti began, bankrolled by capital. Undergirding these exploits were the 'master narratives' of Social Darwinism and the civilising mission, which provided a language to justify colonial rampage and subsequent labour exploitation. The jungle film accompanied these exploits, from D.W. Griffiths' *The Native Heart* in 1901 to the *Tarzan of the Apes* movies produced between 1918 and 1948. As Robinson reminds us, *Tarzan* may have been escapist pulp, but it was also 'social pedagogy', suggesting that 'in a near-primeval chaos an untutored white masculine subject might construct an outpost of civility'.[60]

Tarzan hit the screens at a time of global economic crisis which had the potential of galvanising a working class beyond the divisions created and maintained by race, a time when some of the greatest Black radical intellectuals were making their critiques of race, class, colonialism and imperialism and reaching a wide audience. Tarzan and Jane became emblems of the Depression era, a white couple standing strong in the face of savagery and chaos. Race was the film's 'centering locator'.[61] The film industry in the early twentieth century played a central role in producing the ideological constructs necessary at a critical time in US history; a 'new whiteness' that would lend coherence to a 'national identity in disarray'.[62] It was a tool developed at an opportune time, just when 'a new racial regime was being stitched together from remnants of its predecessors and new cloth accommodating the disposal of immigrants, colonial subjects, and insurgencies among the native poor'.[63]

---

59 Ibid., p. 298.
60 Ibid., pp. 338-9.
61 Ibid., p. 339.
62 Ibid., p. xiv.
63 Ibid., p. xiv.

INTRODUCTION: STITCHING THE NEW RACIAL REGIME

The idea of the racial regime is a particularly generative way for considering how and why race is reproduced and why so much effort is made to maintain it as a mechanism for underwriting capitalism, white supremacism, fascism, colonialism and imperialism, segueing into neocolonialism, and the contemporary global liberal economic and political order. As with all Robinson's work, *Forgeries* privileges showing over telling. So, the methodology employed constantly articulates the realm of representation and that of capitalism in order to show how race becomes a key vehicle for securing white colonial domination, both within the specific context of the US, which he privileges, and more globally. Throughout, Robinson reminds us of the constant challenge by those who reject race as truth. This speaking back necessitates the readaptation of the scripts that help fabricate and uphold racial regimes.

The following example from the book's first chapter, 'The Invention of the Negro', is illustrative of the methodology Robinson uses to demonstrate how late nineteenth-century white supremacism was intricately constructed through a consolidation of material interests and representational technologies backed by finance capital with feet in both camps. During the American Civil War of the 1860s, an alliance between the colonial US government, capitalists and scientists came together to study the 'relative robustness of British Americans, Germans, the Irish, and Blacks' under the auspices of the newly established US Sanitary Commission.[64] Much of the Commission's expenses were paid for by life insurance companies who had a vested interest in the results that would determine who should be insured as recruits to the Union Army. The studies, based on autopsies of (almost exclusively Black) soldiers found that 'the Black male body was more anthropoid, that is, apelike, than the white body'.[65] Such studies underpinned late nineteenth-century ideas about racial inferiority which prevailed despite the fact that the Civil War had freed the slaves. In practice, the role played by Black soldiers in the fight against the South did not translate into them being seen as fully human by the

---

64 Ibid., p. 67.
65 Ibid., p. 69.

newly united post-war nation, a fact which played its part in the failure of the post-slavery Reconstruction era to deliver equality for the formerly enslaved.[66]

The foundations are laid for the 1890s by which time, 'the race science establishment became a critical contributor to the deliberate construction of an American public sphere'.[67] A crucial role was played by the former head of the Sanitary Commission, Frederick Law Olmstead, a landscape architect and the 'father' of Central Park, who went on to design the fairgrounds of the World Columbian Exposition in Chicago where a white American public came to ogle at colonised peoples, stolen artefacts and pillaged plants. By demonstrating how these interests came together, Robinson unveils 'the convergence of the American public culture: the idea of the museum, public spaces, public health, patriotism, and public morality'[68] (similar structures existed in other imperial centres such as Britain and France). The US fairs were financed by 'railroad industrialists' and 'sectors of finance capital', the 'major consumers of the cheapest labour available' who had allied with white supremacists to seize economic control over the US South.[69] When the railroads were originally being built, the labour was provided by slaves. Now, new access to low-cost labour needed to be secured. It is in this context that the Southern Railway Security Company acquired penitentiaries which subsequently became a source of that free Black labour. The funding of expositions such as the World Fairs was a good investment: they wrote the script of Black racial inferiority which legitimated the ongoing super-exploitation of Black labour even after the formal end of slavery. This complex of factors – capitalist, scientific, political and cultural/representational – needs the careful exposition Robinson submits them to in order for the full functioning of racial regimes to come to light.

---

66 W.E.B. Du Bois, *Black Reconstruction in America: 1860–1880*, First edition (New York: The Free Press, 1998).
67 Robinson, *Forgeries of Memory and Meaning*, p. 70.
68 Ibid., p. 71.
69 Ibid., p. 73.

INTRODUCTION: STITCHING THE NEW RACIAL REGIME

RACIAL CAPITALISM AND RECURSIVITY

I told them, that's more important than racial capitalism to me. The racial regime.[70]

The framework of racial regimes encourages an understanding of how modalities of race are in a constant process of cultural reproduction, then and now. It enables us to see these constellations as something that is not purely ideological nor simply a mode of moral panic. In contrast, racial regimes enable the endurance of racial capitalism even when it appears that more numbers have joined the antiracist side. The analysis in *Forgeries* puts more flesh on the bones of Robinson's treatment of racial capitalism in his best-known book, *Black Marxism: The Making of the Black Radical Tradition*. Al-Bulushi describes 'racial capitalism, racial regimes, and the black radical tradition' as the triplet forming Robinson's work.[71] Joshua Myers contends that because the racial regime 'talks about how this thing is moving, how it works, how it operates, how it continuously updates itself in ways that maintain this order, not just the system, but the whole order', it is a more important idea than racial capitalism itself.[72] Put another way, we cannot grasp how racial capitalism proliferates without understanding the reproductive capacities of racial regimes, which are its vehicle.

In *Black Marxism* Robinson develops an historicisation and theorisation of Black radical action and thought that helps us to understand the origins of race and what he calls racialism, in and through capitalism, developing from its European feudalist origins to become the ordering principle for a world system. In this sense, *Black Marxism* is not an attempt to inject a racial reading into the history of capitalism. Rather, the book is testimony to how those who race oppresses and exploits are best placed, not only to parse it, but to propose alternative modes of social and political organisation that derive inspiration from cultural practices and formations that are rejected as primitive in Eurocentric accounts. Crucial to

---

70 Myers and McNeil, 'Cedric Robinson'.
71 Al-Bulushi, 'Thinking Racial Capitalism and Black Radicalism from Africa', p. 261.
72 Myers and McNeil. 'Cedric Robinson'.

this work is an understanding of the importance, for Robinson, of Black radical thought as a collective project of liberation and resistance. Where *Black Marxism* offers us an explanation of the roots and routes of racial capitalism as lived by enslaved Africans and theorised by Black radicals, *Forgeries* parses its reproductive capacities.

How can racial regimes help us think further about racial capitalism, not only as a set of practices, but as a methodological approach that is derived from articulated processes that are often observed separately across space but also across time in ways that resist 'a linear model of temporality'.[73] Race, despite being imbued with the character of fixity, is anything but; it is unstable, adaptive and recursive. Robert Nichols introduces the concept of recursivity to theorise Indigenous dispossession under settler colonialism, a process wherein the theft of land from Indigenous people results in it being made into property where before it was not. Recursivity is a looping procedure, one part of which 'refers directly back to its starting point' but in which 'each iteration is not only different from the last but builds on or augments' the original.[74] Dispossession 'produces what it presupposes'[75] as does racial capitalism. Practices of exploitation and subjugation create categories of inferiorised human beings, who are then made to appear to have been inferior all along. Recursivity refers to the 'dynamic' and 'amplificatory' processes that essentially make dispossession happen,[76] processes that are equally the work of racial regimes. But where does this originate?

A full answer to this question is not the object of this book. However, as Chapter 2 shows, the target of attacks on critical race theory is often history, which version of it can be told, what must be commemorated and what denied in order to leave intact fairy tales of white innocence. The question of how to think historically about race – rather than how to periodise it – is therefore

---

73   Geraldine Heng, *The Invention of Race in the European Middle Ages* (New York: Cambridge University Press, 2018), p. 21.
74   Robert Nichols, *Theft Is Property! Dispossession & Critical Theory*, Radical Américas (Durham, NC: Duke University Press, 2020), p. 9.
75   Ibid.
76   Ibid., p. 91.

important methodologically. The question is taken up in more detail in Chapter 5 where I discuss the establishment of western man, *homo europaeus*, as a figure in need of constant recreation in the effort to shore up western power against the 'racialized outsider'.[77] The question of race's historical evolution is raised in Cedric Robinson's treatment of racial capitalism as a specifically European manufacture. In *Black Marxism*, Robinson begins with an exploration of the emergence of racialism within European feudalism in order to explain why race as a way of thinking about social and economic relations was already available for extension and readaptation under colonialism and imperialism. He argues that racialism comes to legitimate and corroborate 'social organisation as natural' in feudal times. Rather than withering away with the advance of bourgeois society, as Marx and Engels thought it would, it solidifies to 'inevitably permeate the structures emergent from capitalism'.[78] This is racial capitalism.

Racial capitalism is not simply a way of talking about how capitalism or labour relations are racialised, or how bosses rely on racism in their quest for profit. That is the superficial argument relied on by many 'vulgar Marxists' who boil racism down to a tool of exploitation, pitting Black and white workers against each other, negating their common interests. But neither is it sufficient to just state that 'all capitalism is racial capitalism'. While this cuts to the chase of Robinson's argument, that there is no way to theorise capitalism outside of its relationship with racialism because the former relied on the latter to grow and spread, much like simply repeating that 'race is a social construct',[79] it does not explain the question of *how* the racial infused capitalism. Robinson offers us a picture of what this looks like in practice. He does this by taking us through how race went from being a means to tether groups of people from different geographical regions and ethnicities to particular forms of labour during the feudal era, a time of burgeoning intra-European

---

77 Satnam Virdee, *Racism, Class and the Racialized Outsider* (Basingstoke: Palgrave Macmillan, 2014).
78 Robinson, *Black Marxism*, Second edition, p. 2.
79 Patrick Wolfe, *Traces of History: Elementary Structures of Race* (London: Verso, 2016); Alana Lentin, *Why Race Still Matters* (Cambridge, UK; Medford, MA: Polity Press, 2020).

migration, to being applied first to Indigenous and indentured workers and then to African peoples naturalised as slaves. Ideas of racial essentialism were the requirements for capital's advancement, both locally, where workers of different provenances could be sifted and separated, and globally, where the same logic was put to work at the level of entire regions and peoples.

Robinson reads history against the grain of the dominant approach taken by scholars who characterise race as a uniquely modern phenomenon, that really only has purchase, according to some, after the invasion of the Americas in the late fifteenth century, or for others with a more US-centric bent, after the institutionalisation of African slavery in seventeenth-century Virginia.[80] For Robinson, there is no way to disentangle capitalism from racism and nationalism which influenced its 'historical development ... in a most fundamental way. This could only be true if the social, psychological, and cultural origins of racism and nationalism both anticipated capitalism in time and formed a piece with those events that contributed directly to its organization of production and exchange.'[81] As Kieron Turner suggests, Robinson is engaged in entirely overturning the dominant idea that race is peripheral to the history of capitalism and the world order it establishes by engaging in a 'deconstruction of western historiography through the situating of race at the centre of European civilization and its global imperial expansion', a way of legitimating 'the social organisation of exploitation as *natural* by reference to the "racial" components of its elements'.[82] The idea of differentiation as a naturally occurring phenomenon supplies an ordering principle for the subsequent development of the world system.

Robinson's location of the origins of racism in feudal Europe can be generatively considered in relation to Satnam Virdee's emphasis on the significance of racism for European absolutist

---

80   Charlie Post, 'Beyond "Racial Capitalism"', *The Brooklyn Rail*, 2020, https://tinyurl.com/4ue2ud7h (last accessed October 2022).
81   Robinson, *Black Marxism*, Second edition.
82   Kieron Turner, 'Racial Capitalism as a Theory of History', in *The Sage Handbook of Decolonial Theory*, ed. Jairo I. Fúnez-Flores, Sabelo J. Ndlovu-Gatsheni, Ana Carolina Díaz Beltran, Sandeep Bakshi, Augustin Lao-Montes, and Flavia Rios (London: Sage, 2025).

states[83] or Geraldine Heng's meticulous uncovering of the existence of racial logics and systems of rule in Europe in the Middle Ages.[84] For Heng, the reason why race theorists, including until recently myself, have clung so stubbornly to the idea that race is a purely modern phenomenon has to do with the dominant tendency, explored further in Chapter 2, to think of history as a straight line. Because we identify racial thought and governance so emphatically with modern political phenomena – colonialism, imperialism, transatlantic slavery, fascism, the Nazi genocide, Apartheid, Jim Crow segregation, etc. – we have difficulty noting the reliance of premodern systems on remarkably similar logics, resulting in equally egregious oppression. She argues that, in fact, multiple temporalities are in play at different times and in different contexts and that being alive to the fact that, consequently, modern manifestations of race build on or rehabilitate those of the past, allows us to trace their genealogies more closely with the aim of deepening understanding and opening new routes to antiracist consciousness. Heng's attention to mediaeval practices of antisemitism and anti-Irish racism that employed strikingly similar motifs of demonisation and simianisation to those applied to African peoples also sheds light on the fact that racial thinking has not always been bound to skin colour. So-called 'new cultural racism' is just a recurring form.[85] Such an approach, taken together with Robinson's account of race's origins as predominantly intra-European, gives us the tools to think of racisms as co-constitutive.

Taking Robinson's and Heng's approaches together, I find an analytic of racial capitalism most useful as a means to think about the material purpose of producing, reproducing and managing human difference.[86] Heng pays attention to the premodern roots

---

83 Satnam Virdee, 'The Longue Durée of Racialized Capitalism: A Response to Charlie Post', *RACE.ED* (blog), 2021, https://tinyurl.com/56p5mjn4 (last accessed October 2022).
84 Heng, *The Invention of Race in the European Middle Ages*. I take up a further discussion of Virdee's and Heng's contributions in Chapter 5.
85 Stolcke, 'Talking Culture: New Boundaries, New Rhetorics of Exclusion in Europe'. *Ethnographic Authority and Cultural Explanation Current Anthropology*, 1995, 1–24.
86 I use the term management rather than governance here to draw attention to the fact that race acts heuristically at all levels of society, as an idea that plays a role

of race during which time it appears as a way of making sense of the enormity of human variation. She shows, for example, how the Venetian merchant Marco Polo created a taxonomy of human difference in which each category was attached to a value.[87] Robinson emphasises the significance to European civilisation of a logic of differentiation which births racial capitalism. Within the Europe of the early capitalist era, the tendency was to exaggerate 'regional, subcultural and dialectical differences into "racial ones"', naturalising the functions performed by groups of people so as to enable their exploitation and domination.[88] From a methodological standpoint, the aim is to track what tools enable these practices of differentiation, categorisation and valuation. This aids an understanding of race that resists the temptation offered by racial logic itself to cement our reading of race into hardened categories – Black, Muslim, Indigenous, etc. – each of which has its place in a fixed hierarchy and, it is implied, are naturally in competition with each other. Rather, we can observe how modern capitalism develops, using race, at a particular time and place.[89]

Robinson's *Black Marxism* can be situated in a body of twentieth century Black radical scholarship that reconstructs the relationship between race and capitalism through the history of imperialism and slavery.[90] These scholars negated Eurocentric Marxist accounts of slavery as a form of primitive accumulation that fully formed

---

in organisation and planning for individuals, families and communities, as well as political and capitalist elites. An example might be the decision, common among the middle class in societies of the west, about which school to send one's children to or which area to live in. White people might manage our evening around which locations are considered 'safe', based on racialised presumptions.

87 Siddhant Issar, John McMahon, and Rachel H. Brown, 'Rosa Luxemburg and the Primitive Accumulation of Whiteness', in *Creolizing Rosa Luxemburg*, ed. Jane Anna Gordon and Drusilla Cornell (Lanham, MD: Rowman & Littlefield Publishers, 2021), pp. 343–69.

88 Robinson, *Black Marxism*, Second edition, p. 26.

89 Crucially, while what later became differently positioned classes were drawn from long-standing ethnic and religious groups around Europe, it was only opportunistic events during the expansion of mercantilism driven by intense competition among different groups in the merchant class that fix them as 'races'.

90 Destin Jenkins and Justin Leroy, eds., *Histories of Racial Capitalism*, Columbia Studies in the History of U.S. Capitalism (New York: Columbia University Press, 2021).

capitalism, preferencing wage labour, no longer requires. They 'subverted their disciplinary training in supplanting the narrative myths of the episteme of the West that underpinned them through an alternative historical experience of Black critique'.[91] Black Marxists from Oliver Cromwell Cox to Walter Rodney to Claudia Jones, to name but a few, differ in how they view the relationship between race and class or regarding when to date the emergence of racial thought. However, they are united in believing that a full understanding of capitalism cannot relegate race to mere identity, to some unfortunate hangover from a less progressive era, or to see it as just a tool of divide and rule. As Stuart Hall explains, it is not sufficient to see race 'simply as residues or traces of previous modes'; we must observe how distinctions between differently racialised groups were eroded, transformed or indeed preserved over time, remaining 'active structuring principles of the present organisation of society'.[92] That is not to say that race is a permanent feature of human relationships, as some argue, but that it recursively repeats in different ways across a much longer historical time than scholars of race have overwhelmingly tended to think.

The critique of racial neoliberalism motivated many of us in the first decade of the twenty-first century to expose how mythologies of colourblindness and meritocracy operate to deny racial discrimination, domination and exploitation.[93] Contemporary racial discourses build recursively on these older scripts, amplifying their themes and modifying them in response to the renewed demands of racialised and colonised peoples for freedom against the backdrop of the horror of climate crisis, a global pandemic and surging fascisms; today's racial regime. However, the renewed interest in racial capitalism is an opportunity to resituate our critiques. The framework of racial capitalism forces us to think further about what pre-existing social forces precipitated and expanded capi-

---

91 Turner, 'Racial Capitalism as a Theory of History'.
92 Stuart Hall, 'Race, Articulation and Societies Structured in Dominance', in *Sociological Theories: Race and Colonialism* (Paris: UNESCO, 1980), p. 238.
93 Alana Lentin, 'Post-Race, Post Politics: The Paradoxical Rise of Culture after Multiculturalism', *Ethnic and Racial Studies* 37, no. 8 (2014): 1268–85; Alana Lentin and Gavan Titley, *The Crises of Multiculturalism: Racism in a Neoliberal Age* (London: Zed Books, 2011).

talism to become the primary global mode of production beyond developmentalist accounts that start with European feudalism and end with neoliberal globalisation.

Rejecting developmentalism entails seeing that, far from capitalism leaving behind the stage that Marx called primitive accumulation, which depended 'in part on brute force, e.g., the colonial system',[94] violence and dispossession are a permanent fixture of capitalist expansion.[95] Indigenous critique in particular shows that the violent dispossession of land is a permanent fixture of capitalism, a fact that can be seen in the rapacious appetite of mining companies, property developers, universities, agrobusinesses, the tourism and prison industries, etc. for more and more land. As Koshy et al. write, Indigenous anticolonial resistance is not just a struggle for land but a struggle for seeing 'the land as system of reciprocal relations and obligations'.[96] This vision of things, much like Robinson's portrayal of 'the collisions of the Black and white "races"' long before modern European slavery, helps us to see the world otherwise. It is precisely the capacity to see in this way that forms the rhetorical core of much of the discourse on race today, as exemplified by the war on critical race theory, discussed in Chapter 1. To see things from their underside, is not just to wish for a different symbolic order – no more colonial statues, more diverse television, etc. – it is to be able to envision a new world, one which threatens those who benefit from the status quo, or more tragically, those who think they do.

THE CURRENT CONJUNCTURE

Attention to the recursivity of racial capitalism through the recalibrating racial regime helps us parse what Stuart Hall often referred

---

[94] Karl Marx, 'Economic Manuscripts: Capital Vol. I – Chapter Thirty-One', 1867, https://tinyurl.com/2krhmb63 (last accessed October 2022).
[95] For a particularly interesting discussion of this, to be taken up in Chapter 5, see Issar et al., 'Rosa Luxemburg and the Primitive Accumulation of Whiteness'.
[96] Susan Koshy, Lisa Marie Cacho, Josie Byrd, and Brian Jordan Jefferson, 'Introduction', in *Colonial Racial Capitalism*, ed. Susan Koshy, Lisa Marie Cacho, Josie Byrd, and Brian Jordan Jefferson (Durham, NC: Duke University Press, 2022), pp. 8–32, p. 22.

to as the current conjuncture. For Gramsci, the conjuncture was a way of understanding times of crisis and the diverse histories and processes that bring them about. A conjunctural analysis is used to make sense of times of significant change, times which in Gramsci's view, can be ripe for revolution if the particular constellation of events that generate them can be grasped and subverted.[97] In Gramsci's time in 1920s and 1930s Italy, much like today where the fascist Fratelli d'Italia party was brought to government in September 2022, these conjunctural crises often work in the right's favour. At times like these, the various social, cultural and political forces at work in the production of crisis often appear to work in sync, making it even more necessary to do the work of disentangling them.[98] In considering today's racial regime we might ask, as Hall did in his conjunctural analysis of Thatcherism in the UK of the 1980s, 'what is the nature of this ideology which can inscribe such a vast range of positions and interests in it, and which seems to represent a little bit of everybody?'[99]

The new racial regime also involves a wide range of actors with seemingly divergent interests. For example, we cannot simply understand the attacks on the teaching of the history of slavery and colonialism, discussed in Chapter 2, as a matter of an ascendant right wing asserting cultural hegemony because, as we shall see, significant elements of the left are also involved. Therefore, we are drawn to observe what Gramsci called the 'war of position', where 'different fronts of struggle are the various sites of political and social antagonism'.[100] That racism stands opposed to 'antiracism' is a troubling supposition in these circumstances. While our story starts in the next chapter with the manipulation by powerful right-wing actors of local politics, at school and library board meetings, local councils and state governments, we will quickly see that the composition of the new racial regime, as an analytical frame for

---

97   Antonio Gramsci, *Selections from the Prison Notebooks of Antonio Gramsci*, ed. Q. Hoare and G. Nowell Smith (London: Lawrence and Wishart, 1971).
98   Deborah Grayson and Ben Little, 'Conjunctural Analysis and the Crisis of Ideas', *Soundings* 65 (2017): 59–75.
99   Stuart Hall, 'Gramsci and Us', Versobooks.com, 2017, https://tinyurl.com/2f6ke4x4 (last accessed September 2022).
100 Stuart Hall, 'Gramsci's Relevance for the Study of Race and Ethnicity', *Journal of Communication Inquiry* 10, no. 2 (June 1986): 5–27, p. 20.

a conjunctural reading of the present, extends beyond the usual suspects. To see it clearly, we thus need to reassess liberal antiracist conceptions of diversity and representation and think about them as articulated with the banning of the 'wrong' types of antiracist protest; the sometimes obvious, sometimes strange friendships between fascism, coloniality and anti-antisemitism and the cynical mobilisation of the languages of decolonisation and Indigeneity in the pursuit of white supremacist settler domination.[101]

Capturing something I am boldly calling the New Racial Regime is an elusive task, due to the operations of recalibration themselves. It was Stuart Hall who described race as slipping 'around the edge of the veranda and climb[ing] back in through the pantry window',[102] an evocative image I also referred to in my last book *Why Race Still Matters*. That I am returning to this demonstrates that the litheness of race is something I continue to grapple with. The trajectory of this book is a clear example of how race appears to constantly throw up what Étienne Balibar, in 1988, called 'crisis racism'.[103] One is seemingly always confronted with new disasters

---

101 Along these lines, in a web of increasing complexity, racialist structures borrow from antiracist scripts to sustain and reproduce themselves. For example, the depiction of the former British Home Secretary Suella Braverman, named a 'real racist bigot' by members of her own Conservative Party, as a 'Coconut' by a Muslim participant of a pro-Palestine rally in London in November 2023, led to its designer being charged with a racially aggravated public order offence. This followed the attempt to prosecute a young Black man who sent a tweet with a raccoon emoji to the Black Conservative Prospective Parliamentary Candidate Ben Obese-Jecty in objection to Obese-Jecty's racist pronouncements. Both cases represent the contortion of long-standing intracommunal Black critique into a designation of racism by a Brown and Black leadership class complicit in delinking it from the operations of the state and capital they defend. Amine Rumeysa Ergoren, '"Racist Bigot": Tory Backlash Grows over Braverman's Demeaning Remarks', *TRT World*, 2023, https://tinyurl.com/yjxvkm92 (last accessed September 2024); Aina Khan, 'UK Charges Pro-Palestine Protester behind Divisive "Coconut" Placard', *Al Jazeera*, 2024, https://tinyurl.com/favzbsca (last accessed May 2024); Nels Abbey, 'Why Was a Black Man Put on Trial for Using a Raccoon Emoji?' *The Lead*, 2024, https://tinyurl.com/yc4p67ay (last accessed September 2024).
102 Stuart Hall, *The Fateful Triangle: Race, Ethnicity, Nation* (Cambridge, MA: Harvard University Press, 2017).
103 Étienne Balibar, 'Racism and Crisis', in *Race, Nation, Class: Ambiguous Identities*, ed. Immanuel Maurice Wallerstein and Étienne Balibar (London; New York: Verso, 1991), pp. 217–27.

or more cunning obfuscations. However, attention to the workings of the racial regime helps us think, with Balibar, that 'it does not follow from the fact that racism is becoming more visible, that it has arisen from nothing, or almost nothing ... Though it experiences fluctuations, though the tendency comes and goes, it never disappears from the social scene, or at least it remains waiting in the wings'.[104] The presentation of racism as a resurgent 'crisis that is political, moral or cultural'[105] assumes it to be an inevitable outcome of economic crisis which naturally generates anxiety among the working class to be taken out on 'usurping' migrants. Such readings, which continue to fuel the increasingly overtly normalised fascist rhetoric of our times, intentionally whiteout the structural conditions of 'industrialization, the growth of urban poverty, the dismantling of the welfare state and imperial decline'.[106] In other words, they conceal the functioning of racial capitalism in 'the covering conceit of a racial regime'.[107]

The experience of tracking the racial regime inevitably means becoming entrapped in its web. Thus, as you follow the book's progression you will notice that capturing the appearance of the racial regime in the first half of the 2020s, the time of writing, led me to confront what came to be one of the most obdurate problems of our times, the latest, most murderous, phase of the genocide in Palestine. Just as the watchword of the global Palestinian protest movement was that the 7 October uprising did not start in a vacuum but had a century of Zionist colonialism behind it, the challenges underlined by the genocide reveal a web of interconnections that go far beyond the 'Gaza ghetto uprising'[108] and the 'war to save western civilisation', as Israeli president Isaac Herzog called it.[109] For example, we can witness in the Zionist borrow-

---

104 Ibid., p. 218–19.
105 Ibid., p. 217.
106 Ibid., p. 217.
107 Robinson, *Forgeries of Memory and Meaning*, p. xii.
108 Adi Callai, 'The Gaza Ghetto Uprising', *The Brooklyn Rail*, 2024, https://tinyurl.com/b8db443k (last accessed July 2024).
109 Al Mayadeen English, 'Herzog Claims War in Palestine Would Save "Western Civilization"', *Al Mayadeen English*, 2023, https://tinyurl.com/5n94w62y (last accessed January 2025).

ing of the terminology of the war on critical race theory, discussed in Chapter 3, how fascisms here and there nourish, and indeed – understood as a product of the globality of race – *require* each other. In a similar vein, the exemplification of Israel as a success story of racial supremacist nationalism to be emulated by a Europe construed by right-wing pundits such as the British journalist Douglas Murray as 'in decline' due to overly generous, guilt-induced multiculturalism[110] demonstrates the extent to which the genocide in Palestine is at the vanguard of a project to stave off the white supremacist fantasy of 'the great replacement'.[111]

The recalibration of the racial regime for the protection of Zionism as an exemplar of settler colonial rule that requires the elimination of Palestinians[112] and a racial supremacist entity that enacts antisemitism through its fascist expression of Judaism allows us to observe the centrality of race for imperialism and racial capitalism. The problematics thrown up by the genocide include the deepening of the state's use of violence and incarceration with invaluable returns for the arms industry and its satellites, the liberal media's role in propagandising and censorship, the institutional use of ostensibly antiracist policy-making to discipline and punish activists, the capitulation of radical-liberal elements with the forces of the state and institutions such as universities by willingly or unwittingly becoming amenable to cooptation, and what bin-Wahad describes as 'the delusion of electoral politics, which effectively camouflage the military corporate control of every facet of the state and state policies'.[113] At the same time, the adjustments made to the racial regime sharpen minds and instigate a greater determination to resist as shown by the pro-Palestine encampments on university campuses and the direct action of groups such as Palestine Action or Stop Cop City, the movement that began

---

110 Douglas Murray, *The War on the West*, First edition (New York: Broadside, 2022).
111 Renaud Camus, *Le grand remplacement* (Paris: Chez l'auteur, 2015).
112 Jamal Nabulsi, 'The Continuation of Zionist Settler Colonialism', *Al-Shabaka* (blog), 2024, https://tinyurl.com/mvfnffa3 (last accessed January 2025).
113 Dhoruba bin-Wahad, Jared Ware, and Joshua Briond. '"The Last of the Loud" – Dhoruba bin Wahad, Philosopher of the Whirlwind', https://tinyurl.com/33f6j6kp (last accessed September 2024).

in the Weelaunee Forest on stolen Muscogee land in Atlanta to halt the 'opening, renovation, or expansion of facilities for "Public Safety", SWAT Team police training, mostly near predominantly Black communities', mushrooming around the US.[114] It is this dialectical push-pull of the forces of racial fascism, endowed with an immense arsenal, against the People that produces and reproduces the racial regime.

Lastly, we must not lose sight of the so-called war on critical race theory, which spurred my interest to write this book in the first place. Why is so much energy invested in attempting to either annul the teaching of the accurate histories of colonialism and slavery or contain it in tightly circumscribed ways within western curricula? Dhoruba bin-Wahad puts it plainly:

> America could talk all it wants about democracy and freedom, but the reality of the white supremacy construct that is America belies that … This is why they don't want you to teach the truth about America in school. Because all that bullshit they're talking about freedom … all of that shit is bullshit. And they know it's bullshit and it can't be verified by the US's social and political practices.[115]

'Pedagogies that tackle racial power will be most uncomfortable for those who benefit from that power', as critical race educators Leonardo and Porter write.[116] Yet the stress placed on discomfort, anxiety and unease, psychologising and individualising ways to describe an affective state that might overcome the prototypical white student, do not get at the systemic importance of scrubbing these histories or making them more digestible that bin-Wahad gets at. We can come full circle by connecting the war on critical race theory to the attempt to systematically destroy Palestinian knowledge.

---

114 bin-Wahad, 'Rise of Militarized Policing in Response to Black Dissent'.
115 bin-Wahad et al., Millennials Are Killing Capitalism.
116 Zeus Leonardo and Ronald K. Porter, 'Pedagogy of Fear: Toward a Fanonian Theory of "Safety" in Race Dialogue', *Race Ethnicity and Education* 13, no. 2 (July 2010): 139–57, p. xiv.

The obliteration of archives, libraries and universities during the genocide in Gaza is but the latest iteration of a long practice that the Palestinian scholar Karma Nabulsi has named as scholasticide.[117] The archives of the Palestine Research Center, the research wing of the Palestine Liberation Organization, were looted and seized by Israel during the bombing of its building during the invasion of Lebanon in 1982 and a second time from their relocated home in East Jerusalem in 2001.[118] This 'colonial plunder' is followed up by

> a strict system of management, control and 'knowledge production' – laws, rules, norms, methods and archive procedures such as censorship, restricted study, access prohibition/limitation, control over what is declassified (to whom and to what extent), cataloging and labeling according to Zionist codes and terminology that differ from the original Palestinian terminology, signifying Israeli ownership over the material and more.[119]

'Every genocidal regime' has tried to kill the stories of the people it colonises by killing its storytellers, a reality driven home by the assassination of journalists and scholars, most prominently on 6 December 2023, the Palestinian poet and teacher, Refaat Alareer at the age of 44.[120] While following the narrative web this book weaves, one that refuses linearity in its attempt to shed light on the wilful obfuscations planted by the racial regime, it could be useful to return to the maxim that colonialism requires scholasticide, and that this comes in many, more and less overt, forms.

READING *THE NEW RACIAL REGIME*

The grounding purpose of this book is to explore how race is reproduced recursively over time by examining interlock-

---

117 Scholars Against the War, 'Scholasticide Definition', n.d., https://tinyurl.com/mryz2vyz (last accessed January 2025).
118 Sabri Jiryis and Salah Qallab, 'The Palestine Research Center', *Journal of Palestine Studies* 14, no. 4 (1985): 185–7.
119 Rona Sela, 'The Genealogy of Colonial Plunder and Erasure – Israel's Control over Palestinian Archives', *Social Semiotics* 28, no. 2 (15 March 2018): 201–29.
120 Ayman Makarem, 'Zionism from the Standpoint of Its Victims', *YouTube*, 2024, https://tinyurl.com/yxkydmau (last accessed January 2025).

ing aspects of racial regime recalibration in the 2020s. I do not contend that race is a vicious circle that spins indefinitely. Instead, I break down some of the dynamics of race's reproduction via the writing of racial scripts, 'stitched together from remnants of its predecessors and new cloth'.[121] The purpose of this is manifold. First, it draws attention to the utility of ideology to the practice of race as a technology of rule without ceding to the idea, popular on the white left, that race is purely fictional and thus not worth taking seriously. Second, it allows us to think about race as operating in different periods, each of which requires different scripts, even as these borrow from the past and restitch them for today, often seeming to occur concurrently. Third, it permits a knitting together of the realms of representation and narrative with those of governance and political economy: racial capitalism. Lastly, it draws out how racial narratives such as the war on critical race theory, the war on antisemitism, or differently, the rewriting of Indigenous and decolonial resistance as cooptable agenda items for university committees, are written in opposition to alternative scripts. Foregrounding the analysis of Black and Indigenous radicals throughout, I point to their power as sources of revolutionary and emancipatory thought with which to attack and halt the recalibration of racial regimes.

The first chapter, '"A Drop of Poison": What the War on Critical Race Theory Tells Us about the New Racial Regime', redraws the outline of what David Theo Goldberg has called the war on critical race theory as it took shape, from the dying days of Donald Trump's first presidency, spreading from the US across the globe.[122] Far from a new phenomenon, what some refer to as moral panics about the teaching of the accurate history and sociology of race are a recurring, if never identical, fixture. Paying attention to the attacks on the teaching of 'progressive' subjects as a means through which to dismantle public education in a public-private alliance between the state, the private sphere and not-for-profits, the chapter critiques the idea that such attacks are the expressions of an evenly sided

---

121 Robinson, *Forgeries of Memory and Meaning*, p. xiv.
122 David Theo Goldberg, *The War on Critical Race Theory: Or, the Remaking of Racism* (Medford, MA: Polity Press, 2023), p. 37.

'culture war'. Rather, I foreground the historical interrelationships between racial liberalism and racial capitalism to demonstrate how the drive to minimise the role played by the racial regime conceals what the war on critical race theory signals: the centrality of racialist ideology to ensuring continued white dominance.

Building on this analysis, Chapter 2, 'On History and the Technologies of White Forgetting', focuses on the attacks on the teaching and public discussion of the interrelated histories of slavery and colonialism. I discuss the usages of time, arguing that claims that slavery and colonialism were 'of their time' and that colonised Indigenous people should 'get over it' are expressions of how western progressivist interpretations of history are used to repress 'more truthful' accounts. To exemplify how the racial regime is recalibrated through the teaching of history, the chapter spotlights two case studies. The first is the furore over *The New York Times' 1619 Project*. Here, rather than focus exclusively on the right's ample attacks, I engage in a critique of how white leftists used its publication to disparage the intellectual contributions of Black historians and thinkers. My second case study is the so-called 'history wars' that raged in Australia from the 1980s on. Spurred by the Indigenous writer, historian and poet Tony Birch's critique of white progressive historians, this discussion foregrounds the organic knowledge of the Indigenous youth as a means of returning us to the purpose of this aspect of the racial regime: to obscure and contain the thought of the colonised through an institutionalised epistemic racism that is not always straightforwardly expressed purely as a right-wing project.

The conclusion to the second chapter establishes the terrain into which Chapter 3 enters, the counterinsurgent capture of key terms associated with critical race and ethnic studies. In 'Institutionalising Dissent in a Time of Genocide', I argue that both repression and the retrofitting of critical ideas are necessary for 'the persistent efforts of repair' that, as Robinson shows, are entailed by the recapitulation of the racial regime. In the context of Israel's genocide in Gaza, I home in on Zionist tactics of counterinsurgency, targeting critical race and ethnic studies. This involves both full-frontal attacks that accuse the disciplines of antisemitism and the exclusion of Jews as well as the instrumentalisation of the terms of critical race theory, ethnic studies and diversity, equity and inclusion. These two-pronged tactics are used by Zionist organisations to undermine and delegitimate the work of radical educationalists and anticolonial movements. The second part of the chapter engages in a discussion of what Orisanmi Burton calls the 'institutionalisation of dissent'.[123] I consider the affordances and limitations of a critical race epistemology, arguing that its traditional neglect of colonialism and imperialism, despite Indigenous and anticolonial commitments to think relationally and interactively about race, hinder the ability of critical race theory as a discipline to confront Zionist attacks on it and intervene in opposition to the genocide in Gaza. This in turn raises questions about the limitations of academia and related institutions in the west as always already susceptible to cooptation in the interests of imperialism.

Chapter 4, 'Capturing Indigeneity, Colonising Decolonisation', builds on and deepens the discussion in Chapter 3 by turning our attention to how Indigeneity and decolonisation are coopted by imperial projects. I engage with Zionist involvement in the Indigenous Voice to Parliament referendum that was held in Australia on 14 October 2023. The timing, a week after the launching of 'Palestine's Great Flood'[124] – a resounding No vote reiterating the extent of the 'possessive investment in whiteness'[125] – permits me to consider the multiple uses to which Indigeneity can and has been put. Zionist claims of Jewish Indigeneity to Palestine, and their acceptance within settler colonial institutions of Australian higher education call proposals to ensure 'self-determination in Indigenous education' into question, precipitating a critical discussion of the political usages of self-determination over anticolonial resistance. The chapter foregrounds how conceptualisations of Indigeneity, defanged of their ongoing and unassimilable opposition to colonialism, can be put to work for the recalibration of the racial regime. The disciplining and punishment of radical Indige-

---

123 Orisanmi Burton, *Tip of the Spear: Black Radicalism, Prison Repression, and the Long Attica Revolt* (Oakland, CA: University of California Press, 2023).
124 Max Ajl, 'Palestine's Great Flood: Part I', *Agrarian South: Journal of Political Economy* 13, no. 1 (2024): 62–88.
125 Aileen Moreton-Robinson, *The White Possessive: Property, Power, and Indigenous Sovereignty* (Minneapolis, MN: University of Minnesota Press, 2015).

nous thought alongside the sidelining of Indigenous scholars and activists as theorists of their own experience sheds light on the multiple levels at which epistemic erasure and scholasticide are key to the making of the racial regime.

The final chapter, 'Against Definitions', departs from the question of what it means when fascists and white supremacists proclaim themselves the protectors of Jews to examine the contemporary usages of antisemitism for the new racial regime. I analyse how the necessity for the west to secure itself against the 'racialized other'[126] is enacted through a discourse and practice of 'Jewish safety', leading to the establishment of 'Zionist' as a protected identity category. This has rapidly become a means for the chimeric figure of the Jew in need of the west's protection to be employed to legitimate the criminalisation of dissent that accompanies mounting fascism. Here, what Anna Younes calls the 'war on antisemitism'[127] becomes the rationale for the criminalisation of protest, the banning of books, and the building of ever-higher walls and cop cities, protecting the fortressed spaces created by racial capitalism from the 'wretched of the earth'. Considering this, I discuss the debates over the definition of antisemitism, arguing that the quest to institutionalise definitions of ever-more forms of racism presents a danger to any group that is constituted as a threat to the current order because it can be used to further police and exclude. In conclusion, I propose that we must eschew what Robinson referred to as the established terms, the official 'meanings of things' designed by the racial regime and find the collective strength to assert 'humanity indivisible from the collective relation'.[128]

---

126   Virdee, *Racism, Class and the Racialized Outsider*.
127   Anna-Esther Younes, 'Fighting Anti-Semitism in Contemporary Germany', *Islamophobia Studies Journal* 5, no. 2 (1 October 2020).
128   Cedric J. Robinson, *The Terms of Order: Political Science and the Myth of Leadership* (Chapel Hill, NC: University of North Carolina Press, 2016), p. 18.

1
'A Drop of Poison': What the War on Critical Race Theory Tells Us about the New Racial Regime

So Cedric's idea, his concept of racial regime – its veracity, its power – is proven by the fact that much of the counter force against Spring 2020 is what is ideological and cultural. It is anti-critical race theory, which is not about critical race theory at all. It's basically saying we don't want any discussion of liberal multiculturalism. We don't want any discussion about racism because what they're trying to do is shore up the racial regime to convince white people that America can be America again ... that we're going to restore white sovereignty as the natural order of things and we're going to shut these people up because they've been messing you up.[1]

Behind a rash of freedom of information requests being sent to councils across the UK[2] is Don't Divide Us, a 'grassroots movement of all sorts of people' set up to oppose antiracism policies in schools across the UK. Its founding letter responds to what it says is as an attempt to exploit the killing of George Floyd by Minneapolis police on 25 May 2020, 'to promote an ideological agenda that threatens to undermine British race relations'. It says that a nebulous consortium of activists, corporations and institutions is to blame for sowing fear 'in those who would otherwise speak out' against the forced spread of critical race ideology. The founding

---

1 Robin D.G. Kelley and Jordan T. Camp, 'Against Pessimism', *Conjuncture Series* 2, 2022, www.youtube.com/watch?v=euoC8k3iB3o (last accessed October 2022).
2 Personal communication, Penny Rabiger, 18 September 2022.

letter portrays its signatories as the brave few who dare to stand up against an all-powerful 'toxic, racialised agenda' overrunning politics, schools and corporations. Calling racism systemic, institutionalised, widespread, embedded or inherent in society is portrayed as an attack on the gains of 'earlier generations of civil rights activists'; refusing to adhere to principles of colourblindness and recognising racialised differences is asserted as intentionally divisive and as rolling back progress; demanding acceptance of the existence of white privilege breeds racism; using acronyms such as Black and Minority Ethnic (BAME) encourages assumptions of victimhood; criticism of colonialism and attempts at symbolic redress, for example, destroying statues of colonists and slavers, is obsessional and turns 'history into a morality tale'.[3]

Don't Divide Us is run by people linked to the defunct Revolutionary Communist Party and gathered around the online magazine, *Spiked*: 'right-libertarian' iconoclasts with influence over British politics at the highest levels.[4] Its founding letter echoes any of the innumerable statements, politicians' speeches, school board petitions, op-eds, social media feeds and YouTube/Discord/podcasting screeds, in myriad locations, big and small, in a range of countries. Far from being the spontaneous groups of concerned parents and citizens that they portray themselves as, groups such as Don't Divide Us in the UK, Parents Defending Education or Moms for Liberty in the US, are supported by powerful interest groups with a long history of investment in attacks on attempts to bring about even a modicum of cultural change on matters of race and gender.

On the other side of the globe, on 22 June 2021, the Australian Senate voted in support of a motion to reject critical race theory from the national curriculum. Australia had seen its own Black Lives Matter mobilisations throughout the Southern hemisphere winter of 2020. As elsewhere, the protests were spurred by the murder of George Floyd and focused on the local killing of Indigenous

---

3   Don't Divide Us, 'Don't Divide Us', 2020, https://dontdivideus.com/founding-letter (last accessed September 2022).
4   Evan Smith, 'How a Fringe Sect from the 1980s Influenced No 10's Attitude to Racism', *Guardian*, 2020, https://tinyurl.com/j74uu4xz (last accessed January 2025).

people by police in prisons and by vigilantes. The killings have not stopped. In October 2022, a 15-year-old Noongar-Yamatji boy, Cassius Turvey, was killed while he walked home from school in Perth, Western Australia. Other Indigenous children, as young as ten, are locked away in 'cage-like conditions'.[5] In general, the proportion of Indigenous people who are incarcerated tops that of Black people disappeared into the prisons and jails of the US, Brazil or the UK.[6] However, a discourse of disproportionality masks the purposeful carcerality on which the colony was founded and which continues to reproduce the indelible difference between settler and native on which settler colonial racial capitalism depends. This line of difference is drawn and redrawn by the systematic killings of Indigenous people by those with the authority to do so, and to get away with it.

One of the over 550 deaths recorded since the Royal Commission into Aboriginal Deaths in Custody reported in 1991[7] was that of young Warlpiri man, Kumanjayi Walker. The 18-year-old was shot three times and killed by police officer, Zachary Rolfe, in the small town of Yuendumu in the Central Desert region of the Northern Territory in November 2019. Rolfe was found not guilty of the murder. The subsequent inquest was told that 'racism was not "widespread" within the NT police force',[8] despite '"threatening" and "blatantly racist"' texts between Rolfe and his colleagues coming to light.[9] Rolfe, who had fought in the Afghanistan war, was mentored by former SAS soldier, Ben Roberts-Smith, who

---

5   Lorena Allam, 'Warning "Cage-Like" Conditions for Young People in NT Detention Is "History Repeating"', *Guardian*, 2021, https://tinyurl.com/mnnh92p4 (last accessed January 2025).
6   Thalia Anthony, 'Fact Check: Are First Australians the Most Imprisoned People on Earth?' *The Conversation*, 2017, https://tinyurl.com/2vtz67ep (last accessed January 2025).
7   NAA, 'Royal Commission into Aboriginal Deaths in Custody', *NAA*, n.d., https://tinyurl.com/4wzb3h82 (last accessed September 2022).
8   Sarah Collard, 'Kumanjayi Walker Inquest: Racism a "Broader" Issue in NT Police, Superintendent Says', *Guardian*, 2022, https://tinyurl.com/3txay5pp (last accessed January 2025).
9   Samantha Jonscher, '"Blatantly Racist" and "Homophobic" Texts between Zachary Rolfe and Fellow Officers Revealed at Inquest', *ABC News*, 2022, https://tinyurl.com/4a6aja8j (last accessed January 2025).

was accused of war crimes by the *Sydney Morning Herald*.[10] The violence of imperial war works through domestic colonialism and vice versa. Former prime minister, John Howard, who had led the country into battle in Afghanistan and Iraq, stated in 2021 that it was not *his experience* that 'there is underlying racism in Australia'.[11]

In the midst of these cases of murderous racism and impunity the motion to ban critical race theory (CRT) from the Australian curriculum was introduced by Pauline Hanson, whose One Nation party has held an anti-immigration, anti-Indigenous line since its emergence on the Australian political scene in the 1990s, provoking the centre-right, led then by Howard, to move further rightwards ever since. Speaking with disgraced right-wing shock-jock Alan Jones on Sky News Live two days later, Hanson called CRT 'reverse racism against white people'. The One Nation education policy platform is three sentences long, one of which reads, 'There should be no room for Western, white, gender, guilt shaming in any classroom and instead children should be taught the benefits of a merit-based, free-thinking society'. Hanson tells a concerned Jones that 'in America ... five states have passed legislation banning critical race theory in schools. Why shouldn't we do that? Well, we should do it, but I had to take the government kicking and screaming to actually support it.'[12] In fact, despite pro-

---

10   Nino Bucci, 'Ben Roberts-Smith a Mentor to Zachary Rolfe, the NT Police Officer Cleared of Murder', *Guardian*, 2022, https://tinyurl.com/mr5tzjcb (last accessed January 2025). Roberts-Smith's defamation case against the newspaper was funded by Seven West Media (owned by Australian media, property and mining billionaire Kerry Stokes). Roberts-Smith finally lost the case in June 2023.
11   Junkee, 'The ABC Resuscitated John Howard So He Could Deny That Racism Is an Issue in Australia', *Junkee*, 2021, https://tinyurl.com/3mdampad (last accessed January 2025). My emphasis added. In 2024, Howard defended the so-called Northern Territory Intervention, which overrode the Racial Discrimination Act to install a system of racial governance over Indigenous people in remote communities accused en masse of sexual deviance fuelled by alcoholism and gambling. Lillian Rangiah, 'Former PM John Howard Defends NT Intervention after Police Commissioner Apology Speech', *ABC News*, 2024, https://tinyurl.com/3txnftxn (last accessed August 2024).
12   Pauline Hanson and Alan Jones, 'Pauline Hanson on Why One Nation Rejects Anti-White Critical Race Theory', *YouTube*, 24 June 2021, https://tinyurl.com/bp4vxsaf (last accessed January 2025).

gressive noises as to the importance of historical 'truth-telling' and the need for greater representativity in the overwhelmingly white public sphere, the history and sociology of racial colonialism continues to be suppressed across the Australian political spectrum. As Sriprakash et al. make clear, 'Australian education works hard to legitimise and consolidate whiteness and its claims to settle colonial futurities.'[13]

The war on CRT is powered by a network of organisations and lobby groups that have gained traction, particularly but not exclusively in North America, to mobilise parents against the teaching of anything with even the remotest link to CRT. Opposition to CRT has become a rallying point for right-wing activists and pundits. The form taken by the 'war' mirrors earlier incursions by the right into any gains made by antiracism. In the US, the war on CRT merges with long-standing attacks on public education and affirmative action in which schools and universities have been centre stage. There, the apex of attacks on what previously came under the label of 'political correctness' was the US Supreme Court's deliberation on two cases of race-based university admissions that finally brought the already near dead era of affirmative action to a close in 2023.[14] It has triggered legislation outlawing education and training evoking euphemistically termed 'divisive concepts', leading to books being banned, and causing consternation on US school and library boards. It has been the subject of parliamentary debate in the UK. In South Africa, the issue of discrimination in schools attended by poor, Black children is said to be tainted by a CRT that sees 'rights [as] determined by a hierarchy of eternal victimhood'.[15]

In France, so-called 'Islamoleftist' educators have faced sanction from the highest levels of government for importing 'progressive

---

13   Sriprakash Arathi, Rudolph Sophie, and Gerrard Jessica, *Learning Whiteness: Education and the Settler Colonial State* (London: Pluto Press, 2022), p. 74.
14   Lauren Aratani, 'Where Now for Workplace Diversity after Court's Affirmative Action Ruling?' *Guardian*, 2023, https://tinyurl.com/ymshwjk6 (last accessed July 2023).
15   Sara Gon, 'CRT: The Next Challenge for Schools to Face', *Daily Friend*, 2021, https://tinyurl.com/3c5k6bay (last accessed September 2022).

American ideas – specifically on race, gender, post-colonialism' to undermine society, as President Emmanuel Macron put it.[16] A former French Minister of Education Jean-Michel Blanquer asserted that 'indigenist, racialist, and "decolonial" ideologies', imported from North America, were responsible for 'conditioning' the violent extremist who assassinated the school teacher, Samuel Paty in 2020.[17] Then Minister for Higher Education Frédérique Vidal called for an investigation into 'Islamogauchisme' within French universities.[18] This followed her claim on 14 February that Islamogauchisme was having a gangrenous effect on the whole of French society. Seeing the transparency of Vidal's statements as a 'weaponisation of science', the French national research institute, the CNRS, denounced the attempt to 'delegitimise various fields of research, such as postcolonial studies, intersectional studies or research on the term "race," or any other area of knowledge'.[19] The refutation came too late as the folk devil of Islamogauchisme had taken on a life of its own, building on entrenched Islamophobia across the French political board. Despite widespread ridicule that the French education system had become infected by a parasitic Islamic-leftism, 'the polemic spread with the Minister of Education Jean-Michel Blanquer lending support to Vidal, saying in a televised interview on 20 October, that he believed Islamo-gauchisme was '"undoubtedly a social fact"'.[20]

---

16   Norimitsu Onishi, 'Will American Ideas Tear France Apart? Some of Its Leaders Think So', *New York Times*, 2021, https://tinyurl.com/2p9bbuka (last accessed January 2025).
17   Aude Le Gentil, '"Woke", "racialiste", "indigéniste" … Que signifient ces termes, que certains reprochent à Pap Ndiaye?' *Le Journal du Dimanche*, 2022, https://tinyurl.com/ymz96pwj (last accessed January 2025).
18   Bernadette Sauvaget and Simon Blin, '"Islamo-gauchisme": Frédérique Vidal perd ses facultés', *Libération*, 2021, https://tinyurl.com/4ew3je9b (last accessed August 2024).
19   CNRS, '"L'islamogauchisme" n'est pas une réalité scientifique', *CNRS*, 2021, https://tinyurl.com/2s38dvpu (last accessed September 2022).
20   Jean Beaman and Aurélien Mondon, 'The Moral Panic of Islamo-Gauchisme in Service of a Colorblind Approach to Racism', *Contemporary French and Francophone Studies* 27, no. 2 (2023): 261–70, p. 265.

For the self-nominated generals of the war on CRT,[21] critical race theory is a 'drop of poison',[22] one of which is enough to pervert the minds of young people and launch a 'war on the west'.[23] In fact, as shall be discussed in greater detail in Chapter 3, CRT emerged as a specialised rectification to critical legal theory which does not sufficiently account for the extent to which the US legal system is founded upon systemic racial injustice.[24] This fact did not prevent the allegation that children were being indoctrinated with CRT as soon as they entered kindergarten where they were being taught to 'hate America' and 'blame white people' for their 'misfortunes'. The only antidote to the 'white genocide' ushered in by CRT is counter-revolution; a counter-revolution that has swept the west since its launch in 2020.

The war on CRT holds teaching on race and cultural diversity responsible for indoctrination of white students by an ascendant class of 'woke' educators. According to the right-wing political scientist Eric Kaufmann, 'critical social justice content', including CRT, is hegemonic in British schools and students are denied exposure to counter-arguments.[25] On this side of the looking glass, teaching about British colonialism is predominantly approached as a question of pros and cons.[26] The focus on education and training is not incidental; it is in schools and workplaces that hegemonic common sense is shaped. Threats to what Goenpul woman and critical Indigenous scholar Aileen Moreton-Robinson calls the

---

21 David Theo Goldberg, *The War on Critical Race Theory: Or, the Remaking of Racism* (Medford, MA: Polity Press, 2023).
22 Julia Carrie Wong, 'The Fight to Whitewash US History: "A Drop of Poison Is All You Need"', *Guardian*, 2021, https://tinyurl.com/3nxhfpdu (last accessed January 2025).
23 Douglas Murray, *The War on the West*, First edition (New York: Broadside Books, 2022).
24 Richard Delgado and Jean Stefancic, *Critical Race Theory: An Introduction*, Third edition (New York: New York University Press, 2017).
25 Eric Kaufmann, 'The Political Culture of Young Britain' (London: The Policy Exchange, 2022).
26 Members of a WhatsApp group I established in 2022 related this predominant approach to me in November 2022.

'possessive investment in patriarchal whiteness'[27] need to be contained or extinguished at the point when young minds are most malleable. The focus on CRT is but the justification for 'the restructuring and realignment of the curriculum according to the logic of coloniality'. This is expressed in 'the systematic erasure of historically excluded experiences and knowledges, as well as resistance to colonialism, racism, capitalism, slavery, patriarchy, heteronormativity and genocide, and a recommitment to whiteness and Eurocentrism'.[28]

Floating free from any anchoring in its actual tenets then,[29] CRT is made an object of 'debatability',[30] enlisted in struggles over antiracist pedagogy and the recounting and representation of the history of colonialism and slavery that are far from new. Legislative and rhetorical assaults on CRT present it as a totalising discourse, one which stands in opposition to the ideals and aspirations of 'most middle-class Americans, including racial minorities'.[31] Despite the fact that many of the most strident battlers in the war on CRT can indeed be identified as 'racial minorities', the image of middle-class America that anti-CRT warriors paint is a structurally white one. It is a vision of the US beloved of conservatives, where individual families work hard to secure their children's futures, where any incursion by the state to wrest away the earnings from that hard work to redistribute it to the undeserving, indexed as feckless and Black,[32] must be resisted at all costs. Above all, the war on CRT is a counter-reaction to antiracist and decolonial uprising, specif-

---

27 Aileen Moreton-Robinson, *The White Possessive: Property, Power, and Indigenous Sovereignty* (Minneapolis, MN: University of Minnesota Press, 2015), p. 69.
28 Jairo I. Fúnez-Flores, 'Aníbal Quijano: (Dis)Entangling the Geopolitics and Coloniality of Curriculum', *Curriculum Journal (London, England)* 35, no. 2 (2024): 288–306, p. 294.
29 Victor Ray, *On Critical Race Theory: Why It Matters and Why You Should Care*, First edition (New York: Random House, 2022).
30 Gavan Titley, *Racism and Media* (London: Sage, 2019).
31 Benjamin Wallace-Wells, 'How a Conservative Activist Invented the Conflict over Critical Race Theory', *The New Yorker*, 2021, https://tinyurl.com/yc23yxbs (last accessed January 2025).
32 Dana-Ain Davis, 'Narrating the Mute: Racializing and Racism in a Neoliberal Moment', *Souls* 9, no. 4 (6 December 2007): 346–60.

ically the global protests against systemic racism, expressed as a statement – Black Lives Matter – but evoking a rejection of coloniality in its material and symbolic forms and an abolitionist cry to 'change everything'.[33] As discussed in the Introduction, the war on CRT, or in Robin Kelley's terms, 'the war on woke', 'is the perfect example of the functioning of the racial regime'.[34]

How does the idea that CRT is a nefarious ideology that is grooming children and turning them into 'Race Marxist'[35] traitors take hold? What is the 'complex structure in dominance', as Stuart Hall puts it, in which certain messages about race can be decoded by the public?[36] What alarm bells does it sound about the advantages people need to cede for real justice to be attained; a justice that is antiracist, anticolonial and abolitionist in the face of a rapidly dying planet on which the rich and the white are most likely to survive, at least in the interim? As the Black abolitionist organiser and scholar Robyn Maynard notes, 'there's a reason why at this time the right wing is mobilising so that kids can't learn about the injustices of slavery, settler colonialism and genocide, because that orients kids with a strong sense of justice, again to say, what else?'.[37] The purpose of the war on CRT is to obfuscate the functions of racial capitalism at a time of conjunctural crisis. This chapter uses the war on CRT as a lens to explore how a racial regime recalibrates white supremacy. Piggybacking on the racial liberal ideological foundations powering US white supremacy, and

---

33 Ruth Wilson Gilmore and Naomi Murakawa, eds., *Change Everything: Racial Capitalism and the Case for Abolition* (New York: Haymarket Books, 2024).
34 Kelley and Camp, 'Against Pessimism'.
35 James Lindsay, *Race Marxism: The Truth about Critical Race Theory and Praxis* (Independently published, 2022).
36 Stuart Hall, 'Encoding/Decoding', in *Culture, Media, Language Working Papers in Cultural Studies, 1972–79*, ed. Stuart Hall, Dorothy Hobson, Andrew Lowe, and Paul Willis (London: Routledge, 1980).
37 Maynard's work, together with the Michi Saagiig Nishnaabeg scholar, writer and artist Leanne Betasamosake Simpson, to work with young people to 'see themselves as people who can interrupt injustice' stands in polar opposition to the attack on alternative forms of worldmaking that the war on CRT sets in motion. Robyn Maynard, Leanne Betasamosake Simpson, Jared Ware, and Joshua Briond, '"Getting Ready for the Next Act" – on *Rehearsals for Living*', 2022, *Millennials Are Killing Capitalism*, https://tinyurl.com/yh67aa3m (last accessed September 2022).

fanning out across the west in viral force, the so-called war on CRT obscures the myriad ways in which education has always been a site of control and a terrain of struggle.

'WE HAVE SUCCESSFULLY FROZEN ITS BRAND'

The first shots in the war on CRT may well have been fired by 'the right's leading culture warrior', Christopher Rufo,[38] fellow at the right-wing think tank, The Manhattan Institute. While director of the Center on Wealth and Poverty at the right-wing Discovery Institute,[39] Rufo made a documentary, *America Lost*, which blamed a lack of public order – not of houses – for homelessness. For Rufo, individual self-sufficiency, 'a proper sense of limits and public order' is the three-pronged solution to human immiseration under capitalism.[40] Rufo claims to have encouraged Donald Trump to sign an executive order banning antiracism and diversity training 'inspired by Critical Race Theory'.[41] Trump was apparently alerted to the existence of CRT when he watched Rufo's visit to Tucker Carlson, then 'America's most watched cable news host', on Fox News on 3 September 2020.[42] Rufo told Carlson about his research into the impact of what he called 'critical race ideology' on US public life via antiracism, and diversity, equity and inclusion training courses: 'it's absolutely astonishing how critical race theory has pervaded every institution in the federal government'

---

38 Zack Beauchamp, 'Chris Rufo's Dangerous Fictions', *Vox*, 2023, https://tinyurl.com/yzdx4sk4 (last accessed September 2023).
39 The Discovery Institute's mission is to promote western culture, 'conceived by the ancient Hebrews, Greeks and Christians, and elaborated in the American founding'. Discovery Institute, 'Mission', *Discovery Institute*, n.d., www.discovery.org/about/mission/ (last accessed September 2022).
40 Christopher Rufo, 'Homelessness in America: An Overview', *The Heritage Foundation*, n.d., https://tinyurl.com/bdfw9rmj (last accessed September 2022).
41 Fabiola Cineas, 'Critical Race Theory and Trump's Executive Order on Diversity Training, Explained – Vox', *Vox*, 2020, https://tinyurl.com/52856t4k (last accessed September 2022).
42 Zack Beauchamp, 'Why It Matters That Tucker Carlson Is Broadcasting from Hungary This Week', *Vox*, 2021, https://tinyurl.com/2s3tdte9 (last accessed January 2025).

to become 'the default ideology of the federal bureaucracy' and 'weaponised against the American people', he opined.[43]

Rufo's exposé of the 'segregationism, group-based guilt, and race essentialism' he says are underpinned by critical race methodology and driving antiracism programmes across the US public service, came on the back of a series of freedom of information requests he made to the Seattle Office of Civil Rights.[44] He concluded that a unitary critical race ideology was implanting itself via antiracism, and diversity, equity and inclusion training courses after consulting the footnotes of books such as Robin Di Angelo's *White Fragility* and *How to Be an Antiracist* by Ibram X Kendi, the two texts that were most heavily promoted in the wake of the murder of Minneapolis man George Floyd in the summer of 2020. Their footnotes contained references to the works of veteran CRT scholars, in particular, Derrick Bell and Kimberlé Crenshaw. For Rufo, ostensibly innocuous antiracism and diversity training courses and policies were in fact informed by 'radical, often explicitly Marxist, critical-theory texts from the generation of 1968'.[45] From public institutions, Rufo moved on to attack 'woke capital', egging on right-wing Florida governor, Rick DeSantis, to confront Disney 'for promoting CRT and "gender ideology" ... polluting its brand as a family-friendly company'.[46] By 2024, as Chapter 3 details, Rufo was heavily involved in the campaign to unseat the first Black woman president of Harvard, Claudine Gay, for being a 'diversity hire' who was insufficiently repressive of pro-Palestine students.

---

43 Christopher Rufo, 'Critical Race Theory Has Infiltrated the Federal Government, Christopher Rufo on Fox News', *YouTube*, 2021, https://tinyurl.com/4eybzwxb (last accessed 2022).
44 Wallace-Wells, 'How a Conservative Activist Invented the Conflict over Critical Race Theory'.
45 Ibid.
46 Adrian Wooldridge, 'An Anti-Woke Warrior Has US Companies Running Scared', *Bloomberg.com*, 2022, https://tinyurl.com/mtythkhm (last accessed January 2025). In fact, it was Disney workers walking out in protest that forced the company to issue a statement objecting to DeSantis' virulently anti-queer bill, dubbed 'Don't Say Gay', which coming on the back of the earlier 'Stop W.O.K.E' legislation that attacked CRT, prohibits classroom discussion and instruction on matters of gender identity and sexual orientation. Matt Lavietes, 'Here's What Florida's "Don't Say Gay" Bill Would Do, and What It Wouldn't Do', *NBC News*, 2022, https://tinyurl.com/h2tz9t7p (last accessed March 2022).

Race Marxism[47] author James Lindsay is one figure who provides the intellectual fodder for the war on CRT. During discussions of State of New Hampshire House Bill 544 on 'the propagation of divisive concepts' in May 2021, he claimed to be 'a world level expert in critical race theory ... I am a PhD in mathematics who has been studying the relevant academic literature full time, for sixteen hours a day, most days of the week for the last three years'.[48] His fervour contributes to the illusion that it's all hands on deck or bust in the fight to rid society of the CRT scourge. Lindsay provides the lines used to scaremonger among white parents already primed by the racial regime to interpret their very existence, and the survival of the white-coded nation more broadly, as predicated on the disempowering of Indigenous and Black people. Critical race theorists are, according to Lindsay, fomenting nothing short of 'an Antiracist Cultural Revolution against the United States and other western nations in the hopes of opening the door to establishing their Dictatorship of the Antiracists'.[49] This image, constructed from a century of red-baiting[50] and conjoined counterinsurgency against Black radicalism, with a good measure of the antisemitic discourse of globalist Judeo-Bolshevist plotting to boot, easily finds its real target. Critical race theory, Lindsay insists, is a '*Marxian theory*', 'race-Marxism'[51] to be precise, an 'institutional and conceptual virus'.[52] On cue, one father at the rural northwest Nevada Douglas County School district board meeting in October 2021 said, 'I don't know about you, but I don't want Marxist blood in this county.'[53]

---

47 Lindsay, *Race Marxism*.
48 Sam Hoadley-Brill, 'I Still Can't Believe These Clips from James' Testimony on NH HB 544 Haven't Gone Viral', X, 2021, https://tinyurl.com/ms54u87v (last accessed September 2022).
49 Lindsay, *Race Marxism*, p. 413.
50 Charisse Burden-Stelly, 'How Are Anti-Marxism, Anti-Blackness and Anti-Imperialism Connected?' *Arts of the Working Class*, 2022, https://tinyurl.com/3hwnrhy5 (last accessed January 2025).
51 Lindsay, *Race Marxism*.
52 Ibid., p. 21.
53 Kyung Lah Hannah Jack, 'Discussions of Critical Race Theory, Covid-19 Rules Whip up School Board Meetings to the Dismay of Students', *CNN*, 2021, https://tinyurl.com/3j8d597v (last accessed January 2025).

More cooly, warrior in chief Christopher Rufo admits that CRT was purposefully chosen by him as an instrument for mobilisation. CRT, he explained, works better in service of his aims 'to bait the left'[54] than other, more vague, frames such as 'cancel culture' or 'woke', telling the *New York Times* that it is 'the perfect villain'.[55] In March 2021, he posted, 'we have successfully frozen their brand – critical race theory – into the public conversation and are steadily driving up negative perceptions. We will eventually turn it toxic as we put all the various cultural inanities under that brand.' He followed,

> the goal is to have the public read something crazy in the newspaper and immediately think 'critical race theory.' We have decodified the term and will recodify it to annex the entire range of cultural constructions that are unpopular with Americans.[56]

Rufo has certainly misread – or indeed not read – Stuart Hall on the encoding/decoding processes at work in mass communication. As Hall reminds us, it is only within a 'complex structure in dominance' that messages can be decoded by the public. A message about the perverse nature of something being called CRT, whose bearing or otherwise on an actual body of academic work is irrelevant, can only be received by a public primed to receive it as a 'meaningful discourse'.[57] It is the degree to which certain discourses are dominant that determines whether or not they will cut through, or be meaningfully decoded. Thus, the extensive top-down efforts to decodify/recodify CRT, to cite Rufo's confused use of the terms, are exemplary of what Robinson refers to as the 'mechanisms of assembly' of the racial regime.[58]

---

54 Nicole Gaudiano, 'A Key Conservative Instigator of the Critical Race Theory Controversies Says He Now Wants to "Bait" the Left into Fights over Republican-Led "Transparency" Efforts in Schools', *Business Insider*, 2022, https://tinyurl.com/bdfjnzbv (last accessed November 2022).
55 Wallace-Wells, 'How a Conservative Activist Invented the Conflict Over Critical Race Theory'.
56 Christopher F. Rufo, X, 2021, https://tinyurl.com/49jsphfy (last accessed January 2025).
57 Hall, 'Encoding/Decoding', p. 119.
58 Cedric James Robinson, *Forgeries of Memory and Meaning: Blacks and the Regimes of Race in American Theater and Film before World War II* (Chapel Hill, NC: University of North Carolina Press, 2007), p. xii.

Across the US, bans on the teaching of CRT came thick and fast. By 2023, the UCLA CRT Forward Tracking Project[59] had recorded 619 attempts to introduce anti-CRT measures at local, state and federal levels in all but one state in the US.[60] Many of these policies, resolutions and pieces of legislation were fought for at the school district level. For example, on 5 April 2022, the Placentia-Yorba Linda Unified School District in Orange County, California, *voted to prohibit 'classroom teaching' and 'curriculum content' that 'invokes critical race theory'*.[61] Despite the appearances carefully curated by Rufo, the architects of Project 2025, the Heritage Foundation, and an archipelago of astro-turfing organisations, this is a top-down movement at its core. It is spearheaded by committed right-wing ideologues, such as the anti-Disney crusader Florida Governor Ron DeSantis, accused of torturing detainees in his role as Guantanamo Bay Judge Advocate General Corps and an alumnus of the notoriously racist and sexist Yale University Delta Cappa Epsilon fraternity.[62] DeSantis' Stop W.O.K.E (Wrongs to Our Kids and Employees) Act, passed in 2022, effectively prohibits any antiracist or antisexist training in Florida schools and workplaces, claiming that such training is ideologically underpinned by CRT.[63] It was followed up by The Parental Rights in Education – dubbed 'Don't Say Gay' – Act that prohibits 'classroom discussion about sexual orientation or gender identity in certain grade levels' in Florida's primary schools.[64]

---

59 CRT Forward Tracking Project, 'CRT Forward Tracking Project', https://crtforward.law.ucla.edu (last accessed 27 September 2022).
60 Taifha Natalee Alexander, 'Efforts to Ban Critical Race Theory Have Been Put Forth in All But One State – and Many Threaten Schools with a Loss of Funds', *The Conversation*, 2023, https://tinyurl.com/46nuy4yx (last accessed April 2023).
61 CRT Forward Tracking Project, 'CRT Forward Tracking Project'.
62 Al Mayadeen, '"I Was Screaming and He Was Smiling": DeSantis Ran Guantanamo Torture', *Al Mayadeen English*, 2022, https://tinyurl.com/bd984nkv (last accessed January 2025).
63 Katie Reilly, 'Florida's Governor Just Signed the "Stop Woke Act." Here's What It Means for Schools', *Time*, 2022, https://time.com/6168753/florida-stop-woke-law/ (last accessed September 2022).
64 Meredith Johnson, 'The Dangerous Consequences of Florida's "Don't Say Gay" Bill on LGBTQ+ Youth in Florida', *The Georgetown Journal of Gender and the Law* XXIII, no. 3 (2020), https://tinyurl.com/2p9rvzyx (last accessed January 2025).

In 2021, the state of Texas, 'a state built on a towering mountain of African corpses victimized by enslavement and the ongoing cry to "exterminate" Indigenes',[65] passed a bill prescribing how teachers can talk about current events and America's history of racism in the classroom, dubbed the 'critical race theory bill'.[66] As Gerald Horne's account of what he calls the Texan counter-revolution of 1836 shows,[67] the state was birthed 'in the toxically amniotic fluid of white supremacy and shameless profiteering'.[68] It is therefore unsurprising that it is 'in the vanguard of seeking to move the nation rightward on matters such as "Critical Race Theory" or providing an accurate account of Texas's bloodstained history in classrooms, voting rights and other fraught matters'.[69] The war on CRT is a 'brazen attempt to increase white power'.[70]

'ANTI-WOKENESS IS THE PERFECT EXAMPLE OF THE FUNCTIONING OF THE RACIAL REGIME'

I have loosened the drawstring of the grab bag that is the war on CRT and scattered a smattering of its contents on the table. What is clear is that although the war on CRT certainly raises important questions about the content of education curricula in societies structured in racial dominance or, more broadly, how to speak publicly about the practices that denote that structure – slavery, coloniality, Indigenous dispossession and genocide – the discursive form taken by this 'war' means that we are often diverted into a defensive stance where the terms are set by those who wage it. While critical race scholars and antiracists alike have either entered the fray by debating their detractors or by mounting defences of

---

65 Gerald Horne, *The Counter Revolution of 1836: Texas Slavery & Jim Crow and the Roots of U.S. Fascism* (New York: International Publishers, 2022), p. 570.
66 Kate McGee, 'Texas "Critical Race Theory" Bill Limiting Teaching of Current Events Signed into Law', *The Texas Tribune*, 2021, www.texastribune.org/2021/06/15/abbott-critical-race-theory-law/ (last accessed December 2022).
67 Horne, *The Counter Revolution of 1836*.
68 Ibid., p. 76.
69 Ibid., p. 574.
70 Liz Granderson, 'Texas Gerrymandering Is All about Keeping a Grip on White Power', *Los Angeles Times*, 2021, https://tinyurl.com/5crmj5h4 (last accessed January 2025).

CRT, using the ill-boded opportunity for a teachable moment,[71] this approach treats the attacks as though they can be rationally apprehended and opposed on that basis. It is satisfying to be sure to watch a skilled analyst of race, such as Black studies scholar Marc Lamont Hill, debate Christopher Rufo who was clearly uncomfortable when he was asked to 'name something positive that you like about being white'.[72] However, being drawn into debate on race, as Stuart Hall and his colleagues warned us in 1978, dramatises it 'so as to enhance its newsworthiness'. This 'permits institutional definers to establish the initial definition or *primary interpretation of the topic in question*'.[73]

Differently, my question is what does the war on CRT, much like earlier assaults on antiracism which have set education curricula and policy in their sights, tell us about the recursivity of race in the formation and recalibration of racial regimes? Certainly, such attacks are not new. H.L.T. Quan reminds us that 'systematic and sustained attacks against feminist and ethnic studies throughout the 1980s and 1990s, for instance, represent a campaign of deterrence and containment against the democratization and radicalization of knowledge production that ethnic and gender studies teleologically embodied'.[74] With this in mind, I return here to Robin D.G. Kelley's remark that 'anti-wokeness is the perfect example of the functioning of the racial regime'. Kelley's note that the ideas represented by the rubric of CRT need to be 'shut up' in order to 'restore white sovereignty as the natural order of things'[75] signals that the war on CRT is a mechanism to shore up white sovereignty in the face of Black resistance, becoming acute following the mass mobilisations of 2020. This resistance goes beyond the US. George

---

71 Cf. Ray, *On Critical Race Theory*.
72 Marc Lamont Hill and Christopher F. Rufo, 'The Grio Politics: Marc Lamont Hill Interviews Key Opponent of Critical Race Theory', *YouTube*, 2022, www.youtube.com/watch?v=ihnuYXKBGZg (last accessed May 2023).
73 Stuart Hal, Chas Critcher, Tony Jefferson, John Clarke, and Brian Roberts, 'The Social History of a "Moral Panic"', in *Policing the Crisis: Mugging, the State and Law and Order*, Second edition, 35th anniversary edition (London: Macmillan International Higher Education, 2019), p. 58.
74 H.L.T. Quan, 'Emancipatory Social Inquiry: Democratic Anarchism and the Robinsonian Method', *African Identities* 11, no. 2 (1 May 2013): 117–32, p. 122.
75 Kelley and Camp, 'Against Pessimism'.

Floyd's murder resonated with the experiences of racism structuring the lives of Black people and other negatively racialised people, especially those frequently targeted by the repressive institutions of the state. In the settler colonies, these resistances dovetailed with those of Indigenous people standing against carcerality and popular violence, against colonial extraction, and for land back, from Gadigal-Wangal land, where I live, to Wet'suwet'en land in so-called British Columbia where, in 2020, First Nations people formed a blockade against the gas pipeline projected to cut across their lands with dire effects for the wellbeing of land, water and people.

As Cedric Robinson wrote following the beating by Los Angeles police of Rodney King in 1992, which triggered the 'outraged and the betrayed [taking] to the streets', the 'phantasmagoria of "political correctness" and "reverse discrimination"' are a slap in the face to the 'real aspirations of women, workers, the poor and people of colour'.[76] 'Political correctness' and 'reverse discrimination' were terms used in earlier times to discredit attempts to hold back the tide of white supremacy through university admissions processes and curricular modifications. These past dismissals of institutional antiracism efforts are the building blocks on which the war on CRT teeters. It seems that each moment of resistance is pushed back by the reconstruction of the ideology of racial threat, today purportedly posed by the dangers of 'critical race theory ideology'.

Robinson sees 'political correctness', the right's attempt to dismiss attempts to redress the effects of discriminatory policy and dehumanising speech as 'loony leftism' (to use a phrase once beloved of the British tabloid press), as a diversionary tactic to draw attention away from what he calls the *real world* of political correctness.[77] In this real world, 'official mantras evoking democracy, national

---

76   Cedric J. Robinson, 'Race, Capitalism, and the Antidemocracy', in *Cedric Robinson: On Racial Capitalism, Black Internationalism, and Cultures of Resistance*, ed. H.L.T. Quan (London: Pluto Press, 2019), p. 582.
77   Cedric J. Robinson, 'US The Real World of Political Correctness', *Race & Class* 35, no. 3 (January 1994): 73–9; Joshua Myers, *Cedric Robinson: The Time of the Black Radical Tradition*, Black Lives (Cambridge: Polity Press, 2021). Emphasis my own.

security, anti-Communism, anti-terrorism, etc.' cover over interpretations that reground 'imperialism, racialism, anti-capitalism'.[78] In other words, the brutal reality of 'foreign and domestic wars'[79] is what is actually politically correct, but by scoffing at 'political correctness gone mad', those in control of the narrative shift the gaze away from these truths and onto 'those who would oppose sexism, racism, imperialism and chauvinism'.[80] They, not racial capitalism and imperialism, are responsible for any and all social malaise.

During the 1990s panic over multiculturalism, repeated and intensified in the 2000s,[81] Robinson argued that those defending adjustments made in the name of institutional inclusion, principally affirmative action in the US, avoided the concomitant existence of a *racist* multiculturalism that emphasised relative difference in order 'to conceal the prerogatives of power'.[82] Robinson was concerned that complex questions to do both with domestic racism and capitalist exploitation, as well as US militarism in the context of 'imperial decline' and 'the decay of the global economy', were being recentred around an over-simplification of racial identities.[83] The very real concern that Robinson noted in the 1990s was that 'racial capitalism finds its natural end in fascism',[84] a fact which Black people ignore at their peril because it is they who face

---

78 Robinson, 'US The Real World of Political Correctness', p. 73.
79 Myers, *Cedric Robinson*.
80 Robinson, 'US The Real World of Political Correctness', p. 79.
81 Alana Lentin and Gavan Titley, *The Crises of Multiculturalism: Racism in a Neoliberal Age* (London: Zed Books, 2011).
82 Cedric J. Robinson, 'Ota Benga's Flight through Geronimo's Eyes: Tales of Science and Multiculturalism', in *Cedric Robinson: On Racial Capitalism, Black Internationalism, and Cultures of Reisistance*, ed. H.L.T. Quan (London: Pluto Press, 2019), p. 200.
83 Cedric J. Robinson, 'White Signs in Black Times: The Politics of Representation in Dominant Texts', in *Cedric J. Robinson: On Racial Capitalism, Black Internationalism, and Cultures of Resistance*, ed. H.L.T. Quan (London: Pluto Press, 2019), p. 327.
84 Cedric J. Robinson, 'Toward Fascism? Race, the Two Reservations, and the Materiality of Theory', paper presented at Stanford University, The Two Reservations: Western Thought, the Color Line, and The Crisis of the Negro Intellectual Revisited Symposium, 5 March 1994, CRP, cited in Myers, *Cedric Robinson*, p. 209.

the brunt of it.[85] Ruth Wilson-Gilmore agrees, noting that 'unequal institutions – most notably education and the legal system' lay the ground for 'a more secure fascism'.[86]

It is thus unsurprising that the work of concealing the 'prerogatives of power' proceeds on the terrain of education. Right-wing political scientist, Eric Kaufmann's report into the teaching of 'critical social justice concepts', authored for Policy Exchange,[87] a Conservative lobby group masquerading as a 'neutral educational charity', exemplifies this.[88] Kaufmann claims that 40 per cent of school students exposed to these concepts 'felt fearful of being shamed, punished or expelled for voicing their opinions on controversial subjects'.[89] However, his interview questions included such loaded queries as, 'how comfortable would you have been to criticise a Black schoolmate?' In this case the 'prerogatives of power' are to upturn reality by fictitiously placing Black students, teachers and so-called 'critical race ideologues' in the ideational driver's seat. The report makes no mention of the policing of Black, Indigenous, Roma, Traveller and Muslim children and teens in schools, or indeed their exclusion tout court. Muslim pupils in the UK are regularly 'interviewed by the police and counter-terrorism officers without any of the protections they would have if they were charged with an offence' if they are suspected of being 'vulnerable' to radicalisation.[90] Under the countering violent extremism pro-

---

85 Myers, *Cedric Robinson*.
86 Ruth Wilson Gilmore, *Abolition Geography: Essays towards Liberation*, ed. Brenna Bhandar and Alberto Toscano (London; New York: Verso, 2022), p. 87.
87 As the journalist Hamza Syed noted with regards Policy Exchange's report on the *New York Times*' podcast about the Islamophobic Trojan Horse Affair, there is a direct link between the think tank and those at the highest levels of government. Michael Gove who had been the British education minister at the time of the affair, during which a conspiracy against Muslim educationalists led to their removal from any involvement with a successful public school, co-founded Policy Exchange. Hamza M. Syed, *X*, 2022, https://tinyurl.com/y46k95k4 (last accessed January 2025).
88 George Monbiot, 'No 10 and the Secretly Funded Lobby Groups Intent on Undermining Democracy', *Guardian*, 2020, https://tinyurl.com/bddee6yh (last accessed January 2025).
89 Kaufmann, 'The Political Culture of Young Britain', p. 7.
90 John Holmwood and Layla Aitlhadj, 'The People's Review of Prevent' (London: Prevent Watch, 2022), pp. 1–2.

gramme, Prevent, all those in contact with young people including their teachers are required to undergo training to spot the 'vulnerability' that may lead to a young child being referred to the Office of Security and Counter-Terrorism of the UK Home Office.[91]

The school is a site of violence and carcerality. Prisons and schools are linked through the constant presence of police which turns the nominal spaces of education into places of punishment for Black and poor youth,[92] and Indigenous youth.[93] While school policing in the US is notorious, it occurs with increasing frequency elsewhere. For example, the case of 'Child Q', a Black teenage girl who was strip-searched by police in East London after they were called by her school in 2020, reverberated around the world. In France, former minister for education, Jean-Michel Blanquer's plan to install police in schools in response to a so-called 'wave of violence', in what are euphemistically called the 'popular areas' mainly inhabited by the descendants of formerly colonised peoples,[94] was halted following the 2022 elections. Nonetheless, negatively racialised children still describe being stopped and searched by police on their way to and from school.[95]

The end of Covid lockdown brought with it an amping up of punishment in US schools. Many confronted students' traumatic response to mass death by reinstating the school policing that, in many instances, had been removed due to successful campaigning before 2020. As Warren et al. note, the 'whitelash' against police-free schools 'became part of a larger movement to push back against the gains of the antiracist movement, including attacks on

---

91   Ibid.
92   Damien M. Sojoyner, *First Strike: Educational Enclosures in Black Los Angeles* (Minneapolis, MN: University of Minnesota Press, 2016).
93   Sarah Hopkins, 'The School-to-Prison Pipeline: How the Criminal Justice System Fails At-Risk Kids', 2019, https://tinyurl.com/2cmxy7uh (last accessed January 2025).
94   Myriam Roche, 'Blanquer "trouve très positif" le fait d'avoir des policiers à l'école', *Le HuffPost*, 2018, https://tinyurl.com/22h9nmv5 (last accessed January 2025).
95   Front de Mères, 'Les mères avec les lycéens réprimés par la police: ne touchez pas à nos enfants!' *Front de Mères*, 2020, https://tinyurl.com/y47792ez (last accessed January 2025).

the teaching of Critical Race Theory'.[96] Linking the racist policing of school children and the attack on antiracist ideas, the former British Conservative government tried to 'incorporate Black Lives Matter, the left, and environmental activism under its strictures about extremism'[97] in its plans to 'ratchet up' the Islamophobic Prevent agenda in schools.[98] As Chapter 3 shows, as genocide was perpetrated by Israel in Gaza, schools and universities became sites of intense repression and policing. Far from ideas badged 'critical race theory' muzzling free expression, administrators colluded with the state to raid student encampments, shut down protest, and violently arrest, suspend and fire students and educators.

We can trace the looping patterns of recursivity of the racial regime in these developments. Just as 1990s racial ideology in the US plays out in recalibrated ways today, amplified and expanded by the affordances of contemporary media and technology, it was also coherent with earlier iterations of the racial regime. We can note how each cycle deepens the wound in the flesh of those trying to survive, even as illusions of greater freedom and progress are transmitted via the capitalist, political and mediatic success of a chosen few among the negatively racialised, and the superficial affordances of whiteness conditionally extended to a growing number of those whose forebears were previously denied access.

Racial regimes constantly entail 'efforts to repair or alter race as an effective mechanism of social ordering'.[99] Repair or alteration become the order of the day when political control must be reasserted over 'an American order frayed by domestic rebellion and social diversity'.[100] In Robinson's account of the coterminous birth of commercial cinema and the onset of Jim Crow, rebellion

---

96 Mark R. Warren, Jonathan Stith, and Emma Tynan, 'Police-Free Schools: Challenging the "Pandemic-to-Prison" Pipeline', *Equity & Access Pre K-12, The American Consortium for Equity in Education*, 2022, www.ace-ed.org/police-free-schools/ (last accessed January 2025).
97 Holmwood and Aitlhadj, 'The People's Review of Prevent', p. 9.
98 John Holmwood, 'Ratcheting up the Prevent Agenda in Schools', *Discover Society*, 2020, https://tinyurl.com/yt6ukapa (last accessed January 2025).
99 Robinson, *Forgeries of Memory and Meaning*, p. xvi.
100 Ibid., p. 181.

and social diversity had to be contained by the solidification of American nationalism which relies, as Gerald Horne puts it, on a 'class collaboration' forged in whiteness that is fundamental to the establishment and maintenance of settler colonial rule.[101] The same process is noted by Houria Bouteldja, writing of the class collaborationist and racial solidarity of white trade unionists in France from the time of the Third International.[102] As Robinson shows, in the era of mass unemployment at the turn of the twentieth century and with the concomitant consolidation of American finance capital 'no longer originated in London',[103] the potential for uprising among both Black and white workers was fertile. It became imperative in that context to maintain 'political order among this mix of an impoverished majority' and the tool for doing so was 'white racism', a most powerful ideology.[104]

The potential loss of that order was expressed in a 2022 study in which students were asked whether they had been taught that 'white people have unconscious biases that negatively affect non-white people'.[105] The implication, Kemi Badenoch, now the Conservative Party leader, said, was that such teaching makes 'one group of people feel inferior and another group of people feel superior'.[106] Any challenge posed to the alignment of the masses with white possessive power sets the wheels of racial regime construction in motion. Pressing on this point is vital to ensure that recapitulations of the racial regime in the guise of recursive phenomena such as the war on CRT are not minimised as the mere apparitions of 'the culture war' but assessed as endemic to the ideological structure of the racial state.

---

101   Gerald Horne, 'Against Left-Wing White Nationalism', *Monthly Review*, 2021, https://tinyurl.com/5f6fs5xt (last accessed September 2022).
102   Houria Bouteldja, *Rednecks and Barbarians: Uniting the White and Racialized Working Class* (London: Pluto Press, 2024).
103   Robinson, *Forgeries of Memory and Meaning*, p. 181.
104   Ibid., p. 182.
105   Zach Goldberg and Eric Kaufmann, 'Yes, Critical Race Theory Is Being Taught in Schools', *City Journal*, 2022, https://tinyurl.com/yaua9ws7 (last accessed January 2025).
106   Fraser Nelson, 'Kemi Badenoch: The Problem with Critical Race Theory', *The Spectator*, 2020, https://tinyurl.com/2fz2n9k4 (last accessed October 2022).

'DR MARTIN LUTHER KING, JR. WAS MURDERED TWICE'

Ever present in the rhetoric of campaigns like the UK anti-CRT lobby group Don't Divide Us, whose founding letter opened this chapter, is Martin Luther King Jr. It is always a lone sentence, the only one most people can remember, and which many can cite by heart, from Dr King's infamous March on Washington speech: 'I have a dream that my four little children will one day live in a nation where they will not be judged by the colour of their skin but by the content of their character.' Even the leader to end all leaders of the US Black struggle for freedom and equality wanted simply, many claim to sincerely believe, not to be reduced to the colour of his skin. In an impassioned article protesting against Brighton and Hove City Council's antiracism training approach, Don't Divide Us activist, Bola Anike, writes, 'Colour-blindness ... is the essence of an anti-racist approach famously exemplified by Martin Luther King Jnr (a hero of mine).'[107]

In 1999, a civil suit taken by the King family found that 'local, state and federal governments were liable for his death'.[108] King was assassinated in 1968 after years of obsessive discrediting by the FBI under the reign of J. Edgar Hoover and COINTELPRO[109] which had the mission of violently stamping out political radicalism in the US and due to which countless political prisoners, mainly Black, are unfree to this day.[110] As Robin Kelley puts it, 'Dr Martin Luther King, Jr. was murdered twice. First by an assassin's bullet in Memphis and then by killing his revolutionary mes-

---

107 Bola Anike, 'Bring People Together to Tackle Racism Rather than Back Divisive Council Approach', *Brighton and Hove News*, 2022, https://tinyurl.com/8kbf8kpv (last accessed September 2022).
108 Tom Jackman, 'Who Killed Martin Luther King Jr.? His Family Believes James Earl Ray Was Framed', *Washington Post*, 2018, https://tinyurl.com/32jtrx8k (last accessed January 2025).
109 The counterinsurgency programme conducted by the Federal Bureau of Investigation (FBI) under J. Edgar Hoover from 1956 to 1971 that mainly targeted radical Black, Indigenous and communist organisations.
110 National Archives, 'Findings on MLK Assassination', *National Archives*, n.d., www.archives.gov/research/jfk/select-committee-report/part-2d.html (last accessed January 2025).

sage.'[111] 'King's radicalism, including his socialist commitments' and his 'indictment of capitalism'[112] have been traded for what Kelley calls remembrances in the shape of 'special holiday sales.'[113] The power he embodied means that not only was it necessary to eliminate him, but King had to be reconstituted as a floating signifier for everything the US empire tells itself about racial progress and parroted around the world.

We get a palimpsest of Dr King when his words are uprooted from the context of the violence of racial segregation from which he spoke and put to work for the reconstruction of fascism. Hence, Donald Trump, opening the 2020 White House Conference on American History, an event posed in opposition to CRT, said, 'We embrace the vision of Martin Luther King, where children are not judged by the color of their skin but by the content of their character. The Left is attempting to destroy that beautiful vision ...'[114] For his part, reactionary British journalist, Andrew Doyle, who as the parody character, Titania McGrath, initiated a social media pile-on against me in 2021, appeared on the right-wing GB News channel to lambast so-called culture warriors 'who have told us that Martin Luther King's dream of a colourblind society should be abandoned in favour of a system of heightened racial division.'[115]

The work to detach King from both his Black radicalism and anticapitalism[116] and from the campaign waged by the state to per-

111   Robin D.G. Kelley, 'The Dream of Revolution', *Cooperation Jackson*, 2019, https://cooperationjackson.org/blog/dreamofrevolutionrdgk (last accessed January 2025).
112   Andrew J. Douglas and Jared A. Loggins, *Prophet of Discontent: Martin Luther King Jr. and the Critique of Racial Capitalism*, Sustainable History Monographs Project (Athens, OH: The University of Georgia Press, 2021), p. 3.
113   Kelley, 'The Dream of Revolution'.
114   GOP Chairwoman, 2020, *X*, https://tinyurl.com/c5zcjp8p (last accessed September 2022).
115   Andrew Doyle, 'If Culture Warriors Really Are on the Right Side of History, the Future Looks Bleak', *YouTube*, 2022, https://tinyurl.com/mnjtrynj (last accessed January 2025).
116   The day following Martin Luther King Day 2023, former CIA employee from 2003 to 2014, Gail Helt, posted, 'For many of the years I was at CIA, I included this MLK quote as part of my email header: "Cowardice asks the question, is it safe? Expediency asks the question, is it politic? Vanity asks the question, is it popular? But conscience asks the question, is it right? And there comes a time

manently silence him did not begin with the war on CRT. The severing of the instrumentalisation of King's 'dream' from what Cornel West describes as 'his grand fight against poverty, militarism, materialism and racism'[117] has been traced back to 1985 when the Cold Warrior President Ronald Reagan used the 'dream' to oppose affirmative action policies in hiring. Reagan had objected to the Civil Rights Act when it was passed in 1964, but that did not deter him from arguing that 'civil rights laws were designed to stop' quotas based on race or sex.[118]

Similar arguments are used to mobilise against CRT which is posited as discriminatory under the terms of the Civil Rights Act because, according to the *National Review*, it creates 'a hostile environment by continually singling people out for criticism solely on the basis of their skin color'.[119] CRT, according to Christopher Rufo's 'Critical Race Theory Briefing Book', sees all white people as inherently racist, thus legitimating 'antiracist discrimination' against them. It is also anti-meritocratic in that critical race theorists recognise the role of ideological egalitarianism in obscuring the workings of the 'racial contract'.[120] King's dream can be invoked to argue for a universalist vision of racism from which history has been evacuated. Gary Younge recalls Malcolm X's remark that 'this dream of King's is going to be a nightmare before it's over'.[121]

---

when we must take a position that is neither safe, nor politic, nor popular, but one must take it because it is right"'. Gail Helt, *X*, 2023, https://tinyurl.com/3n5ezm89 (last accessed December 2023).

117 Cornel West, 'Martin Luther King Jr Was a Radical. We Must Not Sterilize His Legacy', *Guardian*, 2018, https://tinyurl.com/5c5sx45b (last accessed December 2023); Rufo, 'Critical Race Theory Briefing Book', 2022, https://christopherrufo.com/crt-briefing-book/ (last accessed June 2022).

118 John Blake, 'Why Conservatives Call MLK Their Hero', *CNN*, 2013, www.cnn.com/2013/01/19/us/mlk-conservative/index.html (last accessed December 2023).

119 Samantha Harris, 'Critical Race Theory Is Dangerous. Here's How to Fight It', *National Review*, 2021, https://tinyurl.com/39z5wvzb (last accessed January 2025).

120 Charles W. Mills, *The Racial Contract* (Ithaca, NY: Cornell University Press, 2011).

121 Gary Younge, 'Gary Younge on Martin Luther King: Exclusive Book Extract from The Speech', *Guardian*, 2013, https://tinyurl.com/ypfdtfde (last accessed January 2025).

Malcolm recognised that the speech could be used to paper over the reality of US racial rule and murderously undermine the struggle for Black freedom. The fact that King is so readily invoked to condemn any effort to redress systemic racism, from affirmative action to the teaching of CRT, is paradoxical given the FBI's portrayal of 'King as a "whole-hearted Marxist"'.[122] Today, anti-CRT activists looking for tips on how to lobby their school boards or local councils are advised to define it as 'race-based Marxism'.[123]

IDEOLOGICAL CONSTRUCTS OF RACIAL LIBERALISM

As I return to remember at several junctures throughout this book, any argument which takes hypocrisy as its starting point will do very little to make sense of how the hollowed-out shell of King's 'I have a Dream' speech becomes an instrument for reactionary anti-antiracism. Indeed, the framing of the right's capture of liberal antiracist rhetoric as hypocritical fails to excavate the rooting of modern racial ideology in what Charles Mills calls 'racial liberalism or white liberalism'.[124] A central idea in CRT is the critique of what Richard Delgado calls 'liberal McCarthyism', that is, the efforts of liberal academia to limit the possibilities of a new cadre of Black and Brown students who entered universities in large numbers in the US from the late 1950s on and to stave off any potential for radicalism among them.[125] Racial liberalism, as the legal scholar and civil rights jurist Lani Guinier explains, 'emphasized the corrosive effect of individual prejudice and the importance of interracial contact in promoting tolerance ... without fear of disrupting society as a whole'.[126] In contrast, CRT sets out to 'understand how a regime of

---

122 Douglas and Loggins, *Prophet of Discontent*, p. 3.
123 Rufo, 'Critical Race Theory Briefing Book'.
124 Charles W. Mills, *Black Rights/White Wrongs: The Critique of Racial Liberalism*, Transgressing Boundaries (New York: Oxford University Press, 2017), p. 30.
125 Richard Delgado, 'Liberal McCarthyism and the Origins of Critical Race Theory', *Iowa Law Review* 94 (2009): 1505–46.
126 Lani Guinier, 'From Racial Liberalism to Racial Literacy: Brown v. Board of Education and the Interest-Divergence Dilemma', *The Journal of American History* 91, no. 1 (2004): 92–118, p. 95.

white supremacy and its subordination of people of colour have been created and maintained in America, and in particular, to examine the relationship between that social structure and professed ideals such as the "rule of law" and "equal protection".[127] The attack on white advantage that CRT denotes, whipped up and personalised as an attack on 'your children' by the anti-CRT ideologues, triggers a deep-seated reaction formed by racial liberalism: any challenge posed to it is not only experienced as an undermining of white freedom but also as a rejection of the benevolence on which liberal morality is predicated.

Racial liberalism was not a new feature of the late twentieth century when critical race theorists began to emerge; neither is it confined to the US. From the eighteenth century, an evolving racial liberalism 'restricted full personhood to whites' while advancing a modernist ideology which emphasised 'the importance and rights of the individual'.[128] Freedom, as Tyler Stovall shows for both the US and France,[129] is essentially forged on a white vision, uniting the two nations ideologically despite the hegemonic French rejection of all things American, race first and foremost. Liberal ideas of universalism, reprocessed as colourblindness and meritocracy, initially shaped European colonial benevolence and the 'civilising mission'. In extending the white patriarchal hand of 'progress' to select colonised subjects, colonial administrators enacted internal race-class taxonomies that enabled the division of labour necessary for the smooth running of colonial capitalism and creating the internal class and colour hierarchies that have challenged the newly decolonised nations.[130] W.E.B. Du Bois drew out the ideo-

---

127 Kimberlé Williams Crenshaw, Neil Gotanda, Gary Peller, and Kendall Thomas, 'Introduction', in *Critical Race Theory: The Key Writings That Formed the Movement*, ed. Kimberlé Crenshaw, Neil Gotanda, Gary Peller, and Kendall Thomas (New York: New Press, 1995), p. xiii.
128 Tyler Stovall, *White Freedom: The Racial History of an Idea* (Princeton, NJ: Princeton University Press, 2022), p. 139.
129 Ibid.
130 Frantz Fanon, *The Wretched of the Earth: Frantz Fanon* (New York: Grove Press, 2004).

logical role played by liberalism[131] in support of capitalism as 'a global historical system rooted in class exploitation and colonialism'.[132] In 1936, he wrote that nineteenth-century colonial imperialism replaced empire as 'political rule' with 'empire which was investment' in which 'the philanthropic plan of carrying civilization to the natives became one and the same as the commercial plan of making native labour pay'.[133]

Via the ideological constructs of liberalism premised on the promise of universal individual rights, substantial effort has been put into obscuring the workings of racial rule, as CRT reveals. Racial liberalism conceals exploitation and dispossession as seen in the theft of land, the mass enslavement of inferiorised peoples, and the subsequent imperial and colonial domination that facilitated the extraction of the majority of the world's resources for European enrichment. Despite the rhetoric of emancipation and brotherhood formulated by the progressive white abolitionists of the nineteenth century, in practice, as Sylvia Wynter notes, people of Black African descent were counterposed to the 'fully evolved, thereby only True Human Self ... optimally incarnated in the Western bourgeois liberal monohumanist *homo economicus*'.[134] After the formal end of slavery, forced by the long revolution fought by the enslaved of Haiti at the dawning of the 1800s, Black

---

131 While the political economist Onur Ince remarks that the development of colonial capitalism is contingent on liberal thinking and its ability to deploy the ideology of individual rights and freedoms to contain the actual violence of rampaging colonial expropriation, he is mistaken in thinking that most scholars have treated 'the connection between liberalism and empire primarily as a problem of the politics of representation, culture, or identity' rather than of capitalist reproduction. Onur Ince, *Colonial Capitalism and the Dilemmas of Liberalism* (Oxford: Oxford University Press), p. 15. Cf. Lisa. Lowe, *The Intimacies of Four Continents* (Durham, NC: Duke University Press, 2015).

132 Aldon Morris, Michael Schwartz, and José Itzigsohn, 'Racism, Colonialism, and Modernity: The Sociology of W.E.B. Du Bois', in *Handbook of Classical Sociological Theory*, ed. Seth Abrutyn and Omar Lizardo, Handbooks of Sociology and Social Research (New York: Springer International Publishing, 2021), pp. 121–43, p. 132.

133 Phil Zuckerman, *The Social Theory of W.E.B. Du Bois* (London: Sage, 2004), p. 73.

134 Katherine McKittrick, ed., *Sylvia Wynter: On Being Human as Praxis* (Durham NC: Duke University Press, 2015), p. 47.

people were 'made to embody this most subordinated *wholly human Other* status'.[135] While many have interpreted the Haitian revolution as 'the most concrete expression of the idea that the rights proclaimed in France's 1789 Declaration of the Rights of Man and Citizen were indeed universal',[136] the punishment meted out to Haiti to this day for beating back the French reveals the 'white ignorance'[137] at the heart of this assumption.

Indeed, the legacy of the Haitian revolution is a good prism for considering the politics of the war on CRT. The repackaging of the Black Jacobins' victory in the terms of universalist human rights[138] masks the fact that the ongoing attempt to contain and exploit Haiti[139] is in part a response to 'armed Africans surging to power', freeing themselves from bondage and liberating their nation.[140] Gerald Horne notes that the Haitian overthrow of slavery raised the fear that Black rule over the 'new world' would follow.[141] Britain's support for abolition as a means of positioning itself against the increasingly aggressive slaveholding American republic after 1776,[142] together with the threat posed by insurgent Africans in the Caribbean who could influence those enslaved within the United States itself, meant that the new Republic had to face the 'prospect of a reconfiguration of' a state 'conspicuously based on enslav-

---

135   Ibid.
136   Laurent Dubois, *Avengers of the New World: The Story of the Haitian Revolution*, First Harvard University Press paperback edition (Cambridge, MA: The Belknap Press of Harvard University Press, 2005), p. 3.
137   Mills, *Black Rights/White Wrongs*.
138   Philip Kaisary, 'Human Rights and Radical Universalism: Aimé Césaire's and CLR James's Representations of the Haitian Revolution', *Law and Humanities* 6, no. 2 (1 December 2012): 197–216.
139   Jemima Pierre, 'Haiti: The Second Occupation', *The Public Archive: Black History in White Times*, 2015, https://thepublicarchive.com/?p=4639 (last accessed January 2025).
140   Gerald Horne, *Confronting Black Jacobins: The United States, the Haitian Revolution, and the Origins of the Dominican Republic* (New York: Monthly Review Press, 2015), p. 9.
141   Ibid., p. 10.
142   Gerald Horne, *The Counter-Revolution of 1776: Slave Resistance and the Origins of the United States of America* (New York: New York University Press, 2014).

ing Africans'.[143] By placing insurgent slaves at the heart of history as Horne does, we get a clearer picture of why racial liberalism develops; essentially as a mechanism for quelling revolt and containing the potential for a powerful alliance between Blacks and others among the poor. It is no coincidence, as we shall see in the next chapter, that 'the People's Historian', Gerald Horne's thesis on the counter-revolutionary nature of the founding of the United States as a bastion of slaveholding power against abolitionism is a major touchstone of the war on CRT and related furores about the (re)writing of US American history.

What is certain is that the apparent contradictions of the interweaving of race and liberalism cannot be countered from within liberalism itself. This is where I depart from Charles Mills who ultimately defended the possibility of producing a 'self-consciously antiracist liberalism' out of the ashes of what he portrays as the '(anti-universalist, anti-egalitarian) distortions in mainstream white liberalism'.[144] The way liberal ideology is used as a cudgel to beat radical forms of antiracism with[145] severely questions whether this is possible, or indeed desirable. The opposition set up between 'reasonable' and 'rational' approaches to race and racism and what are proposed as their 'illiberal' and 'extremist' rejection by radical actors is the discursive linchpin of the war on CRT. When liberalism, which hides 'the social as a concrete formation' from view,[146] is applied to attempts at social transformation, it comes up short because the primacy placed on the ideological frames of freedom, equality and tolerance obscures the actual conditions of the eighteenth and nineteenth centuries in which they were developed, at the height of colonialism and slavery. Indeed, the extreme liberal position was often used to argue in favour of the institution of slavery by representing abolitionist fervour as the *anti*liberal stance.[147] The peak of liberalism's success, as seen

---

143 Ibid., p. 14.
144 Mills, *Black Rights/White Wrongs*, p. 201.
145 Arun Kundnani, *What Is Antiracism? And Why It Means Anticapitalism* (New York: Verso, 2023).
146 Himani Bannerji, *The Ideological Condition: Selected Essays on History, Race and Gender* (Leiden: Brill, 2020), p. 43.
147 Domenico Losurdo, *Liberalism: A Counter-History* (London: Verso, 2014).

most prominently in the French and American revolutions, not only coincidentally accompanied slavery's 'maximum development',[148] ideologically it placed individual freedoms over those of the masses. This was primed to favour minoritarian white male property holders and the political interests they represented over those whose unfreedom their gains were based upon.[149] This individualist bent allowed the interpretation of 'the peculiarly American race "problem" as a psychological and interpersonal challenge rather than a structural problem rooted in our economic and political system'.[150]

The ideological framing of the war on CRT rhetorically reasserts a racial liberalism whose tenets are seen as benign in centrist and white left accounts because they are deracinated from their origins as cornerstones of colonialism, racial capitalism and the racial state. An approach to the war on CRT that disconnects it from 'the overall social organisation and relations that form' it[151] see it as a discrete event, one in a series of such events often grouped under the heading of 'the culture wars'. From this perspective, it cannot be understood as continuous with the formation and rearticulation of the racial regime to which liberal ideology is core. Any approach which treats race as tangential, rather than central, to liberalism, capitalism, colonialism or the state cannot contend with something like the war on CRT because the tendency is always to see it as either marginal, trivial or a ruse to distract from what is proposed to be 'the real issue'.

To think through the appearance of the war on CRT as an example of the functioning of the racial regime, we need to pay attention to the interrelationship between the ideological and the material in the enactment of racial rule in the current conjuncture. For this, we need to consider the interplay between racial capitalism and racial liberalism, recalling Du Bois' words on the

---

148   Ibid., p. 35.
149   J. Sakai, *Settlers: The Mythology of the White Proletariat from Mayflower to Modern*, Fourth edition (Oakland, CA: PM Press, 2014).
150   Guinier, 'From Racial Liberalism to Racial Literacy', p. 100.
151   Bannerji, *The Ideological Condition*, p. 43.

inability to extricate the civilising mission from colonialism's capitalist ends.[152] It is to this relationship that I now turn.

NO MERCY!

No Mercy: How Conservative Think Tanks and Foundations Changed America's Social Agenda[153] is the title of a book published in 1996 by Richard Delgado and Jean Stefancic, the authors of the best-known textbook on CRT.[154] The authors track the role of US conservative think tanks and foundations starting in the 1960s in setting off a conservative revolution through their funding of studies and programmes on a range of issues made politically contentious, from immigration to affirmative action and multiculturalism. They detail the role of foundations such as The Pioneer Fund, a 'Nazi endowment',[155] in bringing eugenics back in through the proverbial backdoor to justify the 'purposeful abandonment organised by elites', the slashing of welfare under neoliberalism that leaves the poor to fend for themselves.[156] The role of neoconservatives – 'prominent liberal intellectuals who moved right' – in 'draw[ing] up the very terms of the culture wars' is a well-charted history.[157] Certainly, that the war on CRT 'works better' discursively, in Christopher Rufo's terms, is in large part because it has been fashioned by a well-oiled and abundantly financed machine: the network of right-wing lobby groups that has cultivated the weapon of intractable polarisation around questions of race in order to set the political agenda in favour of conservative financial elites.

---

152   Zuckerman, *The Social Theory of W.E.B. Du Bois*.
153   Jean Stefancic and Richard Delgado, *No Mercy: How Conservative Think Tanks and Foundations Changed America's Social Agenda* (Philadelphia, PA: Temple University Press, 1996).
154   Delgado and Stefancic, *Critical Race Theory*.
155   Steven J. Rosenthal, 'The Pioneer Fund: Financier of Fascist Research', *American Behavioral Scientist* 39, no. 1 (September 1995): 44–61.
156   Gilmore, *Abolition Geography*, p. 304.
157   Andrew Hartman, *A War for the Soul of America: A History of the Culture Wars* (Chicago, IL: University of Chicago Press, 2015), p. 38.

Key actors in the war on CRT are not mere 'concerned citizens' to be sure. The reason why, in Christopher Rufo's language, 'decodifying' CRT and 'recodifying' it to stand for what are depicted as left-wing 'cultural inanities' has proven a viable strategy for the US right becomes clearer when we note Rufo's association with the private, conservative Christian liberal arts Hillsdale College. Rufo's book, *Critical Race Theory: What It Is and How to Fight It* is published by Imprimis, the Hillsdale College publishers. Hillsdale is also home to the Academy for Science and Freedom, established in December 2021 as the Omicron variant of the Covid-19 virus swept the globe. The Academy's response to the pandemic focuses on what it sees as the fiasco of 'government pandemic measures like mask and vaccine mandates, contact tracing, and lockdowns'.[158] The leading scholars within the Academy are major figures of the Great Barrington Declaration, the March 2020 letter encouraging governments to adopt a 'herd immunity' strategy to the pandemic. The declaration is backed by right-wing corporate actors, principally the billionaire Koch brothers through their right-wing non-profit organisation, Americans for Prosperity, whose principal concern was to preserve the fossil fuel industry which took a major hit as a result of the lockdown measures introduced by governments to curb the viral spread. The work put in place by powerful right-wing economic players to undermine the pandemic response had a direct impact on the number of lives lost through the reckless anti-public health policies put in place by political leaders across the US,[159] first among them conservatives such as Florida's DeSantis where Covid deaths have consistently exceeded those in other states.[160]

Bragman and Kotch note the techniques used by various Koch brother-funded lobby groups to popularise the herd immunity

---

[158] Walker Bragman and Alex Kotch, 'How the Koch Network Hijacked the War on COVID', *The Lever*, 2021, https://tinyurl.com/27hbvwks (last accessed January 2025).
[159] Ibid. They remark that the impact of the Great Barrington Declaration also went beyond the borders of the US, influencing the disastrous policies adopted by the UK and Swedish governments.
[160] Chris Persaud, 'Florida Leads Nation COVID Deaths Though Cases Keep Declining', 2022, https://tinyurl.com/3sa5w546 (last accessed September 2023).

strategy through the funding of anti-lockdown protests. Networks established with Koch brother funds in the 1990s, which came to fruition in the Obama-era ultra-libertarian Tea Party movement, proved useful for providing bodies for the protests.[161] One of the groups tapped was FreedomWorks, 'a dark money group tied to Charles Koch instrumental in organizing Tea Party protests in 2009'.[162] A look at the FreedomWorks website finds extensive search results for 'critical race theory', including the May 2021 statement that 'FreedomWorks Foundation's Regulatory Action Center and Building Education for Students Together (BEST) initiative have joined forces to push back against federal control of civics education.'[163] FreedomWorks is only one of a large number of organisations funded by right-wing donors within what Wilson and Kamola call the Koch donor network. They examine the role of Koch money in fomenting a 'campus free speech crisis' which is discursively linked with the war on CRT through the promotion of the idea that authoritarian antiracist students, encouraged by so-called 'Race Marxist' academics, shut down opinion on race and racism that does not toe the line with what Eric Kaufman calls the hegemonic 'left-moralist' agenda' on matters of race.[164]

The Koch Foundation funds Covid and climate change denialism, the war on CRT and campus 'free speech' campaigns, in addition to a whole range of other right-wing agendas. Koch-funded organisations work 'to undermine environmental, health, and labour regulations, to attack unions, privatise education, reduce taxation, and dismantle the social safety net'.[165] It is,

---

161 Jeff Nesbit, 'The Secret Origins of the Tea Party', *Time*, 2016, https://time.com/secret-origins-of-the-tea-party/ (last accessed September 2023).
162 Bragman and Kotch, 'How the Koch Network Hijacked the War on COVID'.
163 Parents Know Best, 'FreedomWorks Foundation Pushes Back against Critical Race Theory in Schools', *FreedomWorks*, 2021, https://tinyurl.com/yc3y2cmm (last accessed February 2025). FreedomWorks shut down in May 2024.
164 Eric Kaufmann, 'Taking on the Social Justice Warriors', *UnHerd*, 2018, https://unherd.com/2018/12/taking-on-the-social-justice-warriors/ (last accessed January 2025).
Kaufmann is an adjunct fellow at the Manhattan Institute where Rufo is a senior fellow.
165 Ralph Wilson and Isaac A. Kamola, *Free Speech and Koch Money: Manufacturing a Campus Culture War* (London: Pluto Press, 2021), p. 13.

therefore, apparent why it would fund *Spiked*, the online publication spawned by the utralibertarian descendants of the Revolutionary Communist Party which, as we have seen, also birthed Don't Divide Us as well as the Festival of Dangerous Ideas where its director, Dr Alka Sehgal Cuthbert, has appeared. 'Spiked's US fundraising arm, Spiked US Inc – received $280,000 from the Charles Koch Foundation' to, among other things, fund its 'Unsafe Space Tour' of US campuses.[166] There are more articles containing the words 'critical race theory' than can be counted on the Spiked website.

Another lead actor in the Koch donor network is the DeVos family foundation. Betsy DeVos served as Secretary of State for Education under Donald Trump. She has been vocal in her opposition to CRT, writing on her website that 'CRT is a Trojan horse used to introduce Marxist concepts into classrooms.' Her article concludes, 'I've long advocated for education freedom, the idea that students should be free to learn wherever, whenever and however works best for them.'[167] 'Education freedom' is a euphemistic reference to the long-standing Republican plan to defund public schools in the US. It was thus no surprise that DeVos chose a conservative education summit held in Florida in July 2022 to propose that the Department of Education should be abolished,[168] a call given wings by Trump as a 2024 electoral promise.[169] The right's attack on teacher autonomy and its support for increased parental involvement is a dog whistle in the right's efforts to entirely roll back public education, a step which would affect the worst off in society, and which many have signalled is a direct attack on Black families in the US, already disadvantaged by the resegregation of public schools that has continued apace since the legal victories of the 1960s that offi-

---

166 Ibid., p. 203.
167 Betsy DeVos, 'Critical Race Theory in Our Schools', *Betsy DeVos*, n.d., https://betsydevos.com/issues/critical-race-theory/ (last accessed October 2022).
168 Julia Shapero, 'Trump's Education Secretary Betsy DeVos Calls for Abolishing the Department of Education', *Axios*, 2022, https://tinyurl.com/2pemhtwx (last accessed January 2025).
169 Rachel Leingang, 'Trump Promised to Shut down the Education Department. Is It Possible?' *Guardian*, 2025, https://tinyurl.com/2c49ykrz (last accessed January 2025).

cially, but often not in reality, brought an end to the doctrine of 'separate but equal'. When 'increased parental involvement' cannot be assured because, it is proposed, intransigent left-wing dominance over public education overrules it, parents are encouraged to take their children out of public schools and state funding is channelled to the private sector. These policy ideas sit at the heart of the Heritage Foundation's Project 2025, its plan to 'dismantle the unaccountable Deep State, taking power away from Leftist elites', turbo-charged by the election in November 2024 of Donald Trump to the US presidency.[170]

Yet, while there are distinct interests at play in the war on CRT, the line that connects right-wing philanthropists, ultra-libertarian pundits, academics and suburban mothers at school board meetings is not as straight and uncomplicated as some suggest. Solely looking at the war on CRT as a right-wing tool to establish cultural hegemony to smooth the path to privatisation for monetary gain tells only a partial story. For example, Richard Seymour doubts the electoral effectiveness of the attacks on CRT in states such as Texas and Florida in 2021, writing that the Koch brothers' brokering of the anti-CRT agenda was less about swinging elections than it was about raising 'the public profile of demands for market-based deregulation in public schools'.[171] However, this utilitarian reading does not get at *why* the war on CRT has been particularly successful as a rhetorical tool to help divert funding from US public schools.

The war on CRT is a counterinsurgent force which is reactive against a growing commitment to antiracist practice, even when (as we shall see in Chapter 3) this has led to the cooptation and subversion of its more radical elements. It is also the case, contra the dominant tendency to downplay the extent to which aspects of critical race thought are present within education, that the war on CRT responds to a growing desire to know more about the workings of race and the experience of racism. Therefore, the

---

170 Project 2025, 'Project 2025 Presidential Transition Project', Project 2025, 2024, 21 2024, www.project2025.org/ (last accessed August 2024).
171 Richard Seymour, 'The Resources of Reaction', *Salvage*, 2021, https://salvage.zone/the-resources-of-reaction/ (last accessed January 2022).

outrage to be found certainly among the – mainly white, but not solely – public against the potential teaching of critical race ideas in schools is not as evenly spread as the anti-CRT ideologues would have it. Nevertheless, the reason why the war on CRT has proved itself an amenable discursive vehicle cannot be uniquely put down to 'plutocratic libertarian' manipulation.[172] Certainly, constructing opposing narratives is made more difficult when one notes the sheer volume of material resources injected into creating a controversy such as the war on CRT. In relation to the Kochs' role in fomenting the campus free speech panic, for example, Wilson and Kamola recommend following the money and resisting taking at face value reports on the extent of a crisis on campuses. The value of this meticulous research cannot be quantified. Nevertheless, when it comes to the confection of outrage around issues of race specifically, from which of course the theme of freedom of speech cannot be divorced,[173] then we need to return to the question, 'Why race?'

WHY RACE?

This question is opened by the framework of racial capitalism as conceived by Cedric Robinson. The attempt to answer it in relation to the success of the war on CRT and similar controversies that have preceded it, and will surely follow, helps us move beyond utilitarian framings and excavate the functions of the racial regime more deeply. As we have seen, CRT is attacked discursively through the appeal to a liberalism whose racialist foundations are cloaked in a language of meritocracy. CRT is presented as unfair to people of colour whose efforts to be treated as equals are undermined by the determination of 'race peddlers' to treat them as less able, a staple of racial neoliberal ideology.[174] For the conservative linguist, John McWhorter, for example, a 'woke racism' subverts antiracism into

---

172 Wilson and Kamola, *Free Speech and Koch Money*, p. 261.
173 Gavan Titley, *Is Free Speech Racist?* Debating Race Series (Cambridge, UK; Medford, MA: Polity Press, 2020).
174 David Theo Goldberg, *The Threat of Race: Reflections on Racial Neoliberalism* (Malden, MA: Blackwell, 2009).

a religion which 'is actively harmful to black people', teaching them that the world is 'set against them'.[175] Right-wing and libertarian proponents of the war on CRT propound the view that progress to redress what are characterised as residual racist sentiments has already been achieved, or at the very least is well underway. Hence, CRT which sees race as structured into the legal, political, social and economic infrastructure of societies whose wealth and power are derived from the arrangements of colonial and racial capitalism and imperialism is presented as denying the extent of that progress.

Thinking about the centrality accorded to progress allows us to flesh out the ideological dimensions of racial capitalism. Considering the connections between ideology and materiality helps explain why it is *race* that recursively captures the public imagination, working as a rallying point for right-wing and libertarian projects. Interrogating this question also helps make sense of what part the *racial* plays in capitalism more broadly. Robinson's emphasis on the role played by racialism in the establishment and development of capitalism contributes a reading of world history since the burgeoning of mercantilism in Europe to which race is central rather than peripheral. The practices of racialist differentiation could be shaped to fit the requirements of ever-expanding capitalist endeavours. The larger and more complex they became, the more human labour was needed for them to operate. As Robinson notes, building on the work of scholars such as Eric Williams in *Capitalism and Slavery*,[176] Europe became wealthy on the backs of enslaved people as the appetite for products from the 'new world' rampantly increased and whole economies were made by their toil. This system of unadulterated exploitation which led to massive loss of life among European crews in addition to transported Africans, at least 400,000 of whom 'died "in transit"',[177] had to be ideologically justified. However, rather than seeing race in purely instrumental terms as a mechanism for advancing capital-

---

175   John H. McWhorter, *Woke Racism: How a New Religion Has Betrayed Black America* (New York: Portfolio/Penguin, 2021), p. 11.
176   Eric Eustace Williams, *Capitalism and Slavery* (London: A. Deutsch, 1964).
177   Cedric J. Robinson, *Black Marxism: The Making of the Black Radical Tradition* (Chapel Hill, NC: University of North Carolina Press, 2000), p. 118.

'A DROP OF POISON'

ist interests by pitting differentially racialised groups of workers against each other, racialism is a way of thinking about human social relations whose potential is fully realised under capitalism. So, it is not that race is commensurate with Black or colonised identities, as we tend to think today. Rather, the application of a racial logic to the mass labour system of slavery first, and that afforded by colonialism later, enabled the financial, political and epistemic dominance of Europe.

Under these circumstances, it was imperative for race to become cemented to the figures of the enslaved and the colonised. As Robinson writes in relation to the former, in the American colonies of the 1600s, 'the invention of the Negro was proceeding apace with the growth of slave labour. Somewhat paradoxically, the more Africans and their descendants assimilated cultural materials from colonial society, the less human they became in the minds of the colonists.'[178] Despite the constant efforts of Africans to rebel and their success in some cases, as the maroon communities and others throughout the Americas and the Caribbean attest, 'African labourers' generated the wealth responsible for the industrial revolution, the growth of a variety of industries in Northern America, and facilitated 'the expansion of colonisation and settlement'.[179] The end of slavery did not end the exploitation, however. The degradation of Black humanity achieved under slavery and the consequent 'rape of Africa', as W.E.B. Du Bois put it bluntly,[180] set the stage for the later European imperial domination and colonisation of Africa.

A real reckoning with the extent to which human degradation was directly responsible for Europe's advancement and the greater comforts enjoyed by its people over time should surely precipitate a mass psychic break. However, for the main part, the minimisation, denial and redefinition of race's significance persists, not only because it continues to benefit capitalism in a variety of ways

---

178 Ibid., p. 120.
179 Ibid.
180 W.E.B. Du Bois, *The World and Africa: An Inquiry into the Part Which Africa Has Played in World History* (New York: International Publishers, 1996), p. 86.

today, but because en masse breakdown needs to be kept at bay. This is where the fictions told about race continue to play their part and 'white ignorance' mobilised.[181] Du Bois tells of 'the lovely British home, with green lawns ... within is a young woman, well trained, well dressed, intelligent and high-minded'. While 'her family is not wealthy', it enjoys a 'sufficient "independent" income'. Du Bois asks, 'how far is such a person responsible for the crimes of colonialism?' He conjectures that she is surely ignorant of the relationship between her comfort and the suffering of thousands. Yet, he remarks, 'ignorance is a colossal crime in itself'.[182]

Du Bois is pointing out the paradox of European civilisation which, on the one hand, has absolved any individual of responsibility for mass murder, rape, theft and destruction, and on the other, preaches the primacy of individual human rights. What this signals is that it is impossible to divorce a discussion of the materiality of race seen in the expansion of capitalism from the ideological leaps that were necessary in order to detach the wealth and comfort of Europeans and white colonists from the reason for that wealth and comfort: the dehumanisation of the majority of the world's population. This is why race continually undergoes evolutions in its discursive expression. So, after slavery ceased to be a profitable means of organising labour, a fact first realised by the British who were only in the position to abolish slavery because of the massive wealth that they had accrued because of it, the logic that centuries of racial practices had instilled could be adapted. But the way racial logic was adapted provided the very means for it to be obscured. Thus, people's natural revulsion for slavery which fuelled the popular abolitionist movement in Britain did not lead to a similar resistance to colonialism. This is because colonial expansion was facilitated by what David Goldberg has called a 'racial progressivism'[183] according to which progress and civilisation was

---

181   Charles W. Mills, 'White Ignorance', in *Race and Epistemologies of Ignorance*, ed. Shannon Sullivan and Nancy Tuana (Albany, NY: SUNY Press, 2007).
182   Du Bois, *The World and Africa*, p. 84.
183   David Theo Goldberg, *The Racial State* (Malden, MA: Blackwell Publishers, 2011).

being brought to Africans, Indians and Indigenous peoples by European invaders.

This is where we see the expanded role of Christian missionaries and humanitarians. Du Bois relates the role of explorers such as Livingstone, who he describes as a humanitarian, who played a primary role in stopping the ivory trade which 'became in the last half of the nineteenth century the scourge of Central Africa'.[184] Livingstone believed that 'trade and commerce was the best and natural way to improve the condition of man'.[185] His role was supplemented by the British imperialist Kirk who had no desire for 'the development and rise of the blacks', but was motivated to end the Arab-run ivory-slave trade in order to enhance British power by 'increasing colonial ownership and serf labour under Britain'.[186] The result was a colonial alliance between Britain and Arab leaders that enabled British colonial expansion in Africa under the guise of 'bringing commerce and missionary effort to the natives'.[187] The stop put to the expansion of slavery solidified the British empire: 'slavery and the slave trade became transformed into anti-slavery and colonialism, and all with the same determination and demand to increase the profit of investment'.[188] However, from the perspective of the ignorant young English woman Du Bois earlier described, this new system was far superior to that of slavery, because those labouring for her comfort were no longer in literal bondage. Moreover, they were being brought civilisation where none, as the story goes, was present.

The predominant view of racism mobilised by the anti-CRT warriors is of a wrongheaded, yet understandable – if not wholly justifiable – way of thinking that was *of its time*. The time nebulously referred to shifts but is usually thought about as the era before the passage of civil rights legislation in the United States or the abolition of slavery, be it for the British, the French, the Dutch or the Portuguese. In any case, this time is past and the important

---

184   Du Bois, *The World and Africa*, p. 112.
185   Ibid., p.113.
186   Ibid.
187   Ibid.
188   Ibid.

thing to remember is that slavery *did* come to an end and legislative and political progress was achieved, no matter that, as we saw in the case of Reagan, it was often opposed by the same people who now claim it is firmly in the past. However, as Black radical, Indigenous and anticolonial actors and thinkers stress, any opposition to racial rule was due to the struggles waged by those degraded by it. This historical fact cannot be left unchallenged by the ideologues of racial liberalism for whom not only is race overwrought in Black, Indigenous and colonised accounts, but crucially, this is so because of the role of whites and Europeans in bringing to a close what is portrayed as an unfortunate relic of history.

Only this fiction is permissible: that while racism may have begun with Europe, it was only European civilisational advancement that could enable its demise. Under this version of events, any 'harking back' to race is tantamount to a slap in the face to that great progressivism that would not have been possible were it not for the existence of European (later white) rule in the first instance. The perversity of this position does not need much belabouring, but it is nonetheless a major component of the racial regime as it continues to be elaborated. Understanding the need for this retelling of history is fundamental for making sense of what is *racial* in racial capitalism. It is not sufficient to explain phenomena such as the war on CRT as an elaborate ruse for masking libertarian oligarchical moves on public education, although that is certainly a factor.

As Du Bois showed with the ending of the ivory-slave trade, the motive is certainly more profit, but the reason why it is *race*, in its ability to morph and reshape, that serves this purpose can only be fully answered by contending with the extent to which denying the degree to which a racial logic has enabled minoritarian enrichment, at the expense of the human majority and the survival of the earth itself is fundamental to the persistence of the status quo, albeit under new guises. The disavowal of the role of race is paramount to the recalibration of the racial regime. Nowhere is this more clear than in the 'history wars' that give substance to the war on CRT.

2
On History and the Technologies of White Forgetting

The work [*Black Marxism*] required a certain destructuring of American and western historiography. For the realisation of new theory we require new history.[1]

This is an orchestrated guerrilla campaign that we are dealing with. If people in the academy feel a need to engage in this battle then they should be prepared to fight with the same guerrilla tactics rather than claim the high moral ground.[2]

In May 2023, the National Conservatism conference was held at Westminster in London featuring an array of the west's most prominent right-wing ideologues. In her address, then British Home Secretary, Suella Braverman, pinpointed the 'radical left' as a threat that must be extinguished. Describing them as perpetually 'ashamed of our history and embarrassed by the sentiments and desires expressed by the British public', Braverman admonished the left for only being able to 'sell its vision for the future by making people feel terrible about our past'. Far from having anything to be ashamed about, Britons should be proud of their history, even those elements more generally acknowledged to be less than admirable: 'The defining feature of this country's relationship with slavery', she said, 'is not that we practised it, but that

---

1   Cedric J. Robinson, *Black Marxism: The Making of the Black Radical Tradition*, Second edition (Chapel Hill, NC: University of North Carolina Press, 2000), p. 307.
2   Tony Birch, '"I Could Feel It in My Body": War on a History War', *Transforming Cultures e-Journal* 1, no. 1 (2006), p. 25.

we led the way in abolishing it.'[3] Little appears to have changed since 2007 when, during the commemoration of the bicentennial of the abolition of slavery at Westminster Abbey, activist Toyin Agbetu mounted a protest, saying, 'This nation has never apologised ... there was no mention of the African freedom fighters ... This is just a memorial of William Wilberforce.'[4]

Braverman's speech parrots increasingly loud, but far from new, calls to resist what is portrayed as the 'orthodoxy' that slavery and colonialism were uniquely negative. Instead, in the spirit of 'viewpoint diversity', a more 'nuanced' approach to domination, exploitation and genocide is encouraged. Nuance, here, amounts to intellectual confusion. For example, it was capitalism, not slavery that 'made Britain rich' according to the former British Conservative politician and free-trade advocate, Daniel Hannan,[5] in a breathtaking act of mental compartmentalisation that exposes his ignorance of the history of both capitalism and slavery. Slavery was universally and perennially practised, and singling out the transatlantic slave trade is 'bizarre' in Hannan's view.[6] Not only was slavery not the unique preserve of the British, Hannan, like Braverman, believes that while courageous British abolitionists fought to defeat the trade in human flesh, it was African monarchs like King Ghezo of Dahomey who fought to keep it. The Dahomey Kings' greed and their willingness to sacrifice their people in order to satisfy it is a recurring theme. Then American Historical Association president, James Sweet, equated the erasure of Dahomean slavery in the Hollywood blockbuster, *The Woman King*, with the right's attack on the teaching of the history of enslavement in the

---

3 Peter Walker, 'Suella Braverman Rails against "Experts and Elites" in Partisan Speech', *Guardian*, 2023, https://tinyurl.com/398kv439 (last accessed January 2025).
4 Press Association, 'Protester Disrupts Slavery Commemoration', *Guardian*, 2007, www.theguardian.com/uk/2007/mar/27/race.world (last accessed January 2025).
5 Daniel Hannan, 'Capitalism Not Slavery Made Britain Rich. It's Time We Stopped Apologising for Our Past', *The Telegraph*, 2023, https://tinyurl.com/45rnus3r (last accessed January 2025).
6 Stephan Heblich, Stephen Redding, and Hans-Joachim Voth, 'Slavery and the British Industrial Revolution', *CEPR*, 2023, https://cepr.org/voxeu/columns/slavery-and-british-industrial-revolution (last accessed January 2025).

US. 'Bad history yields bad politics', he wrote, claiming these historical interpretations to be 'two sides of the same coin'.[7] Calls for 'nuance' on slavery and colonialism from the side of Braverman, Hannan or the Africanist Sweet are wilfully ignorant of the truly multi-layered picture of global racial capitalism that must be painted to understand African involvement in the slave trade. As Kieran Healy reminds us, nuance is not 'a virtue of good sociological theory'.[8]

As W.E.B. Du Bois tells it, the 'ferocity by which the native chiefs, a century earlier, had supplied the demands of English and Dutch traders'[9] was the result of the transformation of the 'mild domestic slavery of the African tribes and of the Arabs and Persians' into chattel slavery to service the 'commercial ends and profits sought by Europe'.[10] This contributed directly to the turning 'backward' of the 'continued development of African civilization ... into chaos, fight, and death'.[11] Yet, attempts to reckon with the extent of this disaster and its ongoing benefits for western economies are constantly met with 'narratives that recycle claims of European (enlightened) exceptionalism and cultural, economic and institutional superiority'.[12] African leaders, by these accounts, were uniquely barbarous, while the wealth that Europe stood to earn by recruiting them for their efforts dissolves out of frame as abolition steps into the spotlight. As Eric Williams famously wrote, 'British historians wrote almost as if Britain had introduced Negro slavery solely for the satisfaction of abolishing it.'[13] This does not stop at Britain's borders. As one professor of economic history, speaking

---

7   James H. Sweet, 'Is History History? Identity Politics and Teleologies of the Present', 2022, https://tinyurl.com/cu7v7hm4 (last accessed March 2023).
8   Kieran Healey, 'Fuck Nuance', *Sociological Theory* 35, no. 2 (2017): 118–27.
9   William Harrison Woodward, *A Short History of the Expansion of the British Empire, 1500–1923* (Cambridge: Cambridge University Press, 1924).
10 W.E.B. Du Bois, *The World and Africa: An Inquiry into the Part Which Africa Has Played in World History* (New York: International Publishers, 1996), p. 117.
11 Ibid., p. 117.
12 Tamira Combrink and Matthias van Rossum, 'Introduction: The Impact of Slavery on Europe – Reopening a Debate', *Slavery & Abolition* 42, no. 1 (2 January 2021): 1–14, pp. 4–5.
13 Eric Eustace Williams, *British Historians and the West Indies* (London: Deutsch, 1966), p. 233.

of the Portuguese, put it, 'Let's at least get this right: white Europeans did not start slavery in Africa. But they ended it'[14] and 'No country ever got rich thanks to the slave trade.'[15]

Frantz Fanon laughs bitterly from the belly of the decolonising world: 'This European opulence is literally scandalous, for it has been founded on slavery, it has been nourished with the blood of slaves and it comes directly from the soil and the subsoil of that underdeveloped world.'[16]

RACE AND TIME

These (tall) tales are everywhere. A micro industry exists devoted to weighing the pros and cons of colonialism and slavery. Books like those by Oxford theologian Nigel Biggar that submit colonialism to a 'moral reckoning'[17] or political scientist Bruce Gilley's, subsequently withdrawn, article, 'The Case for Colonialism',[18] have become beacons of 'heterodox thinking'. The challenge to the dominant Eurocentric historiography on colonialism and slavery is represented by these self-styled free thinkers as having been foisted on the public by the summer of 2020, a time distilled in the common imaginary as a line in the sand. Whether seen as an opportunity to air difficult questions about a previously silenced history or as a dredging up of a past best left precisely *in the past*, the idea that there is a time before and a time after George Floyd – a

---

14   Nuno G. Palma, X, 2023, https://x.com/nunopgpalma/status/1630507975000350721 (last accessed January 2025). This ignores the fact that a century before Wilberforce, the Lusophone African Lourenço da Silva Mendonça was petitioning for 'the complete abolition of the transatlantic slave trade', mobilising Black people across Angola, Brazil, Caribbean, Portugal and Spain. José Lingna Nafafé, *Lourenço Da Silva Mendonça and the Black Atlantic Abolitionist Movement in the Seventeenth Century*, First edition (Cambridge: Cambridge University Press, 2022).
15   Nuno G. Palma, X, 2021, https://x.com/nunopgpalma/status/1370738888415850497 (last accessed January 2025).
16   Frantz Fanon, *The Wretched of the Earth* (London: Penguin Books, 2001), p. 76.
17   Nigel Biggar, *Colonialism: A Moral Reckoning* (London: William Collins, 2023).
18   Bruce Gilley, 'The Case for Colonialism', *Third World Quarterly* (8 September 2017): 1–17.

man whose life was reduced to the event of his murder – is palpable.[19] After this time, those who see history as a 'balance sheet' that shows more 'of which we can be proud than of which we should be ashamed', as former Australian prime minister John Howard once declared,[20] complained they had been silenced. A marauding crowd coming for statues, holidays and textbooks was setting alight all that the white nation holds dear.[21] As Reiland Rabaka notes, 'European modernity, and its postmodern interpretation, has always been and remains one long self-congratulatory and narcissistic narrative.'[22]

The global uprising for Black lives during an unprecedented pandemic lit a metaphoric fire in the police precinct of settler colonialism and racial capitalism. The summer of 2020 was not a radical departure, even as it clearly stands as a significant moment in the history of global antiracism. Yet, its understanding as a watershed moment enables the ever-more radical agendas of the recalibrating forces of white supremacy. The sense of urgency whipped up by what Cedric Robinson calls Black Radical Time – the time of Black resistance[23] which flings the linear order of things

---

19   For example, the book *Against Decolonisation: Campus Culture Wars and the Decline of the West* by Professor of International Relations Doug Stokes has the following blurb: 'Following the killing of George Floyd in 2020, a moral panic gripped the US and UK. To atone for an alleged history of racism, statues were torn down and symbols of national identity attacked. Across universities, fringe theories became the new orthodoxy with a cadre of activists, backed by university technocrats, adopting a binary worldview of moral certainty, sin, and deconstructive redemption through Western self-erasure.' https://tinyurl.com/bxj89swc (last accessed January 2025).

20   Ann Curthoys, 'History in the Howard Era' (Talk to Professional Historians Association, History House, Sydney, 2006), https://tinyurl.com/3x7xjvtk (last accessed January 2025). As Priya Satia remarks, this attitude is shared by a large proportion of the public. She cites the fact: a '2016 study [in which] 43 percent of Britons believe the empire was a good thing, and 44 percent consider Britain's colonial past a source of pride'. Priya Satia, *Time's Monster: How History Makes History* (Cambridge, MA: The Belknap Press of Harvard University Press, 2020).

21   Bronwyn Carlson and Terri Farrelly, *Monumental Disruptions* (Sydney: Aboriginal Studies Press, 2023).

22   Reiland Rabaka, *Africana Critical Theory: Reconstructing the Black Radical Tradition, from W.E.B. Du Bois and C.L.R. James to Frantz Fanon and Amilcar Cabral* (Lanham, MD: Lexington Books, 2010), p. 4.

23   Orisanmi Burton, speaking on his research into Black-led prison rebellions in the US, refers to a political conception of blackness in the tradition of

up in the air – is met by openly fascistic rhetoric and practice justified by the crisis that the uprisings signalled. The idea that time is slipping away and that history is no longer on its side undergirds the message that the west needs saving before it is too late. At the 2023 National Conservatism conference, the historian David Starkey made his epistemic alignments clear when he claimed the left wants 'to replace the Holocaust with slavery in order to wield its legacy as a weapon against Western culture'.[24] First, 'the Jews' and now 'the Blacks'!

The war on CRT is typically classed as a moral panic, characterised by its disproportionate and viral nature.[25] Less significance is given to it as a more continuous process in the ongoing remaking of the racial regime. In fact, we might argue that the characterisation of the war on CRT as sudden, unusual and contagious signals a particular relationship to time that is shared by those fighting to 'reclaim history' from those maligned as wreckers and statue topplers. From this epistemically western perspective, time is understood linearly and as inexorably progressive.[26] Thus, for Robert Tombs, founder of History Reclaimed, a project with strong ties to other actors in the UK anti-woke enclave,[27] to demand the

---

Cedric Robinson or A. Sivanandan that does not tether blackness to Africanness. Orisanmi Burton, Jared Ware, and Joshua Briond, '"Attica Is an Ongoing Structure of Revolt" – Orisanmi Burton on Tip of the Spear, Black Radicalism, Prison Rebellion, and the Long Attica Revolt', *Millennials Are Killing Capitalism*, 2023, https://tinyurl.com/5n8cncpz (last accessed September 2023).

24 Christopher McKeon, 'David Starkey in Bizarre Claim That Left-Wing Wants to Replace Holocaust with Black Lives Matter', *The Independent*, 2023, https://tinyurl.com/5hfd57rb (last accessed January 2025).

25 Nicky Falkof, 'On Moral Panic: Some Directions for Further Development', *Critical Sociology* 46, no. 2 (March 2020): 225–39.

26 As Philip J. Deloria writes in his critique of Yuval Noah Harari's bestseller, *Sapiens*, while western visions of inexorability are grounded in a positive view of human development as continually progressive, in fact inexorability does harm, both 'to Indigenous people – and to all people, as human beings (not species-level sapiens) trying to craft a sustainable future in a moment of climate change and pandemic disease'. Philip J. Deloria, 'Red Earth, White Lies, Sapiens, and the Deep Politics of Knowledge', in *Decolonizing 'Prehistory': Deep Time and Indigenous Knowledges in North America*, ed. Gesa Mackenthun and Christian Mucher (Tucson, AZ: University of Arizona Press, 2021). p. 574.

27 History reclaimed is linked to *Spiked*, the online publication, which is in turn linked to Don't Divide Us, as seen in Chapter 1. Otto English, 'Past Imperfect:

British monarchy and other institutions face up to their involvement in slavery is to deny that 'Britain has long been one of the least racist societies.'[28] It has progressed out of any racism that may have existed in the past. From the other perspective, one that seems perplexed at the onset of the war on CRT and the speed of its spread, laws banning books and educational programmes, the incrimination of antiracist protesters, and the rapid upscaling of openly fascistic rhetoric are reminiscent of another time. The wonderment expressed by the exclamation, 'But it's the twenty-first century!' relates something very specific about what is generally considered to be *the time of racism*.

How we think about time, then, is not neutral. Time is a tool of racialising power. Time can be given or taken away. It has been used to discipline negatively racialised people whose inability or refusal to live within strictures that are expressed in terms of time – wasting time, running out of time – is seen as evidence of their deficiency. The structural reasons for this state of affairs are obscured by the prevalent neoliberal idea that 'bad choices' with regard to the use of time are culturally determined, rather than being the effect of racial governance.[29] As the Black radical anthropologist Damien Sojoyner remarks, this invisibilisation of structural conditions in the 'intense focus on the individual or choice' that western philosophical understandings of time bequeath is inextricable from how we think about the course of history;[30] how we think about how societies came to be as they are today, what we are led to see, and what is hidden from us. Time thus plays a key role in reproducing racial capitalism whose ideo-

---

Astroturfing History', *Byline Times*, 2 September 2021, https://bylinetimes.com/2021/09/02/past-imperfect-part-one-astroturfing-history/; Ralph Wilson and Isaac A. Kamola, *Free Speech and Koch Money: Manufacturing a Campus Culture War* (London: Pluto Press, 2021); Don't Divide Us, 'Don't Divide Us', 2020, https://dontdivideus.com/founding-letter (last accessed September 2022).
28 Robert Tombs, 'Today's History Wars: Ideology, Propaganda, Careerism – History Reclaimed', 16 April 2023, https://historyreclaimed.co.uk/todays-history-wars-ideology-propaganda-careerism/ (last accessed February 2025).
29 Damien M. Sojoyner, 'Dissonance in Time: (Un)Making and (Re)Mapping of Blackness', in *Futures of Black Radicalism*, ed. Gaye Teresa Johnson and Alex Lubin (London; New York: Verso, 2017).
30 Ibid., p. 168.

logical structure is bound up with ideals of progress, development and growth; a movement forward through chronological time that all must be on-board with or be judged as failing. This is echoed in Sylvia Wynter's observation about the different roots of western and non-western culture, the former being the first 'in the history of man in which the social order – and the values which accompany the hegemony of the social order – finds itself transformed into an adjunct to the economic goal, the economic order'.[31] This necessitated an ideological apparatus powerful enough to sustain this bizarre, anti-human state of affairs. The idea of the linearity of time plays a key role in creating and maintaining this ideological infrastructure.

How we consider the organisation of time, then, is a core epistemological question and, as the Dakota historian Philip J. Deloria reminds us, is informed by one's ontological location.[32] From an epistemic perspective based on a view of history as inexorably moving through stages of augmented humanity, there is a constant need to repress histories told from other ontological positions. The Palyku writer, Ambelin Kwaymullina reminds us that in Indigenous systems in contrast,

> the ticking of clocks
> the turning of calendars
> makes nothing happen
> moves nothing closer
> or further away
> from anything else.[33]

For the Kombumerri philosopher, Mary Graham, hierarchically ordered western societies give 'the impression that one is always

---

[31] Sylvia Wynter, 'History, Ideology and the Reinvention of the Past in Achebe's Things Fall Apart and Laye's The Dark Child', in *We Must Learn to Sit down Together and Talk about a Little Culture: Decolonising Essays, 1967–1984*, ed. Demetrius Lynn Eudell (Leeds: Peepal Tree Press, 2022), p. 509.

[32] Deloria, 'Red Earth, White Lies, Sapiens.

[33] Ambelin Kwaymullina, *Living on Stolen Land* (Broome, West Australia: Magabala Books, 2020), p. 12.

on the way to some destination, to a better position, life or world'.[34] The very idea of racism as a series of isolated events that happen and are then moved on from is possible because of the idea of time as a straight line, grounded in western epistemology. This same idea, as we shall see, grounds the notion that negatively racialised people refuse to 'move on', exercising a 'choice' to dwell in the past.

The problem of time, as a cornerstone of historiography, is key to how we think about the idea and practice of race in the present. The very idea that race belongs to a particular time and not another, or that it originates in a certain set of social relations, but not others, is fundamental to how, or whether, race is perceived to be at work today. These questions are fully present in the war on CRT, specifically in the denunciations of any attempt to challenge dominant historical narratives as little more than a vindictive exercise, inducing guilt in a white population for something 'they are not responsible for'; making the proverbial children pay for 'the crimes of their fathers'.[35] The result can be seen in the US College Board's 'purging' of Black writers from the Advanced Placement course on African American history following an attack by Florida's DeSantis,[36] in former Conservative British education secretary Michael Gove's attempt to institute a celebration of 'the distinguished role of these islands in the history of the world',[37] or in the insistence of a previous Australian education minister that the curriculum ensures 'a positive, optimistic view of Australian history'.[38] We find it too in a former French minister of education, Gabriel Attal, lending support to President Macron's 2021 homage to Napoleon by arguing that, as a 'major figure', he must be 'viewed with open

---

34   Mary Graham, 'Some Thoughts about the Philosophical Underpinnings of Aboriginal Worldviews', *Australian Humanities Review* 45 (2008): 181–94, p. 185.
35   John Lloyd, 'Colonialism and Its Discontents', *Quillette*, 2023, https://quillette.com/2023/02/06/colonialism-and-its-discontents/ (last accessed January 2025).
36   Anemona Hartocollis and Eliza Fawcett, 'The College Board Strips down Its A.P. Curriculum for African American Studies', *New York Times*, 2023, sec. U.S., https://tinyurl.com/ynmpbcfa (last accessed January 2025).
37   Anna Leach, Antonio Voce, and Ashley Kirk, 'Black British History: The Row over the School Curriculum in England', *Guardian*, 2020, https://tinyurl.com/5n7mpx9w (last accessed January 2025).
38   Barnes, 'Why Alan Tudge Is Now on the History Warpath', *EduResearch Matters*, 2021, www.aare.edu.au/blog/?p=10987 (last accessed January 2025).

eyes'. As Pierre Tévanien argues, it is notable that it was Napoleon and not his victims that Macron chose to commemorate with the justification that the emperor who reinstated slavery 'is part of us'.[39] Not to be outdone, in July 2023, the Florida State Board of Education approved new standards that 'say students should learn that enslaved people "developed skills" that "could be applied for their personal benefit," and that in teaching about white mob violence against Black people instructors should note the "acts of violence perpetrated *against and by* African Americans"'.[40]

From these perspectives, an overly negative vision of the national past stains it with the taint of race. While it is commonplace to argue that this perspective sets up a distinction between a past in which racism played a role and a present and future which is postracial, this temporal separation is in fact less neat. The argument for postracialism does not merely separate between a putatively racist past and a non- or post-racist present. Rather, the promise of an end to race is written into what Hesse labels the Eurocentric conception of racism which forecloses on its horizons by limiting what it includes.[41] Charles Mills adds that there is no boundary between 'postraciality' and 'preraciality' because the dominant white episteme posits itself as 'aracial' or unconcerned by race, and thus 'always, or always already postracial'.[42] This helps explain why it is the teaching and learning of history that is so obsessed over when it comes to matters of race. Because the dominant account of racism already comprises its end, not only is race designated to a time in the past, but the account of that past must be tempered by a view of race in which it was never more than a mistake, an overreach, or a diversion from the democratic forward march of

---

39   Pierre Tévanien, 'Les Yeux Grands Fermés', *Les Mots Sont Importants*, 2023, https://lmsi.net/Les-yeux-grands-fermes. Translation from French is my own (last accessed January 2025).
40   Lori Rozsa, 'Florida Approves Black History Standards Decried as "Step Backward"', *Washington Post*, 2023, www.washingtonpost.com/nation/2023/07/19/florida-black-history-standards/ (last accessed January 2025). My emphasis.
41   Barnor Hesse, 'Self-Fulfilling Prophecy: The Postracial Horizon', *South Atlantic Quarterly* 110 (2011): 155–78.
42   Charles W. Mills, 'White Time: The Chronic Injustice of Ideal Theory', *Du Bois Review: Social Science Research on Race* 11, no. 1 (2014): 27–42, p. 32.

(western) history. Perhaps we need not tell the history of race at all then, lest we overemphasise its significance in the 'grand scheme of things', asserting a self-fulfilling prophecy, but in reverse.

According to Charles Mills there is a 'white temporal imaginary ... structuring social affect as well as social cognition'.[43] This timeless and raceless conception of time – 'white time' – shapes the telling of history itself. It is this amorphous timelessness which helps construct the abstract universal human ideal against which the negatively racialised and the colonised are positioned. The 'white temporal imaginary' constructs what exists within and outside of time as well as the appropriate uses of time. So not only are colonised people placed outside time itself, their existence pre-colonisation a non-existence, but in being positioned in relation to white moderns, they are 'mastered by time', rather than being its masters. Further, being the beneficiaries of the progress of time despite, in the view of the pro-colonialists, contributing little to that progress, they are not permitted to 'complain' about the impacts on them of domination, dispossession and exploitation. To do so is to ironically dwell too long in the past; ironic because that is where they are racialised as located.

It is not enough to conclude from Mills' discussion, however, that including the history of racial colonial rule in the curriculum is sufficient to rectify the injustices wrought. Indeed, Mills explicitly shows, through a discussion of the philosopher John Rawls' theory of justice, that it is far from adequate to insert 'previously excluded non-White populations' into a normative vision of justice based on an ideal type that is built by and for white people without this being made explicit.[44] The problem is not just that 'the history of racial oppression cannot be admitted into the [white] "socially shared moral geography"';[45] rather, even when it is admitted that the exclusion of the history of racial colonialism must be redressed within mainstream educational institutions, this stops short of

---

43   Ibid., p. 29.
44   Ibid., p. 38.
45   George Lipsitz, *How Racism Takes Place* (Philadelphia, PA: Temple University Press, 2011), p. 29, cited in Mills, 'White Time', p. 39.

rectification.[46] It does not return to people what was taken from them; their lands and property, and certainly not their lives. It can thus still be contained within white time which is located above or outside the actual unrolling of 'modern world history'.[47]

In white time, two relationships to the history of race coexist. On the one hand, there is the right-wing assault on the teaching of the history of slavery, colonisation, genocide and imperialism that is expressed today as the war on CRT. This is exemplified by the position endlessly put forward by right-wing think tanks such as UK-based CIEO, whose report on history and citizenship in the school curriculum in Britain and Australia, 'Teaching National Shame', argues that 'education puts the emphasis on sins rather than achievements'[48] and focuses 'on past wrongdoings rather than celebrating national successes'.[49] However, it is tempting to see this narrative as singularly ascendant and in conflict with a perspective on education that appears more ready to meet the challenge of 'truth-telling'. There are important ways in which both the denial of history and its apparent acceptance coexist within the racial regime. What were previously seen as radical demands for changes in the educational realm can also be formally accommodated within a racially liberal frame. For example, the Australian national curriculum was changed in 2021 to ensure greater 'cross-curricular priority' of Aboriginal and Torres Strait Islander 'histories and cultures'.[50] However, there is often a 'disconnect between policy and practice' when it comes to the actual teaching of Indigenous knowledge.[51] While there may be a laudable aim to redress previous neglect of both this knowledge and the history of invasion and dis-

---

46 Mills, 'White Time', p. 40.
47 Ibid.
48 Tamás Orbán, 'MCC Brussels: Why Cancelling European History Is a Bad Idea', *The European Conservative*, 2023, https://tinyurl.com/3sju379j (last accessed January 2025).
49 Joanna Williams, 'Teaching National Shame: History and Citizenship in the School Curriculum', *The Centre for Independent Studies*, 2022, www.cis.org.au/publication/teaching-national-shame/ (last accessed January 2025).
50 Cathie Burgess and Kevin Lowe, 'Rhetoric vs Reality: The Disconnect between Policy and Practice for Teachers Implementing Aboriginal Education in Their Schools', *Education Policy Analysis Archives* 30 (2022), p. 7.
51 Ibid., p. 4.

possession in the school curriculum, Lowe and Yunkaporta note that 'the curriculum has been written to provide little opportunity for students to explore Aboriginal peoples' own agency in challenging systemic racism'.[52] Sometimes it is in the performance of acceptance rather than in the railing against change that we best observe the operations of the racial regime. Under racial liberalism, those operations require a view of time as linearly progressive. Scratch the surface and we often see that what is named as 'progress' is offered in lieu of a response to a much more obdurate set of problems posed by the persistent realities of racial capitalism.

This progressive 'vibe' thwarts more radical responses and makes them more 'tractable', as Cedric Robinson puts it.[53] We must, therefore, look beyond liberal outrage at anti-woke politics and consider how actors at various points along the political spectrum participate in either denying the relevance of histories told from non-western/non-white ontological positions, or alternatively, in massaging them into a multicultural narrative that is accommodating of national(ist) mythologies.[54] All sides here are invested in historical narratives that are epistemically shaped by the global material and ideological apparatus of racial capitalism, but which do not make this explicit. The epistemology of white time shapes how history is written and taught. This is not a problem that is exclusive to the right because dominant elements on the political left emphasise the same types of abstract universalism that Mills shows stand in the way of a truly rectificatory approach to justice. If the aim of history education is, as the catchphrase goes, to learn from the past, then according to whose account that past is told is all-important. The Martinican writer, Édouard Glissant, pointed

---

52 Kevin Lowe and Tyson Yunkaporta, 'The Inclusion of Aboriginal and Torres Strait Islander Content in the Australian National Curriculum: A Cultural, Cognitive and Sociopolitical Evaluation', *Curriculum Perspectives* 33 (2013), p. 11.
53 Cedric James Robinson, *Forgeries of Memory and Meaning: Blacks and the Regimes of Race in American Theater and Film before World War II* (Chapel Hill, NC: University of North Carolina Press, 2007), p. xi.
54 Cedric J. Robinson, 'Ota Benga's Flight through Geronimo's Eyes: Tales of Science and Multiculturalism', in *Cedric Robinson: On Racial Capitalism, Black Internationalism, and Cultures of Resistance*, ed. H.L.T. Quan (London: Pluto Press, 2019).

to this when he wrote of the absurdity of using official French periodisation to recount Caribbean history. Instead of attempting to see the Caribbean through the externally imposed lens of the colonising nation, Glissant advocates foregrounding the slave trade and its impacts which have had most significance for modern Caribbean societies. Doing this reveals 'a real discontinuity beneath the apparent continuity of our history' given by the French periodisation.[55] It becomes possible to see how the imposition of a '"single" historical time, that of the West', has camouflaged the myriad 'complex sequences' of Caribbean history.[56] These critiques of western time help us to understand the need for what Hannah Elias calls a heterochronic, or multi-layered, approach to history,[57] one that resists the prevailing compulsion to accept history as a line, whose purported start point must be caught up with by those whose inhumanity, or lesser humanity, is posited as standing outside of history peering in.[58]

NEW HISTORY

Similarly opposed to the imposition of 'evenly measured periodicities' onto events in the past, Cedric Robinson advises that the 'ordering of things, that is, their chronological sequencing', is of much less utility than 'the order of things, that is the arrangement of their significances, meanings, and relations'.[59] He thus concludes *Black Marxism* by appealing for a new history, vital for the building of new theory. How can we construct the tools necessary for making sense of the world for the majority of its people when we continue to use the precepts of history handed down from the humanities

---

55 Édouard Glissant, *Caribbean Discourse: Selected Essays*, trans. J. Michael Dash (Charlottesville, VA: University Press of Virginia, 1999), p. 91.
56 Ibid., p. 92.
57 Hannah Elias, 'Time and Race in History Education', 2020, https://renewal.org.uk/time-and-race-in-history-education/ (last accessed September 2022).
58 Anthony Bogues, 'And What about the Human?: Freedom, Human Emancipation, and the Radical Imagination', *Boundary 2* 39, no. 3 (2012): 29–46; Sylvia Wynter, 'Unsettling the Coloniality of Being/Power/Truth/Freedom: Towards the Human, after Man, Its Overrepresentation – an Argument', *CR: The New Centennial Review* 3, no. 3 (2003): 257–337.
59 Robinson, *Black Marxism*, p. 320.

whose very evolution is grounded in the European need to establish 'settlement and order'?[60] In his essay, 'Notes toward a "Native" Theory of History', Robinson writes that an entirely 'new theory of history' is necessary for the 'African Diaspora to assume its historical significance'.[61] It is not sufficient for Black scholars to revise existing theories of history that are 'antithetic to the evolution of Black people' because those approaches to history are inextricable from the facts of 'violence, domination, and exploitation'.[62] There is thus no point in merely correcting 'western paradigms of history' because that will not produce the new history that, as the Bissau-Guinean revolutionary leader Amílcar Cabral pressed home, is fundamental for national liberation.[63] When we start to think in this way about what a reconstruction of history from below means materially for 'the dominant classes' whose continued rule requires 'convenient fairy tales',[64] then we can see why history is such a battleground. The war on CRT as an expression of the new racial regime necessitates holding back the tide of new history which, to follow Robinson, means history, ideologies and epistemologies produced by African peoples (and we can extend this to the negatively racialised, the colonised and the Indigenous more broadly).[65]

In what follows, I turn to two sites in which the struggle for a new history is in play. This struggle is inseparable from the previous discussion of time, specifically the question of whose time we place importance on. If we follow Black, Indigenous and other colonised thinkers, we are drawn to think about time as having been stolen. Yet in racial logic, time stolen becomes time wasted. This has an impact on who we think of as the agents of

---

60 Joshua Myers, *Of Black Study* (London: Pluto Press, 2023), p. 64.
61 Cedric J. Robinson, 'Notes towards a "Native" Theory of History', in *Cedric Robinson: On Racial Capitalism, Black Internationalism, and Cultures of Resistance*, ed. H.L.T. Quan (London: Pluto Press, 2019), p. 53.
62 Ibid.
63 Amílcar Cabral, *Return to the Source: Selected Speeches* (New York: Monthly Review Press, 1974).
64 Du Bois, *Black Reconstruction in America*, cited in Robinson, 'Notes towards a "Native" Theory of History', p. 53.
65 Robinson, 'Notes towards a "Native" Theory of History', p. 53.

history: capitalists or workers, slavers or enslaved, colonisers or colonised, or again proletariat or lumpen. Time is horrific because of 'its covert use in the reinforcement of difference'.[66] By looking to the time of Black (and other colonised, Indigenous) radicalism, as Robinson suggests, we can 'obliterate the difference-making projects of Western society' which make 'racially-charged exploitative practices' logical.[67] Whose version of time, whose account of history do we now see?

First, I look at debates surrounding The New York Times' 1619 Project which triggered right-wing hysteria about the teaching of US history, a focal point of the war on CRT. Centrist and left-wing commentators joined the fray, revealing two key themes which foreground the problem of time and the need for new history. The 1619 Project was accused by American Historical Association president, James Sweet, of having a presentist reading of historical events. Others attacked the project for rejecting a Marxist analysis of history, ironic given the anti-red hysteria in which much anti-CRT rhetoric is drenched. This reading, based on a class-first approach which blames those who are attentive to race for bursting the bubble of historical cross-racial worker solidarity, mobilises a conception of time grounded in Marxist modernity which upholds western societies as inexorably progressive, glossing over the implications that this has for the colonised and negatively racialised. Similar to Sweet, this view implies that to foreground Black radical and Indigenous perspectives on history is to succumb to fashion, thus revealing a deeper and more long-standing attack on Black, Indigenous and colonised epistemologies.

Second, I turn to the example of the 'history wars' that animated Australia in the 1980s and which continue to frame the telling of invasion and colonisation and their persistent impact on Indigenous life, land and waters. The importation of the US American war on CRT conjoins with Australian debates over educational curricula, public memorials and commemorative days.[68] To interrogate how this plays out against the backdrop of the transnational

---

66 Sojoyner, 'Dissonance in Time', p. 90.
67 Ibid., p. 89.
68 Carlson and Farrelly, *Monumental Disruptions*.

war on CRT, I borrow the mash-up phrase, 'Lest We For/Get Over It'.[69] This comment on the appropriate and inappropriate relationship to past and future evokes what Joshua Myers refers to as the "'conceptual incarceration'" of Black people, 'the practice of appropriating the order of things as we knew it and representing it to us through the imposition of a racial regime'.[70] Countering the dominant dictating of what can and cannot be said about the past is Black people's own 'experience of time, history, and memory [which] required us to set terms for studying our own experiences'.[71] What this means for Indigenous people in Australia comes through in Tony Birch's juxtaposition of the knowledge wielded by white liberal historians and by Indigenous youth, respectively. The latter's a priori knowledge of history stands against progressive white settler narrations of colonial history.[72]

THE *1619 PROJECT*

We were told once, by virtue of our bondage, that we could never be American. But it was by virtue of our bondage that we became the most American of all.[73]

Why might a doctor-turned-Secretary of State of Housing and Urban Development open a conference on American history? Held in the great hall of the US National Archives building on 17 September 2020, the conference in question was called by

---

69 This phrase has been used both by the Gamilaroi writer, Luke Pearson, and the settler artist, Sam Wallman. Luke Pearson, 'Lest We Forget over It – Luke Pearson', *IndigenousX*, 2018, https://indigenousx.com.au/luke-pearson-lest-we-forget-over-it/ (last accessed January 2025); Sam Wallman, 'Lest We for/Get over It', *The Australian Museum*, 2021, https://tinyurl.com/528ysawr (last accessed January 2025).
70 Myers, *Of Black Study*, p. 180. Myers borrows the term 'conceptual incarceration' from Wade Nobles, *Seeking the Sakhu: Foundational Writings for an African Psychology* (Chicago IL: Third World Press, 2006).
71 Myers, *Of Black Study*.
72 Sara Ahmed, 'Declarations of Whiteness: The Non-Performativity of Anti-Racism', *Meridians* 7, no. 1 (2007): 104–26.
73 Nikole Hannah-Jones, 'The Possible Plan', in *The 1619 Project: A New American Origin Story*, ed. Nikole Hannah-Jones (New York Times, 2019), p. 26.

US President Donald Trump on Constitution Day to 'defend the legacy of America's founding, the virtue of America's heroes, and the nobility of the American character'.[74] The doctor-politician, Ben Carson began by warning the audience about the 'coordinated attack' being waged from the left on the history, institutions, and heroes of America, giving a rather convoluted lesson about history: 'We're not perfect, we don't have a perfect history, But wise people learn from the past. Unwise people try to bury the past. We get to decide which one we want to be.'[75] As it happens, Ben Carson once worked in Australia where he is reported to have had colleagues who wanted to feel his hair, 'the closest that Carson has come to publicly acknowledging how his personal life has been affected by racism'.[76] His suggestion that only the unwise try to bury the past may have unconsciously recalled the experiences he himself has worked so hard to entomb. We do well to heed Cedric Robinson's warnings about the 'weaknesses and disadvantages' of a psychohistorical approach to history, that it produces a 'highly developed sense of when an event begins to mature into "inevitability"'.[77] Nevertheless, we can observe that giving Ben Carson the first word in that most Trumpian of gatherings, the 2020 Conference on American History, was an effort to fold blackness into American nationalism, an effort that is not confined to actors on the right. A major trigger for the White House Conference was the *New York Times*' Pulitzer-prize winning *1619 Project*, spearheaded by Nikole Hannah-Jones, whose previous journalism on topics such as school segregation has made her a prominent voice on structural racism and antiblackness in the US.[78] The *1619 Project* first appeared as a special edition of the *New York Times*

---

74 Trump White House Archives, 'Remarks by President Trump at the White House Conference on American History', *The White House*, 2020, https://tinyurl.com/mwwatcce (last accessed September 2022).
75 Ibid.
76 Emma Roller, 'Ben Carson on Race, Australia, Evolution, and God's Plan', *The Atlantic*, 2015, https://tinyurl.com/3buxanhz (last accessed January 2025).
77 Robinson, 'Notes towards a "Native" Theory of History', p. 72.
78 Nikole Hannah-Jones, 'Choosing a School for My Daughter in a Segregated City', *New York Times*, 2016, https://tinyurl.com/h6r4236y (last accessed September, 2022).

in August 2019. The 100-page edition gathered ten written essays, a photo essay, as well as poems and fiction. The date, 1619, commemorates the 400th anniversary of the arrival of the first boat carrying African people to the British colony of Virginia. The idea at its core is summarised in its subtitle: 'A New American Origin Story'; the United States must re-evaluate the sacred cow that its founding was an enactment of freedom. Its collected essays were subsequently published in modified book form.[79] In January 2023, an HBO mini-series based on it was released. A dedicated website hosted by the Pulitzer Center offers *1619 Project* educational resources for K-12 students.

The right's revulsion for the *1619 Project* supports W.E.B. Du Bois' 1935 summation of mainstream history as existing 'for inflating our national ego, and giving us a false but pleasurable sense of accomplishment'.[80] Lest this pleasure be taken away, the educational resources accompanying the project were banned in Florida schools under the Stop W.O.K.E Act, with lawmakers in other US states seeking to follow suit.[81] Citizens for Renewing America[82] warns against the ushering in of 'CRT-infused' curricula via 'covert' means such as the *1619 Project* curriculum. For *Race Marxism* and *Cynical Theories* author, James Lindsay, the *1619 Project* aims to 'perpetuate a critical historiography' governed by the CRT principles of pessimism, cynicism and hyperbole. The aim of CRT, he

---

79 Nikole Hannah-Jones and New York Times Magazine, eds., *The 1619 Project: A New Origin Story* (New York: One World, 2021).
80 W.E.B. Du Bois, *Black Reconstruction in America: 1860–1880*, First edition (New York: The Free Press, 1998), p. 609.
81 Sarah Schwartz, 'Lawmakers Push to Ban "1619 Project" from Schools', *Education Week*, 2021, https://tinyurl.com/4nywnvh4 (last accessed January 2025).
82 Citizens for Renewing America, a 'grassroots advocacy organisation' accompanying the Capitol Hill think tank, Center for Renewing America, was founded by Russ Vought, last director of the Office of Management and Budget during Trump's first presidency, described as having 'quietly emerged as an intellectual leader of the GOP's conservative flank'. Bill Allison, 'Trump Acolytes Craft Parallel GOP Universe so Trumpism Lives on', *The Detroit News*, 2021, https://tinyurl.com/2mwv5r23 (last accessed January 2025); Jeff Stein, Josh Dawsey, and Isaac Arnsdorf, 'The Former Trump Aide Crafting the House GOP's Debt Ceiling Playbook', *Washington Post*, 2023, https://tinyurl.com/29c787rp (last accessed January 2025).

argues, is to posit 'the history of the United States as little more than a long series of strategic moves by which white racism – especially anti-black racism – was established and has been and remains maintained as an ordinary and permanent feature of (American) society'.[83] The *1619 Project* thus serves the interests of the 'critical race ideologues' whom Lindsay and his fellow travellers see as in need of rooting out from the US institutions they have infected; education first and foremost. They see an 'anti-liberal' historical revisionism as 'designed "to advance political grievances and earn political points"' by making 'absurd' links between present-day social inequalities and a view of slavery as foundational to the US.[84] Paradoxically, the proposition that a reckoning with the extent of slavery's undergirding of US society will remake democracy anew, strongly expressed in Hannah-Jones' opening essay, echoes this from the other side of the political divide. However, this does not endear her or the project to their right-wing opponents.

This dialectic can also be seen in the efforts of '1776 Unites', a project of conservative Black philanthropic organisation, the Woodson Center.[85] A video on its website claims the *1619 Project* portrays Black people in the US as passive victims and states that 'hope and progress lie within ourselves and within those very American values of self-renewal, freedom and progress towards a more perfect union'.[86] 1776 of course refers to the official Declaration of American Independence on 4 July of that year and Trump's own venture into history, the *1776 Report*, a plan to promote a

---

83 James Lindsay, '1619 Project', *New Discourses*, 2023, https://newdiscourses.com/tftw-1619-project/ (last accessed January 2025).
84 Timothy M. Sandefur, 'Book Review: Debunking the 1619 Project: Exposing the Plan to Divide America, by Mary Grabar', *The Independent Institute*, 2021, www.independent.org/publications/tir/article.asp?id=1753 (last accessed June 2023).
85 The Woodson Center was set up 'to empower community-based leaders to promote solutions that reduce crime and violence, restore families, revitalize underserved communities, and assist in the creation of economic enterprise'. 'About Us', *Woodson Center*, n.d., https://woodsoncenter.org/about-us/ (last accessed September 2022).
86 1776 Unites, 'A New Declaration for America', *YouTube*, 2022, www.youtube.com/watch?v=xdNtmyG48GI, (last accessed September 2022).

'more patriotic education'.[87] As Trump put it in his address to the White House Conference on American History,

> By viewing every issue through the lens of race, they want to impose a new segregation, and we must not allow that to happen. Critical race theory, *the 1619 Project* and the crusade against American history is toxic propaganda, ideological poison, that, if not removed, will dissolve the civic bonds that tie us together, will destroy our country.[88]

According to the American Historical Association, the *1776 Report* was 'a screed against a half-century of historical scholarship, presented largely as a series of caricatures, using single examples (most notably the "1619 Project") to represent broader historiographical trends'. It 'relies on falsehoods, inaccuracies, omissions, and misleading statements' and excises enslaved people, women and Indigenous people from its vision of the founders of the United States as 'godlike men'.[89] Yet, this view was not shared by all within the historical establishment. A letter addressed to the *Times Magazine* by five historians claimed that the *1619 Project* contained 'errors' 'of verifiable fact'.[90] According to journalist Adam Serwer, it was Nikole Hannah-Jones' lead article, 'America Wasn't a Democracy until Black Americans Made It One' and 'American Capitalism Is Brutal. You Can Trace That to the Plantation'[91] by the sociologist Matthew Desmond that drew the most ire.[92] The main

---

87 The President's Advisory 1776 Commission, 'Final Report', 2021, https://tinyurl.com/yv5kphd3 (last accessed September 2022).
88 Trump White House Archives, 'Remarks by President Trump at the White House Conference on American History'.
89 American Historical Association, 'AHA Condemns Report of Advisory 1776 Commission', 2021, https://tinyurl.com/4wahn585 (last accessed September 2022).
90 Victoria Bynum, James M. McPherson, James Oakes, Sean Wilentz and Gordon S. Wood, 'NYT 1619 letter', https://tinyurl.com/3fbese4w (last accessed February 2025).
91 In the book version, these are respectively, Chapter 1, 'Democracy' and Chapter 6, 'Capitalism'.
92 Adam Serwer, 'The Fight over the 1619 Project Is Not about the Facts', *The Atlantic*, 2019, https://tinyurl.com/mvpvr3vn (last accessed January 2025).

contention under discussion was Hannah-Jones' proposition that US independence was declared 'in order to ensure slavery would continue'. 'Every statement offered to validate [this claim] is false', wrote the historians.[93]

The outrage against the project seemed disproportionate given, as Lauren Michelle Jackson remarks, that the arguments made in it were 'not all that provocative' 'by academic standards'. 1619, not 1776, has long been seen as a 'tragic watershed',[94] despite debate over whether we can think of slavery as a system already set in stone at this early date, as the African American historian Nell Irvin Painter comments in her own critique of the project.[95] Notwithstanding the eminently criticisable aspects of the *1619 Project*,[96] not least as Jackson comments its 'impeccable branding',[97] for the historian Nicholas Guyatt, the level of vitriol directed at it by the academic gatekeepers of US history reveals a more prosaic fact: that they were miffed that such a venerable paper as the *New York Times* 'would have published the project without the benefit of their expertise'.[98]

It took an additional three years, with the war on CRT in full swing in 2022, for American Historical Association president, James Sweet, to add his own words of doubt about the *1619 Project*. In his presidential blogpost, he complained that it signifies a tendency to 'read the past through the prism of contemporary social justice issues', begging the question, 'are we doing history that really matters?' What he identifies as a refusal to situate people

---

93 Bynum et al.
94 Lauren Michele Jackson, 'The 1619 Project and the Demands of Public History', *The New Yorker*, 2021, https://tinyurl.com/yc8d4wr4 (last accessed January 2025).
95 Nell Irvin Painter, 'How We Think about the Term "enslaved" Matters', *Guardian*, 2019, https://tinyurl.com/2s4vk2aj (last accessed January 2025).
96 Significantly, the *1619 Project* has been criticised for, among other things, erasing the pre-existence of Indigenous nations prior to 1776, reducing the complex history Hannah-Jones tried to render to a 'single story'. Michelle M. Wright, '1619: The Danger of a Single Origin Story', *American Literary History* 32, no. 4 (1 December 2020): 1–12.
97 Jackson, 'The 1619 Project'.
98 Nicholas Guyatt, 'Opinion: 1619, Revisited', *New York Times*, 2020, https://tinyurl.com/4u4y33xy (last accessed January 2025).

'in their own times' is queried by Sweet as the pursuit of 'contemporary political relevance' rather than serious scholarship.[99] As Kevin Gannon responded, Sweet's choice not to situate his critiques within the discipline of history itself, but to pick examples from journalism and film – the *1619 Project* and the Viola Davis film, *The Woman King* – smacks of (what I will call) misogynoir.[100] It is also reminiscent of Du Bois' point that white scholarship on the events of reconstruction favoured 'selected diaries, letters, and gossip' over authentic and authoritative government records.[101] Sweet hides behind an objection to presentism but, writes Gannon, all history is presentist: 'We are historians, in the present, who are selecting some (certainly not all) "historical facts" from the past in order to narrate, analyze, interpret, and contextualize. At best, we are mapping, or representing, the past; we are certainly not reproducing the past in any exact way.'[102]

The 1776 Report, the White House Conference on American History, and the ensuing battle to expunge curricula of any critical re-evaluation of the role played by slavery are caricaturally hysterical. However, Sweet's article should alert us to the danger of constructing a boundary between the right's obvious disdain for the established methods of history and the acceptable, yet no less partial, approach of many 'bona fide' historians. As Priya Satia writes with direct relevance to Sweet, the overwhelming impetus of the historical discipline is to see historical events as being of their time, thus impossible to submit to 'ethical judgement [without] sufficient passage of time'.[103] This thinking 'shaped the practical unfolding of Empire'[104] by giving it the justificatory narrative of progress, be it of a liberal or Marxist inflection; theories

---

99   Sweet, 'Is History History?'
100 Kevin Gannon, 'On Presentism and History; Or, We're Doing This Again, Are We?' *The Tattooed Professor*, 2022, https://tinyurl.com/yxc3zxzv (last accessed January 2025).
101 Du Bois, *Black Reconstruction in America*, p. 618.
102 Gannon, 'On Presentism and History'; Du Bois, *Black Reconstruction in America*.
103 Satia, *Time's Monster*, p. 7.
104 Ibid., p. 6.

of history which placed 'higher ultimate ends'[105] before all else. Thus, the question of how to tell the history of the relationship of the founding of the United States of America and the institution of slavery that, conjoined with Indigenous dispossession and genocide, enabled it is not two-sided, with Trump et al. on one side and 'established history' on the other. In fact, both lay claim to authority and converge on several principles. The creation of an appearance of a two-sidedness contributes to the formulation of the terms of the racial regime. The place accorded to the *1619 Project*, a flawed exercise from the perspective of a more radical historiography, is instructive as a means of observing how much more work needs to be done to recuperate what, in Cabral's words, was lost when colonised and enslaved people were made to 'leave history, our history, to follow them, right at the back, to follow the progress of their history'.[106]

UNDERMINING BLACK RADICALS

We may be on the verge of fascism and the left-wing is so weak because of a failure to understand history, a failure to do a critique of whiteness and white supremacy particularly by your Euro-American friends who should have been in the vanguard ... For a long time Black people did not have access to historical archives. They did, and yet they were constructing all these fantasies about 1776 as this grand republican, democratic experiment ... No wonder we're in trouble.[107]

That the doyens of academic history were displeased about the audacity of Nikole Hannah-Jones might have been foreseen. That actors on the radical left, including the International Committee of

---

105   Ibid., p. 8.
106   Amílcar Cabral, 'The Nationalist Movements of the Portuguese Colonies: Opening Address at the Conference of Nationalist Organizations of the Portuguese Colonies, Dar Es Salaam, 1965', in *Return to the Source: Selected Texts of Amílcar Cabral*, ed. Tsenay Serequeberhan (New York: Monthly Review Press, 2022), p. 69.
107   Gerald Horne and Briahna Joy Gray, 'Can You Be a Leftist & a Patriot?' 2021, www.youtube.com/watch?v=ZMBcLXijfhE (last accessed January 2025).

the Fourth International via its World Socialist Website (WSWS), converged with anti-CRT warriors in condemning the project may at first glance seem more incongruous. In fact, all the detractors of the project – liberal historians, orthodox Marxists, and anti-CRT warriors alike – converge on the point made by WSWS's David North: the project is 'a false, politically-motivated narrative that makes racism and racial conflict the central driving forces of American history'; a dangerous endeavour, as they see it. In particular, they objected to the *1619 Project*'s suggestion that slavery had a central role in determining socioeconomic inequality in the US today. Like the speakers at the National Conservatism Conference encountered at the opening to this chapter, these socialist authors warn against denying that 1619 'is one episode in the global history of slavery' which 'existed in West Africa "well before the fifteenth century"'.[108] The co-editor of the WSWS book, *The New York Times' 1619 Project and the Racialist Falsification of History*, Thomas Mackaman, put it thus to the Marxist political scientist, Adolph Reed: 'The dominant tendency in academia is to attribute all social problems to race, or to other forms of identity, but the 1619 Project goes farther still, saying that they are all rooted in slavery.'[109]

The historiographical objections raised from the left cannot be disentangled from their political assumptions, framed by an epistemic orientation according to which the foregrounding of race is always motivated by a moralist turn way from politics. Echoing those leading the charge on CRT, to make the historical argument that racism is endemic to US society, is to hold white USians hostage to 'the inescapable fate' of racism as a 'permanent condition'.[110] Their contention that the *1619 Project* is nothing but a 'racialist morality tale' is based on the common misreading of CRT,

---

108 Niles Niemuth, Thomas Mackaman, and David North, *The New York Times 1619 Project: A Racialist Falsification of American and World History* (Oak Park, MI: World Socialist Website, 2019), p. 9.
109 Thomas Mackaman and Adolph Reed, 'An Interview with Political Scientist Adolph Reed, Jr. on the New York Times' 1619 Project', World Socialist Website, 2019, www.wsws.org/en/articles/2019/12/20/reed-d20.html (last accessed January 2025).
110 Niemuth et al., *The New York Times' 1619 Project*, p. 15.

encouraged admittedly by some of its popularised versions, that racism is driven solely by individual white racists. For self-claimed materialists, this failure of thought can only be read as a slippage into an idealism wherein only 'class struggle' constitutes the 'real history of the African American population and the events which shaped a population of freed slaves into a critical section of the working class'.[111] In a provocation well loved by the historian, Gerald Horne, the enslaved should be called 'unpaid workers' if that is what is needed to recognise their status as vital contributors to US wealth.[112]

In the WSWS's vision of things, it is the *1619 Project* that is idealist and also 'irrationalist' for its metaphoric references to racism as something that runs in the DNA of the US.[113] Fanon agreed when he told the First Congress of Negro Writers and Artists in Paris in 1956 that 'it is a common saying nowadays that racism is a plague of humanity. But we must not content ourselves with that phrase.'[114] Nevertheless, the focus on Hannah-Jones' choice of metaphor obscures the fact that, for many on the left, locating race as central rather than incidental to US history, sociology and politics is always seen as politically conspiratorial. It is suspected to be a ploy to shatter the potential for a more radical politics of class unity to the benefit of the apparatchiks of the Democratic Party. Certainly for the WSWS, 'the 1619 Project was developed for the purpose of providing the Democratic Party with a historical narrative that legitimized its efforts to develop an electoral constituency based on the promotion of racial politics'.[115] Therefore, the *1619 Project*, though unique in terms of its reach, is less important in itself than for what it signifies about why the narration of history is

---

111 Ibid., p. 17.
112 Anthony Ballas and Gerald Horne, 'Gerald Horne on The Counter-Revolution of 1836: Texas Slavery & Jim Crow and the Roots of US Fascism', *YouTube*, 2023, www.youtube.com/watch?v=QpNSSu5UdyM (last accessed January 2025).
113 Niemuth et al., *The New York Times' 1619 Project*, p. 7.
114 Frantz Fanon, 'Racism and Culture', in *Toward an African Revolution* (New York: Grove Press, 1994), p. 36.
115 David North, 'Introduction to The New York Times' 1619 Project and the Racialist Falsification of History', World Socialist Website, 2020, www.wsws.org/en/articles/2020/12/04/intr-d04.html (last accessed January 2025).

such a politically divisive focal point in the present. In fact, Sweet's opposition to presentism is disingenuous when we consider the uses to which history is put, which are often – if not always – in opposition to the aim of establishing what Du Bois wrote should be its aim: 'the Truth, on which Right in the future may be built'.[116]

A through-line in the attacks on the *1619 Project* is that to highlight the foundational role played by slavery in the unequal apparatus of US racial capitalism goes against the interests of class solidarity. For example, in her book-length rant against the professional managerial class, Catherine Liu accuses the *New York Times* of permitting a trampling of the 'norms of historical research' for fear of falling out of favour with the 'powerful forces, funders and donors' of the Pulitzer Center.[117] Hannah-Jones' aim is to make race, not class, the 'essential social and economic fault line in America'[118] by claiming that Black people fought for their freedom 'largely alone'.[119] This intentionally fractures the working class, benefiting the 'powerful donors who will support them in publicising its cause'.[120] In Liu's world, not only does discussion of the role of race trammel that of class, but it is always an elite conspiracy to stymy interethnic coalition. The content of this critique lacks novelty to be sure; it echoes what motivated Cedric Robinson, at least in part, to make his critique of the dominant white core of Marxist historiography in *Black Marxism*.[121] What is of interest to me here is less the *1619 Project* itself which suffers from a methodological nationalism that veers explicitly into US patriotism. Public intellectuals such as Hannah-Jones certainly play an outsized role in the 'mission ... to make the ruling class

---

116 Du Bois, *Black Reconstruction in America*, p. 618.
117 Catherine Liu, *Virtue Hoarders: The Case against the Professional Managerial Class* (Minneapolis, MN: University of Minnesota Press, 2021), p. 29.
118 Ibid., p. 31.
119 In response to this complaint, the *New York Times* reworded Hannah-Jones' essay to say that '"some of the colonists" saw the Revolution as a way to preserve slavery' and the project's book version qualified the second controversial statement by adding the words 'for the most part'.
120 Liu, *Virtue Hoarders*, p. 31.
121 Robinson, *Black Marxism*.

look like the photo of America'.[122] Of greater importance is the method of attack chosen by the project's critics which, like figures from within the historical establishment, sought to discredit it on the grounds of scholarliness. This raises important questions about the place of Black radical historiography; questions raised by Robinson and Du Bois, as well as Sylvia Wynter, Saidiya Hartman and Gerald Horne, among others, about the meaning of calling, not merely for the inclusion of previously 'silenced' voices,[123] but the reorientation of the entire epistemology employed in building theory on the basis of historical accounts; what is meant by Robinson's call for a new history.

It is impossible to disentangle the question of 'new history' which drives the epistemic orientation of thinkers working in the Black radical, anticolonial, Indigenous and decolonial traditions and the attempts to discredit their scholarship from a simplistic class-first politics which shares more than it is willing to admit with both the political centre and the more extreme right wing. A case in point is the attacks from the left on the Black historian Gerald Horne whose book, *The Counterrevolution of 1776*, 'deals precisely with [the] fraught matter' of the role played by slavery in 'the revolt against British rule in 1776'.[124] The book informs Hannah-Jones' argument in the *1619 Project* that fear of an uprising of the enslaved against their captors in alliance with the British is what precipitated the American revolution. Far from the revolution being fought to end slavery, as the orthodoxy goes, Horne's research is used to make the case that the Declaration of Independence 'protected the institution of slavery'; that 'it was a slaveholders' revolt in essence'.[125] For this, his work has been lambasted as 'worse than inaccurate'.[126] Yet,

---

122 Jennifer C. Pan, 'Adolph Reed: We Must Avoid Race Reductionism', *Jacobin*, 2023, https://tinyurl.com/mk8anx2x (last accessed January 2025).
123 Michel-Rolph Trouillot, *Silencing the Past: Power and the Production of History* (Boston, MA: Beacon Press, 2015).
124 Gerald Horne, 'Gerald Horne Answers Adam Hochschild about 1619', *Konch*, Winter 2022, https://tinyurl.com/47b5mjkc (last accessed January 2025).
125 Ballas, 'Gerald Horne on The Counter-Revolution of 1836'.
126 Fred Schleger, 'Gerald Horne's Counter-Revolution against 1776', World Socialist Website, 2021, www.wsws.org/en/articles/2021/03/18/horn-m18.html (last accessed January 2025).

ON HISTORY AND THE TECHNOLOGIES OF WHITE FORGETTING

for Horne, the arbitration of accuracy is a fig leaf concealing questions such as from whose perspective history should be told, who can be permitted to tell it, and who may participate in the arising discussions which, contrary to the conservativism of the appeals to the 'norms of historical research', are under constant regeneration in response to new scholarship.

Crucial to the undermining of Horne's and others' scholarship is the white left's deep discomfort with the facts of history that paint a less rosy picture of interracial solidarity than the one it advances. For Black scholars such as Horne, Du Bois, Robinson or Manjapra,[127] it was the resistance of the enslaved, or the fear of a repeat of previous uprisings, that precipitated the demise of slavery more than anything else. Because of the tendency among 'our friends on the left' not to think of the enslaved as 'unpaid workers', and thus as a class, it seems incomprehensible to them that the roots of abolition should be looked for, not in London, but in 'Tacky's Revolt' in Jamaica in 1760 which shook London to its core and anticipated the epochal Haitian revolution, 1791–1804, where the London elite realised that class struggle amongst the enslaved could cause not only a loss of life for European invaders but, more importantly, the loss of investments.[128] For Horne then, Hannah-Jones' contention that the enslaved mainly fought alone is not as far-fetched as her outraged detractors contend.

Far from joining forces with Black and Indigenous people before or after emancipation, Horne's further claim is that the overwhelming tendency of European newcomers to North America was towards class collaboration with elites. This cross-class solidarity helped consolidate US American whiteness as a structure of power. Horne is not the first to undermine leftist orthodoxies; 40 years earlier, the popular historian and revolutionary, J. Sakai, went a step further by provocatively stating that 'while there were many exploited and poverty-stricken immigrant [colonising] individuals, these ... Euro-American workers as a whole were a privileged labor stratum [which] had, instead of a proletarian con-

---

127 Kris Manjapra, *Black Ghost of Empire: The Long Death of Slavery and the Failure of Emancipation* (London: Scribner, 2023).
128 Horne, 'Gerald Horne Answers Adam Hochschild about 1619'.

sciousness, a petit-bourgeois consciousness that was unable to rise above reformism'.[129] His book, *Settlers*, was widely discredited, for example, by *Race Traitor* editor, Noel Ignatiev, who accused Sakai of denying that 'for European-Americans who think that revolution is necessary, what better use could there be of their time, intelligence, and energy than the effort to crack open white society?'[130] In fact, this was more an aspiration of Marxist antiracists like Ignatiev than it was reality.

According to Moufawad-Paul, *Settlers* was snidely dismissed by white leftist historians 'because it attempts to expose historical and material foundations of … US American, settler-colonial society' despite its use of the conventions of dialectical materialism to arrive at its conclusions.[131] Once again, rather than responding to Sakai's call for a need to analyse the intersections of race and class and the pernicious question of why 'the white working class most often refused radicalization',[132] the response is to accuse Sakai of advancing a racial ontology over a class analysis. In fact, like the anticolonialists Frantz Fanon or Samir Amin, Sakai precisely foregrounds the question of class when asking why historically white people in North America 'form a labour aristocracy' rather than becoming revolutionary and joining with Black and Indigenous and other negatively racialised workers to overthrow the ruling class. In posing these questions, Sakai does not deny the possibility that white workers 'can change sides and consciousnesses',[133] but he wants to know why, on the whole, they did not. This fact is not confined to the US. With regards to the history of Black-white relationships in Liverpool, the city with the oldest Black community in Europe,[134] hostility to interracial relationships was expressed

---

129 J. Sakai, *Settlers: The Mythology of the White Proletariat from Mayflower to Modern*, Fourth edition (Oakland, CA: PM Press, 2014).
130 Noel Ignatiev, *How the Irish Became White* (London: Routledge, 2015).
131 Joshua Moufawad-Paul, 'J. Sakai's "Settlers": A Meta-Review', 2010, https://tinyurl.com/mpv7d5kc (last accessed January 2025).
132 Ibid.
133 Ibid.
134 Jessica Moody, *The Persistence of Memory: Remembering Slavery in Liverpool, 'Slaving Capital of the World'* (Liverpool: Liverpool University Press, 2020).

by most people, 'as working-class people, as lower-middle class people based on their own stereotypes'. Black people's experience told them the white people among whom they lived were not the mere dupes of elites.[135]

Nonetheless, attacks on the attempts by Black, Indigenous and colonised scholars to reconstruct history, in the tradition set out by Du Bois,[136] reveal the extent to which class collaboration continues to take precedence for many on the left leading elements among it to make what Charisse Burden-Stelly has called 'asinine proclamations like "patriotic socialism"'.[137] Certainly, as a cultural theorist, Catherine Liu has no scholarly authority to speak on the history of US slavery. Yet, she has been adopted by 'some of our friends on the left who also don't seem to have that much knowledge of slavery ... [who] ... like to accuse black people of what they call identity politics'.[138] The accusation of identity politicking takes the place of engagement with Black historiography or any other accounts critical of established positions on US history. The insistence from some leftist voices that veering from these accounts equates to explaining all of history 'from the existence of a supra-historical emotional impulse'[139] – race – gives fodder to a right whose agenda is as anti-communist as it is racist. It is odd then that Liu is comfortable in the reactionary right's orbit, but indeed she can be best situated in the 'Tucker Carlson Left' which coalesces 'around a grab bag of positions, including defending traditionalism, an embrace of nationalism, and the rejection

---

135   Shelda-Jane Smith, Stephen Small, and Chantelle Lewis, 'Hidden Histories: Liverpool Is an African City', *Surviving Society Podcast*, 2023, https://surviving society.co.uk/portfolio/hidden-histories (last accessed January 2025).
136   Cedric Robinson sees Du Bois' *Black Reconstruction in America* as an attempt to develop a 'theory of history', emphasising mass action in the section 'Du Bois and the Reconstruction of History and American Political Thought' in Chapter 9 of *Black Marxism*. Robinson, *Black Marxism*, p. 349.
137   Charisse Burden-Stelly, P.M. Irvine, and Breht O'Shea, 'W.E.B. Du Bois: Radical Black Peace Activism', *Revolutionary Left Radio*, 2023, https://revolutionary leftradio.libsyn.com/web-du-bois-radical-black-peace-activism (last accessed August 2023).
138   Ballas and Horne, 'Gerald Horne on The Counter-Revolution of 1836'.
139   Niemuth et al., *The New York Times' 1619 Project*, p. 8.

of "wokeness"'.[140] This is evidenced in her thanking of the Koch brothers' funded *Spiked* magazine[141] for publishing the first review of her book.[142] We can read her in Koch-adjacent *Quillette* magazine,[143] known for its publication of eugenicist pseudoscience posing as 'dangerous ideas'.[144] *Spiked's* intellectual guide, the sociologist Frank Furedi, spoke at the 2022 far-right CPAC conference hosted by fascist Hungarian premier, Victor Orbán[145] as well as at the 2023 National Conservatism Conference which opens this chapter.[146]

My argument is not that Liu or other 'patriotic socialists' represent a majoritarian impetus of a radical left-wing structured in whiteness. Rather, the insistence on a universalist antiracism that refuses to contend with the far from satisfactory history of white class collaboration across the west stands in the way of building alternative possibilities in the face of mounting fascism, as Horne notes in the extract at this beginning of this section. The fact that this continues to thwart the left is the reason that Robinson called for new history to be written before new theory could be elaborated. In *Black Marxism* he details how Du Bois' attempt to write such a history was a reaction against the propagandists of the US

---

140   Comrade Motopu, 'The PMC Meets the Tucker Carlson Left', *Libcom*, https://libcom.org/article/pmc-meets-tucker-carlson-left (last accessed September 2022).
141   Liu, *Virtual Hoarders*.
142   Catherine Liu, X, 2021, https://mobile.x.com/bureaucatliu/status/135237 8401756045314 (last accessed September 2022).
143   'Who Funds Quillette?' *Pinkerite*, 2022, www.pinkerite.com/2022/09/who-funds-quillette.html (last accessed 30 August 2023).
144   Catherine Liu, 'How Liberal Elites Use Race to Keep Workers Divided – and Justify Class-Based Inequities', *Quilette*, 2021, https://tinyurl.com/s33f5a9r (last accessed January 2025).
145   Ravi Bali, 'Ex-Marxist Furedi Joins Racist Authoritarians at CPAC Hungary – Marxist-Humanist Initiative', 2022, https://tinyurl.com/2s44kwvj (last accessed September 2022).
146   She was also interviewed on the *Aufhebunga Bunga* podcast, hosted by Alex Hochuli, formerly associated with *Spiked* predecessor *Living Marxism* and its various offshoots in the UK, Alex Hochuli and Catherine Liu, 'The Worst Class', *Aufhebunga Bunga* 176, 2021, www.patreon.com/posts/176-worst-class-47450171 (last accessed January 2025); Tony Belletier, 'Part II. "Turd Positionism": On Alex Hochuli and Other Softcore Trumpists', *Washington Babylon*, 2021, https://tinyurl.com/2y8zhm4f (last accessed January 2025).

historical establishment such as William Dunning and his colleagues who were motivated by nationalism, naked racism and paternalism[147] to oppose the relative freedoms for Black people during the period of Reconstruction following the American civil war (1865–77).[148]

It was not only the entrenched antiblackness of these historians that Du Bois lambasts in the concluding chapter of *Black Reconstruction* for their propagandistic approach to history. He also advanced 'both a critique of the ideologies of American socialist movements and a revision of Marx's theory of revolution and class struggle'. These perspectives did not give due credence to the importance of 'mass action' as a basis for a theory of history,[149] 'specifically the capacities of the Black masses to take steps decisive to their own liberation'.[150] In *Black Reconstruction*, Du Bois' aim, according to Robinson, was to confront the messy truths of US history in order to write a 'political work' that, through asking hard questions of 'the nationalist and reactionary American intelligentsia' and 'the political left', sought to 'alert and instruct revolutionary Black leadership'.[151] To understand why socialists seemed so 'ill-equipped to deal with the Black worker' it was necessary to return to what Du Bois saw as the fundamental contradiction of the US, namely, its constitution on the grounds of slavery.[152] Du Bois, his previous rejection from the scholarly canon having been more recently rectified,[153] thus, gives the *1619 Project* the imprimatur it apparently lacks by reiterating its core point. Yet, without a hint of irony, as Joshua Myers notes, one of the signatories of the historians' letter, Sean Wilentz, referred to Du Bois' critique in the 'Propaganda of History' to accuse the *1619 Project* of the same!

---

147 Du Bois, *Black Reconstruction in America*.
148 Sean Wilentz, 'Touchstone Texts: The Historical Works We're Reaching for Today, Part 1' (134th Annual Meeting of the American Historical Association, New York, 2020), cited in Myers, *Of Black Study*, p. 42.
149 Robinson, *Black Marxism*, p. 350.
150 Ibid., p. 353.
151 Ibid., p. 350.
152 Ibid., p. 355.
153 Aldon Morris, *The Scholar Denied: W.E.B. Du Bois and the Birth of Modern Sociology* (Oakland, CA: University of California Press, 2017).

The investment made in ensuring the continued hegemony of established accounts is laid bare by the debates around the 1619 Project. The undermining of Black, Indigenous and colonised scholarship on all sides reveals the extent to which the refusal to relinquish power motivates so much of what is presented as ostensible scholarly debate. This is not just a feature of the increasingly dangerous attacks on knowledge from the right under the guise of the war on CRT. As Du Bois' frustrations with the US left in the 1930s reveal, long-standing problems of racism and paternalism mean that the white left is often ill-equipped to mount a defence against what needs to be understood, not only as an anti-black counter-offensive, but one which, as it has always been, is also anti-communist at its heart.[154] By splitting hairs over identity politics, the left emerges impoverished and those who face the greatest degree of domination, exposed further still.[155] Turning now to the case of Australia's 'history wars', I ask whether scholars are ready to fight what Tony Birch says must be a 'guerrilla war', a struggle for the new history Robinson says is indispensable.

IT'S IMPORTANT TO GET THE TRUTH DONE

A Guardian Australia investigation has revealed nine suspicious anomalies have been found by ground-penetrating radar scans at the former government-run Kinchela Aboriginal Boys' Training Home near Kempsey on the New South Wales north coast. The Missing Children Project report found the 'suspicious anomalies' should be considered for excavation as they show similar GPR signals to other confirmed human burials.[156]

The technical language of the 7 September 2023 *Guardian* newspaper report coats the facts: at least nine sites of possible clandestine

---

154   Charisse Burden-Stelly, *Black Scare/Red Scare: Theorizing Capitalist Racism in the United States* (Chicago, IL: University of Chicago Press, 2023).
155   Michael Richmond and Alex Charnley, *Fractured: Race, Class, Gender and the Hatred of Identity Politics* (London: Pluto Press, 2022).
156   Sarah Collard and Lorena Allam, 'Ground-Penetrating Radar: How the Discovery of "Clandestine" Anomalies Could Reveal Buried Truths', *Guardian*, 2023, https://tinyurl.com/cwbwbrt5 (last accessed January 2025).

graves had just been uncovered on the grounds of the former euphemistically named 'home'. There, Indigenous children such as Uncle Roger Jarrett were made to 'walk down the line'.

> They would put 30 this side and 30 that side and they'd send this boy down. You'd have to punch him hard and if you didn't punch him hard enough, the staff would walk behind you and belt the crap out of you with a cane. If it was not hard enough for them, they'd send you down the line.[157]

The chairperson of the Kinchela Boys' Home Aboriginal Corporation (KBHAC), Uncle James Michael 'Widdy' Welsh, said he hoped there would be nothing there if the government funded the further excavation his organisation called for, 'but with the way that those people were and the way that they flogged us, it wouldn't surprise me at all'.[158] In a media release published by KBHAC, various comments emphasised the need for truth-telling. 'For the future, it's important to get the truth done, because a lot of stuff has been covered over by the government', Uncle Roger Jarrett said. The truth is a weapon, but it is blunted by its constant and systemic denial. In his 1920 collection, *Darkwater*, Du Bois recalls his time as a teacher. In front of the classroom, he was faced with the question, 'Do you trust white people?' He felt the need to 'rise and lie' for the student's 'salvation and the world's'. Yet, he writes, 'all the while you are lying and every silent level, silent eye knows you are lying'.[159] There is great investment in white lies. The extent of massacres, land theft and child removal enacted by white settlers was minimised from the early days of colonisation when 'media reports, official enquiries, depositions and the like invariably attempted to calculate the numbers of "white" or non-Indigenous deaths more

---

157 Lorena Allam and Sarah Collard, 'Revealed: Multiple Sites of Possible Secret Graves Discovered at Stolen Generations Institution for Children', *Guardian*, 2023, https://tinyurl.com/mrxp3u4j (last accessed September 2023).
158 Ibid.
159 W.E.B. Du Bois, Honorée Fanonne Jeffers, and Manning Marable, *Darkwater: Voices from within the Veil* (Brooklyn, NY: Verso, 2021), p. 78.

scrupulously that they did when addressing Indigenous deaths'.[160] What purpose the truth serves in these circumstances is called into doubt when its telling is so often met with violence.

The violence of denial is on constant display in response to revelations such as those at Kinchela. A supposedly satirical letter published by the right-wing Australian magazine, *Quadrant*, from a fictitious history professor to an equally fictitious concerned high school history teacher, claims that 'we teach our students to understand truth-seeking as an exercise in identifying where they (those in the past) were wrong, and we (enlightened historians of today) are right about their manifold errors'.[161] Australia's colonial ideologues dismiss Roger Jarrett's memories as unreliable and thus not constitutive of 'the truth'. The real truth, as one of their number, the journalist and popular historian Keith Windschuttle wrote, is that 'there were no stolen generations'.[162] The 400–600 other boys incarcerated at Kinchela Boys Home were never forcibly taken from their parents and communities,[163] in Windschuttle's estimation. His book, *The Fabrication of Aboriginal History*[164] concludes that the 'small number' of Aboriginal children removed from their families does not constitute genocide as has been established by the vast majority of scholarship that concurs with Indigenous experiential knowledge. The few removals he concedes took place were 'almost all based on traditional grounds of child welfare'.[165]

In fact, as many as one in three Indigenous children are said to have been stolen between 1910 and 1970, during the period

---

160 Raymond Evans and Bill Thorpe, 'Indigenocide and the Massacre of Aboriginal History', *Overland*, no. 163 (June 2001): 21–39.
161 Simon Kennedy, 'History as She Is Taught', *Quadrant Online*, 2023, https://tinyurl.com/3n6sysvb (last accessed January 2025).
162 Keith Windschuttle, 'Why There Were No Stolen Generations (Part One)', *Quadrant Online*, 2010, https://quadrant.org.au/magazine/2010/01-02/why-there-were-no-stolen-generations/ (last accessed January 2025).
163 Kinchela Boys Home Aboriginal Corporation, 'History of Kinchela Boys Home', n.d., https://kinchelaboyshome.org.au/kinchela-boys-home/history-of-kinchela-boys-home/ (last accessed September 2023).
164 Keith Windschuttle, *The Fabrication of Aboriginal History* (Sydney: Macleay Press, 2002).
165 Windschuttle, 'Why There Were No Stolen Generations (Part One)'.

known officially as the Stolen Generations.[166] Yet for Windschuttle, there was no racist motivation. Rather, 'government officers and religious missionaries wanted to rescue children from welfare camps and shanty settlements riddled with alcoholism, domestic violence, and sexual abuse'.[167] Over a century later and some 20 years after the 2007 Northern Territory Emergency Response, when the Australian federal government suspended the Racial Discrimination Act to enact a suite of restrictive policies, including the sequestering of welfare payments and the effective dismantling of the Northern Territory Land Rights Act,[168] the same racist stereotypes continue to impose a hegemonic 'truth' on the lived realities of Indigenous people.

The Northern Territory Emergency Response was ideologically framed by a fight to preserve the sanitised account of Australia as a 'quiet' and peaceful continent which conveniently avoided the existence of Indigenous peoples.[169] It was triggered in 1997 with the publication of the 'Bringing Them Home Report' on the removal of Indigenous children from their families between the mid-1800s and the 1970s. Then prime minister, John Howard, refused to apologise for the state's systemic child theft, the purpose of which was to forcibly assimilate Indigenous people, dissolving Indigeneity into whiteness until it completely disappeared. For Howard, the treatment of Indigenous people was a 'blemish' on Australia's history, but present generations could not be held accountable for the misdeeds of their forbears. The affair, and indeed colonialism writ large, was placed strictly in the past. The formal government apology to the Stolen Generations came only in 2008. For his part, Howard continues to defend his refusal to apologise, saying in 2021 that it was meaningless to apologise for a past generation from a contemporary vantage point.[170] While the national apology was

---

166 The Healing Foundation, 'Who Are the Stolen Generations?' n.d., https://tinyurl.com/yn9nbryw (last accessed September 2023).
167 Windschuttle, 'Why There Were No Stolen Generations (Part One)'.
168 Bruce Petty, 'The NT Intervention and Human Rights' (Amnesty International, 2021).
169 Evans and Thorpe, 'Indigenocide and the Massacre of Aboriginal History'.
170 Shubha Krishnan, 'John Howard Has Criticised Kevin Rudd's 2008 Apology to the Stolen Generations', *SBS News*, 2022, https://tinyurl.com/3metpjys (last accessed January 2025).

one of the recommendations of the 'Bringing Them Home' report, it is a widely shared view among Indigenous people that its effects were purely symbolic given the ongoing removal of Indigenous children today at rates higher than during the official Stolen Generations.[171] Indigenous people fighting for justice for their families remind us that 'Sorry means you don't do it again.'[172]

The effects of the Northern Territory Emergency response, or the NT Intervention as it is colloquially known, continue to reverberate. The Intervention placed restrictions on Indigenous communities to resolve what was claimed to be widespread child sexual abuse within them. However, as the Darumbal and South Sea Islander writer and scholar Amy McQuire makes clear, neither it nor the 'Stronger Futures' policy that followed have resulted in a reduction in child abuse. Instead there have been more suicides and a massive increase in incarceration, particularly of women and children.[173] In 2023, the state of Queensland too suspended the Racial Discrimination Act to enable it to make legal a practice that had been 'going on for years', the imprisonment of children in police watchhouse cells for up to 40 days.[174] In July 2023, the Queensland Corrective Service encouraged applicants to 'Unlock your potential at the new men's correctional centre', in offering more than 800 new jobs.[175] This adds to two youth detention centres approved for the state in 2023.[176] As Orisanmi Burton clearly states, in the US

---

171 Calla Wahlquist, 'Indigenous Children in Care Doubled since Stolen Generations Apology', *Guardian*, 2018, https://tinyurl.com/43uhtz86 (last accessed January 2025).

172 Larissa Behrendt, *After the Apology* (Sydney: Pursekey Productions, 2017).

173 Amy McQuire, 'Mainstream Feminism Still Blind to Its Racism', *IndigenousX*, 2018, https://indigenousx.com.au/amy-mcquire-mainstream-feminism-still-blind-to-its-racism (last accessed January 2025).

174 Ben Smee, 'Queensland Government Repeatedly Ignored Warnings Two Years Ago of Youth Prison Overcrowding', *Guardian*, 2023, https://tinyurl.com/4zvazkp2 (last accessed January 2025).

175 Queensland Corrective Services, 'Unlock Your Potential at the New Men's Correctional Centre near Gatton in the Lockyer Valley', *Queensland Corrective Services*, 2023, https://tinyurl.com/4e5fyf28 (last accessed November 2023).

176 Queensland Government, 'New Youth Detention Centre to Be Built at Woodford', *Ministerial Media Statements*, 2023, https://statements.qld.gov.au/statements/97712 (last accessed September 2023).

'prisons are war. They are state strategies of race war, class war, colonization, and counterinsurgency.'[177]

The same is true of Australia. A group of detained teens who held a rooftop protest against conditions at the Banksia Hill youth detention centre in Western Australia in 2023 were described as terrorists by the state's premier as they were apprehended and removed to an adult prison by the police 'regional operations group, polair [aviation command] and the K9 [dogs] unit'.[178] In the midst of what breathless media reports describe as an Indigenous youth crime epidemic in Alice Springs, white mobs called for vigilante violence against Indigenous people and the government responded in June 2023 with new alcohol restrictions. As Arrernte/Luritja woman Catherine Liddle pointed out, 'funding cuts to family and youth services, and Aboriginal voices being ignored' explain the crisis facing criminalised young Indigenous people.[179] Again, white and Black accounts of 'the truth' conflict.[180] Uprisings against the violent structures of colonial governance are painted as illegitimate. Consequently, Indigenous history is configured as a story of perpetual dysfunction and not of resistance to recursive dispossession.[181]

GUERRILLA TACTICS

Facts may be told and retold, and indeed they are. However, truth-telling knocks against a structurally white historical disci-

---

[177] Orisanmi Burton, *Tip of the Spear: Black Radicalism, Prison Repression, and the Long Attica Revolt* (Oakland, CA: University of California Press, 2023), p. 3.
[178] Grace Burmas, James Carmody, David Weber, and Zathia Bazeer, 'Riot at WA Detention Centre over as Footage Shows Armed Officers Confronting Teens on Roof', *ABC News*, 2023, https://tinyurl.com/3tsjxjee (last accessed January 2025).
[179] Carly Williams, Kirstie Wellauer, and Tahnee Jash, 'This Arrernte Teenager Is Helping to Address Youth Issues in Alice Springs. But He Needs More Support', *ABC News*, 2023, https://tinyurl.com/5czwaavc (last accessed January 2025).
[180] Amy McQuire, *Black Witness: The Power of Indigenous Media* (St Lucia: University of Queensland Press, 2024).
[181] Robert Nichols, *Theft Is Property! Dispossession & Critical Theory*, Radical Américas (Durham, NC: Duke University Press, 2020).

pline whose internal conflicts often resemble 'a family drama'.[182] For Tony Birch writes, intellectual discussions held without a commitment to political solidarity often 'only feign pluralism in support of the status quo and the maintenance of their own authority'.[183] The notion of the 'history wars', like the 'culture wars' more broadly, gives the appearance of two opposed sides evenly waged in battle. However, as Birch suggests, the question remains, to what extent are settler historians who work to uncover the truth of colonial history committed to following through on the implications of this uncovering? As he alludes in his review essay, 'The Abacus of History', acute focus on the 'crude and deliberately anti-intellectual polemic' of conservative ideologues such as Keith Windschuttle often redirects us from the question of why Indigenous critiques are overlooked and negated.[184]

The work of reconstructing a 'new history', then, has had to contend with a political landscape that, even when periodically attenuated by acknowledgements of past wrongdoing and promises to 'do better', rests back on the self-satisfaction that, as the progressive maxim goes, 'we are better than this'.[185] One of the major books written on the 'history wars' is instructive as to how the largely white body of progressive Australian historians treats academics such as Geoffrey Blainey who is credited with coining the phrase 'black armband view of history' to refer to the scholarly movement that began in the 1970s to address the evasion of the truth of colonial invasion. Blainey provided John Howard with much of the intellectual fodder for his position on colonial history and was called 'arguably our greatest living historian' by a recent education minister.[186] The progressive white historian authors of *The History Wars*

---

182 Tony Birch, 'The Abacus of History. "The History Wars" by Stuart Macintyre and Anna Clark and "Whitewash: On Keith Windschuttle's Fabrication of Aboriginal History" by Robert Manne (Ed)', *Australian Book Review* 255 (October 2003).
183 Birch, 'I Could Feel It in My Body', p. 19.
184 Birch, 'The Abacus of History'.
185 Robyn Cadwallader, ed., *We Are Better than This* (Hindmarsh, South Australia: ATF Press, 2015).
186 Emily Ross and Rachael Dwyer, 'First, It's Not an Instruction Manual: 3 Things Education Ministers Need to Know about the Australian Curriculum', *The Conversation*, 2021, https://tinyurl.com/4dum22kr (last accessed January 2025).

provide a litany of Blainey's anti-Indigenous and anti-immigration opinions yet still conclude that he 'is not a racist'[187] because he was merely 'concerned with the incorporation of immigrants into the host society' and not 'exclusion on grounds of race'.[188]

White Australian historians' ability to appraise Blainey as an 'unconventional historian' and a 'superb teacher'[189] supports Birch's critique of the role of 'left or liberal historians' in the 'history wars'[190] and his lack of enthusiasm for a debate on the telling of colonial history that insists on an 'adherence to "civility"'.[191] He insists that 'this debate is not about the sanctity of the footnote. It is a political struggle',[192] a struggle in which left and liberal historians are largely missing in action. Yawuru historian, Shino Konishi notes the tendency to stress the pseudohistorical nature of the work of right-wing defenders of Australian colonialism without sufficient regard for 'how such spurious claims of Aboriginal cultural dysfunction might impact on Indigenous readers'.[193] Moreton-Robinson reminds us that the predominance of non-Indigenous researchers within Indigenous studies in Australia, stemming from their origins in colonialist anthropology, mutes critical approaches grounded in 'distinctive Indigenous theories and methodologies'.[194] All of this flows into the choice of what to notice and what to ignore. For example, the police killing of Indigenous teenager TJ Hickey in

---

187   Stuart Macintyre and Anna Clark, *The History Wars*, New Edition (Melbourne: Melbourne University Press, 2004), p. 170. Birch also picks up on this in his review.
188   Ibid., p. 170. It can be safely assumed that Blainey was not objecting to the incorporation of British people, who still represent the highest number of immigrants into Australia. The worry was about migrants who could not easily – or at all – be folded into the structures of whiteness, undermining white Australian claims to sovereignty.
189   Ibid., p. 182.
190   Birch, 'I Could Feel It in My Body', p. 20.
191   Ibid., p. 21.
192   Ibid., p. 21.
193   Shino Konishi, 'First Nations Scholars, Settler Colonial Studies, and Indigenous History', *Australian Historical Studies* 50, no. 3 (3 July 2019): 285–304.
194   Aileen Moreton-Robinson, 'The Past, Present & Future of Indigenous Studies in Australia', *Australian Academy of the Humanities*, 2023, https://tinyurl.com/yw8732ck (last accessed January 2025).

inner city Sydney in 2004 received much less attention from historians than the 'Bringing Them Home' report. This killing, only one of the countless times Indigenous life has been snuffed out by the state, could not be safely placed in the past; it was of the here and now. Liberal historians are 'good people [who] respect the discipline',[195] but perhaps they did not want to be aligned with Indigenous youth rising up in anger against the colony. Perhaps they prefer the fiction that Indigenous people have mainly given up their struggle.

This is what we find in Ghassan Hage's classic treatise on Australian racism, *Against Paranoid Nationalism* which 'conveys the sense of an anticolonial stance', while in fact reproducing colonial logic.[196] Hage tacitly justifies Australian paranoiac nationalism by couching it as being 'in constant fear of decolonisation' despite having been 'built on the attempted decimation of the Indigenous population'.[197] He believes the colony's paranoia is unwarranted because 'Australia's Indigenous people are no longer capable of engaging in any significant anti-colonial political practices of this kind'.[198] Here the 'unfinished business of Indigenous sovereignty'[199] is severed from material questions such as land and reparations and cloistered in the realm of the unconscious. The white public can shed its paranoid fears because, in the estimation of the antiracist scholar Hage, Indigenous resistance is moot. In contrast, Indigenous scholars and activists, call us to 'recognise the autonomy' of Indigenous people's voices which would also mean listening when they say the struggle is far from over.

Thus, it is not only that well-meaning historians stay stuck in the 'footnotes', as Tony Birch puts it, it is also telling whose footnotes

---

195 Birch, 'I Could Feel It in My Body', p. 22.
196 Maria Giannacopoulos, 'Nomophilia and Bia: The Love of Law and the Question of Violence', *Borderland E-Journal* 10, no. 1 (2011), p. 10.
197 Ibid., p. 11.
198 Ghassan Hage, *Against Paranoid Nationalism: Searching for Hope in a Shrinking Society* (Annandale, NSW: Pluto Press, 2003), p. 48, cited in Giannacopoulos, 'Nomophilia and Bia', p. 11.
199 Aileen Moreton-Robinson, *The White Possessive: Property, Power, and Indigenous Sovereignty* (Minneapolis, MN: University of Minnesota Press, 2015), p. 141.

they frolic amid. Indigenous 'intellectuals, historians, academics and community leaders' are 'spoken about, not to' in ways that are at times 'more offensive and poorly constructed than the work produced by historians on the right'.[200] Rather than speaking to Indigenous people in a patronising manner[201] or in 'feigned outrage' when they are critical, historians 'should be prepared to fight with the same guerrilla tactics' as the right, which has no similar need to 'claim the high moral ground'.[202] Birch, attuned to Indigenous teenagers who protested after TJ Hickey's killing, noted that they were 'acting from a profound sense and knowledge of what has happened to other Indigenous communities and generations of Indigenous children who came before them'.[203] This knowledge is their history book. This chimes with Orisanmi Burton's account of his methodology for 'digging in the archives' of Black-led prison rebellions. As he explains, he uses,

> Black radical and revolutionary sources of knowledge as the starting point and then also engaging with the state archive, but the state archive is secondary. I don't start with the state archive and then pepper the analysis with, you know, quotations from *The Black Panther*, or whatever. I start with people who lived this struggle, with their claims, and then from there I dig.[204]

'LEST WE FORGET/OVER IT'

I like to encourage as many Aboriginal people as possible to consider history instead of law. I think it's really important – especially in the context of the last ten years of the so-called

---

200 Birch, 'I Could Feel It in My Body', p. 23.
201 One young Australian historian, Yves Rees, innocently confesses to understanding that history as a discipline 'was and remains implicated' in the work of colonisation and concludes that white historians may need to 'look to' the voices of Indigenous historians. This is all very well, but it is no meaningful response to Birch's provocations. Yves Rees, 'The Book That Changed Me: How Priya Satia's Time's Monster Landed Like a Bomb in My Historian's Brain', *The Conversation*, 2022, https://tinyurl.com/59dz2yem (last accessed August 2022).
202 Birch, 'I Could Feel It in My Body', p. 23.
203 Ibid., p. 26.
204 Burton et al., 'Attica Is an Ongoing Structure of Revolt'.

'history wars' in Australia – that we take control of the telling and owning and representation of our own history.[205]

Gumbaynggirr historian and lifelong militant, Gary Foley, an instigator of the Aboriginal Tent Embassy set up on the grounds of the Australian federal parliament in 1972, wrote in 2011 about 'one hundred years of the Aboriginal resistance in Australia'.[206] Indigenous people need to study their own history because racial regimes, despite possessing a history, as discussed in the Introduction, 'are unrelentingly hostile to their exhibition'. Indeed, 'a discoverable history is incompatible with a racial regime and ... so are its social relations'.[207] There is thus great investment 'by interested cultural and social powers'[208] in creating the conditions for this undiscoverability. The 'patchwork' nature of the racial regime, and the 'chaotic' methods by which race is produced means that it is insufficient to merely expose 'the invention of raced subjects'. For Robinson, it is the 'alchemy of the intentional and the unintended' that produces and recalibrates racialised power.[209] Without tracing these overlapping and confusing historical processes, attacking that power remains constantly gruelling. Yet, Robinson and other writers in the Black Radical Tradition, as well as Indigenous and colonised activists and thinkers, show us that the chinks in the armour of the racial regime appear at the moments at which resistance is actualised. Foley frames his account of history in terms of the 'struggle' because 'the situation for us today seems to me to be actually worse than it was when I was seventeen years old and I got the fire in my belly. So, this sort of history is even more important to understand.'[210]

The fight over the narration of history in the Australian settler colony rages on over a decade since Foley's writing. The Gamilaroi writer Luke Pearson employs a mash-up of 'two of the most

---

205 Gary Foley, 'Black Power, Land Rights and Academic History', *Griffith Law Review* 20, no. 3 (January 2011), p. 608.
206 Ibid., p. 609.
207 Robinson, *Forgeries of Memory and Meaning*, pp. vii–viii.
208 Ibid., p. viii.
209 Ibid., p. vii.
210 Foley, 'Black Power, Land Rights and Academic History', p. 618.

popular phrases in Australia': 'Lest we forget/over it'.[211] Australians are called on not to forget the sacrifice of its soldiers in foreign wars, while Indigenous people are told to get over the consequences of the history of invasion and 'the knowledge that there will continue to be senseless and preventable Aboriginal deaths'.[212] While the valour of the ANZACs[213] is ritualistically exalted, the battles fought by Indigenous resisters in the Frontier Wars are forgotten. While the deaths of Australians at war are mourned, the massacres of Indigenous peoples, the dispossession of their lands, the cultural genocide they continue to experience, as well as their ongoing 'vulnerability to premature death' are endlessly minimised.[214] Again, the common framing of this in terms of hypocrisy misses the mark, for as already noted, there are ways in which more truthful tellings of Australian history can sit within the overall structure of coloniality, and even strengthen it further by conceding to some of the facts in the understanding that they pertain purely to the 'foreign country' of the past.[215]

Indeed, the 'history wars' that have raged between settler historians of different political stripes have not succeeded in overturning the material effects of invasion and colonisation',[216] and also because of the divergent concerns of differently positioned 'truth tellers'. Central to the struggle over how to tell the history of Australia since invasion is the question of what such a telling should achieve. While right-wing actors condemn any semblance of doubt cast on the overwhelmingly 'peaceful' nature of white settlement, their counterparts on the left, despite their faithfulness to uncovering brutal truths, nevertheless commit to an Australian futurity that conflicts with Indigenous demands for decolonisation. The representation of the past and its constant appearance

---

211 Pearson, 'Lest We Forget over It – Luke Pearson'.
212 Ibid.
213 The Australian and New Zealand Army Corps.
214 Ruth Wilson Gilmore, *Golden Gulag: Prisons, Surplus, Crisis, and Opposition in Globalizing California*, American Crossroads (Berkeley, CA: University of California Press, 2007), p. 21.
215 David Lowenthal, *The Past Is a Foreign Country* (Cambridge: Cambridge University Press, 1985).
216 Robinson, *Forgeries of Memory and Meaning*, p. vii.

in the structures of Australian settler colonialism are not purely discursive. Neither do they align with a neat parcelling out into right- and left-wing readings of the national-colonial relationship to a period denoted as being in and of the past. Rather, 'systems of education are linked to foundational acts of seizing and occupying Indigenous lands and waters, and dispossessing and exploiting Indigenous peoples'.[217] The same is true of the public discussion and memorialisation of Australian nationhood, none of which can be disentangled from the dispossessing, divisive and extractive operations of racial capitalism.[218] Like in the broader international context, framing attacks on the truth of history purely in terms of a reactionary right fighting an interminable 'culture war' is to miss how a white settler culture structured in dominance is globally invested in moving beyond a past, whether that past is understood as glorious or shameful.

'Get over it' may be vocalised by the right, but by seeking to mobilise the truth of history for the aims of 'reconciliation'[219] rather than the more radical demands of land back, reparations and decolonisation, settler historians more politely request that 'we all' do just that. This leads us back to the overarching argument, following Robinson, that a 'new history' is indispensable for overturning the bases on which interpretations of social reality are offered in the form of a racial regime. Yet, at every turn, and from all sides, this work is thwarted by those ultimately invested in the recalibration of their own versions of the racial regime. As H.L.T. Quan remarks, 'Robinson's way of doing history/theory ... holds the promise that just beyond the official and fictive narratives lie the richness and rewards of the real and its possibility for liberationist subjectivities with different ontologies' and for this reason, like fugitivity and marronage was for plantation owners, it is a fright-

---

217 Sriprakash Arathi, Rudolph Sophie, and Gerrard Jessica, *Learning Whiteness: Education and the Settler Colonial State* (London: Pluto Press, 2022), p. 43.
218 Ibid., p. 45.
219 Danielle Hradsky, 'Invasion or Reconciliation: What Matters in the Australian Curriculum?' *Monash Lens*, 2021, https://tinyurl.com/3ae4673b (last accessed January 2025).

ening prospect for purveyors of official historical narratives.[220] I bear this in mind as I turn now to consider the counterinsurgent refutations and instrumentalisations of CRT and ethnic studies in the service of imperialism at a time of genocide.

---

220 H.L.T. Quan, 'Emancipatory Social Inquiry: Democratic Anarchism and the Robinsonian Method', *African Identities* 11, no. 2 (1 May 2013): 117–32, p. 126.

3

Institutionalising Dissent in a Time of Genocide

The present work attempts to alter the terms of interpretation: proposing constant trembles in racial regimes; persistent efforts to repair or alter race as an effective method of social ordering; and a succession of alterations in race discourses (cultural, religious, scientific, etc.).[1]

To struggle is to overturn the logics of a racial regime that uses security to justify dispossession, military rule, and the denial of the most basic rights. To struggle is to begin building the future in the present, to prefigure a post-apartheid/post-Zionist society.[2]

General Mark Milley retired as Chairman of the Joint Chiefs of Staff, the highest-ranking military officer in the US Army, at the end of September 2023. Two weeks later, he spoke at his alma mater, Belmont Hill School, on the occasion of its centennial:

> It's been the bloodiest week and bloodiest day in Judaism since the Holocaust ... This is no time for moral equivalency. Hamas is not a resistance organisation defending some cause of liberty

---

1 Cedric James Robinson, *Forgeries of Memory and Meaning: Blacks and the Regimes of Race in American Theater and Film before World War II* (Chapel Hill, NC: University of North Carolina Press, 2007), p. xvi.
2 Robin D.G. Kelley, 'Yes, I Said "National Liberation"', Verso, 2016, https://tinyurl.com/bdzh4sfw (last accessed January 2025).

and freedom ... Their charter calls for the slaughter of all Jews.[3] And in 1945, we, the world, said 'never again,' and we must say 'never again' today ... We, the United States of America, we stand for something, and today we stand for Israel.[4]

What else would a retired US general say a mere week after Palestinian fighters pierced the fence separating Gaza, the largest open-air prison in the world, rising up in anticolonial resistance on 7 October 2023? As Fayez Sayegh wrote in 1965, from the mid-1940s on, 'the United States was available as a willing candidate' replacing Britain as a 'more powerful and more militant supporter' of Zionism,[5] making Israel 'a condensation of Western colonial and imperial power'[6] and hence vital for continued US hegemony. Nevertheless, Milley's words may trigger cognitive dissonance for naïfs who expect consistency with their antiracism. After all, two years earlier, while still chairman of the Joint Chiefs of Staff, during a widely reported US Congress House Armed Services Committee hearing, Milley had become embroiled in the war on CRT.[7] Republican Congressman Matt Gaetz wanted the Defence Secretary Lloyd Austin to appraise the committee on how 'the Department' should 'think about critical race theory'. Referring to the 'stand-down regarding extremism', a mandatory

---

3 In fact, the 2017 Hamas charter states, 'Hamas affirms that its conflict is with the Zionist project not with the Jews because of their religion. Hamas does not wage a struggle against the Jews because they are Jewish but wages a struggle against the Zionists who occupy Palestine. Yet, it is the Zionists who constantly identify Judaism and the Jews with their own colonial project and illegal entity.' Patrick Wintour, 'Hamas Presents New Charter Accepting a Palestine Based on 1967 Borders', *Guardian*, 2017, https://tinyurl.com/2262rsuz (last accessed January 2025).
4 Nick Stoico, 'General Mark Milley Voices Support for Israel, Denounces Hamas as a "Terrorist" Group in Speech at Belmont Hill School', *BostonGlobe.com*, 2023, https://tinyurl.com/2p8y77tj (last accessed October 2023).
5 Fayez Sayegh, *Zionist Colonialism in Palestine* (Beirut: Palestine Liberation Organization Research Centre, 1965), p. 16.
6 Max Ajl, 'Palestine's Great Flood: Part I', *Agrarian South: Journal of Political Economy* 13, no. 1 (2024): 62–88, p. 63.
7 Copp, 'Austin, Milley Push back on Lawmakers' "Critical Race Theory" Accusations', *Defense One* (23 June 2021), https://tinyurl.com/mt7kz4yx (last accessed February 2025).

training session for military personnel following the revelation that some had joined in the 6 January 2021 fascist riot on Capitol Hill, Gaetz said, 'it did not help our military, it hurt our military'. In particular, 'it caused servicemen to otherise one another' and 'I've heard those sentiments most frequently from units that are majority-minority.'

There was a clear attempt to implicate Austin, a Black former four-star general, in this line of questioning. So to allay concerns he might condone any 'otherisation', Austin denied the military teaches CRT. But his response was not enough for another committee member, Mike Waltz, who had evidence that, in fact, a seminar on 'Understanding Whiteness and White Rage' *had* been held at the United States Military Academy at West Point.[8] Taking a different tack to Austin's denials, Mark Milley responded that he thought CRT was 'important, actually'. Indeed,

> I want to understand white rage and I'm white and I want to understand it. So, what is it that caused thousands of people to assault this building and try to overturn the Constitution of the United States of America? What caused that? I want to find that out. I want to maintain an open mind here and I do want to analyse it. It's important that we understand that, because our soldiers, sailors, airmen, marines, and guardians, they come from the American people, so it is important that the leaders now and in the future do understand it.[9]

It should really be of no surprise that General Milley can extol the virtues of CRT for learning about 'white rage' *and* declare unequivocal support for Israel against 'Hamas terrorists'. After all, the defence contractor, RTX Corporation (formerly Raytheon) which teamed with the Israeli company, Rafael Advanced Defense Systems, to manufacture Israel's Iron Dome system used to intercept short-range missiles, has also run an antiracism training

---

8   Michael Conte, 'Top US General Hits back against "offensive" Republican Criticism and Defends Pentagon Diversity Efforts', *CNN*, 2021, https://tinyurl.com/4u4db66m (last accessed January 2025).
9   Ibid.

programme,[10] which Christopher Rufo wrote, 'relies heavily on critical race theory and manipulative pedagogical techniques'.[11]

Israel's latest genocidal onslaught on the Palestinian people that began in October 2023 indeed proves that such hypocrisy is core to racial logic: we can do to you what we cannot do to others. What may be seen as surprising, however, is the way that some among those fighting for CRT's survival responded to Mark Milley's comments. Speaking on MSNBC, for example, the Black historian, Keisha N. Blain, said of Milley, 'I think frankly it was one of the most powerful speeches that I've heard in defence of critical race theory.'[12] On the one hand, that Blain, or indeed her fellow historian, Ibram X Kendi, who joined her on the panel, used Milley's defence of CRT as a teachable moment is understandable in the face of the onslaught against it. On the other, it raises important questions about how CRT, which springs from 'a deep discontent with liberalism',[13] could have been defended in this context without a passing mention of the militarism and imperialism that Milley represented.

---

10   In a similar vein, Arun Kundnani points out the hypocrisy of the CEO of the world's largest finance company in the world, Blackrock, remarking that 'racism was a "deep and longstanding problem in our society and must be addressed on both a personal and systemic level"'. Needless to say, this did not lead him to ending 'investment in arms manufacturers like Boeing, General Dynamics, Lockheed Martin, and Raytheon, which supply the weapons for the US wars in the Middle East'. Arun Kundnani, *What Is Antiracism? And Why It Means Anticapitalism* (New York: Verso, 2023). In addition, the fact that Meta moved to cancel its Diversity, Equity and Inclusion programmes in the weeks before Donald Trump's inauguration for his second presidency reveals the cynicism of their corporate adoption in the first place and the limitations of foregrounding this in analyses. Adria R. Walker, 'Meta Terminates Its DEI Programs Days before Trump Inauguration', *Guardian*, 2025, www.theguardian.com/us-news/2025/jan/10/meta-ending-dei-program (last accessed January 2025).
11   Christopher F. Rufo, 'The Woke Defense Contractor', *City Journal*, 2021, www.city-journal.org/article/the-woke-defense-contractor/ (last accessed January 2025).
12   'Critical Race Theory Helps Explain How Race, Racism Permeates the Law and Society, Says Professor', *MSNBC*, 2021, https://tinyurl.com/nx9zd9pw (last accessed January 2024).
13   Richard Delgado and Jean Stefancic, eds., *Critical Race Theory: The Cutting Edge*, Third edition (Philadelphia, PA: Temple University Press, 2013), p. 3.

It helps here to consider the Counterinsurgency Field Manual, a document 'prepared under the direction of the Chairman of the Joint Chiefs of Staff' that proposes a 'holistic approach aimed at weakening ... insurgents'.[14] Counterinsurgency is presented as different to traditional warfare because its focus is not on defeating a threat militarily. Rather, it adopts 'an adaptive and flexible mindset to understand' local populations and, hence, the grievances that propel insurgency.[15] Although the Field Manual is primarily used during operations of the US military overseas, as Dylan Rodríguez writes, it can be seen as providing the ideological paradigm for 'domestic war'.[16] Mark Milley's performed willingness to learn about white rage signals the US military's role in counterinsurgency, dedicating significant resources to gaining 'an intimate knowledge' of 'insurgency strategy and narrative to anticipate and counter their operations'.[17] It is, therefore, 'completely logical that the US military Joint Chiefs of Staff are providing a kind of analytical frame that can be extracted and resituated to offer a critical analysis'. Black historians welcoming his endorsement of CRT beg Rodríguez's question: 'Are we actually playing into this?'[18]

The slipperiness of these stories about Mark Milley captures a two-sided process that was made more widely visible during the Gaza genocide. This process is framed by Zionism as an aggregator of global white supremacy and bulwark of western civilisation, a theme I elucidate in greater detail in Chapter 5's discussion of the utility of anti-antisemitism for what Dylan Rodríguez calls 'white reconstruction'.[19] Here we can observe the coming together of two wars, the war on CRT and what the Palestinian race scholar Anna Younes calls the 'war on anti-Semitism'. In Younes' account,

---

14 Chairman of the Joint Chiefs of Staff, 'Counterinsurgency' (Joint Publication, 2018), p. x.
15 Ibid., p. III-4.
16 Dylan Rodríguez, *White Reconstruction: Domestic Warfare and the Logics of Genocide*, First edition (New York: Fordham University Press, 2021), p. 45.
17 Chairman of the Joint Chiefs of Staff, 'Counterinsurgency', p. III-4.
18 Dylan Rodríguez and Jared Ware, 'Insurgency & Counterinsurgency 101 with Dylan Rodríguez', 2024, *Millennials Are Killing Capitalism Live!*, https://tinyurl.com/3ptj9sy6 (last accessed February 2024).
19 Rodríguez, *White Reconstruction*.

the ostensible fight against antisemitism wields the repressive and technical apparatuses of the state to manage 'non-white migration in an ethnically diverse yet white supremacist Europe'.[20] Far from being concerned with the protection of all Jewish people from racism, the war on antisemitism is waged 'by managing, criminalizing, and targeting migrant, refugee, and of colour communities with the figure of the Palestinian anti-Semite as its main culprit'.[21] Its modus operandi bears similarities to Rodríguez's account of counterinsurgency as 'politically directed warfare as a modality of racial statecraft that is versatile, durable, and transnational'.[22] This state-approved antiracism, as Chapter 5 explicates in greater detail, is instrumentalised to contain, police and punish people already and increasingly constructed as belonging to enemy populations, becoming a key operation of racial regime recalibration.

The war on antisemitism piggybacks on the war on critical race theory, painting CRT and related disciplines, ethnic studies primarily, as uniquely antisemitic, providing the theoretical underpinnings for pro-Palestinian radicalism, and being purportedly hostile to Jews whose allegiance to Zionism goes unquestioned. During the Gaza genocide, schools and universities, already primed by the authoritarianism and conjoined 'state philosemitism'[23] of the war on antisemitism resulting in the repression of pro-Palestine speech and the targeting of Palestinians and their supporters, became sites of full-throated state repression from New York to Amsterdam, Berlin and Paris. Emory University, close to the site earmarked for the building of Atlanta's privately funded 'Cop City', saw some of the worst police violence against

---

20 Anna-Esther Younes, 'Fighting Anti-Semitism in Contemporary Germany', *Islamophobia Studies Journal* 5, no. 2 (1 October 2020), pp. 252–3. In Younes' account, the ostensible fight against antisemitism wields the repressive and technical apparatuses of the state to manage 'non-white migration in an ethnically diverse yet white supremacist Europe'.
21 Ibid., p. 252.
22 Rodríguez, *White Reconstruction*, p. 45.
23 Houria Bouteldja, 'State Racism(s) and Philosemitism or How to Politicize the Issue of Antiracism in France?' *Parti des Indigènes de La République*, 2015, https://tinyurl.com/ys99wcfjblique (last accessed January 2025).

students and staff in April 2024.[24] University administrators in the US responded to pro-Palestine student encampments by putting a plan of action in place for the start of the academic year 2024–25: an effective 'indefinite state of emergency' involving 'more militarization, more law enforcement, more criminalization, and more consolidation of institutional power'.[25]

In Germany, the biggest newspaper, *Bild*, published photographs of academics who signed an open letter objecting to police repression of a student protest for Palestine, calling them 'perpetrators'.[26] This violence, surveillance and subjugation, using charges of antisemitism to suppress pro-Palestine action,[27] coalesced with attacks

---

24 Timothy Pratt, '"Like a War Zone": Emory University Grapples with Fallout from Police Response to Protest', *Guardian*, 2024, https://tinyurl.com/23mct7a7 (last accessed January 2025).
25 Carrie Zaremba, 'U.S. Universities Spent the Summer Strategizing to Suppress Student Activism. Here Is Their Plan', *Mondoweiss*, 2024, https://tinyurl.com/29md6h96 (last accessed January 2025).
26 James Jackson, X, 2024, https://x.com/derJamesJackson/status/1788979608286539819 (last accessed January 2025).
27 Since 7 October 2023, individuals associated with highly funded Zionist, right-wing pressure groups, such as Canary Mission and Accuracy in Media, have doxed and harassed campus activists, leading even to physical injury. In Germany, where the Boycott, Divestment, Sanctions movement was already deemed antisemitic by the Bundestag in 2019, pro-Palestine speech within universities has effectively been banned and repression of artists, activists and academics is rife. Regular arrests are made of people calling for a ceasefire or carrying slogans such as 'Stop the Genocide', despite courts deeming such slogans legal. In the UK, school and university students have been referred to the Islamophobic counter-terrorism Prevent programme for 'displaying support for Palestine'. In October 2023, the French interior minister made an instruction, instantly defied by protestors, for all pro-Palestine protests to be banned. Social media are used to target students, teachers and academics who speak out against the genocide, from the UK to Palestine. In November 2024, violent rampages by Israeli football fans in Amsterdam were met with condemnations of local residents for allegedly responding with 'antisemitic pogroms'. This allowed Dutch authorities to pass legislation including taking away the passports of dual citizens and migrants' temporary residency permits. Student encampments to protest the genocide set up in universities across Europe, North America and Australasia have been met with brutal police and vigilante violence. Students and staff have been suspended or fired and misconduct proceedings used against them. Pro-Palestine chants and slogans have been explicitly banned. This intensified in the academic year 2024–25. For example, Harvard University effectively banned 'any substantive critique of Israel, making classes, panel talks, or vigils subjects of scrutiny.'

on CRT, blamed for providing the theoretical underpinnings for pro-Palestinian radicalism and labelled antisemitic for allegedly excluding Jews. Amid these discursive machinations, concepts such as CRT, woke and diversity, equity and inclusion (DEI) received unprecedented public attention, and were made debatable in the service of Zionist apologia, dovetailing with the right's onslaught discussed in the previous two chapters.

In constitutive tension with this process, ideas from critical race and ethnic studies, as well as administrative apparatuses – most prominently DEI policies – are used to configure antisemitism as both an overlooked and a more pressing form of racism in an effort to suppress anticolonial, and specifically pro-Palestine action and speech within educational settings. To examine this, unlike analyses that focus overly on the dissonance of the US army taking up CRT or RTX Corporation employees sitting down to excavate their unconscious bias, I trace some of the routes taken when critiques grounded in analyses of race are uprooted from their radical origins and transplanted to the centres of power. While this chapter foregrounds critical race, ethnic studies, and DEI, the next excavates the commodification of Indigeneity for the ends of

---

Shraddha Joshi and Asmer Asrar Safi, 'Harvard's New Speech Rules Continue Their Pattern of Repression', *The Nation*, 2025, https://tinyurl.com/5ybpza4j (last accessed February 2025); Brittney McNamara, 'Harvard Students Doxxed for Israel-Palestine Letter Speak out', *Teen Vogue*, https://tinyurl.com/p4zxw476 (last accessed January 2025); James Bamford, 'Israel's War on American Student Activists', *The Nation*, 2024, https://tinyurl.com/2pd37euc (last accessed January 2024); Amanda Yen, 'Columbia Students Allegedly Sprayed with Putrid Chemical at Pro-Palestine Rally', *The Daily Beast*, 2024, https://tinyurl.com/4rsbph8e (last accessed January 2024); Hebh Jamal, 'Pro-Palestinian Speech Is Now Effectively Banned in German Universities', *Mondoweiss*, 2023, https://tinyurl.com/ys4bxu5a (last accessed January 2024); Jad Salfiti, 'Nobel Winner Joins Push to Boycott German Cultural Institutions over Gaza', *Al Jazeera*, 2024, https://tinyurl.com/jy4e79dy (last accessed January 2024); Nandini Naira Archer, 'Prevent Referrals for Children Expressing Pro-Palestine Solidarity', *openDemocracy*, 2024, https://tinyurl.com/3536f324 (last accessed February 2024); The New Arab Staff, 'Germany: Two Courts Say Pro-Palestinian Slogans "legal"', *The New Arab*, 2023, https://tinyurl.com/5dnf592x (last accessed February 2025); Katherine Hearst, 'Social Media Surveillance Creates a "Culture of Fear" on UK Campuses', *Middle East Eye*, https://tinyurl.com/ytfne9ex (last accessed 23 January 2024); Josephine Solanki, 'A Disturbing Pattern of Repression Is Emerging in Europe', *Al Jazeera*, 2025, https://tinyurl.com/4zmrefsy (last accessed February 2025).

Zionism in alliance with white settlerism. These chapters focus on the extraction and retrofitting of ideas for intentionally, and sometimes unintentionally, obfuscating, counterinsurgent purposes. The uprisings against Israel's genocide in Gaza, which galvanised the Arab, Indigenous, Black and Brown youth, uniting them with their white counterparts in new and unexpected ways, shines light on the capacity of states, aided by elites, ever-more diversified along class and racial lines, to utilise the very terms of antiracist critique to undermine their efforts. This, I argue in the final section of the chapter, is exemplary of the current racial regime whose flexibility is assured via the partial incorporation of antiracist theories and racialised experience.

These counterinsurgent tactics not only use the language of antiracism to isolate and repress certain racialised subjects while elevating others, they also shield elites from among the abjected group whose investment in 'gentrifying disciplines'[28] places a distance between them and the masses whose condition their scholarship is supposed to contribute towards improving. In considering this I think through some of the epistemological limitations of CRT and studies of race and ethnicity more broadly, as well as the institutional constraints placed on them within the western academy. How do these two factors at times disable scholars from thinking relationally and interactively[29] about race, colonialism and imperialism and how might this be linked to the surprising silence on the genocide in Palestine from some quarters? We might provocatively recall the Black Liberation Army's call to Black intellectuals to join the struggle instead of 'laying back theorizing and writing essays in a vacuum, or in various black bourgeoisie publications' and demand the same from all antiracist scholars today.[30]

---

28 Alison Reed, 'Gentrifying Disciplines: The Institutional Management of Trauma and Creative Dissent', in *Antiracism Inc.: Why the Way We Talk about Racial Justice Matters*, ed. Felice Blake, Paula Ioanide, and Alison Reed (Santa Barbara, CA: Punctum Books, 2019), pp. 129–58.

29 David Theo Goldberg, 'Racial Comparisons, Relational Racisms: Some Thoughts on Method', in *Theories of Race and Ethnicity: Contemporary Debates and Perspectives*, ed. Karim Murji and John Solomos (Cambridge: Cambridge University Press, 2015), pp. 251–62.

30 Black Liberation Army, 'Message to the Black Movement: A Political Statement from the Black Underground', n.d., https://archive.lib.msu.edu/DMC/

'MOVEMENT MOOCHING'

I grew up in a place where the authorities proclaimed: 'the proletariat of the world unite.' In today's conception of intersectionality, haters of Jews unite. In the Soviet Union, there were good nations and bad nations – good nations were part of the struggle against the global capitalists and bad nations were opposed to it. In woke ideology, there are good identities and bad identities. In this worldview, the most victimized identity is Palestinian and the worst identity is Israeli, that which represents the last colonial project. Intersectionality unites woke progressive theory with the most primitive forms of antisemitism.[31]

Thus opens *Woke Antisemitism*, a book by David L. Bernstein, founder and chief executive of the Jewish Institute for Liberal Values, a lobby group founded in 2021 'to "build a strong counter-movement" to oppose "Critical Social Justice" within the Jewish community' in the United States.[32] The author of the book's foreword is former Soviet Jewish *refusenik* and hard-right Israeli politician, Natan Sharansky. In December 2023, Sharansky penned an article in the US Jewish magazine, *Tablet*, arguing that the support shown by Black Lives Matter activists for 'Hamas' murderous rampage' on October 7 was proof that the Jewish community had been wrong to 'set our differences aside and unite in the struggle against racism' after the murder of George Floyd in 2020.[33] Sharansky mobilises the well-worn trope of antisemitism as a 'particularly "Black problem"' which, Michael Richmond claims, simply 'gives white people the opportunity to call Black

---

AmRad/messageblackmovement.pdf, p. 9 (last accessed February 2025). My thanks to Dylan Rodríguez for mentioning this document in group communication.
31 David L. Bernstein and Natan Sharansky, *Woke Antisemitism: How a Progressive Ideology Harms Jews* (New York: Wicked Son, 2022), p. 12.
32 Arno Rosenfeld, 'Jewish "Harper's Letter" Tied to Opaque Foundation, Republican Megadonor', *The Forward*, 2021, https://tinyurl.com/3kx8rmht (last accessed January 2025).
33 Natan Sharansky, 'Our False Partners', *Tablet Magazine*, 2023, www.tabletmag.com/sections/news/articles/our-false-partners (last accessed January 2025).

people "racist"'.[34] The myth of disproportionate Black antisemitism ignores the differential structural conditions affecting Black people and white Jews. This was summed up by Martin Luther King in 1968 during his conversation with Rabbi Everett Gendler when he said that 'there is absolutely no anti-Semitism in the black community in the historic sense of anti-Semitism'.[35] Antisemitism, as Chapter 5 makes clear, has always been and continues to be a European political project.

The accusation that Black people are uniquely antisemitic is not unrelated to Sharansky's comment made 20 years earlier to then Israeli prime minister, Ariel Sharon, that 'the main battlefield for the future of the Jewish people lies in American academia'.[36] It was there that 'left-wing antisemitism' had been allowed to bloom with the tacit permission of 'liberal American Jews', duped into alliance with 'questionable bedfellows'.[37] Zionists like Sharansky peddle in the Red Scare that unfolded 'jointly' and 'recursively' with the Black Scare[38] which 'characterized Black agitation, protest, unrest, or dissent as dangerous, antithetical to the interests of the United States, and/or spurred by or susceptible to outside agitation'[39] going back to at least the 1930s.[40] It is against this history that Zionist

---

34 Michael Richmond, 'On "Black Antisemitism" and Antiracist Solidarity', *New Socialist*, 2020, https://newsocialist.org.uk/black-antisemitism-and-antiracist-solidarity/ (last accessed January 2025).
35 King Jr Martin Luther and Gendler Everett, 'A Conversation with Martin Luther King', *The Rabbinical Society*, 1968, https://tinyurl.com/3fdzwx5z (last accessed January 2025).
36 Sharansky, 'Our False Partners'. Undoubtedly, this groundwork, laid long before 2023, led to the Israeli newspaper *Haaretz* to run a stream of articles in the aftermath of 7 October making claims such as 'the State of Israel is confronted with an unprecedented enemy: woke "chicks"'. Shir Reuven, 'Medinat Israel Nitzav Mul Oyev Khasar Takdim: Efrochei Ha' Woke', *TheMarker*, 2023, https://tinyurl.com/25rmdm4y (last accessed February 2024).
37 Sharansky, 'Our False Partners'.
38 Charisse Burden-Stelly, *Black Scare/Red Scare: Theorizing Capitalist Racism in the United States* (Chicago, IL: University of Chicago Press, 2023), p. 6.
39 Ibid., p. 5.
40 Kendall Thomas, 'Rouge et Noir Re-read: A Popular Constitutional History of the Angelo Herndon Case', in *Critical Race Theory: The Key Writings That Formed the Movement*, ed. Kimberlé Crenshaw, Neil Gotanda, Gary Peller, and Kendall Thomas (New York: New Press, 1995), pp. 465–94.

critics zone in on Black Palestine solidarity activists, often mobilising well-worn antisemitic tropes, such as the 'scourge of cultural Marxism', in so doing.[41] Propagandists pose as defenders of Jews against antisemitism, but a principal target of their actions are Jews themselves who they see as being forced to embrace 'radical woke ideology... to maintain their standing' in an 'ultra-progressive milieu', a watchword for Black, or more generally radical antiracist, movements.[42]

On message, the Israeli newspaper *Haaretz* accused 'young Black activists' of 'movement mooching ... land[ing] upon Gaza as their next social-justice journey'.[43] The word mooching of course evokes the supposed thievery of the 'benefits scrounger', or the 'welfare queen', words associated with the 'war on drugs' used to criminalise 'predominantly Latinx and Black communities',[44] and to invoke the fecklessness of the activist. It exemplifies Younes' argument that the 'war on antisemitism' operates according to the logic previously epitomised by the 'war on drugs'. In fact, Black solidarity with Palestine has a long history which, following a not yet concluded period of 'Afro-Zionism',[45] 'crystallised during the anti-colonial turn and particularly after the 1967 war'.[46] In 1970,

---

41 Russian Jewish émigrés have a specific function in advancing the 'Race Marxism' thesis proposed by James Lindsay, as escapees from Soviet indoctrination who find themselves confronted by it once more in the guise of US ethnic studies. Such is the position taken by Elina Kaplan, co-founder of Constructive Ethnic Studies, just one of the lobby groups established amid a well-organised campaign to defang the teaching of ethnic studies in US high schools. Angelica Stabile, 'Soviet Immigrant, Registered Democrat Warns Critical Race Theory Resembles Marxist Curriculum', *Fox News*, 2021, https://tinyurl.com/mnehfu3s (last accessed January 2025).
42 Bernstein and Sharansky, *Woke Antisemitism*, p. 131.
43 David Christopher Kaufman, 'Black Activists, the Hamas War to "Liberate Palestine" Is Not Your Battle', *Haaretz*, 2024, https://tinyurl.com/4z86b9ph (last accessed January 2025).
44 Younes, 'Fighting Anti-Semitism in Contemporary Germany', p. 250.
45 Clayton Vaughn-Roberson, 'The "Jewish Question" in the Black Mind: The Image of World Jewry in African American Socialism', *Journal of Civil and Human Rights* 3, no. 2 (1 December 2017): 62–93.
46 Noura Erakat and Marc Lamont Hill, 'Black-Palestinian Transnational Solidarity: Renewals, Returns, and Practice', *Journal of Palestine Studies* 48, no. 4 (192) (2019): 7–16.

Black Panther Party leader Huey Newton connected the Black and Palestinian experiences saying, 'Black people in America have been persecuted; therefore it is easy for us to identify with other people who are suffering.'[47] He recognised that 'some people who happen to be Jewish and who support Israel will use the Black Panther Party's position that is against imperialism and against the agents of the imperialist as an attack of anti-Semitism. We think that this is a back-biting, racist tactic and we will treat it as such.'[48]

Zionist counterinsurgency has long had a hand in repressing Black radical thought and praxis as Black people in the US joined the majority of the world's population in the decolonised zones in siding with Palestinian resistance to Israeli settler colonialism. The targeting of Black movements runs alongside a campaign waged in the field of education where any teaching, research, or student activism focused on Palestine comes under attack. Its tactics have been adopted by the flurry of other organisations dedicated to fighting antisemitism, conflated with 'defending the Jewish state'.[49] One tactic is to create an ideological divide between palatable 'moderate' Black leaders and their purportedly radical, violent counterparts, deemed to pose a specific threat to Jews. Jewish involvement in the Black struggle for civil rights is presented as having been denied by 'Black nationalists' who threaten the historical Black and Jewish alliance.[50]

This narrative is repeated today in the high school 'FAIRStory Curriculum' disseminated by the Zionist and anti-CRT lobby group, the Foundation Against Intolerance and Racism (FAIR).[51]

---

47 Huey P. Newton and Toni Morrison, *To Die for the People: The Writings of Huey P. Newton* (San Francisco, CA: City Lights Books, 2009), p. 197.
48 Ibid., p. 199.
49 Arno Rosenfeld, 'Dark Money, Questionable Partners behind New Group Fighting Antisemitism', *The Forward*, 2021, https://tinyurl.com/mvyx5w2p (last accessed January 2025).
50 Anti-Defamation League, 'Murder and Extremism in the United States in 2021', *ADL*, 2022, www.adl.org/resources/report/murder-and-extremism-united-states-2021 (last accessed January 2025).
51 Its lesson plan on slavery promises to increase students' 'proficiency in debating alternative interpretations of historical events.' FAIRStory Curriculum, 'Lesson Plans', n.d., www.fairstory.org/curriculum/lesson-plans/ (last accessed February 2024).

The curriculum cleanses the history of Black-Jewish solidarity of any mention of US Jewish participation in the structures of white supremacy to evoke a picture in which Jewish allyship with Black people during the civil rights movement was reciprocated by Black allyship with 'the American Jewish community and ... Israel'.[52] The Zionism of both W.E.B. Du Bois and Martin Luther King, which Kelley and Alahmed among others have contextualised and troubled,[53] is presented as testimony to Black people's abiding allegiance to Jewish Americans whose interests are presented as interchangeable with those of Israel and who, in the FAIRStory narrative, 'represented a disproportionate number of white people involved in the [civil rights] struggle'.[54] As Kelley signals, around the pivotal year of 1967 there was a significant shift among Black USians away from the Black-Jewish alliance and towards a 'shared analogy of oppression' in which Black people rising up in the urban rebellions of that year identified with Palestinians under violent occupation.[55] In the context of the US state's repression of radical Black activism, and any movement associated with it, it became imperative for US imperialist-aligned Zionists to promote the idea that 'the vast majority of Black America enthusiastically embraced Zionism'.[56] With the passing years, and especially after the mutual solidarity extended between Black people and Palestinians in 2014 following the state murder of Mike Brown in Ferguson, Missouri,[57] the two-pronged counterinsurgent strategy of both overt and covert repression of activists and the cooptation of Black icons and ideas built pace. The latter came to a head with the *Washington Post*'s revelations of a leaked WhatsApp group chat of a 'group of billionaires and business titans working to shape U.S. public opinion of the war in Gaza' which stressed 'getting Black Leaders to condemn

---

52 Ibid.
53 Robin D.G. Kelley, 'From the River to the Sea to Every Mountain Top: Solidarity as Worldmaking', *Journal of Palestine Studies* 48, no. 4 (192) (2019): 69–91; Nadia Alahmed, 'From Black Zionism to Black Nasserism: W.E.B. Du Bois and the Foundations of Black Anti-Zionist Discourse', *Critical Sociology* 49, no. 6 (September 2023): 1053–64.
54 FAIRStory Curriculum, 'Lesson Plans'.
55 Kelley, 'From the River to the Sea to Every Mountain Top', p. 73.
56 Vaughn-Roberson, 'The "Jewish Question" in the Black Mind', p. 87.
57 Erakat and Hill, 'Black-Palestinian Transnational Solidarity'.

Anti-Semitism', naming 'Jay-Z, LeBron James or Alicia Keys'.[58] On Martin Luther King Day 2024, the official account of the Israeli government tweeted a quote attributed to Dr King: 'Darkness cannot drive out darkness, only light can do that',[59] a twisted echo of Benjamin Netanyahu's, later deleted, claim that the genocide of Gaza was a 'struggle between the children of light and the children of darkness, between humanity and the law of the jungle'.[60]

ARREST IN THE OFFICE OF DIVERSITY, EQUITY AND INCLUSION

The Gaza genocide unmasked the role played by Zionist counter-insurgency in the wider war on CRT, directing our attention to this longer history. In the US, this was thrown into relief with the forced resignation of Harvard's first Black woman president, Claudine Gay, in a campaign spurred by Christopher Rufo.[61] Rufo was backed by Harvard donor Bill A. Ackman, who blamed the 'reverse racism' of the 'powerful' diversity, equity and inclusion (DEI) 'movement' for Gay's promotion.[62] Her supposed failure to condemn Palestine activists at Harvard harshly enough was wrapped in allegations of

---

58 Hannah Natanson and Emmanuel Felton, 'Business Titans Privately Urged NYC Mayor to Use Police on Columbia Protesters, Chats Show', *Washington Post*, 2024, https://tinyurl.com/34u5fu7c (last accessed January 2025).
59 Israel, X, 2024, https://x.com/Israel/status/1483108452146819077?s=20 (last accessed February 2024).
60 The New Arab Staff, 'Netanyahu Deletes Palestinian "Children of Darkness" Tweet', *The New Arab*, 2023, www.newarab.com/news/netanyahu-deletes-palestinian-children-darkness-tweet (last accessed January 2025).
61 The plan to oust Gay was explained by Christopher Rufo, echoing his previous openness regarding his strategy on CRT, as noted in Chapter 1. On 20 December 2023, Rufo posted, 'We launched the Claudine Gay plagiarism story from the Right. The next step is to smuggle it into the media apparatus of the Left, legitimizing the narrative to center-left actors who have the power to topple her. Then squeeze.' Christopher F. Rufo, X, 2023, https://x.com/realchrisrufo/status/1737209215738069232?mx=2 (last accessed January 2025). On 3 January, Rufo followed with 'SCAPLED: Harvard president Claudine Gay resigns', quickly followed up by '*first tweet should read SCALPED'; Posts by @realchrisrufo, 2024, X, https://x.com/realchrisrufo/status/1737209215738069232 (last accessed January 2025).
62 Bess Levin, 'Bill Ackman Claims Martin Luther King Jr. Would Have Been against Diversity, Equity, and Inclusion – and Yes, He Was Serious', *Vanity Fair*, 2024, https://tinyurl.com/wfv2pf8j (last accessed January 2025).

plagiarism which cast aspersions on her scholarly credentials as a Black woman in academia.[63] In fact, Gay's only mistake was to fail to carry out Harvard's commitment to white supremacy by not suppressing pro-Palestine students 'well enough'.[64]

For the Black scholar Keeanga-Yamahtta Taylor,[65] Gay's dismissal indicates how the charge of antisemitism is deployed as a tool of antiblack counter-attack by groups such as the New York-based Jewish advocacy group, the Anti-Defamation League (ADL). The ADL was made subject to global outrage for defending Trump appointee Elon Musk's twice-repeated performance of a Nazi salute at the January 2025 presidential inauguration as 'an awkward gesture in a moment of enthusiasm, not a Nazi salute'.[66]

---

63 During a House Committee on Education and the Workforce hearing on antisemitism on US college campuses on 5 December 2023, New York Republican Congresswoman Elise Stefanik repeatedly asked Gay whether 'calling for genocide of Jews' violates Harvard's policies on bullying and harassment. 'Calling for genocide of Jews' refers to the chant commonly heard at pro-Palestine rallies, 'From the river to the sea, Palestine will be free.' Gay's response that the answer depends on the context was touted as proof enough that she could not guarantee the safety of Jewish students. Madeleine A. Hung and Joyce E. Kim, '"Victory": Claudine Gay's Resignation from the Harvard Presidency Comes as a Win for Her Critics', *The Harvard Crimson*, 2024, https://tinyurl.com/yf6t9ym6 (last accessed January 2025).

64 As Harvard historian of slavery, Walter Johnson wrote, the university overreacted to 'perceived threats of antisemitism'. He describes the firing and evicting of a Harvard University graduate students and residential adviser who sought to protect students participating in a 'die-in' protest while their faces were being filmed at close range by a counter-protestor, an incident twisted in the right-wing media as an act of aggression on his part. In reality, Palestinian students and their supporters endured 'being shouted at from passing cars or other pedestrians – "suicide bomber," "terrorist," "fuck you and fuck Palestine, fuck all of you," "so did you murder your way into Harvard the way Hamas murdered their way into Israel," "go back to your country, you don't belong here" – and spat on during a demonstration'. Aaryan Morrison, 'On White Supremacy and Zionism: A reflection on Claudine Gay's tenure as President of Harvard University', *Mondoweiss*, 2024, https://tinyurl.com/hssbhwp9 (last accessed January 2025); Keeanga-Yamahtta Taylor, 'The Campaign against D.E.I.', *The New Yorker*, 2024, www.newyorker.com/news/our-columnists/the-campaign-against-dei (last accessed January 2025); Walter Johnson, 'Living inside a Psyop', *N+1*, 2024, https://tinyurl.com/mpwmnuk6 (last accessed January 2025).

65 Taylor, 'The Campaign against D.E.I.'

66 Anti-Defamation League, *X*, 21 January 2025, https://tinyurl.com/mwrunxrv (last accessed February 2025).

Such groups are part of a network of organisations set up with significant donor funding[67] ostensibly to fight antisemitism in the US, instigating a model which can be replicated elsewhere. These groups help to construct a narrative according to which radical opponents of racism and colonialism, especially anyone standing with Palestinians, is the 'real racist'.[68] In the counterinsurgent aim of stamping out pro-Palestine mobilisation, a range of mechanisms are employed, including repression and criminalisation through law and policy. The ADL promotes a carceral approach to tackling racism which it characterises as 'hate', thus not only decoupling individual acts of racist aggression from the operations of the racial state but also establishing a framework for the generalisation of racism to any perceived vilification on the basis of group affiliation.[69] Its reach into the arenas of liberal antiracism and education

---

67   According to Rosenfeld, 'Ronald Lauder, the cosmetics billionaire and president of the World Jewish Congress, pledged $25 million in December 2019, for the Anti-Semitism Accountability Project, or ASAP, which includes a Super PAC that can back candidates. Earlier that year, Robert Kraft, owner of the New England Patriots, put up $21 million and got others to add $10 million more for the Foundation to Combat Anti-Semitism, a group focused on leveraging social media and that is unrelated to the Combat Anti-Semitism Movement.' Rosenfeld, 'Dark Money, Questionable Partners'.

68   As the Heritage Foundation's Project Esther, launched in October 2024 to, as Yoav Litvin puts it, 'crush anticolonial resistance' states, what it calls the 'global Hamas support network' hides behind the label 'pro-Palestinian' to advance a 'virulently anti-Israel, anti-Zionist, and anti-American'. It must be attacked by building a 'silent majority', a 'broad coalition of willing and able partners to leverage existing – *and, if required, work to establish additional* – authorities, resources, capabilities, and activities'. Yoav Litvin, 'Project Esther: A Trumpian Blueprint to Crush Anticolonial Resistance', 2024, https://tinyurl.com/3d55j97x (last accessed January 2025); The Heritage Foundation, 'Project Esther: A National Strategy to Combat Antisemitism', *The Heritage Foundation*, 2024, https://tinyurl.com/ybv9hp97 (last accessed January 2025).

69   Dylan Rodríguez notes the ADL's strong reliance on a carceral approach to 'hate' in the League's 2021 'Audit of Antisemitic Incidents' which states, 'law enforcement agencies should use data from the FBI, Department of Education and NGOs such as ADL and Stop AAPI Hate to anticipate where hate incidents are most likely to occur and to proactively contact community members and institutions to strengthen relationships and collaboration'. Dylan Rodríguez, 'How the Stop Asian Hate Movement Became Entwined with Zionism, Policing, and Counterinsurgency', *Critical Ethnic Studies*, 2024, www.criticalethnicstudiesjournal.org/blog (last accessed May 2024).

and training exemplifies the routes through which progressive ideas and practices become more tractable modes for establishing a hegemonic consensus on what constitutes, and more crucially, what does not constitute racism.

The ADL's cementing of the definition of racism as hate bonds it to speech acts and couches the effects of racism in an amorphous feeling of unsafety experienced by individuals, thus detaching it from institutional and state power. The international reach of this partial definition is made possible by the fact that it coheres with a generalised understanding of racism as 'volitional' and morally vicious,[70] rather than systemically reproduced within racial institutions undergirded by a racial regime. This smooths the long-standing effort to embed hate speech legislation and to support and promote organisations that frame themselves as 'anti-hate' rather than antiracist. This approach promotes criminological methods to target 'hate', enabling the use of state violence to suppress and punish any and all radical Black, Indigenous and anticolonial protest that targets and exposes the violence of state racism and colonialism and imperialism.[71] The use of a blend of state violence, lawfare[72] and rhetorical undermining, undeterred by facts, leading to censorship, loss of employment, incrimination, and even physical harm is not new. In the US, it goes back to at least 1967[73] when the ADL 'laid into' the Student Nonviolent Coordinating Committee (SNCC) for its "'pro-Arab, Soviet and

---

70 J.L.A. Garcia, 'Philosophical Analysis and the Moral Concept of Racism', *Philosophy & Social Criticism Philosophy & Social Criticism* 25, no. 5 (1999): 1–32.
71 Rodríguez, 'How the Stop Asian Hate Movement Became Entwined'.
72 The use of the law to thwart political opponents. Natasha Roth-Rowland, 'Waging Lawfare', *Jewish Currents*, https://jewishcurrents.org/waging-lawfare (last accessed January 2024).
73 The ADL's 'strong allegiance with the U.S. state' and commitment to 'its civilizing mission of settlement, and to capitalist individualism as the framework for rights' was already evident in its earlier collaboration with the House Un-American Activities Committee's anti-communist witch-hunt. From these early days, the ADL played a formative role in affixing antisemitism to anti-Zionism, using education and advocacy to cement the idea of a dizzying rise in antisemitism across the west in which antisemitism is measured by anything from teenagers swastika daubing to pro-Palestine activism. Rodríguez, 'How the Stop Asian Hate Movement Became Entwined'.

racist lines" on the Arab-Israeli conflict'.[74] From 1969 on, the ADL and other Israel-aligned groups played a significant role in using US anti-terrorism law to criminalise Palestinian activists and consequently restrict aid to Palestine.[75]

The effect of the ADL's early dominance over antiracism education and policy, leading to it being 'viewed by legislators and media as an authority on Jewish, Black, Muslim, LGBTQ, immigrant and other civil rights'[76] has been to destabilise antiracist organisations 'that sought to discuss racism and white supremacy in terms of state power and dispossession'.[77] The ADL is behind 'expanding DEI programming to address rising antisemitism'.[78] This may appear paradoxical given the claim by figures aligned with the war on CRT that DEI policies fuel antisemitism by making space for pro-Palestinian speech and action, which they deem antisemitic. However, when taken with the ADL's role in the suppression and criminalisation of Black and anticolonial radicalism, its outsized role in shaping and promoting what Sean Malloy calls a 'counter-insurgency against the radical energies of the 60s and 70s' in the form of DEI policy is entirely logical as a means of racial regime recalibration.[79] Because DEI is an administrative function of institutions like universities, 'the enforcement of anti-Zionism' can be outsourced 'to universities themselves', thus avoiding litigation.[80] Because those leading the charge in the war on antisemitism have successfully made the case that 'Zionist' is a protected identity

---

74 Michael R. Fischbach, *Black Power and Palestine* (Stanford, CA: Stanford University Press, 2020).
75 Palestine Legal and the Center for Constitutional Rights, 'Anti-Palestinian at the Core: The Origins and Growing Dangers of U.S. Antiterrorism Law', 2024, https://tinyurl.com/56sxftv4 (last accessed January 2025).
76 Emmaia Gelman, 'The World Upside-down: Zionist Institutions, Civil Rights Talk, and the New Cold War on Ethnic Studies', *Critical Ethnic Studies* 8, no. 2 (2023), https://tinyurl.com/bkbh65r7 (last accessed February 2025).
77 Emmaia Gelman, 'The Anti-Defamation League Is Not What It Seems', *Boston Review*, 2019, www.bostonreview.net/articles/emmaia-gelman-anti-defamation-league/ (last accessed February 2025).
78 Taylor, 'The Campaign against D.E.I.'
79 Emmaia Gelman, Amira Jarmakani, and Sean Malloy, 'DEI', *Institute for the Critical Study of Zionism Podcast*, 2024, https://criticalzionismstudies.org/2024/04/01/amira-sean-dei/ (last accessed 25 April 2024).
80 Ibid.

inextricable from 'Jewish', DEI mechanisms can be used to punish pro-Palestinian speech and action and protect Zionists, even when they violate the rights and freedoms of their opponents.[81]

On 30 April 2024, as the president of Columbia University called in a highly militarised NYPD to violently evict students who had set up an encampment to protest the university's investments in corporations that profit from Israel's genocide in Palestine,[82] I read a post on X by Princeton student and encampment participant, Aditi Rao, which perfectly encapsulates this:

> Lmao someday I'll be able to process what it felt like being arrested, detained, and booked in Princeton's DEI[83] office and how when I emerged the entire community of 'the country's most apathetic university' was there ready to de-arrest us. Processing someday, relishing now.[84]

The ideological fodder fuelling this institutional repression is the 'new antisemitism' thesis first posited in a book of the same title by the ADL's directors in 1974, and recapitulated in 2002 by Pierre-André Taguieff in the French context as *La Nouvelle Judeophobie*.[85] Both versions construe Arabs, Muslims and those whom Taguieff called 'third worldists' as responsible for an antisemi-

---

[81] This approach is generalised far beyond the US. For example, the equity, diversity and inclusion policy of Macquarie University in Sydney includes the IHRA working definition of antisemitism – 'Antisemitism is a certain perception of Jews, which may be expressed as hatred toward Jews. Rhetorical and physical manifestations of antisemitism are directed toward Jewish or non-Jewish individuals and/or their property, toward Jewish community institutions and religious facilities.' No definition of any other form of racism is included. Macquarie University, 'Equity, Diversity, and Inclusion Policy', *Macquarie University*, n.d., https://policies.mq.edu.au/document/view.php?id=296# (last accessed February 2024).
[82] Sarah Shamim, '"Divest from Israel": Decoding the Gaza Protest Call Shaking US Campuses', *Al Jazeera*, 2024, https://tinyurl.com/yn7v5zc7 (last accessed January 2025).
[83] Diversity, Equity and Inclusion.
[84] Aditi L. Rao, *X*, 2024, https://tinyurl.com/n52etvxx (last accessed January 2025).
[85] Pierre-André Taguieff, *La Nouvelle Judéophobie* (Paris: Fayard – Milles et une nuits, 2002).

tism deracinated from its European origins. However, in the US account, the authors of *The New Antisemitism*, Forster and Epstein, argued that following their 'economic, social, and political inclusion', US Jews faced a new form of antisemitism from the left which 'opposed "establishment" interests – especially Israel – without regard for the fact that they were ... also Jewish interests'.[86] This argument antisemitically essentialises all Jews as white, as wealthy and as Zionist. It contributes to the age-old demonisation of Jews as aligned with power and opposed to 'ordinary' people and thus cements the alliance between the war on antisemitism and the far right.

Taking up the theme in 2021, Pamela Paresky, a researcher with the 'contrarian' right-wing Heterodox Academy, argued that US Jewish students are alienated by their university experience because of the enforcement of 'current social justice ideology' which 'relies on narratives of greed, appropriation, unmerited privilege, and hidden power – themes strikingly reminiscent of familiar anti-Jewish conspiracy theories'.[87] These ideas are endlessly repeated by Zionist groups who paint pro-Palestinian activism on campuses as a threat to Jewish student safety, the allegations that resulted in the removal of Claudine Gay, and that fuel the incrimination, doxing and violence faced by student and academic activists. This is despite the fact that while pro-Palestine student encampments were met not only with police repression but with violent attacks by Zionists, it was the students who were painted as a threat to safety and maligned as terrorists.

'JEWS NEED NOT APPLY'

Just as anti-CRT warriors insist that the precepts of CRT exclude white children by focusing on Black history to their detriment, Zionist groups in California, such as the AMCHA Initiative and the 'heavily funded campus-oriented Zionist advocacy group', StandWithUs' have waged a campaign against ethnic studies which

---

86 Gelman, 'The World Upside-down'.
87 Pamela Paresky, 'Critical Race Theory and the "Hyper-White" Jew', *Sapir* 1, Spring (2021).

they insinuate excludes Jews and antisemitism from its curriculum.[88] On 25 October 2023, the AMCHA Initiative, which has 'a history of obsessive attempts to silence criticism of Israeli policy and label supporters of Palestinians' rights as anti-Semites',[89] coordinated an open letter signed by 115 organisations, addressed to the University of California leadership.[90] The signatories made use of 'Hamas' recent terrorist attack on Israeli civilians' to further a campaign, already underway since 2016, to derail Assembly Bill 101, signed by California Governor Gavin Newsom in 2021, 'which mandated that all California high school students complete an ethnic studies course in order to graduate'.[91] Notwithstanding the incongruity of the state mandating education in ethnic studies, a curriculum that originated in the radical anticolonial struggles of the late 1960s, the attack on the bill was exemplary of the tactics of the war on antisemitism. The efforts of Zionist groups to undermine high school ethnic studies led to the imposition of so-called 'guardrails' that 'enact anti-Arab, anti-Palestinian censorship' by restricting the teaching of 'hard truths about racism and colonialism'.[92] Sixty years of militating for the provision of ethnic studies

---

88   Editors, 'Resisting the New McCarthyism: Rabab Abdulhadi Discusses AMCHA's Smear Campaign, Palestinian Resistance, and the U.S. Solidarity Movement', *Solidarity* (blog), 2014, https://solidarity-us.org/p4220/ (last accessed January 2025).
89   Nora Barrows-Friedman, 'Amcha Attempt to Block "Palestinian Voices" University Course Fails', *Electronic Intifada*, 2015, https://tinyurl.com/2phxk4mh (last accessed January 2025).
90   AMCHA Initiative, '115 Organizations Urge Rejection of UC Ethnic Studies Council Proposal Following Condoning of Terrorism', 2023, https://tinyurl.com/37b4xu89 (last accessed January 2025).
91   UC Ethnic Studies Faculty Council, 'Letter to Governor Newsom and Superintendent Thurmond', *Google Drive*, 2023, https://tinyurl.com/rptfvx43 (last accessed January 2025). The Zionist campaign to halt the provision of ethnic studies in California schools had antecedents going back to 2016 when California Governor Jerry Brown signed new legislation that established an advisory council to develop a model curriculum for ethnic studies in high schools (Christine Hong, personal communication). Valerie Strauss, 'Critics Slam Draft of California Ethnic Studies Curriculum as Far-Left Propaganda', *Washington Post*, 2019, https://tinyurl.com/mr3fz8d4 (last accessed January 2025).
92   Of the three guardrails listed, the second, the requirement to 'not reflect or promote, directly or indirectly, any bias, bigotry, or discrimination against any person or group of persons on the basis of any category protected by Education

in US schools, a campaign led by 'historically marginalized and disenfranchised communities of colour and Indigenous communities, especially students and youth subjected to structural racism and colonial conditions',[93] had come under attack because, per the title of an article scandalously published in the journal *Ethnic and Racial Studies*,[94] to ethnic studies, 'Jews need not apply'.[95]

The Zionist campaign in California succeeded in removing 'all sections discussing Palestine and any criticisms of Israel' from the ethnic studies curriculum.[96] However, as the AMCHA Initiative's October 2023 open letter demonstrates, this was not the end of the story. It was clear that any attempt to research 'power by centring the lived experiences of oppressed racialized people of colour and

---

Code Section 220', was noted in a letter by Governor Newsom to be of particular importance. A warning was included to 'some vendors [who] are offering materials that may not meet the requirements of AB 101' to be particularly mindful of this stipulation, a direct result of Zionist campaigns against the purported antisemitism of the originally drafted ethnic studies curriculum. UC Ethnic Studies Faculty Council, 'Letter to Governor Newsom and Superintendent Thurmond'.

93   Ibid.

94   The Coalition of Liberated Ethnic Studies wrote a letter of protest to the *Ethnic and Racial Studies* editor in protest at the publication of the article by a staffer for StandWithUs, a US-based Zionist lobby group, Daniel Ian Rubin, in 2023. As the letter details, StandWithUs 'provides customized research and helps pro-Israel activists around the world implement effective strategies on the ground'. The organisation's 'About Us' statement betrays its mission: 'We are inspired by our love of Israel, our belief that education is the road to peace, and our commitment to stand up for Israel and the Jewish people. StandWithUs is an international, non-partisan education organization that supports Israel and fights antisemitism.' 'Open Letter to the Editors of Ethnic and Racial Studies', *Google Docs*, 2023, https://tinyurl.com/mryrwrus (last accessed February 2024).

95   Daniel Ian Rubin, '"Liberated" Ethnic Studies: Jews Need Not Apply', *Ethnic and Racial Studies* 47, no. 3 (17 February 2024): 506–25.

96   According to Friedland, 'Specifically, groups took issue with the Arab-American section of the 2019 ESMC model curriculum which included sections such as "Direct Action Front for Palestine and Black Lives Matter," "Call to Boycott, Divest, and Sanction Israel," "Comparative Border Studies: Palestine and Mexico," as well as a citation of the Nakba, the historic displacement of Palestinians in 1948 at the hands of the state of Israel, as a central reason for many Palestinians' migration to America.' Naomi Friedland, 'The Battle over California's Ethnic Studies Curriculum', *New Voices*, 2022, https://newvoices.org/2022/06/23/the-battle-over-californias-ethnic-studies-curriculum/ (last accessed January 2025).

indigenous people'[97] was to be presented as a direct challenge to Jewish people. Although it had been forcefully cleansed of any mention of Palestine, AMCHA continued to describe the ethnic studies curriculum as 'material that provides a one-sided, biased and hateful narrative about Israel and Jews ... laden with anti-Zionism, [that] will incite antisemitic animus and behaviour towards Jewish students'.[98]

The similarity with the rhetorical themes of the war on CRT mapped in Chapters 1 and 2 wherein white children are allegedly victimised by truthful accounts of the history of slavery and colonialism is evident. As the director of the Institute for the Critical Study of Zionism, Emmaia Gelman writes, anti-antisemitism activists 'espouse Trump-era white nationalist arguments against critical race theory' in terms that 'mask their conservative allegiances and the centrality of Zionism to their work'.[99] In the equation drawn by Jewish Zionist opponents of CRT, the framework discriminates against Jews by positing a binary 'oppressor-oppressed' view, which they associate with a 'habit of descending to antisemitism' as Jews do not 'fit neatly in either category' because they are antisemitically associated with having privilege. This, they propose, leads to a 'simplification' of the 'Israeli-Palestinian conflict' wherein Israel is – erroneously in their view – cast in the role of oppressor.[100] Here, the alignment of Jews with whiteness is clear. In a contradictory fashion, however, Bernstein and Lawrence claim that to insist that the grand majority of US Jews are structurally located as white is to deny Jews' minoritised status. Hence, while working to systemically undermine CRT and ethnic studies, unlike their counterparts in the broader war on CRT, Zionist activists coopt

---

97 UC Ethnic Studies Faculty Council, 'Letter to Governor Newsom and Superintendent Thurmond'.
98 AMCHA Initiative, '10,000 Demand UC Reject Ethnic Studies Requirement from Faculty Supporting Hamas Terrorism', *AMCHA Initiative*, 2023, https://amchainitiative.org/10k-petition-uc-reject-proposal/ (last accessed January 2025).
99 Gelman, 'Zionist Institutions, Civil Rights Talk, and the New Cold War on Ethnic Studies'.
100 David Bernstein and Peter D. Lawrence, 'Critical Race Theory and the Jewish Community', *Jewish Virtual Library*, 2022, https://tinyurl.com/yspbxcak (last accessed January 2025).

concepts from these approaches and apply them to Jewish Zionists who, they argue, are excluded and discriminated against by the ethnic studies curriculum because it takes an anticolonial standpoint and names Palestine as a site of struggle against Israeli settler colonialism.

Such a tactic, however, can arguably only gain traction in a terrain characterised by an essentialised interpretation of race as identity which wilfully ignores the role of the racial regime in hiding the politically performative function of identity creation from view. As the authors of the 2012 pamphlet, 'Who Is Oakland: Anti-Oppression Activism, the Politics of Safety, and State Co-optation' remark, 'it is a well-worn activist formula to point out that "representatives" of different identity categories must be placed "front and center" in struggles against racism, sexism, and homophobia. But this is meaningless without also specifying the content of their politics.'[101] The logic of privileging the voice of 'those affected' is coopted by Zionists. Thus, institutional commitments to policy measures such as the adoption of the International Holocaust Remembrance Alliance's working definition of antisemitism, and the conflation of pro-Palestine activism with a 'threat to Jewish safety', as we shall see in Chapter 5, paradoxically re-racialises Jews as Zionists, now formulated as an 'ethnic identity' in need of protection within a commitment to DEI, a framework to be divergently instrumentalised or condemned as the circumstances require.

THE INSTITUTIONALISATION OF DISSENT

> Thousands of students could have been able to go to school and have books and have housing, but instead, our Chancellor, who is a very cruel man, decided to send thousands of dollars' worth of state funding paid for by the taxpayers into the trash ... What job do I have if the students don't have a future?[102]

---

[101] CROATOAN, 'Who Is Oakland: Anti-Oppression Activism, the Politics of Safety, and State Co-optation', *Escalating Identity*, 2012, https://tinyurl.com/tkscj5nt (last accessed January 2025).

[102] Black political science professor, Tiffany Willoughby-Herard spoke these words as she was arrested by police at a pro-Palestine demonstration and solidarity encampment at the University of California Irvine on 15 May 2024. The

A new opportunity structure in the war on CRT created by the genocide clearly revealed how the tools of analysis developed through the radical conjoining of theory and praxis in spaces carved out by Black, Brown, Indigenous, Muslim and other negatively racialised scholar-activists, within and without the university, could, and was being, harnessed as a technology of power. However, this subversion was not the result solely of a well-oiled lobby's machinations. As with the discussion in Chapter 1 of the impact of highly funded pressure groups on public education, through a range of tactics from disinformation to the infiltration of school and library boards, I seek to avoid an analysis that overemphasises the power of lobbyists and sees them as exceptional and at a remove from the regimes of imperial power that produce them. In particular, in the case of Palestine, the argument that '"The Lobby" made us do it' presents the US backing of Israel as irrational rather than as 'pound for pound ... the best investment the US has ever made'.[103] This slant takes attention away from the linchpin role Israel plays, not just for US might, but as the 'purest expression of Western power, combining militarism, imperialism, settler colonialism, counterinsurgency, occupation, racism, instilling ideological defeat, huge profitable war-making and hi-tech development into a manticore of destruction, death, and mayhem'.[104] Thus the tendency to see the unrelenting support given to Israel, even at the apex of its genocidal assault on Palestinians, as due directly to the outsized influence of Zionist Jewish groups, such as the ADL, is part of what Max Ajl calls the 'misreading' of Palestine. He further questions the idea that there is a '"national interest" from which the Lobby diverts US power' from an historical materialist perspective which foregrounds the centrality of violence to the history of capitalist accumulation.[105] The

---

New Arab Staff, 'US Professor Praised for Gaza Student Protest Backing', *The New Arab*, 2024, www.newarab.com/news/us-professor-praised-gaza-student-protest-backing (last accessed September 2024).
103 Max Ajl, 'Misreading Palestine', *Ebb Magazine*, 1 (2024).
104 Ibid.
105 Max Ajl, 'Palestine's Great Flood: Part II', *Agrarian South: Journal of Political Economy: A Triannual Journal of Agrarian South Network and CARES* 13, no. 2 (June 2024): 187–217.

national interest argument, such as that made by the realist International Relations scholars John Mearsheimer and Stephen Walt,[106] assumes that what is in the best interests of the US is also good for the rest of humanity, while nothing could be further from the case. This is not to deny the destructive impact of Zionist organisations and fronts, particularly on those whom the state holds in its sights, radical Black, Muslim and Indigenous people first and foremost. On the contrary, any analysis of this impact should stress Zionism's role as integral to the racial regime, both materially in terms of its centrality to the military-technological complex[107] and global counterinsurgency, and ideologically as the terms within which western civilisation and white supremacy remake themselves today, as Chapter 5 shows.

Zionist use of the war on CRT to repress and criminalise pro-Palestine teaching and activism demonstrates not solely that white supremacy comes in many ethnicities but that, as per the terms of the new racial regime, it requires multiculturalism to reconstruct itself.[108] Zionism becomes a focal point for global white supremacist mobilisation via the use of a superficial antiracist language that can be mobilised for racial colonial, and indeed pro-genocidal, ends. However, Zionism merely crystalises a wider and deeper phenomenon in which 'the appropriation, incorporation, and neutralisation of antiracist discourses [become] a unique technology to advance racism'.[109] Taking this wider view allows us to shift our focus away from the dynamics described in the previous section and towards the institutional settings in which concepts developed to theorise racist structures and racialised experience can be 'used to construct the current racial regime' and the various epistemological outlooks they presage.[110]

---

106 John J. Mearsheimer and Stephen M. Walt, *The Israel Lobby and U.S. Foreign Policy* (New York: Farrar, Straus and Giroux, 2008).
107 Antony Loewenstein, *The Palestine Laboratory: How Israel Exports the Technology of Occupation around the World* (London: Verso Books, 2023).
108 Rodríguez, *White Reconstruction*.
109 Felice Blake and Paula Ioanide, 'Introduction: Antiracism Incorporated', in *Antiracism Inc.: Why the Way We Talk about Racial Justice Matters*, ed. Felice Blake, Paula Ioanide, and Alison Reed (Punctum Books, 2019), pp. 17–39, p. 20.
110 Ibid., p. 21.

In theorising what he calls 'the long Attica rebellion', Orisanmi Burton describes 'the strategy of encapsulating the potentially disruptive claims, demands, and tactics of movements within liberal institutions and discourses, which transform them into routinized processes that legitimize rather than challenge established authority'.[111] Understanding these processes of the 'institutionalisation of dissent' is vital if we wish to disrupt the 'weaponized reforms [that] will continue to thwart the development of revolutionary and abolitionist projects as well as their analysis and historicization'.[112] However, it is difficult to individuate the source of the problem identified by Burton because it points to a complex of institutional, theoretical and political conditionings. The need to defend against the targeting of CRT has required a unity that can impede analysis of the impact of certain epistemic differences among scholars. A blurring of the distinctions between CRT as it was originally formulated by legal scholars and allied yet distinct areas such as US critical ethnic studies, Black studies, or the British sociology of race descended from the Birmingham School that produced *The Empire Strikes Back* sometimes makes this discussion even more difficult.[113] Therefore, it can be challenging to discern whether some frameworks of analysis are more amenable than others to exposing the institutionalisation of dissent.

Perhaps the hard-fought struggle for the institutional legitimacy of CRT, and the fact that those slim gains are so undermined, makes some of its proponents reticent to use their tools of critique to parse a genocide. The tenuous situation of contested fields like race and ethnic studies often force scholars into a defensive position from which accommodations with power are made that ultimately uphold the racial regime. Nevertheless, many, including most prominently Black women academics, such as the Black radical political theorist Tiffany Willoughby-Herard whose words

---

111 Orisanmi Burton, *Tip of the Spear: Black Radicalism, Prison Repression, and the Long Attica Revolt* (Oakland, CA: University of California Press, 2023), p. 17.
112 Ibid., p. 17.
113 Centre for Contemporary Cultural Studies, *The Empire Strikes Back: Race and Racism in 70's Britain* (London: Routledge, 1982).

open this section, have exemplified the opposite tendency.[114] Can paying attention to the differences between theoretical-political orientations within areas of scholarship that are often rhetorically collapsed together be an instructive guide to why some have been more ready than others to act and speak on behalf of Palestine?

Although some forms of opposition incur risk no matter who they are embodied by, the ability of an individual to take a risky political stance is conditioned by how they are positioned vis-à-vis the institution which in turn is dependent on class, race, gender, sexuality, disability or migration status. Therefore, it is more useful to concentrate on two interrelated structural problems, one more particular, the other more universal. First, what political commitments must exist within a field of study to help guard against cooptation or, when it occurs, to analyse the reasons for it and fight back? Second, what is inherent to what Sylvia Wynter calls the 'central mechanisms which integrate and regulate our present world system ... the prescriptive categories of our present order of knowledge, as disseminated in our present global university system and its correlated textbook industry'[115] that thwarts both analysis and fighting back? The genocide in Gaza sharpens my concern that, notwithstanding the need to defend it from attack, critical race theory itself – rather than what it is taken to be by the right – may be somewhat constrained as a framework for an internationalist, anticolonial, anti-imperialist critique. Its tenets thus need to be supplemented by other analytics more adept for theorising what race critical scholar David Theo Goldberg calls the relational form taken by 'racial conception and racist practice'.[116]

---

114   In addition, Professor Ruha Benjamin, a leading voice in the Sociologists for Palestine campaign organised by members of the American Sociological Association in 2024, denounced the building of Cop City and linked it to the genocide in Palestine during her honorary degree address at Spelman College on 22 April 2024. *Middle East Eye*, X, 2024, https://tinyurl.com/4472n6z4 (last accessed January 2025).
115   Sylvia Wynter, '"No Humans Involved": An Open Letter to My Colleagues', *Forum N.H.I.: Knowledge for the 21st Century* 1, no. 1 (1994), p. 7.
116   Goldberg, 'Racial Comparisons, Relational Racisms', p. 1273.

ANTICOLONIAL AND ANTI-IMPERIAL ABSENCES

As the critical race and decolonial sociologist Ali Meghji argues, the US academy has thrown up a range of theories of race, including CRT, 'that study US society bifurcated from the country's past and present imperial and colonial relations'.[117] I agree with him that the solution is not to jettison CRT and I have been inspired by his proposition of a theoretical synergy between decolonial and critical race approaches. He argues that a 'both and' approach to CRT and decolonial thought recognises that 'social reality can be studied from different theoretical viewpoints, and that this theoretical pluralism is essential for understanding' particular issues of race, structures and processes in their full complexity.[118] However, the Kanaka Maoli scholar, J. Kēhaulani Kauanui has also suggested that CRT may not be open to synergy given its neglect of 'land and indigeneity ... in relation to the study of racial formations and the legal construction of race'.[119] Although her 2008 argument does

---

117 Ali Meghji, *A Critical Synergy: Race, Decoloniality, and World Crises* (Philadelphia, PA: Temple University Press, 2023).
118 Ali Meghji, 'Towards a Theoretical Synergy: Critical Race Theory and Decolonial Thought in Trumpamerica and Brexit Britain', *Current Sociology* 70, no. 5 (September 2022), p. 652. In a paper with the Wonnarua and Kamilaroi critical race scholar Debbie Bargallie, we suggested that the classical CRT theory of 'interest convergence', as first applied by Derrick Bell in his analysis of the limitations of US civil rights legislation, helps understand why an approach to combatting racism that focuses on 'racial complaint' against the institutions that produce and reproduce racism is counterproductive. Debbie Bargallie and Alana Lentin, 'Beyond Convergence and Divergence: Towards a "Both and" Approach to Critical Race and Critical Indigenous Studies in Australia', *Current Sociology* 70, no. 5 (September 2022): 665–81. I also appreciate the growing scholarship bridging critical race and critical Indigenous scholarship that recognises the racial character of colonial regimes, the specificities of settler colonialism, and the independence of Indigeneity from both of these. Cf. Jennifer Darrah-Okike, 'Theorizing Race in Hawai'i: Centering Place, Indigeneity, and Settler Colonialism', *Sociology Compass* 14, no. 7 (July 2020); Evelyn Nakano Glenn, 'Settler Colonialism as Structure: A Framework for Comparative Studies of U.S. Race and Gender Formation', *Sociology of Race and Ethnicity* 1, no. 1 (January 2015): 52–72; Nikki Moodie, 'Decolonising Race Theory', in *The Relationality of Race in Education Research*, ed. Greg Vass, Jacinta Maxwell, Sophie Rudolph, and Kalervo N. Gulson, First edition (Abingdon, UK: Routledge, 2017), pp. 33–46.
119 J. Kēhaulani Kauanui, *Hawaiian Blood: Colonialism and the Politics of Sovereignty and Indigeneity*, Narrating Native Histories (Durham, NC: Duke University Press, 2008), p. 10.

not take into account attempts to apply a critical race approach to Indigenous issues,[120] Kauanui raises the pertinent fact that CRT, with what she calls its 'singular logic in explaining racial subordination in relation to whites and the construction of whiteness', elides the question of genocide. She claims that 'rather than simply a logic of subordination or discrimination, critical race theory fails to consider how whiteness constitutes a project of disappearance for Native peoples' through assimilation.[121]

While I do not agree with Kauanui that CRT analyses whiteness *merely* in terms of 'privilege',[122] it is worth asking why much of critical race scholarship has focused on questions of systematic discrimination and the consequent marginalisation and exclusion of people of colour within the confines of single states, generally the US, without setting that in the context of US settler colonialism and its status as the imperial hegemon. Goldberg argues that the dominance of methodological nationalism within CRT and much of what I have called 'racism studies', to distinguish them from race scholarship,[123] mirrors 'post-war area studies', which operates on a 'presumptive model of geographic discreteness, on incontrovertible and reductive cultural, socio-political and legal uniqueness'.[124] This gives the impression that it is possible to compare the operations of race across national contexts. In fact, as Goldberg reminds us, noting the germinal work of theorists such as C.L.R. James, Frantz Fanon and Albert Memmi, among others, it is the colonial condition that is constitutive of 'racial conception and racist expression'.[125] And while 'it is not that racism is reducible only to

---

120 Cf. Bryan Brayboy, 'Toward a Tribal Critical Race Theory in Education', *The Urban Review* 37, no. 5 (2005): 425–46. Debbie Bargallie, *Unmasking the Racial Contract: Indigenous Voices on Racism in the Australian Public Service* (Canberra: Aboriginal Studies Press, 2020).
121 Kauanui, *Hawaiian Blood*, p. 10.
122 Ibid., p. 10.
123 Alana Lentin, '(Not) Doing Race: "Casual Racism", "Bystander Antiracism" and "Ordinariness" in Australian Racism Studies', in *Critical Reflections on Migration, 'Race' and Multiculturalism: Australia in a Global Context*, ed. Martina Boese and Vince Marotta (London; New York: Routledge, Taylor & Francis Group, 2017), p. 125.
124 Goldberg, 'Racial Comparisons, Relational Racisms', pp. 1272–3.
125 Ibid., p. 1273.

some narrow connection to colonial subjection and repression, ordering and governmentality',[126] it also cannot be elided in preference of analyses of racism that isolate it within discrete, nationally bounded case studies or within individuated institutions without considering them relationally and interactively in a colonially constituted global schema undergirded by the racial regime.

A further suggestion made by Goldberg is that the methodologically nationalist and comparativist methodology of much racism studies lends itself to a narrow focus on 'those states considered to exhibit the most extreme and extremely different modes of state racism'[127] in order to overturn this dominant reading and to draw out their similarities instead. This engenders the development of typologies of racist states, the most recent example of which is the designation of Israel as an Apartheid state, similar to pre-1994 South Africa. As the Palestinian scholar, Lana Tatour, argues, however, the designation of Apartheid as a crime against humanity under international law, 'offers only a limited and partial understanding of the situation [as] Israel is a settler-colonial state that is practising both apartheid and permanent occupation'.[128] This argument and the warning that cloistering the analysis of Israeli settler colonialism in what have paradoxically become the more acceptable terms of Apartheid, running the risk of dissolving decolonisation into what Tatour calls 'liberal projects of equality', are well taken. However, it neglects the fact that South Africa itself was a project of settler colonial domination driven by Apartheid rules and racial capitalist logics.[129]

As Robin D.G. Kelley argues with regard to Patrick Wolfe's elision of Africa in his theorisation of settler colonialism, 'in South Africa white settlement was both a structure and a process, not an

---

126   Ibid., p. 1273.
127   Ibid., p. 1272.
128   Lana Tatour, 'Why Calling Israel an Apartheid State Is Not Enough', *Middle East Eye*, 2021, https://tinyurl.com/yszyhurs (last accessed January 2025).
129   Neville Alexander, John Samuel, and Karen Press, *Against Racial Capitalism: Selected Writings*, ed. Salim Vally and Enver Motala, Black Critique (London: Pluto Press, 2023).

event'. Missing this 'eliminates the settler from African history'.[130] Thus, it is not only that applying the analytic of Apartheid to Israel ignores its settler colonial status, but that failing to draw out the relationality between South Africa, Rhodesia, Namibia, Algeria, Israel, the Anglo settler colonies, etc. reinscribes the methodological nationalism Goldberg warns that a critical race, and more broadly as Meghji suggests, a sociology of race analytic lends itself to. Echoing Goldberg, Meghji argues that 'much sociology of race tends to be characterised by a methodological nationalism in which it becomes sociologically viable – and advisable – to study racism within the confines of particular, discrete nation states'.[131] Meghji's appeal to the sociology of race to learn from the history of anticolonialism is grounded in the need to forge the transnational solidarities that are 'successful and necessary in the struggles for social justice'.[132]

The fact that political attacks on CRT, ethnic studies, decolonial thought, etc. blur the theoretical and political divergences between them does not mean that important epistemological differences do not exist between approaches. Drawing attention to this is useful for understanding both what theoretical tools are most operable in the face of imperialist counterinsurgency, and in practical terms, where accomplices for the struggle against it can be found. In considering how critical race ideas are both attacked and repurposed in the war on antisemitism, we should be aware of the varying genealogies of different areas of study related to race. CRT, launched by a group of legal scholars of colour who first gathered in the early 1980s at Harvard and Los Angeles, grew in reaction to white, Marxist-inflected US critical legal theory. These origins are different to those of Black studies which were 'always grounded in Black intellectual history'[133] and were committed to

---

130 Robin D.G. Kelley, 'The Rest of Us: Rethinking Settler and Native', *American Quarterly* 69, no. 2 (2017): 267–76, p. 269.
131 Ali Meghji, 'What Can the Sociology of Race Learn from the Histories of Anti-Colonialism?' *Ethnicities* 21, no. 4 (August 2021): 769–82, p. 778.
132 Ibid., p. 780.
133 Abdul Alkalimat, *The History of Black Studies* (London: Pluto Press, 2021), p. 22.

'a revalorisation of their "racial blackness"'[134] despite also being a 'bureaucratic response to social movements'.[135] In the particular moment of the late 1960s catapulted by the San Francisco State University Black Student Union-led Third World Strike for Black Studies[136] and what later became ethnic studies on US campuses, an 'insurgent narrative structure that facilitates the adjoining of vastly disparate human oppressions and rebellions into an ostensible totality of shared, radical agency against empire, conquest, criminalization, and enslavement' emerged.[137]

Black studies was born in violence as the 'guerilla war' launched by the Black Students Union at San Francisco state in 1968–69 and the administration's heavily policed counter-attack demonstrates. Moreover, despite Rojas' findings that the Black studies programmes that insisted on being 'community controlled' were superseded by those where 'its advocates were able to navigate the university's bureaucratic environment' and turn them into a more 'traditional academic enterprise',[138] the fight to preserve Black and ethnic studies continues. In many locations outside the US of course they have never been assured,[139] or indeed have never existed. Nevertheless, in keeping our attention trained on how institutions

---

134 Sylvia Wynter, 'On How We Mistook the Map for the Territory, and Re-imprisoned Ourselves in Our Unbearable Wrongness of Being, of Désêtre: Black Studies toward the Human Project', in *Not Only the Master's Tools: African-American Studies in Theory and Practice*, ed. Lewis R. Gordon and Jane Anna Gordon (Boulder, CO: Paradigm, 2006), pp. 114–15, cited in Joshua Myers, *Of Black Study* (London: Pluto Press, 2023), p. 55.
135 Fabio Rojas, *From Black Power to Black Studies: How a Radical Social Movement Became an Academic Discipline*, Johns Hopkins paperback edition (Baltimore, MD: The Johns Hopkins University Press, 2010), p. 4.
136 Joshua Myers, *Cedric Robinson: The Time of the Black Radical Tradition*, Black Lives (Cambridge: Polity Press, 2021).
137 Critical Ethnic Studies Editorial Collective, 'Introduction: A Sightline', in *Critical Ethnic Studies: A Reader*, ed. Nada Elia, David Hernández, Jodi Kim, Shana Redmond, Dylan Rodríguez, and Sarita Echavez (Durham, NC: Duke University Press, 2016), p. 2.
138 Rojas, *From Black Power to Black Studies*, p. 95.
139 For example, in 2023 the historian of Africa, Professor Hakim Adi, was dismissed by Chichester University in the UK leading to the suspension of the Masters course in the History of Africa and the African Diaspora he taught. 'Justice for the Chichester 14!', *CrowdJustice*, 2024, www.crowdjustice.com/case/mres-phd-student-campaign/ (last accessed June 2024).

domesticate dissent, Black and ethnic studies too risk entrapment in the comparativism that Goldberg warns against. Rojas remarks that Black studies advocates who did not see themselves 'in service to the African American community ... viewed black studies as comparable to area studies, such as Africa or China studies'.[140] The Critical Ethnic Studies Editorial Collective warns that institutionalised ethnic studies often cede to a 'compartmentalization of human suffering into relatively discrete historical episodes and geographies' which in fact resist such 'coherence'.[141] Nevertheless, in shining a light on 'colonization, land displacement, chattel enslavement, wars of conquest, apartheid and segregation, physical genocide, forced labor migration, and more',[142] the concerns of Black studies and ethnic studies differ substantively to those of CRT in their original conception.

Contra the argument for relationality and interactivity proposed by Goldberg which presages the commitment to bridging race studies, anticolonialism, decoloniality and Indigenous critique, the Black philosopher Tommy Curry criticises the tendency to conflate general studies of race, particularly those of a postcolonial nature, with CRT. He argues that to do so negates the 'nationalist and revolutionary fervour' of its originators.[143] For Curry, the impetus for foundational CRT was 'the reality and unchanging nature of racism in America and social advocacy necessary to combat it'.[144] The contributions of CRT, unlike philosophy's 'attempt to market Blackness'[145] is to 'confront whites as whites – and nothing more – ... not part of a colonial heritage'.[146] The use of the word 'heritage' here sits uncomfortably with the reality of ongoing colonisation, expressed in Moreton-Robinson's critique of US whiteness studies: 'the question of how anyone came to be white or black in

---

140   Rojas, *From Black Power to Black Studies*, p. 95.
141   Critical Ethnic Studies Editorial Collective, 'Introduction: A Sightline', p. 2.
142   Ibid., p. 2.
143   Tommy J. Curry, 'Will the Real CRT Please Stand up? The Dangers of Philosophical Contributions to CRT', *Crit: A Critical Legal Studies Journal* (2009), pp. 1–47, p. 1.
144   Ibid., p. 26.
145   Ibid., p. 2.
146   Ibid., p. 5.

the United States is inextricably tied to the dispossession of the original owners and the assumption of white possession.'[147]

An example of the distinction between CRT and Black and ethnic studies can be seen in the way founding critical race theorists, Crenshaw, Gotanda, Peller and Thomas discuss the utility of a critical race approach for an analysis of globalisation in the introduction to the 1995 collection *Critical Race Theory: The Key Writings That Formed the Movement*. The authors note the need for an 'adequate account of the connections between racial power and political economy in the New World Order'. 'Left liberal' debates on globalisation, they argue, privilege a focus on class to the detriment of revealing how 'beyond abstract allusions to "rich" and "poor" nations', globalisation is 'legitimised by racial power'.[148] In particular, CRT can explain the existence of 'the "South in the North"', or how 'a certain brand of racial politics' has been mobilised to buffer the massive upwards distribution of resources and opportunity within the US. While the authors note that the same 'brand' of politics are 'used to justify relatively open border policies toward our Northern neighbours, even as we close off our borders to those from the South', they do not name these processes as imperialist, resulting from the hegemonic status of the US in world politics.[149]

In fact, neither imperialism nor colonialism are analysed in great depth in *The Key Writings* save in passing or in relation to Harold Cruse's description of the Black experience in the US as 'domestic colonialism'.[150] Rather, Richard Delgado's piece, 'The Imperial Scholar' uses the term metaphorically to recount the exclusion of

---

147 Aileen Moreton-Robinson, *The White Possessive: Property, Power, and Indigenous Sovereignty* (Minneapolis, MN: University of Minnesota Press, 2015), p. 50.
148 Kimberlé Williams Crenshaw, Neil Gotanda, Gary Peller, and Kendall Thomas, 'Introduction', in *Critical Race Theory: The Key Writings That Formed the Movement*, ed. Kimberlé Crenshaw, Neil Gotanda, Gary Peller, and Kendall Thomas (New York: New Press, 1995), p. xxx.
149 Ibid., p. xxx.
150 Gary Peller, 'Towards a Critical Cultural Pluralism: Progressive Alternatives to Mainstream Civil Rights Ideology', in *Critical Race Theory: The Key Writings That Formed the Movement*, ed. Kimberlé Crenshaw, Neil Gotanda, Gary Peller, and Kendall Thomas (New York: New Press, 1995), p. 144.

Black legal theorists by 'a closed circle' of white civil rights scholars 'writing for and citing each other'.[151] While Delgado's observation that the exclusion of 'minority scholars' is infantilising and racist is important, this metaphorisation of imperialism elides a crucial argument made by the decolonial activist and writer Houria Bouteldja. In her anti-Zionist critique of the Miss Provence contestant, April Benayoum, Bouteldja states that, as a French citizen, she does not exclude herself from such critiques:

> no French person is innocent, starting with me ... Not only am I not innocent – because I am French – but I am also a criminal ... My crime rests on one tangible fact: the share of imperialist revenues between the Western ruling classes and the white, and to a lesser extent non-white, working classes.[152]

This troubles analyses that isolate the current forces of racism within individual societies or discrete institutional settings from how they are produced as a result of the processes that set racial capitalism in motion and which, through the recalibrating racial regime, have been elaborated upon over centuries. With specific regard to the role of Zionism for global imperialist white supremacy, it is not merely that parallels can be drawn between the Palestinian and the Black experience, for example, but that the 'common rootedness in white settler-colonialism' of Israel and the US necessitates

---

151   Kimberlé Williams Crenshaw, Neil Gotanda, Gary Peller, and Kendall Thomas, 'Intellectual Precursors: Early Critique of Conventional Civil Rights Discourse', in *Critical Race Theory: The Key Writings That Formed the Movement*, ed. Kimberlé Crenshaw, Neil Gotanda, Gary Peller, and Kendall Thomas (New York: New Press, 1995), p. 3.
152   Houria Bouteldja, 'Clavreul, Césaire et moi. De l'Innocence des uns et de la Conscience des autres'. – UJFP Antisémitisme', 2021, https://tinyurl.com/muvnferx (last accessed January 2025). As Anna Younes also puts it, 'one can be anti-racist, but not antiimperialist, or the other way around. Separating one from the other however doesn't solve the problem – it rather turns the whole issue around race into a circular logic, always revolving around what it actually is not about, or only revolving around anatomized and split off aspects of it, but never the whole picture.' Susan Neiman and Anna-Esther Younes, 'Antisemitism, Anti-Racism, and the Holocaust in Germany: A Discussion between Susan Neiman and Anna-Esther Younes', *Journal of Genocide Research* 23, no. 3 (2021): 420–1.

a relational analysis that draws out their material and ideological co-dependencies.[153] This is so even while we resist 'the language of "sharing a common enemy"' because, as Erakat and Lamont Hill remind us, it 'undermines an analysis of key historical and contemporary differences between Black and Palestinian struggles' and obscures the existence of Arab antiblackness.[154]

I have suggested that CRT's limitations as a tool for analysing and resisting coloniality and imperialism may be due to the resistance, strongly expressed by Curry, to extend CRT beyond its 'nationalist' commitments. However, CRT is taken by many to mean much more than what it was first coined to represent. Kimberlé Crenshaw herself wrote that CRT is 'now used as interchangeably for race scholarship as Kleenex is used for tissue'.[155] The question then of why so many critical scholars have remained silent in the face of genocide while their colleagues have faced up to the violence of university administrations and the carceral state might then be answered by looking to what Sylvia Wynter terms 'the classificatory logic of our present Humanities and Social Sciences'.[156] Wynter offers her critique in response to the not-guilty verdict in the police beating of Rodney King in 1992. She wrote 'an open letter to my colleagues' in which she addressed the police use of the 'acronym N.H.I.' (No Humans Involved). The acronym denotes the dehumanisation of 'young Black males who belong to the jobless category'[157] which she traced back to 'the classificatory logic' of the 'issue of "race"' which forms the basis of 'our present order of knowledge'.[158] The fact that the term 'No Humans Involved' exists denotes an epistemic problem at the core of western academia. The scapegoating of 'jobless young Black males' in the post-civil rights era in the US is tied to the function of the '*Lack* of the human', which has

---

153 Greg Burris, 'Birth of a (Zionist) Nation: Black Radicalism and the Future of Palestine', in *Futures of Black Radicalism*, ed. Gaye Theresa Johnson and Alex Lubin (London; New York: Verso, 2017), p. 169.
154 Erakat and Hill, 'Black-Palestinian Transnational Solidarity', p. 10.
155 Kimberlé Williams Crenshaw, 'The First Decade: Critical Reflections, or "a Foot in the Closing Door"', *UCLA Law Review* 49, no. 5 (2002), p. 1361.
156 Wynter, 'No Humans Involved', p. 7.
157 Ibid., p. 1.
158 Ibid., p. 3.

also been applied to other peoples faced with 'group annihilation' such as Jews and Armenians.[159] Like for Robinson, Wynter locates the origins of the problem in Europe, of which the US is an extension and whose continued global hegemony cannot be understood unless it is understood as an empire, and not merely a state.

Wynter wrote to her colleagues because she took their general acceptance of controlling 'disciplinarian thinking'[160] to mean that they are unable to offer a vision of knowledge wherein the classification 'No Humans Involved' would be untenable. The given epistemic and institutional structure could not offer an alternative to the intellectual 'Bantustans' in which Black scholars have been trapped since the end of segregation in the US.[161] Wynter cites Bradley's critique of US Black intellectuals who refuse to confront the 'systemic nature of the rules which governed their exclusion from the mainstream conception of the United States', resulting in their cloistering in 'black literature' and 'black history'.[162] Myers follows Wynter to make the case for Black study, rather than institutionalised Black studies. Black study is not merely an attempt to rectify the lies told about Black people. 'Understanding the devalorisation of Black people was only the "map".'[163] The aim of centring 'the particularism of Black thought and thinking' was rather to chart the territory of which the 'map' is but a representation.[164] As many Black radicals have insisted, the territory of Black studies is necessarily internationalist, for how could it be otherwise? The consequences of ignoring this 'was part of a multiculturalist move that remade Black Studies into "African-American Studies"' in order to replicate for the Black middle class in the US 'what the Euro-American literary canon did and continues to do for the generic, because white, and hegemonically Euroamerican middle class'.[165]

---

159 Ibid., p. 2.
160 Myers, *Of Black Study*, p. 90.
161 Wynter, 'No Humans Involved', p. 8.
162 Ibid., p. 8.
163 Myers, *Of Black Study*, p. 56.
164 Ibid., p. 55.
165 Wynter, 'On How We Mistook the Map for the Territory', p 110, cited in ibid., p. 56.

This echoes the late ethnicity, race and migration studies scholar Gary Okihiro's critique of what became of the Third World Liberation Front's 1968 demands for a Third World Curriculum. For Okihiro, Third World Studies was 'an academic field of inquiry that never existed because it was extinguished at birth'.[166] Ethnic studies was 'enfolded into the neoliberal institutional mandates of the university through a particular proliferation as commodified and domesticated "difference"'.[167] The resistance mounted to this enfolding, seen most acutely in the fight-back by groups such as the Coalition for Liberated Ethnic Studies against Zionist manipulations of the terms of DEI to argue for the dissolution of the field, is notable. Contrasted with the general silence of CRT in the face of such attacks, could this be due to the nationalist focus on which Curry insists, or indeed Kennedy's remark that CRT advanced 'the exclusion thesis ... the belief that the intellectual contributions of scholars of color are wrongfully ignored or undervalued?'[168] While Kennedy refutes the extent to which he believes this was the case for Derrick Bell, for example, who exercised his choice to leave Harvard in protest against the failure to hire Black women scholars, it might be suggested that the commitment to rectifying institutional exclusion sits uncomfortably with CRT's foundational critique of US society as endemically, and thus irrevocably, racist.

Perhaps despite Derrick Bell's pessimistic realism about the likelihood of full inclusion for Black people, when taken with its national orientation, CRT's commitment to 'advocating for racial justice' can but be caught in a mire: on the one hand, the system is irretrievably racist; on the other, it must be worked within to achieve some redress. Curry rejects precisely this impetus, one he associates with the deployment of CRT in education and its uptake by white scholars. The problem, he observed, with focusing 'almost exclusively on whiteness as an obstacle to "school equity"

---

166 Gary Y. Okihiro, *Third World Studies: Theorizing Liberation* (Durham, NC: Duke University Press, 2016), p. 1.
167 Critical Ethnic Studies Editorial Collective, 'Introduction: A Sightline', p. 3.
168 Randall L. Kennedy, 'Racial Critiques of Legal Academia', *Harvard Law Review* 102, no. 8 (1989), pp. 1745–6.

and "educational opportunity"'[169] is that it leads to CRT becoming 'subservient to the larger integrationist ideal of American democracy'.[170] This move away from the mission of teaching Black people 'what they need to thrive *as Blacks in America*'[171] means that the 'rewriting of knowledge' that Wynter claims should be the aim of Black studies is no longer possible for CRT because, per Curry, in accepting the normative terms of integration, it must work perversely within a system endemically poised against Black people. From this perspective, one can either pragmatically defend 'equity policies against assault', as proposed by Crenshaw,[172] or believe they are beyond saving, but one cannot radically 'challenge our system of scholarship rooted in its own sanctified categories' as Sylvia Wynter claims we must.[173]

Kimberlé Crenshaw, probably the most well known of the scholars at the origin of the critical race movement, claims that CRT is addressed to 'any person who really cares about a democracy's capacity to constantly interrogate itself, to constantly improve itself'. Asked on MSNBC in 2021 whether CRT was Marxism, she answered that its founders 'just wanted to do better with the laws that are embedded in our constitution'.[174] Consequently, of the bans on CRT she says, 'anyone who really believes that this is the core to democracy has to be outraged, frightened, and

---

169 Tommy Curry, 'Saved by the Bell: Derrick Bell's Racial Realism as Pedagogy', *Philosophical Studies in Education* 39 (January 2008), p. 35.
170 Ibid., p. 36.
171 Ibid., p. 37.
172 The demand for inclusion and/or the redress of discrimination within an 'endemically' racist system creates a tension within CRT, recognised by one of its founders, the legal scholar Mari Matsuda. She turns to Du Boisian double consciousness to note 'the dissonance of combining deep criticism of law with an aspirational vision of law', arguing that CRT affords critics the ability to use an inherently legal system against itself. Crenshaw, 'The First Decade', p. 1370; Mari Matsuda, 'Looking to the Bottom: Critical Legal Studies and Reparations', in *Critical Race Theory: The Key Writings That Formed the Movement*, ed. Kimberlé Crenshaw, Neil Gotanda, Gary Peller, and Kendall Thomas (New York: New Press, 1995), pp. 63–79.
173 Wynter, 'No Humans Involved', p. 15.
174 The Reidout, 'Creator of Term "Critical Race Theory" Kimberlé Crenshaw Explains What It Really Is', *MSNBC*, 2021, https://tinyurl.com/2nva7jw2 (last accessed January 2025).

activated by this effort to ban specific ways of thinking.'[175] The African American Policy Forum she leads set up its #TruthBeTold campaign to 'defend truth' against the 'well-funded, orchestrated disinformation campaigns against critical race theory, intersectionality, and other forms of racial and gender justice discourse.'[176] Crenshaw presents the campaign's mission as a fight to 'perfect' US democracy. It is those who resist truth-telling on race who actually 'disdain America'. In contrast, she says, 'I think we are the true Americans because we believe in the project. They are not the true Americans because they're willing to cover up what the sins are.'[177]

It begs asking what Crenshaw believes these sins are. Students at Cornell University reported that during her 20 February 2024 speech at their campus, 'she mentioned the attack on free speech, affirmative action by the Supreme Court, and other liberal anxieties'. However, she failed to connect the assault on Black thought to the criminalisation of speech and action for Palestine 'at a time when Cornell is repressing their students for being Pro-Palestinian.'[178] In fact, she has failed to mention Palestine at all, even while students at both the universities she holds chairs in, UCLA and Columbia, were being violently attacked by police and Zionist mobs. Crenshaw remained silent even though intersectionality, the theory she has been credited with elaborating, has been attacked for supposedly lending legitimacy to Hamas because, according to its Zionist detractors, it promotes a 'sectarian morality'.[179] In contrast, as the US Democratic Party geared up to replace Joe Biden with his vice-president Kamala Harris as the presidential nominee in the 2024 US elections, Crenshaw posted that sharing a few words with Harris at the African American culture event, Essence Festival, presented

---

175   Molly Kaplan, 'Kimberlé Crenshaw on Teaching the Truth about Race in America', *At Liberty Podcast*, 2021, www.aclu.org/podcast/kimberle-crenshaw-teaching-truth-about-race-america-ep-168 (last accessed October 2022).
176   African American Policy Forum, 'Truth Be Told', AAPF, n.d., www.aapf.org/truthbetold (last accessed October 2022).
177   Kaplan, 'Kimberlé Crenshaw on Teaching the Truth about Race in America'.
178   Momodou Taal, X, 2024, https://x.com/MomodouTaal/status/1759781076061356347?s=20 (last accessed January 2025).
179   Julian Adorney, 'Why Does the Intersectional Left Defend Hamas?' *Quillette*, 2023, https://quillette.com/2023/11/28/why-intersectional-leftists-defend-hamas/ 20 (last accessed January 2025).

by Coca-Cola, 'was not only an honor, but an encouragement to continue to do the work that Black women have done for decades'.[180]

This capacity of racial liberalism to incorporate negatively racialised elites and to subsume and water down critiques of race and colonialism by capturing their ideas[181] within institutions of the state, higher education and the non-profit sector is far from new. Despite the extensions of foundational CRT beyond its original scope and demands, as noted, it was instigated not only as a critique of the insufficiencies of both 'the liberal and critical poles'[182] but also 'in a confrontation within institutions of higher learning over curricular and hiring matters'.[183] These institutional struggles often have the effect of 'airbrushing' anything that is 'left of the "left"'.[184] Mumia Abu-Jamal reminds us that the ability of Black radical intellectuals to engage 'in external conflicts that are deemed "controversial" by the media projectors of the status quo' is thwarted by the fact that they must work 'in an academy already under siege by market forces and political interference'.[185] Yet the Africana scholar Reiland Rabaka takes a harsher line. For him, Joy James is right to critique 'the intellectual inferiority, intellectual timidity, pseudosubstance, propensity to perform, and lack of radical political courage on the part of many, if not most, contemporary black academics'.[186]

---

180 Kimberlé Crenshaw (@sandylocks), X, 2024, https://x.com/sandylocks/status/1810739113165033731 (last accessed January 2025).
181 Olúfẹ́mi O. Táíwò, *Elite Capture: How the Powerful Took over Identity Politics (and Everything Else)* (Chicago, IL: Haymarket Books, 2022).
182 Kimberlé Crenshaw Neil Gotanda, Gary Peller, and Kendall Thomas, eds., *Critical Race Theory: The Key Writings That Formed the Movement* (New York: New Press, 1995), p. xxvii.
183 Crenshaw, 'The First Decade', p. 1370.
184 Joy James, 'Seven Lessons in One Abolitionist Notebook', in *In Pursuit of Revolutionary Love: Precarity, Power, Communities* (Winstone: Divided Publishing, 2022), pp. 32–3.
185 Mumia Abu-Jamal, 'Intellectuals and the Gallows', in *Imprisoned Intellectuals: America's Political Prisoners Write on Life, Liberation, and Rebellion*, ed. Joy James, Transformative Politics Series (Lanham, MD: Rowman & Littlefield, 2003), p. 179.
186 Reiland Rabaka, *Africana Critical Theory: Reconstructing the Black Radical Tradition, from W.E.B. Du Bois and C.L.R. James to Frantz Fanon and Amilcar Cabral* (Lanham, MD: Lexington Books, 2009), p. 303.

Joy James' interrogation of the trajectory of abolitionism from 'radical street and prison movements'[187] to the academy – the terrain of 'white collar abolitionists'[188] – trenchantly reminds us that institutional incorporation downgrades and obscures community-based 'theory as a verb'.[189] In the case of the political trajectories of Black studies and abolitionist activism traced by James, 'the weapon of theory'[190] was, and continues to be, developed by the radical communities formed by Black militants, many of whom continue to organise behind bars as the 'Imprisoned Black Radical Tradition'.[191]

This discussion reveals that the clash between the 'Negro intellectual' in the US and the 'black world', pointed out over half a century ago by Harold Cruse, still exists.[192] We can continue to agree with Cruse that, on the whole, the world in which 'the Negro intellectual' can find acceptance is 'the predominantly white intellectual world'.[193] There are still very few ways to exist within elite institutions, and these become increasingly circumscribed the more a negatively racialised intellectual wears their radicalism on their sleeve. However, it is also true that what James calls a 'managerial ethos' allows an apparent radicalism to exist and even to thrive within academia and the non-profit sector. A 'neo-radicalism' can be found organising '"radical" conferences and "lecture movements"' and emulating 'corporate structures and

---

187 Joy James, 'Anti-Racist Algorithms in Abolition Alchemy', in *In Pursuit of Revolutionary Love: Precarity, Power, Communities* (Winstone: Divided Publishing, 2022), p. 50.
188 Ibid., p. 53.
189 Joy James and K. Kim Holder, 'The Limitations of Black Studies', in *In Pursuit of Revolutionary Love: Precarity, Power, Communities* (Winstone: Divided Publishing, 2022), p. 65.
190 Amilcár Cabral, 'The Weapon of Theory', in *Address Delivered to the First Tricontinental Conference of the Peoples of Asia, Africa and Latin America Held in Havana in January, 1966* (Havana, 1966).
191 James, 'Anti-Racist Algorithms in Abolition Alchemy'.
192 Harold Cruse, *The Crisis of the Negro Intellectual: A Historical Analysis of the Failure of Black Leadership*, New York Review Books Classics (New York: New York Review Books, 2005), p. 453.
193 Ibid., p. 453.

behaviour'.[194] As Cedric Robinson wrote of W.E.B. Du Bois at an earlier time, academics can be 'blinded by the elitism characteristic of [their] class prerogative'.[195] Today, the dividing line that separates Du Bois from most of his colleagues in academia remains the same: standing unequivocally with the masses and embracing 'increasingly radical convictions to socialism and communism'.[196] Today, that dividing line is represented by Palestine.

Despite Du Bois' lifelong commitment to internationalism, anti-colonialism and anti-imperialism, this did not extend to Palestine. In 1948, he argued that 'a million displaced Jews are begging to be allowed to migrate to Palestine, where there is room for them, where there is work for them to do, where what Jews have already done is for the advantage, not simply of the Jews, but of the Arabs'.[197] The Orientalist rhetoric of Du Bois' Zionist appeal sits uncomfortably with his trenchant critiques of US racism and imperialism. However, according to Nadia Alahmed, by the 1956 Suez crisis, a glimpse that Du Bois' position had changed could be gleaned in 'Suez', his pro-Nasser poem, the man he positions 'as the figure bearing the truth about the neo-colonial nature of the conflict'.[198] The position taken in the poem 'became the pillar of Black anti-Zionist discourse'.[199] Perhaps the distance placed between Du Bois and the academy that grew ever larger until he eventually chose exile in Ghana rather than remaining in the US, 'a nation where the

---

194   Joy James, '"Sorrow, Tears and Blood" Disavows the Talented Tenth', in *In Pursuit of Revolutionary Love: Precarity, Power, Communities* (Winstone: Divided Publishing, 2022), p. 13.
195   Cedric J. Robinson, 'DuBois and Black Sovereignty: The Case of Liberia', *Race & Class* 32, no. 2 (1990), p. 39.
196   Phillip Luke Sinitiere, 'Comrades in the Struggle for Black Freedom: Gerald Horne and W.E.B. Du Bois', *Phylon (1960–)* 59, no. 1 (2022), p. 111.
197   W.E.B. Du Bois, 'The Ethics of the Problem of Palestine', Special Collections and University Archives (University of Massachusetts Amherst Libraries: W. E. B. Du Bois Papers, 1948), http://credo.library.umass.edu/view/full/mums312-b209-i090 (last accessed January 2025).
198   Alahmed, 'From Black Zionism to Black Nasserism', p. 1062. The poem's second stanza reads: Israel, as the West betrays / It murdered, mocked, and damned, / Becomes the shock troop of two knaves / Who steals the dark man's land?
199   Ibid., p. 1063.

political climate was frequently hostile and unforgiving',[200] aided him to see what was obscure to him less than a decade earlier.

PRESSING THE WEAK POINTS OF THE RACIAL REGIME

In the context of Israel's genocide in Palestine, the dynamics described above can be seen as countering what Abdaljawad Omar calls the 'political potential' of the Palestinian resistance to propel new analytical tools,[201] just as other traditions of resistance have always done. Their proliferation spurs a litany of counterinsurgent tactics that are always experimental and reactive, rather than static, because they are born out of the necessity for regimes to constantly repress mushrooming resistance.[202] In a macabre sense then, the genocide conducted by Israel in Gaza presents a unique crystallisation of racial regime recalibration in which both the repression and the retrofitting of ideas can be thought of as an iteration of the 'mechanisms of assembly' of the new racial regime.[203] Robinson's important reminder in this chapter's epigraph, that racial regimes are susceptible to 'constant trembles', suggests that we should work on uncovering what is entailed in the 'persistent efforts of repair' that lead to successive 'alterations in race discourses' in order to press on their weak points.[204] For such alterations become necessary only because the racial regime is constantly being challenged and undermined.

Aditi Rao's experience in the Princeton DEI office cited earlier expresses the contradictory capacities of the racial regime. As we have come to understand, racial regimes are 'necessarily articulated with accruals of power'. They thus make use of whatever are the

---

200 Charisse Burden-Stelly and Gerald Horne, *W.E.B. Du Bois: A Life in American History*, Black History Lives (Santa Barbara, CA: ABC-CLIO, 2019), p. 187.
201 Louis Allday, 'An Interview with Abdaljawad Omar on October 7th and the Palestinian Resistance', *Ebb Magazine*, 2024.
202 Dylan Rodríguez and Jared Ware, 'Insurgency & Counterinsurgency 101 with Dylan Rodríguez', *Millennials Are Killing Capitalism Live!* https://tinyurl.com/2cjbwxw5 (last accessed February 2024).
203 Robinson, *Forgeries of Memory and Meaning*, p. xii.
204 Ibid., p. xvi.

'more tractable materials'[205] in a process of constantly reactive elaboration. The DEI office may be an apparatus, as well as a physical space, more tractable for the wielding of state and imperial power. Yet, the students' de-arresting of Rao reveals that racial regimes are defined by their incompleteness, never entirely successful due to being subject to continual resistance. It is thus humanity's impulsive embrace of indivisibility 'from the collective relation' that racial regimes are conscripted to contain.[206] This work is one of human management through a naturalised account of the world as ordered according to the narrative that race provides. However, the attempt to portray the world as composed of 'natural orderings' is constantly undermined by 'the archaeological imprint of human agency [that] radically alienates the histories of racial regimes from their own claims of naturalism'.[207] Robinson cites Edward Said who pushes back against Michel Foucault's totalising theory of power:[208] 'in human history there is always something beyond the reach of dominating systems, no matter how deeply they saturate society, and this is obviously what makes change possible'.[209]

That it is Said whom Robinson turns to is salient for my discussion in this chapter, because I have written it while what some have described as a 'global Intifada'[210] is unfurling.[211] It was Said who demonstrated that, to understand the idea of Zionism, it must be regarded 'from the standpoint of its victims'.[212] As the powerful are those who are usually permitted to establish the terms of comprehension or analysis of a given power structure, to flip the script

---

205 Ibid., p. xi.
206 Cedric J. Robinson, *The Terms of Order: Political Science and the Myth of Leadership* (Chapel Hill, NC: University of North Carolina Press, 2016), p. 18.
207 Robinson, *Forgeries of Memory and Meaning*, p. xiii.
208 Greg Burris also makes this connection. Burris, 'Birth of a (Zionist) Nation'.
209 Edward W. Said, *The World, the Text, and the Critic*, cited in Robinson, *Forgeries of Memory and Meaning*, p. xii.
210 Franck Magennis, 2024, https://x.com/franckmagennis/status/1785799835611705827?s=12 (last accessed January 2025).
211 AJLabs, 'Mapping College Campus Protests', *Al Jazeera*, 2024, www.aljazeera.com/news/2024/4/29/mapping-pro-palestine-campus-protests-around-the-world/ (last accessed May 2024).
212 Edward W. Said, 'Zionism from the Standpoint of Its Victims', *Social Text*, no. 1 (1979), p. 7.

and regard this power from the viewpoint of its targets is to radically retell both its history and its constantly adapting present. The epistemic question is key, therefore, to the recursive process of racial regime recalibration, making the realm of education/knowledge a front line for the securing of ideological hegemony. The knowledge of colonised, Indigenous and Black people, which the Palestinian represents in a particularly acute fashion, must thus also be secured. This takes various forms including through '"conceptual incarceration," the practice of appropriating the order of things and representing it to us through the imposition of a racial regime', a process that Black radical thinkers have comprehensively analysed.[213] The role of academia vis-à-vis Black life has been to intentionally chisel it 'away from western ontological practices' through a 'vast array of sordid technological and ideological schemes that cohered imperial projects',[214] practices that Zionist ideologues have played a leading role in buttressing. However, this is never announced. Joy James reminds us that 'the academy never said, "Oh, I have a blueprint for you." That's not what it does, but it will take our blueprints for survival and turn them into texts, documents, or syllabi.'[215]

The constant push-pull of repression and what Too Black calls the 'regularly scheduled laundering of the State developed over centuries of conquests' needs to be understood for resistance to be tactical. This laundering, he writes in the context of the containment of Black rage following mass uprisings, such as the Black Lives Matter protests of 2020, develops in three stages: 'Incubation, Labor, and Commodification'. During the incubation phase, the state creates the conditions for rage to be unleashed. This is followed by the labor stage which takes mass uprisings and layers

---

[213] Myers, *Of Black Study*, p. 180. Myers attributes 'conceptual incarceration' to Wade Nobles, 'Understanding Human Transformation: The Praxis of Science', in his book *Seeking the Sakhu: Foundational Writings for an African Psychology* (Chicago, IL: Third World Press, 2006), pp. 71–86.
[214] Damien M. Sojoyner, *Against the Carceral Archive: The Art of Black Liberatory Practice*, (New York: Fordham University Press, 2023), p. 57.
[215] Joy James and Rebecca A. Wilcox, 'How the University Deradicalises Social Movements', in *In Pursuit of Revolutionary Love: Precarity, Power, Communities* (Winstone: Divided Publishing, 2022), p. 146.

elite Black interests on top of them 'to conceal class interests and collapse the labor of Black Rage into the grips of capital'. Finally, during commodification, Black rage, now under the purview of the elite, can be fully integrated into the state 'ready to be withdrawn as a labor-crushed commodity to be bought, sold, or repressed by white capital for the next cycle'.[216]

Due to the position Zionism occupies for western imperialism, the global Intifada is less susceptible to commodification even as processes of cooptation can be observed in the liberal attempt to contain the movement to divest from the machinery of Israeli settler colonialism.[217] Nevertheless, the recalibration of the racial regime in response to acute pressure from below on its weak points is at work over time amid this phase of Israel's genocide, unleashed on the people of Palestine in October 2023. In the next chapter, I look at another dimension of this as evidenced by the settler capture of Indigeneity and decolonisation.

---

216 Too Black, 'Laundering Black Rage', , *Black Agenda Report*, 2022, https://tinyurl.com/afethehz (last accessed July 2022).
217 Rodríguez, 'How the Stop Asian Hate Movement Became Entwined'.

4

Capturing Indigeneity, Colonising Decolonisation

Fanon and Césaire maintained that colonialist racialism, at the onset inspired by the material needs of capitalism, had disrupted bourgeois ideology and the modern world's social order. Still inhibited by the embedding of the European Enlightenment into their consciousness, they needed only to realize further that they were not faced with a rational order gone awry, but the exhaustion of a rationalist adventure in the wilderness of an irrational (i.e., racial) civilization. It seems more and more apparent that a metropolitan elite, whose domination and rule are increasingly disoriented by racialism, cannot hope to achieve a stable world order conspiring with a frenetic petit-bourgeois elite in the Third World. We shall have few occasions for such concerns or their implications if we are preoccupied with what he said she said.[1]

Landing on the pages of *Al-Jazeera* on 10 October 2023, an article by Middle East historian Mark Levine told us that Frantz Fanon's claim that 'colonialism is not a thinking machine, nor a body endowed with reasoning faculties'[2] is 'profoundly wrong' with regards to Israel. Due to its 'very powerful and longstanding logic and rationalities', there are no 'plausible scenarios in which Palestinians acquire the means to deploy "far greater violence" vis-à-vis

---

1 Cedric J. Robinson, 'The Appropriation of Frantz Fanon', *Race & Class* 35, no. 1 (1 July 1993), p. 305.
2 Frantz Fanon, *The Wretched of the Earth* (London: Penguin Books, 2001), p. 61.

Israel/the Zionist entity'.[3] In reality, on 10 October it was impossible to predict what Palestinian resistance fighters could achieve. Middle East Peace Project's president, Daniel Levy, argued that on 7 October 'Israel's sense of invincibility and security with the status quo came crashing down'.[4]

Al-Aqsa Flood had placed Fanon on many lips. The 'flint warrior' (*guerrier-silex*), as Aimé Césaire called him[5] to evoke his 'incendiary writing style',[6] was summoned to make sense of actions that many insisted had to be regarded with greater nuance. The Fanon of *The Wretched of the Earth*, whose deliberations on the 'unusual importance' of violence[7] have long made even avowed leftists in the west uneasy and indignant, was posthumously reprimanded. Beyond this, however, what the summonsing of Fanon drew out was a sense of impunity within western academia to rein in and domesticate the will of the colonised to strive for resistance or, as Abdaljawad Omar put it, to 'undermine the principles of decolonization and its accompanying tumult'.[8] Omar was responding to a more widely disseminated and discussed article, 'Vengeful Pathologies', by the *London Review of Books* US editor Adam Shatz.[9] In it, Shatz failed to heed Healy's warning about calling for nuance, 'typ-

---

3   Mark Levine, 'Fanon's Conception of Violence Does Not Work in Palestine', *Al Jazeera*, 2024, https://tinyurl.com/587ah45v (last accessed January 2025).
4   Daniel Levy and Middle East Monitor, 'Gaza and the End of Israeli Invincibility: MEMO in Conversation with Daniel Levy', *Middle East Monitor*, 2024, https://tinyurl.com/yc69ry43 (last accessed January 2025). And as George Jackson notes, 'what [western military experts] cannot afford to admit is that even with this numerical superiority they cannot win. They're learning this in every theatre of combat.' George Jackson, *Blood in My Eye* (Baltimore, MD: Black Classic Press, 1972), p. 84.
5   Aimé Césaire, *Moi, laminaire: poèmes*, Points 438 (Paris: Éd. du Seuil, 1991).
6   Jane Hiddleston, 'The Incendiary Breath, Interview by Barbara Burns', 2023, https://mhra.org.uk/news/2023/03/15/the-incendiary-breath.html (last accessed January 2025).
7   Fanon, *The Wretched of the Earth*, p. 35.
8   Abdaljawad Omar, 'Hopeful Pathologies in the War for Palestine: A Reply to Adam Shatz', *Mondoweiss*, 2023, https://tinyurl.com/3pyxkrx2 (last accessed January 2025).
9   Adam Shatz, 'Vengeful Pathologies', *London Review of Books*, 2023, www.lrb.co.uk/the-paper/v45/n21/adam-shatz/vengeful-pathologies (last accessed January 2025).

ically a holding manoeuvre ... what one does when faced with a question for which one does not yet have a compelling or interesting answer'.[10] Rather, drawing on the recently published biography of Fanon he was promoting as the genocide unfolded, he decried the binarism which he wrote inspired 'Hamas's admirers on the "decolonial" left, many of them ensconced in universities in the West' to invoke Fanon's 'controversial first chapter'[11] when they asked, 'What did y'all think decolonisation meant?'[12]

For Adam Shatz, 'the ethno-tribalist fantasies of the decolonial left, with their Fanon recitations and posters of paragliders,[13] are indeed perverse', but ultimately 'less consequential than that of Israel'.[14] To make his point, he quotes from Palestinian writers

---

10   Kieran Healey, 'Fuck Nuance', *Sociological Theory* 35, no. 2 (2017): 118–27, p. 119.
11   Shatz, 'Vengeful Pathologies'.
12   Shatz references a post on X by Najma Sharif Alawi, 2023, https://x.com/najmamsharif/status/1710689657757769783 (last accessed January 2025). An interesting discussion of the article 'Decolonization Is Not a Metaphor' by Eve Tuck and K. Wayne Yang referenced in this and similar posts is engaged by the hosts of JDPOD. They critique Unangax̂ NYU professor Eve Tuck for making a statement condemning Hamas (although this was apparently made as the result of pressure following her signing of a statement 'condemning Israel's "settler colonialism, apartheid, and occupation"'). However, their wider critique of the paper focuses, in a similar manner to my discussion of CRT's limitations in Chapter 4, on its elision of US imperialism. JDPOD, 'Decolonization Is Not a Metaphor', *JDPOD*, 2024, https://podcastaddict.com/podcast/jdpod/5412870 (last accessed January 2025); Max Rosenberg, 'Facing Backlash, NYU Indigenous Studies Director Condemns Hamas Attack', *The College Fix*, 2023, https://tinyurl.com/2s3b8atw (last accessed January 2025).
13   In this regard, it is worth recalling that three young people of colour were charged under the UK Terrorism Act for supporting 'a banned organisation' by displaying stickers with a drawing of the Hamas paragliders who flew over the fence from Gaza on 7 October. Sky News, 'Three Guilty of Terror Offence for Displaying Images of Paragliders at Pro-Palestine March', *Sky News*, 2024, https://tinyurl.com/45ucm6rm (last accessed June 2024). Many were critical of left-wing media personality Aaron Bastani for tweeting about the incident: 'These morons are doing the *opposite* of expressing solidarity with Palestinians, and helping the cause of Palestinian self-determination. They are idiots helping to undermine the tens of thousands of others on this demo. Childish indecency isn't politics.' Aaron Bastani, *X*, 2023, https://x.com/AaronBastani/status/1713252027961168031 (last accessed October 2023).
14   Shatz, 'Vengeful Pathologies'.

who share his position, invoking an intimacy with them about the nefarious influence of 'the radical left's cult of force' by referring to an email he received 'from the Palestinian historian Yezid Sayigh', a senior associate at the Carnegie Middle East Center in Beirut.[15] In dismissing the consequentiality of Hamas' actions, which Omar proposes displays a failure to conduct a 'more sober analysis' of its motivations which goes beyond the Israeli explanation of 'vengeance and wanton bloodshed', this genre of writing also uses Palestine to discipline a global movement and the radical thought it studies and generates as praxis. In Kerry Sinanan's careful exposition[16] of Shatz's later 'shield for Zionist apologism' in an article titled 'Israel's Descent',[17] she notes that authors like Shatz reference anticolonial, Black radical and, here specifically, Palestinian authors to bolster their argument that there are correct and incorrect ways to resist a brutal settler colonial regime. This discussion points to the questions driving this chapter.

How does 'critical counterinsurgency'[18] act to curb and disarm radical thinking by folding it into the operations as usual of the colonial academy? How do the calls for nuance and against binary thinking articulate with an institutional drive within the imperial core to 'decolonise' and 'indigenise' practices of learning and teaching and in so doing legitimise and secure colonial continuities and settler futurities? For the racial regime under recalibration non-performative commitments 'to social justice and Indigenous self-determination'[19] cannot be understood straightforwardly as tools of decolonisation, even when at their best they intellectually invigorate genuinely radical learners. Rather, when understood as part of what Yellowknives Dene scholar Glen Coulthard names

---

15 Omar comments that the 'Palestinian scholar Yezid Sayigh ... has historically downplayed the Palestinian struggle and suggested its incapability of significantly impacting the international system.' Omar, 'Hopeful Pathologies in the War for Palestine'.
16 Kerry Sinanan, 'Critical Counterinsurgency and Zionism', *The Massachusetts Review*, 2024, https://massreview.org/node/11983 (last accessed December 2024).
17 Adam Shatz, 'Israel's Descent', *London Review of Books*, 2024, www.lrb.co.uk/the-paper/v46/n12/adam-shatz/israel-s-descent (last accessed September 2024).
18 Sinanan, 'Critical Counterinsurgency and Zionism'.
19 Western Sydney University, 'Indigenous Futures Decadal Strategy 2023–2032: Building the Next Generation of Indigenous Leaders', 2023.

'a seemingly more conciliatory set of discourses and institutional practices that emphasise our *recognition* and *accommodation*' by the Canadian state, the establishment of processes of non-performative decolonisation can be understood as a counterinsurgent response to 'Indigenous anticolonial nationalism' and decolonial insurgency more broadly.[20]

An analysis that foregrounds the racial regime goes further than one which privileges counterinsurgency to highlight the dialectics that the scenarios in this chapter excavate. As I have shown, the recursive manoeuvres of racial regime recalibration respond to direct challenges to racial colonial domination and the projects of intellectual legitimation that accompany them. As such, efforts to coopt, tame and even inhabit and replace the knowledge systems of Black, Indigenous and colonised people must be seen as a response to something greater than immediate insurgency. What Indigenous, decolonial and Black radical thought at their most liberatory bring to the fore is the suggestion of a life to be lived entirely otherwise to the modern colonial capitalist world system. So, it is not only that this thinking is cut off at the knees by counterinsurgent practices of cooptation within the very colonial institutions it radically opposes. There is also a real tendency to reject it that comes from both the westernised right and the left. The rejection that can be seen in some quarters of the interpretive frameworks of settler colonialism and decolonisation grounded in critical Indigenous and anticolonial politics and worldviews cannot be merely responded to with more accurate interpretations. Rather, this negation of Black radical, Indigenous and decolonial frames signals an impossibility to think, following Robinson, that what the 'massive uprising of slaves in 1831 in Jamaica' and similar freedom struggles wished for was 'the preservation of the ontological totality granted by a metaphysical system that had never allowed for property in either the physical, philosophical, temporal, legal, social, or psychic senses'.[21] In other words, as Fred

---

20   Glen Sean Coulthard, *Red Skin, White Masks: Rejecting the Colonial Politics of Recognition* (Minnesota, MN: University of Minnesota Press, 2017), p. 15.
21   Cedric J. Robinson, *Black Marxism: The Making of the Black Radical Tradition*, Second edition (Chapel Hill, NC: University of North Carolina Press, 2000), p. 168.

Moten intimates, what Robinson achieves in *Black Marxism* is not merely a critique of the historical conditions that produced racial capitalism, but through that critique to show that what 'emerges [is] a "revolutionary consciousness"' that is structured by *but underived from*[22] 'the social formations of capitalist slavery, or the relations of production of colonialism'.[23] Such a revolutionary consciousness is much less susceptible to being folded into either liberal or leftist structures in the west. This fact is what is at stake in the efforts to undermine it from all directions.

To examine these tensions, this chapter calls attention to the Zionist claim that Jews, not Palestinians, are Indigenous to Palestine and to how this is used to rupture solidarity between Indigenous and Palestinian people. In a key case, I examine the involvement of Zionist figures in a referendum held in Australia in October 2023 to decide whether an Indigenous Voice to Parliament should be enshrined in the constitution and the ramifications this has for understandings of settler colonialism and racial capitalism. When set against the 'Indigenising' efforts undertaken by colonial institutions of higher education within a framework of recognition and reconciliation that has a domesticating effect on long-standing Indigenous political struggles, this alliance raises significant questions for the meaning of 'self-determination' under uninterrupted settler colonial rule.

'CREATED AS A PEOPLE IN A LAND'[24]

Nova Peris: 'It's a myth that you have no connection to the land of Israel but you know us, as First Nations people in Australia we've never ceded our sovereignty and like you, you've never

---

22 Emphasis added.
23 Fred Moten, 'The Subprime and the Beautiful', *African Identities* 11, no. 2 (May 2013): 237–45; Robinson, *Black Marxism*, p. 169.
24 At the opening of the Indigenous Embassy Jerusalem on 1 February 2024, the Deputy Mayor of Jerusalem, Fleur Hassan-Nahoum, said, 'My dear friends here from different First Nations communities from around the world, they know that the very definition of Indigeneity is when you are created as a people in a land. The Jewish people became the Jewish people in this land.' Friends of Zion Museum, 'Excerpt of Jerusalem Deputy Mayor Fleur Hassan-Nahoum's Speech', *Vimeo*, 2024, https://vimeo.com/909050435 (last accessed January 2025).

ceded your sovereignty and you have that deep connection and that's what I want to do, is to tell your truth.'

Fleur Hassan-Nahoum: 'Thank you for recognizing our indigeneity, for coming to visit us and for really being a voice of truth for Israel and the Jewish people.'[25]

On 1 February 2024, some four months into the genocidal assault on Gaza, the Indigenous Embassy Jerusalem – 'the one hundredth embassy to be opened in the State of Israel'[26] – was inaugurated. Addressing the diverse Indigenous people gathered at the opening event,[27] the head of the Friends of Zion Museum which hosts the Embassy, the 'prominent U.S. evangelical leader [and] prolific author', Mike Evans[28] said, 'you are going to be the ambassadors to your nations that's going to be sparking a flame of love.'[29] As the Ngati Porou activist and scholar, Tina Ngata writes, the Māori and Polynesian instigators of the Indigenous Embassy, which stems from the Aotearoa-based Indigenous Coalition for Israel, are not representative of Māori people who overwhelmingly stand

---

25 Friends of Zion Museum, 'Nova Peris from Australia at Our FOZ Museum', *YouTube*, 2024, www.youtube.com/watch?v=27otCknDS34 (last accessed January 2025).
26 Gil Haskel, Chief of State Protocol, Israeli–Ministry of Foreign Affairs addressing the opening of the Indigenous Embassy Jerusalem on 1 February 2024. Friends of Zion Museum, 'Highlights of the 1 February Opening Event', *YouTube*, 2024, https://youtu.be/tNAjsnH2VHU (last accessed January 2025).
27 According to a report in the Australasian online Jewish news website, J-Wire, 'Indigenous Embassy Jerusalem is an international project and opens with strong expressions of support from indigenous leaders from around the world: Singapore, Taiwan, Samoa, American Samoa, Hawaii, Tahiti, New Caledonia, Solomon Islands, Australia, Papua New Guinea, Cook Islands, Tonga, Fiji, New Zealand, Native American chiefs and paramount chiefs from Southern Africa.' J-Wire, 'NZ Indigenous Organisation Leads Opening of Indigenous Embassy in Jerusalem', *J-Wire*, 2024, https://tinyurl.com/9k5eabh7 (last accessed January 2025).
28 Ben Lorber and Aidan Orly, 'Why Did an Antisemitic Christian Zionist Have the Chutzpah to Declare That He'd Be Leading a Holocaust March?' *Religion Dispatches*, 2022, https://tinyurl.com/3bpaxfrv (last accessed January 2025).
29 Friends of Zion Museum, 'Highlights of the 1 February Opening Event'.

with Palestine.[30] Rather, they represent the interests of a nexus of Christian Zionist and 'far-right conservative lobby groups closely linked to the tobacco and oil industries'.[31] No one associated with the coalition 'has a public record of defending Indigenous political rights in Aotearoa, nor in the lands which they are Indigenous to'.[32] The purpose of public displays of Indigenous support for Israel is not to appeal to Indigenous people, among whom support for Israel is scant though well-funded, but to help embed the idea that Jews are Indigenous to Palestine. Thus, despite the minority appeal of Zionism among Indigenous people in Aotearoa and elsewhere,[33] examining how settler colonial legitimation builds upon counterclaims to Indigeneity sheds light on the polyvalent uses of Indigeneity for the racial regime.

Israel's cultivation of 'Indigenous diplomacy' has been gathering pace over recent years. The Zionist state's memorialisation of Indigenous soldiers who fought in the World War I Battle of Beersheba allows it to position itself as a champion of 'Aboriginal servicemen against Australia's erasure of that history',[34] thus effacing the settler colonial status it shares with Australia and replacing it with the fiction of shared Indigeneity with Aboriginal and Torres Strait Islanders. When we consider this in relation

---

30 According to Ngata, the Aotearoa-based Indigenous Coalition for Israel can effectively be whittled down to two main figures, the Māori Sheree Trotter, the wife of 'Perry Trotter, pākeha Christian bible teacher and director of the Israel Institute of New Zealand' and 'Alfred Ngaro, who is a self-described Christian Zionist, and also an anti-LGBTQI marriage rights, pro-conversion therapy, anti-abortion, ex-National MP who *left* the National Party because it wasn't conservative enough for him.' Author Tina Ngata, 'Make No Mistake – There Is No Indigenous Support for Israel', *Tina Ngata.com*, 2024, https://tinangata.com/2024/03/04/make-no-mistake-there-is-no-indigenous-support-for-israel/ (last accessed January 2025).
31 Ibid.
32 Ibid.
33 Noura Mansour, 'Indigenous-Palestinian Solidarity Networks Challenging Settler Colonialism in Australia', *Near East Policy Forum*, 2023, https://tinyurl.com/jrbr23c7 (last accessed February 2025); 'To Palestine with Love – A Message for Peace from Turtle Island', *Indigenous Solidarity with Palestine*, 2023, https://tinyurl.com/yc6vavms (last accessed January 2025).
34 Micaela Sahhar, 'Where Is Palestine in the Anzacs' Palestine Campaign? Israel and the Struggle for Indigeneity in Commemorative State Practice', *Middle East Critique* 33, no. 2 (2024), p. 256.

to the discussion of the usurpation of antiracism by anti-antisemitism in both Chapters 3 and 5, this tactic of what Micaela Sahhar calls 'associative indigenization' can be seen as a key technology of the racial regime.[35] Instigating this discussion should not lead to a rejection of Indigenous politics as exclusionary and essentialising as some accounts would have it. For example, Nandita Sharma's strongly worded proposition that 'all autochthonous discourses', be they of the far right or those that espouse 'metaphysical indigeneity in sovereign futures of "decolonial love" (L. Simpson 2013)', 'produce migrants as the negative others of National-Natives'[36] does not stand up to practical scrutiny. Most Indigenous groups do not oppose migration, and many take an active stance of solidarity with migrants as the example of the Aboriginal Passport Ceremony, wherein Aboriginal activists ceremonially presented passports to refugees cast and out and maligned by the Australian state, testifies.[37] Nevertheless, making the case that in practice, most Indigenous people stand in 'solidarity with Black, Brown, and other groups of people who most acutely experience the effects of global capital and colonialism'[38] does not mean that there are not significant ways in which Indigenous politics and people can become vectors for colonial agendas.

Nova Peris' trip to Israel in March 2024, which included a stop at the newly opened Indigenous Embassy, stood out as one such vector. The Olympian athlete and former member of the Australian Senate, and a descendant of the Gija, Yawuru and Muran Clan of the Iwatja people of East and West Kimberley and West Arnhem lands, respectively, had earlier claimed that the 'Indigenous flag and chants have been misappropriated at pro-Palestine

---

35 Ibid.
36 Nandita Rani Sharma, *Home Rule: National Sovereignty and the Separation of Natives and Migrants* (Durham, NC: Duke University Press, 2020), p. 14.
37 Joseph Pugliese, 'For the Instantiation of Migrant Decolonising Practices', *Centre AltreItalie* 59 (2019), https://tinyurl.com/yp53ypra (last accessed January 2025).
38 Crystal McKinnon, 'Enduring Indigeneity and Solidarity in Response to Australia's Carceral Colonialism', *Biography* 43, no. 4 (2020): 691–704.

rallies'.³⁹ Climbing Masada with a born-again Christian actor, Peris evoked the 1992 Mabo decision, which overturned the doctrine of terra nullius and led to the passage of the 1993 Native Title Act.⁴⁰ She credited the decision not to the five Indigenous Meriam people led by Eddie Mabo who brought the case to the High Court, but to 'Ron Castan and these Jewish lawyers who sat down on Mother Earth with my people ... and overturned that decision'.⁴¹ This narrative minimises the ten-year legal battle of the Meriam people to have their right 'to possession, occupation, use and enjoyment of (most of) the lands of the Murray Islands' (Mer) recognised.⁴² Peris' explanation that she was motivated to 'tell the truth' on Israel by 'Jewish people having empathy for my people' because of a shared Indigeneity denies the competing truth that 'neither Jewish faith nor Jewish spiritual practice is land-based'.⁴³ In contrast, for Indigenous people, 'the spiritual nature of the world is incorporated into one's connection to place, home, and country'.⁴⁴

A likely source for Peris is the Melbourne Jewish tax lawyer and former head of the Australia/Israel & Jewish Affairs Council, Mark

---

39 Dechlan Brennan, 'Debate Rages as Nova Peris Claims Aboriginal Flag', *National Indigenous Times*, 2024, https://tinyurl.com/hw6jstkz (last accessed December 2024).
40 'The new doctrine of native title replaced a seventeenth century doctrine of terra nullius on which British claims to possession of Australia were justified on a wrongful legal presumption that Indigenous peoples had no settled law governing occupation and use of lands. In recognising that Indigenous peoples in Australia had prior rights to land, the Court held that these rights, where they exist today, will have the protection of the Australian law until those rights are legally extinguished.' AIATSIS, 'The Mabo Case', *Australian Institute of Aboriginal and Torres Strait Islander Studies*, 2023, https://aiatsis.gov.au/explore/mabo-case (last accessed December 2024).
41 Rova Media, 'Why ABORIGINAL Australians Stand with ISRAEL: Nova Peris in Conversation with Nate Buzz', *YouTube*, 2024, www.youtube.com/watch?v=JDlT-bi4g4g (last accessed January 2025).
42 AIATSIS, 'The Mabo Case'.
43 Michelle Berkon, 'Nova Peris' Apologism for Colonialism and Genocide', *Pearls and Irritations*, 2024, https://johnmenadue.com/nova-peris-apologism-for-colonialism-and-genocide/ (last accessed January 2025).
44 Aileen Moreton-Robinson, *The White Possessive: Property, Power, and Indigenous Sovereignty* (Minneapolis, MN: University of Minnesota Press, 2015), p. 15.

Leibler, whose firm's offices has a boardroom named after Ron Castan.[45] As a founder of the Victorian Aboriginal Legal Service, in 1993 Castan asked Leibler's firm to take on the native title claim of the Yorta Yorta people pro bono.[46] The Yorta Yorta case was the first tried under the then new Native Title Act which is seen by Gary Foley 'as significant an act of dispossession as occurred in 1788'.[47] Although it recognised the fiction of terra nullius in theory, in practice the Mabo decision only upheld native title in areas of the continent where freehold title did not exist. However, where it did exist, 'the Aboriginal people had been dispossessed, without compensation, and had little or no chance of succeeding in any native title claims'.[48] The decision was thus a mechanism for undermining Indigenous people's demand for land rights.[49]

To succeed in a claim under the Native Title Act, 'an Indigenous group must demonstrate a continuing traditional connection to the area subject to claim from the time of sovereignty to the present'.[50] Effectively, whether or not Indigenous people can prove an unsevered connection to culture, based on Eurocentric anthropological interpretations of what that culture consists in, is used to 'authenticate ... Indigeneity for access to welfare, citizenship, or Native title'.[51] Invasion, colonisation and the genocide enacted

---

45 Arnold Bloch Leibler, 'Boardrooms Dedicated to Lawyers Who Shaped ABL', *Arnold Bloch Leibler*, n.d., https://tinyurl.com/3hnw6r23 (last accessed July 2024).
46 Michael Gawenda, *The Powerbroker: Mark Leibler, an Australian Jewish Life* (Clayton, Victoria: Monash University Publishing, 2020).
47 Gary Foley, 'Native Title Is Not Land Rights', *Koori Web*, 1997, https://tinyurl.com/ysk87mn8 (last accessed July 2024).
48 Ibid.
49 The US Supreme Court decision in the 1823 case of Johnson's Lessee v. McIntosh established a similar mechanism in US law wherein 'aboriginal title' introduced 'the right to use and occupy lands, but not to own it 'with the implied 'power of alienation'. Joanne Barker, 'The Corporation and the Tribe', in *Colonial Racial Capitalism*, ed. Susan Koshy, Lisa Marie Cacho, Josie Byrd, and Brian Jordan Jefferson (Durham, NC: Duke University Press, 2022), p. 40.
50 David Ritter, 'The Judgement of the World: The Yorta Yorta Case and the "Tide of History"', *Australian Historical Studies* 35, no. 123 (April 2004), p. 106.
51 Aileen Moreton-Robinson, 'Race and Cultural Entrapment: Critical Indigenous Studies in the Twenty-First Century', in *Critical Indigenous Studies: Engagements in First World Locations*, ed. Aileen Moreton-Robinson (Tucson, AZ: University of Arizona Press, 2016), p. 115.

upon Indigenous people have made it near impossible for such continual connection to be substantiated in colonial law. Thus, the Yorta Yorta were dismissed based on the argument that the '"tide of history" had undoubtedly washed away any traditional rights that the indigenous people may have previously exercised'.[52] Effectively, the judgment 'evoked notions of an inevitable submergence of ancient customs ... a traditional Aboriginal past obliterated by the blind and relentless power of Western civilisation'.[53] Successive scare campaigns convinced the public that any ceding of rights would lead to Indigenous 'reacquisition' of land owned by settlers,[54] part of the ceaseless efforts to secure 'white possession'.[55] As the Tanganekald, Meintangk, Bunganditj and Potaruwutj legal scholar Irene Watson writes, despite loud voices proclaiming that 'native title claims place the backyards of Australians under threat', in reality, 'the guarantees of protection of non-Aboriginal property rights were well secured and were not threatened by the High Court in the decision of Mabo'.[56]

Mark Leibler's intervention on behalf of the Yorta Yorta spearheaded his firm's commitment to 'more pro-bono work as a percentage of its fee revenue than any other Australian firm'[57] and a move away from his previous sole commitment to Jewish Zionist activism. It led in 2000 to conservative Prime Minister John Howard naming him a director of Reconciliation Australia, the body established after the dissolution of the Council for Aboriginal Reconciliation whose call for treaty Howard rejected in preference of positioning sovereign Indigenous peoples as just

---

52   Federal Court of Australia, Members of the Yorta Yorta Aboriginal Community v. State of Victoria & Ors [1998] FCA 1606 (Federal Court December 18, 1998). Cited in Ritter, 'The Judgement of the World', p. 107.
53   Ritter, 'The Judgement of the World', p. 121.
54   This claim was made by the premier of the State of Victoria during the Yorta Yorta case in the 1990s and repeated during the 2023 Indigenous Voice to Parliament campaign. Gawenda, *The Powerbroker*; Jack Latimore, 'Fake Letter Scaremongering about Indigenous Land Claims Sparks Outrage', *The Age*, 2023, https://tinyurl.com/3tx55awp (last accessed January 2025).
55   Moreton-Robinson, *The White Possessive Property*.
56   Irene Watson, 'Aboriginal Recognition: Treaties and Colonial Constitutions, "We Have Been Here Forever ..."', *Bond Law Review* 30, no. 1 (2018): 7–18.
57   Gawenda, *The Powerbroker*, p. 195.

'another "cultural tributary"' of state multiculturalism.[58] According to his unofficial biographer, Leibler disagreed with the position taken by Howard, discussed in Chapter 2, on the impacts of colonisation on Indigenous people who he saw as having faced injustices with ongoing effects that had to be 'urgently addressed'.[59] However, Leibler and Howard bonded over Israel which had his government's unwavering support.

Leibler's early positioning within 'colonial governance that works through the medium of state recognition and accommodation'[60] undoubtedly cemented the ties of loyalty that link him to many of the most recognised figures in Indigenous officialdom in Australia, in particular, Guugu Yimithirr man Noel Pearson, a 'radical centrist'[61] who had done his articles as a lawyer in Leibler's firm and whom Foley describes as one of an 'A-team, hand-picked, self-appointed Aboriginal spokespeople'.[62] On 26 May 2017, Leibler sat between Pearson and Alyawarre woman Pat Anderson, the co-chair of the Uluru Dialogue, during the reading of the Uluru Statement from the Heart,[63] 'issued by First Nations to the Australian people' calling for 'constitutional reforms to empower our people'.[64] He was present at the closed regional consultation organised by and for Indigenous communities in Western Sydney in the lead-up to the signing of the Uluru Statement, 'observing with his hands behind his back'.[65] As the Wiradjuri and Gamilaroi poet and

---

58   Moreton-Robinson, *The White Possessive Property*, p. 149.
59   Gawenda, *The Powerbroker*, p. 201.
60   Coulthard, *Red Skin, White Masks*, p. 38.
61   Tim Rowse, 'Noel Pearson, Radical Centrist', *Inside Story*, 2021, https://insidestory.org.au/noel-pearson-radical-centrist/ (last accessed January 2025).
62   Gary Foley, 'The Struggle for Aboriginal Rights', *Socialist Alternative* 95 (2005), https://kooriweb.org/foley/essays/pdf_essays/marxism_foley.pdf (last accessed January 2025).
63   Uluru Statement from the Heart, 'View the Statement', *Uluru Statement from the Heart*, n.d., https://ulurustatement.org/the-statement/view-the-statement/ (last accessed July 2024).
64   Eddie Synot, 'Arresting the Tide of History: The Uluru Statement from the Heart', *TWAILR*, 2020, https://tinyurl.com/hcaetxf3 (last accessed July 2024).
65   Lorna Munro, 'But Who Was the Old White Man at the Closed Community Consultations Leading Up to the Uluru Convention?' *The Sunday Paper* 3 (July 2024).

artist Lorna Munro asked, who was this 'old white man' and why 'had he inserted himself into our discourses'?[66]

As many Indigenous critics have noted, the Uluru process resulted in those gathered calling for 'Treaty, truth-telling and a voice ... based on the assertion of Aboriginal sovereignty'.[67] Yet in the end what was prioritised was an Indigenous Voice to Parliament to be enshrined in the Australian constitution. To achieve this a referendum was required. This effectively meant '97% of the population voting on what they think is best for 3% of a sovereign people'.[68] More trenchant critics have questioned whether the regional consultations had been inclusive at all[69] and the ultimate meeting at Uluru was not endorsed by all of the Anangu Traditional Landowners of Uluru-Kata Tjuta National Park.[70]

---

66 Ibid.
67 Michael Mansell, 'To Kill a Treaty', *Tasmanian Aboriginal Centre*, 2023, https://tacinc.com.au/2023/07/to-kill-a-treaty/ (last accessed January 2025).
68 Roxanne Moore, 'Yesterday, I Was a No. Today, I'm a Yes. Here's Why', *Crikey*, 2023, https://tinyurl.com/38hhcjkw (last accessed September 2024).
69 For example, Ngarla Kunoth-Monks tells that she and her mother, the veteran Arrernte and Anmatyerre activist and actor, Rosalie Kunoth-Monks, attended one of the 13 regional consultative dialogues held with local Indigenous communities in the run-up to the signing of the Uluru Statement from the Heart in the course of 2016. However, to the 'big meeting', 'mum actually refused to go', Kunoth-Monks told Grant Leigh Saunders. 'We discussed around that, and we came to the same conclusion that it wasn't going to represent us and our sovereignty in our country.' Ngarla Kunoth-Monks and Grant Leigh Saunders, 'How Will You Feel the Next Day Whether YES or NO?' *YouTube*, 2023, www.youtube.com/watch?v=RqZZetHpafs&t=1028s (last accessed January 2025). During an address at the National Press Club in Canberra in November 2022, the co-chair of the Uluru Dialogue, Cobble Cobble, and South Pacific Islander woman and constitutional lawyer, Megan Davis, explaining the procedures followed during the trial dialogue held at the Melbourne law school said, 'we also banned significant leaders from the movement because of their cynicism about government and the country changing and that wasn't great for a law reform proposed like a law reform process, so we wouldn't allow many of them to speak'. National Press Club of Australia, 'IN FULL: Megan Davis & Pat Anderson AO, Address to the NPC on the Uluru Statement from the Heart', *YouTube*, 2022, www.youtube.com/watch?v=lVVt1qfjwfY (last accessed January 2025).
70 The chairperson of APY Law and Culture, Murray George, said days before the meeting that 'I have written to the Referendum Council to say the Tjilpis are insulted that the Referendum Council did not respect protocol and procedure

For many Indigenous people there is an undeniable line from the discredited Recognise campaign to Yes23, the campaign to bring about a Yes vote in the 14 October 2023 referendum.[71] For Arrernte, Anmatjerre, Alyawerr woman Ngarla Kunoth-Monks, for example, 'a lot of our people see the Voice as just a dressed-up version of recognition ... I think that the biggest danger would be a push towards assimilation.'[72] The attempted assimilation of Indigenous people has been the agenda since their naming upon colonisation as 'British subjects'.[73] The campaign to enshrine the Indigenous Voice to Parliament was defeated on 14 October 2023 by 60.6 per cent of voters. Notwithstanding the so-called 'Black No' campaign led by Indigenous dissenters,[74] the success of the No vote was the result of the racist argument that the Voice to Parliament would precipitate settler dispossession. That the vote took place a week after Israel's incursion into Gaza threw the question of Zionist involvement in the Yes campaign's core into relief.[75] For Mark Leibler there was no inconsistency between his position after 7 October that 'in a world in which genocidal enemies persist, powerlessness for the Jewish people is a sin'[76] and his support for an Indigenous Voice. The bridge is his belief in the shared Indigeneity

---

before they called a meeting for discussion on having Anangu/Aboriginal people all over Australia included in Australia's Constitution.' Cited in Lindy Nolan, *Driving Disunity: The Business Council against Aboriginal Community* (Port Adelaide: Spirit of Eureka Publications, 2017), p. 86.
71   Amy McQuire, 'Voting on "The Voice": Will It Fight Racist Violence?' *Black Justice Journalism* (5 January 2023), https://tinyurl.com/mwntneh2 (last accessed January 2025).
72   Kunoth-Monks and Saunders, 'How Will You Feel the Next Day?'
73   Watson, 'Aboriginal Recognition'.
74   As Lorna Munro remarks, 'Blackfullas who criticised the Yes23 campaign in the lead-up to the referendum started to be referred to as the Black NO vote, even though a lot of us didn't want this referendum to happen in the first place. The average white Australian has no right to decide for us whether we exist or not or how we should proceed in righting the wrongs of the past.' Munro, 'But Who Was the Old White Man?'
75   As co-chair of both the Expert Panel on Constitutional Recognition of Aboriginal and Torres Strait Islander peoples and Referendum Council, Mark Leibler had been present at the signing of the Uluru Statement from the Heart at Yulara in 2017. Munro, 'But Who Was the Old White Man?'
76   Mark Leibler, X, 2023, https://x.com/LeiblerMark/status/1717761156939731111 (last accessed January 2024).

of Jewish and Aboriginal people[77] (as long as they support Israel).[78] Nevertheless, in the same year in August he cited Pearson who 'has often described our two peoples as sharing a land-based identity – historical and spiritual ... Noel also says that Indigenous Australians can and must resist victimhood, as the Jewish people have done, even in the face of persistent racism and victimisation.'[79]

The racial neoliberal discourse of resilience rather than victimhood is bathed in a Zionist language of resurgence against the feminised Jewry of the diaspora.[80] While mobilising the social justice language of Indigenous solidarity – in 2019 Leibler's firm renamed its Reconciliation Action Plan Committee the Indigenous Solidarity Network[81] – Indigeneity here is wielded not to oppose colonial power, but to uphold it, for both Palestine and Australia.[82]

---

77   In February 2024, Leibler sought legitimation from 'prominent and highly regarded Indigenous leaders such as Marcia Langton and Nova Peris' to condemn 'attempts by extremist pro-Palestinian groups to hijack the cause of Indigenous Australians, as well as their attempt to deny that Jews are indigenous inhabitants of Israel'. Bruce Hill, 'Drawing a Corrupt Comparison', *Australian Jewish News*, 2024, www.australianjewishnews.com/drawing-a-corrupt-comparison/ (last accessed January 2025).
78   As Munro reminds us, Leibler intervened to try to stop Palestinian writer Susan Abulhawa from attending the Adelaide Writers' Week to participate in a panel chaired by the Martu writer Karen Wyld in March 2023 by lobbying the government to refuse her a visa. Munro, 'But Who Was the Old White Man?'
79   Paige Taylor, 'Jews "Recognise Indigenous Ties to Land"', *The Australian*, 2023, https://tinyurl.com/yzdam4rp (last accessed January 2025). As Leah House remarks, 'as we watch Israel's current genocidal bombardment, no one with a conscience would call Palestinians "Indigenous Israelis." Why then do so many insist on referring to us as "Indigenous Australians"?' Leah House, 'Rejecting Normalisation from Here to Palestine', *The Sunday Paper* 3 (July 2024).
80   Ronit Lentin, 'A Yiddishe Mame Desperately Seeking a Mame Loshn: Toward a Theory of the Feminisation of Stigma in the Relations between Israelis and Holocaust Survivors', *Women's Studies International Forum, Links Across Differences: Gender, Ethnicity, and Nationalism* 19, no. 1 (1996): 87–97.
81   Arnold Bloch Leibler, 'Indigenous Solidarity', *Arnold Bloch Leibler*, n.d., www.abl.com.au/indigenous-solidarity/ (last accessed July 2024).
82   As Leibler said of Australia following the government's decision to hold the referendum in 2022, 'setting aside Israel, there is no better country in the world for Jews to live in'. For Pearson, 'the Jewish community represents what Indigenous Australians want: maintaining their own culture, their own traditions, while being fully integrated members of society'. Deborah Stone, '"Elated": Leibler Optimistic on Next Steps for Uluru Statement', *The Jewish Independent*, 2022, https://tinyurl.com/4vevupc6 (last accessed July 2024).

For many among both those who support Palestine and racists for whom Leibler is but a Jewish 'globalist' with a plan to use the Indigenous '3% as a battering ram against the rest of the country',[83] his involvement in Indigenous politics is simply Jewish Zionist manipulation. The antisemitism that accompanied the virulently racist anti-Indigenous right-wing campaign for a No vote in the referendum must not be discounted. However, for the purposes of my discussion, this affair signals the degree to which Indigenous claims can be wielded to secure colonial power. For Black Peoples Union president, Yuin man Keiran Stewart-Assheton, far from Indigenous recognition in the Australian constitution being an expression of majority Indigenous will, it represents a 'very individualistic, very capitalist approach' which is 'at odds with First Nations culture'.[84] It can also be seen as a response to the unity displayed by Indigenous people protesting 200 years of British invasion in 1988. It was then that the Business Council of Australia implemented a plan 'focussing on "reconciliation" and constitutional recognition and through that to land tenure, business contacts with Aboriginal organisations, direct employment and creating a sympathetic new leadership among Aboriginal and Torres Strait Islanders'.[85] Neither reconciliation nor recognition involved 'reparations and land back or ending ... occupation'.[86]

Indigenous leadership on the Voice to Parliament is consistent with support for Zionism, because 'when we look at their principles and even their outlook on other colonies across the world, we see that they ultimately support settler colonialism'.[87] If Zionism, as the Belgian Jewish Trotskyist Abram Leon put it, is 'the product of the last phase of capitalism, of capitalism beginning to decay [that] pretends to draw its origin from a past more than two thousand years old',[88] this pretence seeks to give it an imprimatur of legit-

---

83   Ibid.
84   Keiran Stewart-Assheton and Alana Lentin, 'Interview with Black Peoples Union President Keiran Stewart-Assheton', conducted 27 June 2024.
85   Nolan, *Driving Disunity*, p. 4.
86   Munro, 'But Who Was the Old White Man?'
87   Stewart-Assheton and Lentin, 'Interview with Black Peoples Union President'.
88   Abram Leon, 'The Jewish Question', *Marxists.org*, 1942, www.marxists.org/subject/jewish/leon/ (last accessed January 2025). Leon was murdered by the Nazis at Auschwitz in 1944.

imacy that white settlers cannot access. Colonial assimilation dressed in the cloak of Indigenous self-determination, from the Recognise to the Yes23 campaign, and to whatever succeeds them, propels Australian racial capitalism which, since the introduction of a modicum of access to native title, has increasingly relied on the cultivation of 'Indigenous engagement' with business.[89] By positing Jews as Indigenous to Palestine and seeking alliances, however ersatz, among Indigenous peoples worldwide, Zionism too manipulates Indigeneity, and some Indigenous people, to suit the agenda of settler colonial racial capitalism.

These strategies are not new. Lenape historian Joanne Barker has demonstrated 'how the core foundational definitions of the legal status and rights of "corporations" and "Indian tribes" in the US worked to cement US capitalist imperialism.[90] The way the legal infrastructure was crafted over time to ensure that Indigenous dispossession has always been part of the structures engendered by racial capitalism[91] points to the impossibility of separating ostensibly cultural and political-economic questions. Thus, the attempt to construct a mutuality between Zionists and Indigenous people cannot merely be dismissed as manipulation. Rather, it signals that whitened representations of culture unmoored from 'Aboriginal epistemologies'[92] are appealed to, not to further decolonisation but to thwart it. For Watson, for example, 'in Aboriginal law the land speaks for itself: can you ask the land to say "yes" to its own destruction? Can First Nations agree to sell the land? I say "no." We have no lawful authority to do this and yet we are asked to do it over and over and over again.'[93] This is echoed by âpihtawiko-

---

89 Nolan writes that the Business Council of Australia prioritises 'Indigenous Engagement'. It worked with multinational companies to roll out the highly criticised 'reconciliation action plans' 'which give businesses a model for planning their engagement with Indigenous communities'. Nolan, *Driving Disunity*, pp. 2–3.
90 Barker, 'The Corporation and the Tribe', p. 34.
91 Susan Koshy, Lisa Marie Cacho, Brian Jordan Jefferson, and Jodi A. Byrd, 'Introduction', in *Colonial Racial Capitalism*, ed. Susan Koshy, Lisa Marie Cacho, Jodi A. Byrd, and Brian Jordan Jefferson (Durham, NC: Duke University Press, 2022), pp. 8–32.
92 Watson, 'Aboriginal Recognition', p. 15.
93 Ibid., p. 16.

sisân (Métis-Cree) writer Mike Gouldhawke who writes that 'land is the terrain upon which all our relations play out, and it can even be seen as a living thing itself, constantly shaping and being shaped by other life forms'.[94] As Fanon recognised in *The Wretched of the Earth*, during the period of decolonisation 'the colonialist bourgeoisie ... decides to carry out a rearguard action with regard to culture, values, techniques, and so on'.[95] Indeed the aims of capitalist colonialism are unachievable without the occupation of this terrain. Colonialism has always 'attempted to destroy the people's culture in order for those people to become appropriate citizens'.[96]

FAKING ANGELA DAVIS: AN ANALOGY

The preceding discussion opens several avenues that help us to think more clearly about racial regime recalibration. As I have been showing, constant resistance to the racial regime exposes its instability and the necessity of repair. The efforts to recalibrate the racial regime thus entail trial and error as this is always somewhat of a scramble. The 1930s Scottsboro Boys affair, in which a group of nine Black teenagers were wrongly accused of raping two white women, led to 'the racial barriers established less than fifty years' earlier beginning to disintegrate as communist organising on their behalf united workers across racial lines.[97] As a consequence, as discussed in the Introduction, 'with the largest movie studios now under the hegemony of the largest factions of capital, namely, the Morgan and Rockefeller groups, a significant proportion of Hollywood's productions in the 1930s provided justification for the re-establishment of overt Black repression, American colonialism, and domestic fascism'.[98] The role of American cinema, as Robinson shows throughout

---

94 Mike Gouldhawke, 'Land as a Social Relationship', *Briarpatch Magazine*, 2020, https://tinyurl.com/ytwc46x3 (last accessed January 2025).
95 Fanon, *The Wretched of the Earth*, p. 44.
96 Cedric J. Robinson, 'The First Attack Is an Attack on Culture', in *Cedric Robinson: On Racial Capitalism, Black Internationalism, and Cultures of Resistance*, ed. H.L.T. Quan (London: Pluto Press, 2019), p. 130.
97 Cedric J. Robinson, 'Blaxploitation and the Misrepresentation of Liberation', in *Cedric J. Robinson: On Racial Capitalism, Black Internationalism, and Cultures of Resistance* (London: Pluto Press, 2019), p. 222.
98 Ibid., p. 223.

Forgeries of Memory and Meaning, is to discipline and calm the social forces that move against the order installed by the state and capital through recourse to nationalist and moralistic white mythologies. The challenge facing the studios in the 1970s was to respond to the consensus among Black people, and I would add too, Indigenous people organised in radical groups such as the American Indian Movement, many working-class and/or undocumented immigrants, and those who had been radicalised in opposition to US imperialist war, that integration was 'a liberal conceit'.[99]

Here enters Blaxploitation in Robinson's account, conceding to the fact that 'Black social protest was an emergent force from a community with a historical dimension and an urgent moral impulse.'[100] However, this acknowledgement that it was no longer possible for cinema to underwrite a full-throttled integrationism could not at the same time yield to Black Power's 'more muscular postures'.[101] The Blaxploitation industry thus reinvigorated the jungle and plantation genres of the Great Depression, focusing on the 'Bad Black woman' to double down on the vision of urban (Black) life in the US as pathological and perverse.[102] In these representations, capitalism is disappeared and replaced by the banditry and vigilantism of the Black (and poor white) female protagonist. To achieve the look, however, at a time of Black Power, the films appropriated 'Angela Davis' public image' by representing their central characters as approximations of her while 'eviscerating the original's intellectual sophistication, political and organizational context, doctrinal commitments, and most tellingly, her critique of capitalist society and its employment of gender, race, and class.'[103]

---

99   Ibid., p. 221.
100   Ibid., p. 222.
101   Ibid.
102   Ibid., p. 225. This analysis has similarities to Patricia Hill Collins' delineation of the different 'controlling images' used to discipline Black women and rein in protest in the US. Patricia Hill Collins, *Black Feminist Thought: Knowledge, Consciousness, and the Politics of Empowerment* (New York: Routledge, 2000).
103   Robinson, 'Blaxploitation and the Misrepresentation of Liberation', p. 225. In *Contextualizing Angela Davis*, Joy James argues that it is necessary to juxtapose the persistence of Davis' radical image with her more recent championing of 'centrist liberalism'. Joy James, *Contextualizing Angela Davis: The Agency and Identity of an Icon* (London: Bloomsbury Academic, 2024), p. 175.

Robinson concludes that, by faking Angela Davis, movies gave audiences the risk-free 'vicarious thrill of participation into primitive excesses'.[104]

We see in this discussion how the recalibrating racial regime, adjusting in recognition of the masses' opposition to the status quo ante which takes different forms from the more overtly radical to community resistance against the everyday degradations of systemic racism, appropriates to undermine. Robinson's critique could well be mobilised to explain the tendency of capitalism to 'commodify, celebritize, and corporatize any and everything, by any means necessary'.[105] What the Zionist inhabitation of Indigeneity through attempted alliances with local Indigenous peoples shows is the degree to which this is immanent to the securing of settler colonial regimes. It is not only, as the Palestinian scholar Steven Salaita puts it, that 'appeals to Native authority become inscribed in the very language of Israeli settlement'.[106] It is that in the case of Zionists, as the last chapter also showed, their involvement in the local politics of antiracism, and in this case Indigeneity, serves not only as an attempt to cement Zionist legitimacy over Palestine and consequently justify genocide but also to intervene in solidarity efforts in Australia and elsewhere. So, as Robinson illustrates with the example of Blaxploitation, resistance is recognised and in response domesticated and subverted, but it is also inhabited – not just ventriloquised – in service of power.

The effects of this are not just representational, seeking in the case of Zionist self-presentations as Indigenous to occupy the space of native legitimacy in the public eye. They are also obfuscatory in the sense that the various layers of Zionism as a political project, combining settler colonialism, rampant nationalism and imperialism as the apotheosis of racial capitalism as the driving

---

104 Robinson, 'Blaxploitation and the Misrepresentation of Liberation', p. 226.
105 Joshua Briond, 'Rock-a-bye Baby: On the State's Legitimation of Juneteenth and Liberal Concessions as Political Anesthetization in Slavery's Afterlives', *Hampton Institute*, 2021, www.hamptonthink.org/read/tag/carceral (last accessed January 2025).
106 Steven Salaita, 'Inter/Nationalism from the Holy Land to the New World: Encountering Palestine in American Indian Studies', *Native American and Indigenous Studies* 1, no. 2 (2014): 125–44, p. 130.

force of western civilisation, can be hidden from view. One aspect of this is the exceptionalisation of Zionism from multiple directions. From the Zionist perspective, Jewish claims on Palestine cannot be written off as comparable to other settler colonial regimes because of Jews' 'contractual connection to the land reiterated in the Bible'[107] and 'Jews' historic status as a colonised people and Zionism as an anticolonial movement'.[108] From the opposing side, Zionism is also exceptionalised as 'still ongoing and incomplete, marking a critical divergence from historical precedents of settler colonial projects that either reached a conclusion or underwent significant transformation'.[109] However, this view, which the Palestinian political scientist Tariq Dana reaches because Israel is 'faced with the indomitable and unrelenting Palestinian resistance', denies the myriad practices of resistance that continue in older settler colonies too.[110]

In contrast, it is more useful to draw out the similarities between different settler colonial regimes historically[111] and their emplacement within the totality of colonial racial capitalism continuously. As Stasiulis and Yuval-Davis observe, 'whatever their variations in historical genesis and development, settler societies share certain common features and challenges pertaining to the coexistence of diverse indigenous and migrant collectivities'.[112] This is not to deny political, geographical and representational particularities, but to

---

107 Ilan Troen and Carol Troen, 'Indigeneity', *Israel Studies* 24, no. 2 (2019): 17–32, pp. 21–2.
108 Derek J. Penslar, 'Zionism, Colonialism and Postcolonialism', *Journal of Israeli History* 20, no. 2–3 (2001), p. 87.
109 Tariq Dana, 'Notes on the "Exceptionalism" of the Israeli Settler-Colonial Project', *Middle East Critique* 33, no. 2 (2024), p. 169.
110 Ibid.
111 Kauanui discusses the similarities between settler colonialism in Hawai'i and Palestine. J. Kēhaulani Kauanui, 'Decolonial Self-Determination and "No-State Solutions"', *Humanity Journal*, 2019, https://tinyurl.com/2farbknb (last accessed January 2025).
112 Daiva Stasiulis and Nira Yuval-Davis, 'Introduction: Beyond Dichotomies – Gender, Race, Ethnicity and Class in Settler Societies', in *Unsettling Settler Societies: Articulations of Gender, Race, Ethnicity and Class*, ed. Daiva Stasiulis and Nira Yuval-Davis (London: Sage, 1995), p. 1.

start with the principle that 'resistance remains'[113] in the face of the widespread notion that 'native elimination' is a 'completed story'.[114] From my perspective which stresses the recalibrating processes of the racial regime as being always in response to push-back from those it targets for discipline, exploitation and attempted elimination, this helps us to more clearly identify those processes in order to trace how they are resisted and how that resistance in turn is disciplined.

The various joint public-private initiatives to discipline Indigenous resistance – reconciliation, recognition and representation – allow us to trace overlaps between these and Zionist assertions of Jewish self-determination. In her letter on the topic of Indigeneity to Leanne Betasamosake Simpson, the Palestinian and Canadian scholar, Sabrien Amrov makes two remarks that evoke the complex under discussion here. First, she notes the 'huge push to promote Indigenous representation in our institutions of higher education' in Canada. Second, 'young adults who proudly identify as Zionists on TikTok are recycling words like "Indigenous," authentic/original ancestry, as a way to keep a grip on power'.[115] On the one hand, the fact that because it 'comes from a knowledge system, languages, and academic practices that were designed to reproduce colonialism', the term Indigeneity cannot but be 'appropriated and remade by colonialism'. On the other hand, Indigenous remains useful 'in building transnational relationships between movements for liberation'.[116] It is therefore important to preface any discussion of the political usages of Indigeneity by colonising power with the observation that Indigenous resistance persists and transnational alliance grows despite cooptation. However, it is also important to track how colonial institutions such as universities – much like Blaxploitation's manipulation of Black radical personas – are adept

---

113 Keiran Stewart-Assheton and Jasper Cohen-Hunter, 'Internalised Colonialism and the Inevitability of Resistance', *The Sunday Paper* 3 (July 2024).
114 Rana Barakat, 'Writing/Righting Palestine Studies: Settler Colonialism, Indigenous Sovereignty and Resisting the Ghost(s) of History', *Settler Colonial Studies* 8, no. 3 (2018), p. 352.
115 Leanne Betasamosake Simpson and Sabrien Amrov, 'Indigenous: A Conversation', *The Funambulist Magazine* (25 October 2023), https://thefunambulist.net/magazine/redefining-our-terms/indigenous (last accessed January 2025).
116 Ibid.

at creating the impression of radicality and subversiveness. My argument is that within an institutional context that purports to promote Indigenous knowledge-building and the empowerment of Indigenous people but in which pro-Palestine anticolonial, pre-resistance speech and action are punished, Zionist proclamations of Indigeneity can be sustained. This is because a depoliticised understanding of Indigeneity is privileged in practice while a language of self-determination is used to describe what is in fact Indigenous inclusion. This then calls into question the practical remit of the notion of self-determination itself, and whether the clash between its hegemonic and subaltern understandings can be overcome in favour of the latter.

When understood in tandem with the questions raised in the last chapter about the conceptual limitations of our theoretical frameworks caught within the constraints of the western academy, and the discussion of how oppressive definitions of antisemitism are used to police an antiracist imaginary, this raises important considerations of strategy against the racial regime.

'SELF-DETERMINATION IS A FRONT FOR ASSIMILATION AND EXPLOITATION'[117]

We understand that for many Indigenous Australians, the language of reconciliation no longer best captures the imperative of self-determination.[118]

---

117 Marcia Langton, 'Preface: Self-Determination as Oppression', in *Australia's Policy towards Aborigines, 1967–1977*, ed. H.C. Coombs, *Report Minority Rights Group* 35 (London: Minority Rights Group, 1978). Paradoxically, the Aboriginal writer and academic Marcia Langton who made this statement in 1978, during more radical times, in 2024 took a strong stance against Indigenous people who stood with Palestinians. She claimed that 'Blak sovereignty' activists had misrepresented Indigenous people's stance on Palestine, stating, 'First, they claim that "Indigenous Australians feel solidarity with Palestinians". This is false; it is the view of a tiny few, if put in those words. Most of us are aware of the complexity and that there is very little comparable in our respective situations, other than our humanity. Second, they refuse to condemn Hamas. I am aghast and embarrassed. They do not speak for me ... No legitimate Aboriginal leader will permit our movement to be associated with terrorists.' The Jewish Independent, 'Australia Day or Invasion Day, It's No Place for Palestinian Partisanship', *The Jewish Independent*, 2024, https://tinyurl.com/ypdabsa5 (last accessed January 2025).

118 Arnold Bloch Leibler, 'Indigenous Solidarity'.

'It's ironic', wrote the Zionist propagandist Hen Mazzig in 2020 about why he is 'hated' for believing 'in Israel's right to exist': 'I am the embodiment of intersectionality. I'm the son of an Iraqi mother and North African Berber (Amazigh) father. I grew up in an underprivileged community, a gay boy in the closet who then became an openly gay man.'[119] Mazzig, who has been paid by the Israeli government,[120] brands himself as 'a globally-recognised speaker, educator, and digital influencer'.[121] He is also on the Advisory Board of Jews Indigenous to the Middle East and North Africa (JIMENA), a US organisation set up to combat what it calls 'revisionist history', which portrays Israel 'as a white, European colonial outpost in the Middle East and ignores the fact that over half of Israel's Jewish population descend from Mizrahi and Sephardic Jewish refugees from Middle Eastern and North African countries who fled Antisemitic persecution in the 20th century'.[122] Both Mazzig and JIMENA's executive director, Sarah Levin, trade in the language of antiracism and Indigenous rights to brownwash settler colonialism. JIMENA was integral to the attacks on ethnic studies in California discussed in Chapter 3, using principles that 'seem in line with ethnic studies' goal of teaching about the experiences of marginalised groups' to embed Zionist propaganda in the public school curriculum.[123] In an article bemoaning criticisms of the organisation,[124] Levin mobilised the language of self-determination:

---

119 Hen Mazzig, 'Why Some People Hate Hen Mazzig', *Medium*, 2020, https://tinyurl.com/mt4v5mz5 (last accessed January 2025).
120 Aiden Pink, 'Did This Pro-Israel Superstar Work as a Secret Agent on College Campuses?' *The Forward*, 2018, https://tinyurl.com/3wv84x3v (last accessed July 2024).
121 Hen Mazzig, 'Hen Mazzig', n.d., www.henmazzig.com/ (last accessed July 2024).
122 JIMENA, 'Jewish Refugees from Arab Countries', *JIMENA*, n.d., www.jimena.org/about-jimena/ (last accessed July 2024).
123 Gabi Kirk, 'Authors of California Ethnic Studies Curriculum Decry Cuts to Arab Studies', *Jewish Currents*, 2021, https://tinyurl.com/2xhmb6rk (last accessed January 2025).
124 Solomon Brager, 'When Settler Becomes Native', *Jewish Currents*, 2021, https://jewishcurrents.org/when-settler-becomes-native (last accessed January 2025).

What is most sad is that a Jewish publication seems intent on undermining Jewish self-determination (Zionism) while lifting up the rights of other indigenous groups in their quest for political self-determination ... The piece was exclusively aimed at discrediting the claim that Jews are entitled to our right to self-determination.[125]

To be sure, the belief that 'a Jewish nation has been in existence since Moses received the tablets of the law on Mount Sinai'[126] and that 'the Land of Israel' is central to Jewish self-understandings is widespread and hegemonic.[127] However, as the Israeli historian Shlomo Sand argues based on archaeological and textual records, this is largely a myth invented in the late nineteenth century to give legitimacy to the emerging idea of Jewish nationhood against a backdrop of fully developed European *Herrenvolk* nationalism.[128] The Palestinian intellectual Ghassan Kanafani, assassinated by Israel in 1972, further reminds us that 'Judaism had ceased to be a national bond for nearly two thousand years' and 'among the world's Jews, there was certainly not an ethnic kinship.'[129] The specific use of a language of Indigeneity with regards to the Jewish claim on the land between the Euphrates River and the Mediterranean Sea seems to be more recent. Steven Salaita remarks on a 2008 reference to Israel by a Canadian MP as the 'aboriginal [sic] homeland of the Jewish people across space and time', noting the appropriation of 'the language of Indigenous peoplehood' as used by the native peoples of Turtle Island.[130] While the concept of Indigeneity is contested among Palestinians,[131] for the Palestinian scholar Jamal Nabulsi it 'articulates the power to reclaim *all* Pal-

---

125 Sarah Levin, 'Jewish Indigeneity to Israel by Sarah Levin', *JIMENA*, 2021, www.jimena.org/jewish-indigeneity-to-israel/ (last accessed January 2025).
126 Shlomo Sand, *Invention of the Jewish People* (London: Verso, 2019), p. 16.
127 Troen and Troen, 'Indigeneity'.
128 Sand, *Invention of the Jewish People*.
129 Ghassan Kanafani, *On Zionist Literature* (Oxford: Ebb Books, 2022), p. 7.
130 Steven Salaita, *Inter/Nationalism: Decolonizing Native America and Palestine*, Indigenous Americas (Minneapolis, MN: University of Minnesota Press, 2016), p. 17.
131 Lila Abu-Lughod, 'Imagining Palestine's Alter-Natives: Settler Colonialism and Museum Politics', *Critical Inquiry* 47, no. 1 (2020): 1–27.

estinians as Indigenous to *all* of Palestine'.[132] Furthermore, it is a powerful rallying call for solidarity across territorial boundaries with other peoples dispossessed by settler colonialism as seen in the political alignments of Palestinians and the American Indian Movement going back to the 1970s who, with 'their Black Panther counterparts looked at the global liberation struggles for inspiration and solidarity'.[133]

This counterhegemonic unity triggers the Zionist appropriation of Indigeneity. Sarah Levin consciously mirrors 'Indigenous studies [which] understands that land is life',[134] claiming 'for Jews, like most indigenous groups, the spiritual is political and also ecological, and we should not be afraid to lean into deep connections to the land of Israel.'[135] Moreover, she repackages the long-standing Zionist myth that Palestine was a 'land without a people' by arguing that recognising Jews as the Indigenous people of 'Israel' benefits Palestinians 'and all other indigenous Middle Eastern peoples'. Following this statement up by writing that 'we should build relationships with other indigenous Middle Eastern communities and support them as they strive for land-rights, cultural survival, and self-determination', Levin makes clear that Palestinian Indigeneity can be severed from the actual land of Palestine. It is clear by referring to 'the rights of Palestinians' that, at best, they could be accommodated within a Jewish state which she conceives as 'our 2,500-year-old cry for freedom and self-determination'.[136] In posthumous response, Edward Said puts it pithily:

> Jews had a claim, I've never denied that, of course they have. But is it a claim that can tell a Palestinian, 'well, you better leave this house because I got it three thousand years ago? I mean, it's true I come from Brooklyn or from Poland, but I have a bigger right

---

132 Jamal Nabulsi, 'Reclaiming Palestinian Indigenous Sovereignty', *Journal of Palestine Studies* 52, no. 2 (2023), p. 30.
133 Majd Abu Amer, 'Distinguishing Solidarity and Changing the Interlocutor towards Rethinking Indigeneity in Palestine and Rethinking Palestine Indigenously', *28*, 2021, https://tinyurl.com/nayrwumk (last accessed January 2025).
134 Koshy et al., 'Introduction', p. 11.
135 Levin, 'Jewish Indigeneity to Israel by Sarah Levin'.
136 Ibid.

to this house than you do, so get out.' I'm sorry, I disagree with that.[137]

In her discussion of the spread of Indigeneity as a way of conceptualising what it means to be Palestinian, Lila Abu-Lughod raises concerns that alert us to the processes of recuperation that even the most radical of conceptualisations are susceptible to. This is not to problematise the concept itself, as is the wont of opponents of 'identity politics' who blame 'anti-racism for divisions on the left since the 1970s'.[138] Rather, it is to note the well-tested propensity of the state to integrate and subvert oppositional discourses. While Salaita points to how US multiculturalism can accommodate 'both colonial desire and communal racism' within a vision of racism as 'individualistic failure or ignorance' rather than the product of the colonial racial state, this does not necessitate an adherence to liberal multiculturalism, universalism or humanism. Zionist claims to Indigeneity are also upheld by the far right across the Global North which has itself appropriated the language of Indigeneity to assert its legitimacy in the face of the white supremacist 'Great Replacement' theory. Nevertheless, both Salaita and Abu-Lughod alert us to the way the recognition of Jewish Indigeneity to Palestine in explicit negation of Palestinian claims to the land can mobilise the very language of Indigenous sovereignty and self-determination to discipline and punish Palestinians and their supporters.

Abu-Lughod points to the tokenisation and culturalisation to which Indigenous people are submitted by the Australian state, notably finding it incongruous to think about an acknowledgement of country performed on 'unceded Palestinian land', as we hear daily on campuses, public institutions and even on television in Australia. However, she tempers her scepticism by noting the power in Indigenous acknowledgements of country that carry

---

137   Heba M. Khalil, 'Edward Said: Claims to the Holy Land (Israel and the Occupation of Palestine)', *YouTube*, 2016, www.youtube.com/watch?v=x2z-7kEAy6mI (last accessed January 2025).
138   Michael Richmond and Alex Charnley, *Fractured: Race, Class, Gender and the Hatred of Identity Politics* (London: Pluto Press, 2022), p. 5. Richmond and Charnley make this claim of the Black USian political scientist Adolph Reed.

'a different valence' when addressed by an Indigenous person in recognition of another's sovereignty.[139] This is echoed by Brenna Bhandar who notes the use of land acknowledgements, most often by 'racialized settlers and Indigenous peoples [who] bear a disproportionate burden of repression for their work on Palestine',[140] 'to speak about the complicity of the state of Canada and its public institutions in the colonisation of Palestinian lands'.[141] However, Taylor Miller draws attention to the institutionalised perfunctoriness of land acknowledgements at the University of Arizona 'that are in every email including the email that I received when they're like, "we're deploying chemical munitions on your students"'.[142] This dialectic alerts us to the necessity of sitting with the complexities of attempts to 'Indigenise' institutions such as universities. These questions are particularly pressing given the choice of some academics to remain 'conspicuously and persistently silent'[143] in the face of genocide. Yet, beyond discussions of complicity and double standards contained in Abu-Lughod's suggestion that an Israeli acknowledgement of 'unceded Palestinian land' would signal a point of no return is the question of what the various decolonising and Indigenising projects that universities established on 'stolen land' – as the acknowledgements alert us to – permit.

Projects such as *Towards Braiding*, a project of the arts/research collective, 'Gesturing Towards Decolonial Futures' in British Columbia, aim to 'rewrite the story' of how institutional Indigenising initiatives usually end: with a breakdown of communication

---

139 The discussion still lingers on the qualitative difference between national liberation struggles and Indigenous claims within the settler colonial state. However, signalling the need for more attention to be paid across locations, Abu-Lughod welcomes the Uluru Statement from the Heart as a demand for 'sovereignty', something even its proponents did not claim it did. Abu-Lughod, 'Imagining Palestine's Alter-Natives', p. 17.
140 Brenna Bhandar, 'A Land Acknowledgment in a Different Key: Palestine, Solidarity and the Disruption of the Liberal Script', *Middle East Critique* 33, no. 3 (2024), p. 7.
141 Ibid., p. 3.
142 Taylor Miller and Alex Aviña, '"Landscape of Deathmaking": The Palestine/Mexico Border', 2024, *The East Is a Podcast*, https://player.fm/episodes/429184778 (last accessed January 2025).
143 Bhandar, 'A Land Acknowledgment in a Different Key', p. 2.

between organisations and the Indigenous people brought in to '"Indigenize" and/or "decolonize"'.[144] As Bargallie and Fernando note, 'recent moves to Indigenize the curriculum and to decolonize the university ... have glossed over race and racism, excluding, misrepresenting and devaluing critical voices through epistemic racism'.[145] However, despite such critiques stressing that there is an incommensurability between Indigenous demands and colonial institutions, the project's leaders risk reproducing the confines from which Indigenous resistance attempts to break free. For example, *Towards Braiding* names 'refusal to engage' as a factor in 'non-generative organisational decision-making'.[146] However, Glen Coulthard upsets the assumption that there are pathways of goodwill that can radically alter the terms within which Indigenous people are expected to operate. Writing about the blockades engaged in by Indigenous land and water defenders in Turtle Island, Coulthard draws attention to the skill of the 'state and corporate powers' in 'recuperating the losses incurred as a result of Indigenous peoples' resistance by drawing our leaders off the land and into negotiations where the terms are always set by and in the interests of settler capital'. The only answer is 'a massive transformation in the political economy of contemporary settler-colonialism' without which 'any efforts to rebuild our nations will remain parasitic on capitalism'.[147] In making these critiques, Coulthard distinguishes between different approaches to Indigenous self-determination, between those that 'remain dependent on a predatory economy that is entirely at odds with the deep reciprocity that forms the cultural core of many Indigenous peoples' relationships with land' and those that 'challenge the relationship

---

144 Elwood Jimmy, Vanessa Andreotti, and Sharon Stein, 'Towards Braiding', *Musagetes*, 2019, https://decolonialfutures.net/wp-content/uploads/2019/05/braiding_reader.pdf, p. 7 (last accessed September 2024).
145 Debbie Bargallie and Nilmini Fernando, eds., 'Introduction: Articulating a Critical Racial and Decolonial Liberatory Imperative for Our Times', in *Critical Racial and Decolonial Literacies: Breaking the Silence* (Bristol: Bristol University Press, 2024), p. 3.
146 Jimmy et al., 'Towards Braiding', p. 34.
147 Glen Sean Coulthard, 'For Our Nations to Live, Capitalism Must Die', *Unsettling America*, 2013, https://unsettlingamerica.wordpress.com/2013/11/05/for-our-nations-to-live-capitalism-must-die/ (last accessed January 2025).

between settler-colonization and free-market fundamentalism'.[148] However, another reading, by Joseph Massad, questions the ability of the very concept of self-determination to be anything other than a 'principle designed to limit the claims of anticolonial nationalism and enhance the claims of colonialism'.[149]

Massad critiques the ultimate inability of Lenin's socialist conception of 'the self-determination of nations'[150] to defeat its 1918 Wilsonian deployment with the 'explicit aim of equat[ing] the powerful and the powerless' and thus positing 'self-determination as a mask for the "right of conquest"'.[151] He demonstrates how, throughout the history of the twentieth century, European government representatives used the very concept of self-determination developed to address the discrimination and marginalisation faced by Yiddish-speaking Jews and insisted upon by the socialist Jewish Bund to uphold the rights of colonisers. For example, British Prime Minister Lloyd George 'in a speech written for him by Robert Cecil and Jan Smuts', the Afrikaner prime minister of South Africa from 1919, argued that 'self-determination should apply to the German colonies in Africa'.[152] The same Russian socialist concept was used by 'European Jewish colonists' in Palestine who, like their white South African counterparts, 'began to use self-determination in earnest when they parted ways with their British colonial sponsors after 1939'.[153] While an interlude instigated by the 1955 Bandung Conference saw an attempt to reverse the colonial cooptation of the principle of self-determination, this was short-lived due to the success of 'European settler-colonies and European colonising countries by 1970' to defeat it in the United Nations (UN).[154] In effect, the principle established by Wilson and mirrored in the

---

148 Ibid.
149 Joseph Massad, 'Against Self-Determination', *Humanity Journal* 9, no. 2 (2018).
150 Vladimir Ilyich Lenin, *The Rights of Nations to Self-Determination*, 1914, www.marxists.org/archive/lenin/works/1914/self-det/ (last accessed January 2025).
151 Massad, 'Against Self-Determination', p. 167.
152 Ibid., p. 168.
153 Ibid., p. 170.
154 Ibid., p. 173.

claim by Sarah Levin of JIMENA that all Indigenous peoples in the Middle East, including Israeli Jews, should enjoy 'land-rights, cultural survival, and self-determination', placed 'oppressor' and 'oppressed nations'[155] on a par.

In the context of Palestine, the deployment of jus sanguinis rights to nationality seen in the 'fantastical claims that Jews have across history formed one race that shares one blood rendering them one people and one nationality from the dawn of time', given ongoing coloniality on the international stage, has permitted Zionists to claim jus soli, or rights over the land.[156] The predominance of a racialist conception of nationality which cohered in the nineteenth-century articulation of race, *Herrenvolk* ideology and nationalism[157] means that the necessarily fictitious product of racial science – 'relations of blood' – trumps the relational attachments to land on which Indigenous claims are based. This is why it is also vital to oppose the ubiquitous references on social media throughout the genocide to a 2012 Johns Hopkins University study claiming to 'prove 97.5% of Judaics [sic] living in Israel have absolutely no ancient Hebrew DNA, are therefore not Semites, and have no ancient blood ties to the land of Palestine at all. Whereas 80% of Palestinians carry ancient Hebrew DNA and thus are real Semites.'[158] The point is not to claim the reverse is true, but to highlight that any recourse to genetics or blood in the assessment of Indigeneity, which is a social and material relation of coloniser versus colonised, reproduces the terms of racial rule.

What we see in effect is the racial colonial technology of blood quantum used to determine Indigeneity and plot 'native elimination' through assimilation[159] being deployed by the Zionist colonial project to assert not only supremacy but also legitimacy. This assertion moves via a detournement of self-determination which is

---

155   Lenin, *The Rights of Nations to Self-Determination*.
156   Massad, 'Against Self-Determination', p. 175.
157   Robinson, *Black Marxism*.
158   The study did not in fact include Jewish people living in Israel in the sample. Blair Simpson-Wise, 'Study Misrepresented in Jewish Ancestry Claim', *Australian Associated Press*, 2024, https://tinyurl.com/mr2xdtef (last accessed January 2025).
159   Patrick Wolfe, *Traces of History: Elementary Structures of Race* (London: Verso, 2016).

made into a question of bioracial destiny, detached from the reality of everyday Indigenous existence on the land. As Kauanui shows, in Hawai'i the implementation of a 50 per cent blood quantum rule to assess Indigeneity has thwarted the building of 'Kanaka Maoli political power because it is ultimately about exclusion, while it also reduces Hawai'ians to a racial minority rather than an Indigenous people with national sovereignty claims'.[160] Not all Indigenous claims of self-determination are elusive because of a reliance on blood quantum to designate Indigeneity specifically. For example, since 1967 the Australian state has eschewed blood quantum in favour of 'a three-part definition of "Aboriginal" … composed of (1) descent, (2) self-identification and (3) community recognition'.[161]

However, when we consider the fact that all western colonial regimes implement a racialist conception of nativeness – that is, one of inherent, recursive differentiation – then we can see the implication of Massad's warnings about the capacity for the concept of self-determination to lead to Indigenous freedom. As Kaunaui puts it, for the US state, 'people's racial difference has to be proved as part of their claim to sovereignty'.[162] Whatever the mechanism used to assess racial difference, including euphemisms for race such as ethnicity, descent or heritage, the fact that Indigenous people are not entirely free to determine their own parameters of self-identification outside the structures of coloniality continues to hamper the horizons of self-determination. There is also of course a spectrum of stances among Indigenous people. For some, self-determination flows from the assertion of sovereignty and therefore stands independent of colonisation, while for others, self-determination is a western, colonial framework that has been imposed upon Indigenous peoples. Many Indigenous people also engage in a pragmatic politics of reconciliation with the colonial

---

[160] J. Kēhaulani Kauanui, *Hawaiian Blood: Colonialism and the Politics of Sovereignty and Indigeneity*, Narrating Native Histories (Durham, NC: Duke University Press, 2008), p. 10.
[161] Sana Nakata, 'Who Is the Self in Indigenous Self-Determination?' in *Indigenous Self-Determination in Australia*, ed. Laura Rademaker and Tim Rowse, *Histories and Historiography* (Canberra: ANU Press, 2020), p. 340.
[162] Kauanui, *Hawaiian Blood*, p. 9.

state that they see as paving the way for self-determination over Indigenous policy domains.[163] For example, First Nations in Turtle Island did not choose 'the bizarre child of American colonialism that is federal Indian law'. They have therefore had to navigate 'the contradictions of colonial-capitalism' to 'overcome colonial dependency relations, grow social infrastructure, and ensure the welfare of their citizens'.[164] This, however, is different to the top-down efforts to institute practices of self-determination.[165] In the Australian context these have most often not differed meaningfully from discrete 'self-management' initiatives[166] all within a context of the 'foundational sovereign conflict' between the colonial state and Indigenous people.[167]

When we put these political-historical discussions together with Coulthard's assertion that 'for our nations to live, capitalism must die',[168] or as Simpson puts it, 'communities standing up and saying no to the idea of tearing up the land for wealth',[169] we can critically consider how self-determination is deployed by 'institutional entrepreneurs'[170] within higher education. Following Massad, the question of whether Palestinian liberation can be achieved

---

163 Laura Rademaker and Tim Rowse, 'How Shall We Write the History of Self-Determination in Australia?' in *Indigenous Self-Determination in Australia*, ed. Laura Rademaker and Tim Rowse, First edition, Histories and Historiography (Canberra: ANU Press, 2020), pp. 1–36.
164 David Myer Temin, 'Misreading Indigenous Politics: A Eulogy for the Eurocentric Left', *Developing Economics*, 2024, https://developingeconomics.org/2024/07/20/misreading-indigenous-politics-a-eulogy-for-the-eurocentric-left/ (last accessed January 2025).
165 Jon Altman, 'Self-Determination's Land Rights: Destined to Disappoint?' in *Indigenous Self-Determination in Australia*, ed. Laura Rademaker and Tim Rowse, First edition, Histories and Historiography (Canberra: ANU Press, 2020), pp. 227–45.
166 Rademaker and Rowse, 'How Shall We Write the History of Self-Determination in Australia?'
167 Elizabeth Strakosch, 'The Technical Is Political: Settler Colonialism and the Australian Indigenous Policy System', *Australian Journal of Political Science* 54, no. 1 (2019), p. 116.
168 Coulthard, 'For Our Nations to Live, Capitalism Must Die'.
169 Leanne Betasamosake Simpson and Naomi Klein, 'A Conversation with Idle No More's Leanne Simpson', 2013, https://tinyurl.com/458n32x7 (last accessed January 2025).
170 Rhonda Povey, Michelle Trudgett, Susan Page, and Stacey Kim Coates, 'Full Article: Workers United: A Non-Assimilatory Approach to Indigenous

via recourse to the recognition of the right to self-determination serves both as a method to assess the parameters of possibility for liberation and to ask whether 'a massive transformation, a massive decolonization'[171] is even a goal within universities operating on unceded Indigenous lands. Indigenous academics Michelle Trudgett from the Wiradjuri Nation and the Aboriginal Australian Susan Page cite the United Nations Declaration of the Rights of Indigenous People (UNDRIP) to assert that 'self-determination, rather than advocacy, has the potential to reposition Indigenous peoples within institutions, placing Indigenous matters at the heart of the higher education sector and potentially disrupting current practices that can entrench Indigenous disadvantage'.[172] The Indigenous Futures Decadal Strategy 2023–2032 lays out Western Sydney University's commitment to 'the self-determination of Indigenous Australians'.[173] Crucial for the achievement of its aim of ensuring their 'cultural, social and economic autonomy' is the development of 'institutional procurement practices that create business and entrepreneurship opportunities',[174] and the development of 'a suite of employability skills designed to serve Indigenous People and communities and to enhance professional and industry capacity to deliver effective services for Indigenous Australians'.[175] Important also is the embedding of 'a suite of leadership opportunities' for Indigenous staff and students.[176]

Leadership in Higher Education', *International Journal of Qualitative Studies of Education*, 2024, p. 5.
171 Betasamosake Simpson and Klein, 'A Conversation'.
172 Susan Page and Michelle Trudgett, 'Cementing Indigenous Self-Determination in Australian Universities', *Future Campus*, 2024, https://futurecampus.com.au/2024/05/02/cementing-indigenous-self-determination-in-australian-universities/ (last accessed January 2025).
173 Western Sydney University, 'Indigenous Futures Decadal Strategy 2023–2032', p. 5.
174 Procurement is also a priority for the law firm Arnold Bloch Leibler which aims in 2025 'to continue to update and promote the First Nations Procurement List and Procurement Questionnaire to increase the percentage of spending by the firm with First Nations businesses'. Arnold Bloch Leibler, 'Priorities for 2025', *Arnold Bloch Leibler*, https://tinyurl.com/4e6tv564 (last accessed February 2025).
175 Western Sydney University, 'Indigenous Futures Decadal Strategy 2023–2032', p. 6.
176 Ibid., p. 9.

The argument that 'self-determination and autonomy require that Indigenous people have genuine participation and authority'[177] mirror's Gary Foley's claim that 'self-determination means Aboriginal control of Aboriginal Affairs. It means political and economic independence.'[178] However, Foley's couching of self-determination within sovereignty reveals a different understanding to that deployed in the UNDRIP and on which university policy relies. As Moreton-Robinson explains, 'the unfinished business of Indigenous sovereignty continues to psychically disturb patriarchal white sovereignty'.[179] It therefore stands necessarily opposed to the sovereignty asserted by the Australian state and its institutions. Indeed, in its deliberations on the UNDRIP, the US insisted that the right to self-determination 'does not confer a right for Indigenous peoples to be independent or self-governing within nation states, nor does it confer permanent sovereignty over resources'.[180] In finally agreeing to ratify the declaration, the four states where 'almost half of the Indigenous population of the world lives'[181] 'repossessed' it, making their ratification into a virtuous act which evidences their 'good intentions' as 'benevolent states' in their relations with Indigenous peoples.[182]

The UNDRIP expressly places 'the question of land and territorial rights ... outside' its purview.[183] We might consider this alongside the fact that many of the universities currently engaging in 'decolonising' and 'Indigenising' strategies in white settler colonial states are what, in the US, have been named 'land grab universities'; universities funded with 'almost 11 million acres of land taken from nearly 250 tribes, bands and communities'.[184] The

---

177 Page and Trudgett, 'Cementing Indigenous Self-Determination in Australian Universities'.
178 Gary Foley and Padraic Gibson, 'The Use and Abuse of History in the Voice Referendum Debate', *Overland Journal*, 2023, https://tinyurl.com/muynshsd (last accessed July 2024).
179 Moreton-Robinson, *The White Possessive Property*, p. 143.
180 Ibid., p. 183.
181 The US, Canada, Australia and New Zealand.
182 Moreton-Robinson, *The White Possessive Property*, p. 187.
183 Massad, 'Against Self-Determination', p. 182.
184 Tristan Ahtone, 'Lost and Found: The Story of Land-Grant Universities', *High Country News*, 2020, www.hcn.org/issues/52-4/editors-note-lost-and-found-the-

so-called 'land grants' funded 52 universities in the US with the passage of the Morrill Act, 'a law signed in 1862 to broaden access to higher education'.[185] In Australia, with no treaties having been signed with Indigenous peoples, the process was more direct. The land of the Gadigal people on which the University of Sydney was built was 'divided into grants for John White, Thomas Rowley and George Johnston' on 28 May 1793.[186] A riposte might be that by engaging in processes of Indigenisation, universities are recognising and repairing these historical thefts. However, we might ask what such processes are also permitting and concealing. As la paperson puts it,

> Universities are land-grabbing, land-transmogrifying, land-capitalizing machines. Universities are giant machines attached to other machines: war machines, media machines, governmental and nongovernmental policy machines. Therefore the terms of the struggle in the university are also over this machinery – deactivating its colonizing operations and activating its contingent decolonizing possibilities.[187]

For Miller, 'the capitalistic rhizomatics of The University, where all theories and formulations must point to profit maximization' obviate the fact that the student encampment for Palestine at the University of Arizona 'was attacked and rapidly dismantled, three separate times, causing great damage to the land and

---

story-of-land-grant-universities/ (last accessed January 2025).
185   Robert Lee, Tristan Ahtone, Margaret Pearce, Kalen Goodluck, Geoff McGhee, Cody Leff, Katherine Lanpher, and Taryn Salinas, 'Land Grab Universities: Overview', *Land-Grab Universities*, www.landgrabu.org/ (last accessed July 2024).
186   Billy Griffiths, 'An Aboriginal History of the University of Sydney', *Down City Streets*, n.d., https://tinyurl.com/3fjmwufe, p. 1 (last accessed February 2025).
187   La paperson, *A Third University Is Possible* (Minneapolis, MN: University of Minnesota Press, 2017), p. 36. I acknowledge Taylor Miller's article where she cites la paperson's comments. Taylor Miller, 'The University of Arizona's Institutionalized Border Violence', *The New Inquiry*, 2024, https://thenewinquiry.com/the-university-of-arizonas-institutionalized-border-violence/ (last accessed July 2024).

its caretakers'.[188] There is a direct link between universities built on occupied Indigenous lands, investments in the machinery of war fuelling genocides and undergirding the mass incarceration of Indigenous people – 'perhaps more universities promote more jails'[189] – and the need to whitewash the extent of complicity with the maxim of 'self-determination in Indigenous education'.[190] This is thrown into relief when we consider the case of Ben Gurion University, 'founded to incentivize Jewish settlement' in the Palestinian Naqab Desert in 1969[191] and the role of settler academics in promoting the recognition of the Bedouin Palestinians who live there 'as indigenous under international law'.[192] As the anthropologist of Israeli expertise Maya Wind shows, 'Israel simultaneously worked to concentrate the Naqab's Indigenous Bedouin Palestinian population and appropriate their lands', a major vector for which was the university's expansion.[193] Although the call to recognise the Bedouin as Indigenous was first made by Bedouin professor Ismael Abu-Saad based on his observation of 'the similarities between the conditions faced by Native Americans and by the Naqab Bedouin', it is not shared by all Bedouin people.[194] Nevertheless, it was taken up by Israeli scholars, principally the critical geographer Oren Yiftachel who, Tatour claims, promoted a culturalist interpretation of Indigeneity that 'became hegemonic' but which negates its more political potential.[195] She shows how this interpretation which frees Indigeneity from 'an earlier approach, which limited "indigenous peoples" only to those "first/original inhabitants"' allows Yiftachel and his colleagues to argue that 'the

---

188   Miller, 'The University of Arizona's Institutionalized Border Violence'.
189   Stefano Harney and Fred Moten, *The Undercommons: Fugitive Planning & Black Study* (Wivenhoe New York Port Watson: Minor Compositions, 2013).
190   Western Sydney University, 'Indigenous Futures Decadal Strategy 2023–2032'.
191   Maya Wind, *Towers of Ivory and Steel: How Israeli Universities Deny Palestinian Freedom* (London: Verso, 2024), p. 78.
192   Lana Tatour, 'The Culturalisation of Indigeneity: The Palestinian-Bedouin of the Naqab and Indigenous Rights', *The International Journal of Human Rights* 23, no. 10 (2019), p. 1575.
193   Wind, *Towers of Ivory and Steel*, p. 79.
194   Tatour, 'The Culturalisation of Indigeneity', p. 1575.
195   Ibid., p. 1576.

indigenous concept enables (mutual) recognition and flexibility'. This in turn makes way for 'the transformation ... of Israeli Jews from a settler, to a non-colonizing, homeland group'.[196] The recognition of Bedouin Indigeneity is thus established to permit settlers to become native.[197] It also acts to separate Bedouins from the rest of the Palestinian nation who do not benefit from the same recognition as Indigenous under international law, thus enacting a classic colonial move of divide and conquer.

The University of Ben Gurion, through its role in 'the development of the Naqab as the new regional home of Israeli military bases',[198] participates in the constant dispossession of the Bedouin through the judicial system which deprives them of their land, resulting in the destruction of their homes and their consequent displacement.[199] It hosts the BGUrban laboratory, founded in 2018 and headed by Oren Yiftachel, which 'works in cooperation with the Negev Sustainability Center' contributing to advancing the UN Sustainable Development Goals[200] which the Indigenous Decadal Strategy at Western Sydney University also claims to align with.[201] Given that 'a sustained policy of concentrating the Bedouin population' has led to the criminalisation of their villages and their concentration in 'seven Israeli-designed urban centers' and 46 villages, 'either unrecognized or only semi-recognized by the Israeli state',[202] it is important to draw attention to an urban studies centre – BGUrban – established by an expansive and

---

196 Oren Yiftachel, Batya Roded, and Alexandre (Sandy) Kedar, 'Between Rights and Denials: Bedouin Indigeneity in the Negev/Naqab', *Environment and Planning A: Economy and Space* 48, no. 11 (2016): 25–6, cited in Tatour, 'The Culturalisation of Indigeneity', p. 1578.
197 Raef Zreik, 'When Does a Settler Become a Native? (With Apologies to Mamdani)', *Constellations* 23, no. 3 (2016): 351–64.
198 Wind, *Towers of Ivory and Steel*, p. 80.
199 Morad Elsana, 'Indigenous Peoples' Land: The Case of Bedouin Land in Israel', *California Western International Law Journal* 49, no. 1 (2019): 61–79.
200 Ben Gurion University, 'BGUrban Lab', *Ben-Gurion University Research Portal*, n.d., https://cris.bgu.ac.il/en/equipments/bgurban-lab (last accessed July 2024).
201 Western Sydney University, 'Indigenous Futures Decadal Strategy 2023–2032'.
202 Wind, *Towers of Ivory and Steel*, pp. 78–9.

extractive university and led by an Israeli champion of Bedouin Indigeneity whose 2018 talk at Melbourne University was titled 'Terra Nullius in Hebrew?'[203] This riffs off the title of the Introduction to Yiftachel et al.'s 2018 book, with its tellingly placed question mark, '*Terra Nullius* in Zion?' Notably, the authors open with an anecdote about a Hamas rocket launched in retaliation against Israel's 2014 war on Gaza which fell into the livestock pen of a Bedouin village designated by Israel as an 'open area'. Their focus is on an Israeli court's rejection of a civil rights group's application on behalf of the Bedouin that they be supplied 'with defensive facilities similar to those provided to nearby Jewish settlements', immediately setting the problem facing the Bedouin up not as one of colonisation by Israel but of unequal citizenship rights in the face of Hamas rockets.[204]

What these discussions point to is that, just as the recognition of Indigeneity in international law forecloses on the possibility for self-determination to bring about 'land rights and "restitution" of stolen lands' in the case of Palestinians,[205] neither can it be used to challenge the settler colonial university in any way that could give true meaning to the term 'decolonisation'. Moreover, self-determination, as enshrined within the UNDRIP as well as in practical application,[206] entails the proviso that it cannot be 'used to deny any peoples their right to self-determination'.[207] This means that it could potentially be used simultaneously to uphold the rights of others to assert Indigeneity, such as Zionist students within universities engaged in 'Indigenising' initiatives. While in a settler colonial state such as Australia, who can self-define as Indigenous can come under contestation,[208] it is nonetheless clear that

---

203 Connor Melbourne Law School, 'Oren Yiftachel Seminar', *Melbourne Law School*, 2018, https://tinyurl.com/5en78t8a (last accessed January 2025).
204 Alexandre Kedar, Ahmad Amārah, and Oren Yiftachel, *Emptied Lands: A Legal Geography of Bedouin Rights in the Negev* (Stanford, CA: Stanford University Press, 2018), p. 2.
205 Massad, 'Against Self-Determination', p. 183.
206 Rademaker and Rowse, 'How Shall We Write the History of Self-Determination in Australia?'
207 Nakata, 'Who Is the Self in Indigenous Self-Determination?' p. 338.
208 Ibid.

it applies to peoples whose lands are occupied by a foreign power. However, within a political landscape in which a structure of liberal multiculturalism dilutes Indigenous claims[209] and submits them to processes of state recognition, it is possible to imagine a scenario, for example, within university Indigenising initiatives, where divergent claims to Indigeneity clash, such as if Indigenous staff and students take an openly pro-Palestinian stance.[210] When we place this alongside the extent of Zionist involvement in the spaces of Indigenous politics, this raises concerns about whether, by choosing the framework of self-determination rather than other more radical alternatives, Indigenous initiatives in academia do not hinder the possibility for them to uplift and safeguard transnational solidarity with other Indigenous movements engaged in anticolonial resistance, from Palestine to Kanaky to West Papua.

RECOLONISING RESISTANCE (AFTER ROBINSON)

In the ninth month of the genocide in Gaza, the winners of the Dan David Prize, 'the largest history prize in the world', awarded by the Dan David Foundation at Tel Aviv University, built 'on the site of the Palestinian village Sheikh Muwannis',[211] were announced.

---

209 Elizabeth A. Povinelli, *The Cunning of Recognition: Indigenous Alterities and the Making of Australian Multiculturalism* (Durham, NC: Duke University Press, 2007); Moreton-Robinson, 'Race and Cultural Entrapment'.
210 For example, Mark Leibler is a member of the University of Melbourne's University Council. The university has been undergoing a Dhoombak Goobgoowana – truth-telling – process revealing the extent of its 'hoarding of Indigenous remains and employment (and celebration) of eugenicists, massacre perpetrators and Nazi sympathisers'. However, Leibler, who undoubtedly supports this endeavour, encouraged people to speak out against the university's chancellor's refusal to single out antisemitism, saying instead that '"all forms of racism" deserved attention'. Leibler also reprimanded other university leaders for not, in his opinion, enforcing their own policies and disciplining pro-Palestine activists on Australian university campuses. Paul Daley, 'One Exclusive Australian Institution Is Facing up to Its Deeply Racist Past While Another Backs Away from It', *Guardian*, 2024, https://tinyurl.com/46r858u3 (last accessed January 2025); Noah Yim and Natasha Bita, 'Leibler's Lament at Uni Chief's Anti-Semitism Response', *The Australian*, 2024, https://tinyurl.com/3nyxfupd (last accessed January 2025).
211 Elhalaby, 'No Palestinians Involved: An Open Letter to My Colleagues', *Past and Future Present(s)*, 2023, https://tinyurl.com/5n7z6spr (last accessed January 2025).

Among them were scholars of slavery and decolonisation, including the Black historian Keisha Blain whose commendation of General Mark Milley's defence of critical race theory we encountered in the last chapter. Despite widespread public condemnation, none of the awarded renounced the prize. In a 2023 blog post, 'No Palestinians Involved: An Open Letter to My Colleagues', the Palestinian scholar Esmat Elhalaby evoked Sylvia Wynter's open letter to her colleagues, 'No Humans Involved' (see Chapter 3). He noted the transformation of the Dan David prize from an award of $1 million to 'three well-established scholars and artists' annually to one of $300,000 for nine 'junior scholars (no more than 15 years beyond their PhD) working in the "historical disciplines"', linking this shift to the public withdrawal from the prize of the historian of slavery, Catherine Hall in 2016.[212] Responding to Elhalaby's letter, an 'Open Letter from Black Faculty' was signed by Black scholars at the University of Toronto at Tkaronto. In it they recognised 'the connection between two plights across geography and time', that of the Black USians written about by Wynter and that of Palestinians. They also noted that to accept the Dan David prize is a 'false choice that can be easily misappropriated and used to turn us against our common interests in anticolonial and decolonial futures'.[213]

The misuses of decolonisation, decoloniality, Indigeneity and anticolonialism abound. For example, Elhalaby critiques the volume *Unacknowledged Kinships* co-edited by the Israel studies scholar, Derek Penslar, which draws together Zionism and postcolonialism to argue 'that Zionism cannot be understood as "colonial" because it was both an anti-colonial nationalist movement (even "subaltern") not a colonial enterprise'.[214] Penslar first made this argument in 2001, claiming then that there had been a failure to consider 'anticolonialism (Zionism as an act of resistance by a colonized people) and postcolonialism (the Zionist project as akin to state-building projects throughout twentieth century Asia and

---

212 Ibid.
213 PACBI, X, 2023, https://x.com/PACBI/status/1638964845088505858/photo/1 (last accessed January 2025).
214 Esmat Elhalaby, 'A Dying Postcolonialism', *The Abusable Past*, 2024, https://abusablepast.org/a-dying-postcolonialism/ (last accessed July 2024).

Africa)'.[215] Penslar's proposition that Zionism has anticolonial elements works analogically via his counterfactual discussion of the Indian historian Partha Chatterjee's tracing of intellectual trends in nineteenth-century westernised colonised thought with which he claims 'the Jewish intelligentsia in nineteenth century Europe bore much in common'.[216] The anticolonialism of Zionism is thus more of a mood, an imitating of 'anticolonial national movements' in India and elsewhere, than an actuality. In making this claim, Penslar perfectly exemplifies the dominant tendency in postcolonial studies, remarked on by Cedric Robinson, in which 'the text is everything'.[217]

For Elhalaby, Penslar and his fellow travellers rely on a particular reading of postcolonialism, principally attributed to the theorist Homi Bhabha. Bhabha's emphasis of '"hybridity" and "instability"' is positioned contra Edward Said, believed by the Israeli scholars who dabbled in postcolonial theory in the 1990s to have been surpassed by Bhabha.[218] Perhaps Said's depiction of 'Zionism from the standpoint of its victims' was insufficiently poststructuralist.[219] The work of racial regime recalibration retrofits the Zionist project, conceived by the Zionist ideologue Theodor Herzl as a 'rampart of Europe against Asia, an outpost of civilisation as opposed to barbarism'[220] to emulate anti- and/or postcolonialism, pitting purportedly evenly weighted indigeneities against each other to present a picture of 'complexity' to the measure of liberal imperialism's demands. There is of course no Indigenous subject who exists outside the colonial relationship and 'the people who

---

215 Penslar, 'Zionism, Colonialism and Postcolonialism', p. 85.
216 Ibid., p. 91.
217 Morgan Ndlovu, *Performing Indigeneity: Spectacles of Culture and Identity in Coloniality*, Decolonial Studies, Postcolonial Horizons (London: Pluto Press, 2019), p. 87.
218 Elhalaby, 'A Dying Postcolonialism'; Ella Shohat, 'The Potcolonial in Translation: Reading Said in Hebrew', *Journal of Palestine Studies* 33, no. 3 (2004): 55–75.
219 Edward W. Said, 'Zionism from the Standpoint of Its Victims', *Social Text*, no. 1 (1979).
220 Theodor Herzl, *The Jewish State: An Attempt at a Modern Solution of the Jewish Question*, The Internet Archive, 1904, https://tinyurl.com/bdvatj3t (last accessed January 2025), p. 32.

became Indigenous subjects were also those who either became, or were already, victims of the colonial project'.[221] None of this denies the fact that people experience their existence as Indigenous, but it does mean that Indigenous peoples were constituted under colonialism and subjectified through race.[222] In the real world, Zionists do not exist in the 'liminal' space 'between colonial, anticolonial and postcolonial discourse and practice'[223] that Penslar places them in at all. Rather, as Elhalaby remarks, echoing the invocations of 'nuance' with which this chapter opens, while 'complexity' is presented as 'the order of the day', as bombs rain down on Palestinians in Gaza, scattering the body parts of children whose parents gather them in plastic bags, in fact 'the history of colonialism ... become[s] clearer by the hour'.[224]

The summonsing of postcolonialism to 'nuance' Zionist colonialism, like the rewriting of history to Indigenise Jews in an act of self-racialisation that imposes a language of blood on diverse peoples, united by religion not provenance to lay claim to another's land, allows for a close observation of the recalibrating racial regime. It is thus unsurprising that Robinson took postcolonial theorists to task for their 'appropriation of Frantz Fanon' demonstrating how the question of Palestine brilliantly exemplifies postcolonial theory's participation in 'ignoring the uncompromising call to arms in colonial exploitation'.[225] Much like Adam Shatz's invocation of Fanon to discipline the Palestinian resistance today, Robinson claims that literary theorists such as Homi Bhabha, Gayatri Spivak and Henry Louis Gates set out to mishandle the 'Fanonian tradition' with the express aim of making it 'appear woefully mistaken if not harmless'.[226] But the target of their 'recolonisation' of Fanon, which is achieved through the dismissal of his

---

221 Ndlovu, *Performing Indigeneity*, p. 12.
222 Moreton-Robinson, 'Race and Cultural Entrapment'.
223 Penslar, 'Zionism, Colonialism and Postcolonialism', p. 85.
224 Elhalaby, 'A Dying Postcolonialism'.
225 Madhava Prasad, 'The "Other" Worldliness of Postcolonial Discourse: A Critique', *The Critical Quarterly* 34, no. 3 (1992): 74–89, cited in Robinson, 'The Appropriation of Frantz Fanon', p. 88.
226 Robinson, 'The Appropriation of Frantz Fanon', p. 88.

contribution as having 'little to offer *all* victims of oppression',[227] resulting in the erasure of 'the violence, the exploitativeness, the reality of colonialism',[228] is not Fanon himself, for 'after all Fanon is dead',[229] but Edward Said (and other Fanonists). As Robinson reminds us, these scholars who followed Fanon in raising uncomfortable truths about the role of Indigenous elites in the capitalist economy were themselves 'involved in liberation movements'.[230] Robinson claims that what these radical Third World scholars 'now represent, and what Fanon once embodied, is the sustained attempt to locate and subsequently advertise a fixed and stable site of radical, liberationist criticism and creativity'. In this sense, they 'do sound like the Fanon whose attitude toward the colonised intellectual was rather extreme'.[231]

It is this 'extremism' and the efforts to contain it that should be tracked as academics rush to explain, contain or just expediently ignore the Palestinian resistance. Edward Said asked in 1979, in the face of 'Western intellectuals talking exclusively and endlessly about Palestinian "terror," ... what is meant to be the response of a desperate, dispersed, and expatriated people to the state and the movement that has violently attacked them at home and from abroad for almost a century?'[232] In his discussion of 'Palestine's Great Flood', Max Ajl notes that the attention on 'the post-7 October Israeli brutality applied to the Gaza strip' is accompanied by a 'diffuse rhetoric of Palestinian agency, centralisation of Palestinian voices, and solidarity with undifferentiated Palestinians' in opposition to the uplifting of 'the organised national movement and its factions and exile formations'.[233] The pragmatism of a 'narrow elite' that results in the creation of 'a reality in which the very notion of resistance is lost in the annals of a compromised

---

227 Ibid., p. 84.
228 Ibid., p. 85.
229 Ibid., p. 87.
230 Ibid., p. 88.
231 Ibid.
232 Said, 'Zionism from the Standpoint of Its Victims', p. 55.
233 Max Ajl, 'Palestine's Great Flood: Part II', *Agrarian South: Journal of Political Economy: A Triannual Journal of Agrarian South Network and CARES* 13, no. 2 (June 2024): 187–217, p. 187.

reality' in Palestine itself is mirrored in the academic drive to domesticate and repackage decolonisation and anticolonialism in a wrapping that is palatable for the business of academia. As this chapter has shown, the Zionist capture of Indigeneity finds points of accommodation with the taming of self-determination for the requirements of the western political order, finding a home in the neoliberal settler colonial university. These dynamics demonstrate with evidence Ajl's warning that 'more accommodationist positions vis-à-vis Palestine and Israel' can be taken in 'academic and popular spheres' on the grounds that 'it is Palestine itself which is radical' rather than the armed resistance against colonisation.[234] In the final chapter, I turn to the usages of antisemitism for the recalibration of white supremacy in the present continuum of fascism of which Zionism is currently our most overt example.

---

234 Ibid., p. 210.

5
Against Definitions

The first attack is an attack on culture. Marx refused to accept the terms, the language, the conceptualizations of the society which he was addressing. He could not accept them because he understood them to be distortions, because he understood them to be very pointed, very clearly related to distortions, to the oppression of a people.[1]

This war is a war that is not only between Israel and Hamas. It's a war that is intended – really, truly – to save western civilization, to save the values of western civilization.[2]

On 31 July, a violent crowd descended on Southport in Northern England. Burning police cars and throwing bricks through the windows of a mosque, the crowd had been galvanised by false far-right rumours that the 17-year-old who had stabbed three young girls to death at a dance workshop the previous day was a Muslim.[3] The riots quickly spread through the country. The Canadian conservative social commentary media website, Western Standards, shared a post from @NiohBerg, the 'British-Iranian Jewish Nationalist Zionist' X account that read, 'I don't think I've ever seen the British rise up and take to the streets like this. The energy has

---

1   Cedric J. Robinson, 'The First Attack Is an Attack on Culture,' in H.L.T. Quan ed. *Cedric Robinson: On Racial Capitalism, Black Internationalism, and Cultures of Resistance* (London: Pluto Press, 2019), p. 71.
2   Al Mayadeen English, 'Herzog Claims War in Palestine Would Save "Western Civilization"', *Al Mayadeen English*, 2023, https://tinyurl.com/5n94w62y (last accessed January 2025).
3   Hannah Al-Othman, Josh Halliday, Nadeem Badshah, and Vikram Dodd, 'Keir Starmer Says Southport Rioters Will Feel "Full Force of the Law"', *Guardian*, 2024, https://tinyurl.com/yaf8pynr (last accessed January 2025).

shifted'.[4] Pressing play on the video of the riot, the crowd can be heard chanting 'England till I die' and 'Tommy, Tommy, Tommy Robinson'. The previous weekend, the far-right Islamophobe had organised what he called 'the "biggest patriotic rally" the UK had ever seen',[5] uniting disparate elements of the rabidly Islamophobic, anti-migrant far right with conspiracists bred during the Covid lockdowns, Christian elements, and a flurry of Israeli flag bearers. Asked by reporter, Richard Hames why he had come, a man holding one of these flags said, 'stand with Israel. Palestine was never a place. Here to make a difference'.[6]

It has not escaped the notice of the Palestine movement that the far right's rush to 'stand with Israel' contradicts its foundations on a bedrock of antisemitism, of the old kind. Far right-wing ideologues are defending Zionists by engaging in Holocaust denial. One of their number, the author of the Islamophobic screed *The Strange Death of Europe*,[7] Douglas Murray, took to the pages of *The Jewish Chronicle*, the 'oldest continuously published Jewish newspaper in the world', to make the denialist claim that unlike Hamas on 7 October 2023, the Nazis were 'rarely proud' of 'shooting Jews in the back of the head all day and kicking their bodies into pits'.[8] In France, the left-wing party *La France insoumise*, was criticised for refusing to attend the March Against Antisemitism held in Paris on 12 November 2023 by the president of the French National Assembly and the Senate. However, party leader Jean-Luc Mélenchon's rejection of the invitation to attend aptly pointed to the absurd fact that 'first to respond to the invitation was the *Ras-*

---

4   Dave Naylor, 'WATCH: Furious Residents Riot Outside Scene of Daycare Slaughter Chanting "English till I Die"', *Western Standard*, 2024, https://tinyurl.com/3wafu3j4 (last accessed September 2024).
5   Tom Symonds, 'Thousands Join Tommy Robinson March in London', *BBC*, 2024, www.bbc.com/news/articles/ce4qd4e4e1vo (last accessed September 2024).
6   Novara Media, 'Tommy Robinson and His Supporters "Take Over the Streets"', 2024, *YouTube*, www.youtube.com/watch?v=rx2FoBCC-mY (last accessed January 2025).
7   Douglas Murray, *The Strange Death of Europe: Immigration, Identity, Islam* (London: Bloomsbury, 2018).
8   Douglas Murray, 'Why Must Jews Watch Their Backs as London Mobs Cheer?' *Jewish Chronicle*, 2023, https://tinyurl.com/4urkf5kt (last accessed January 2025).

semblement national', the far-right party led by Marine Le Pen, the inheritor of her father's fascist *Front national* party.[9]

Defending her presence at the march, Le Pen stated, 'we are where we ought to be'.[10] Her remark is nothing more than an echo of the belief among the dominant class in France that this is indeed correct. As the French Marxist sociologist Ugo Palheta notes, Le Pen's prominence within the anti-antisemitism 'movement' manufactured by the French state belongs to the 'mediatic and political normalisation of the extreme right' in France. It serves to endorse the severing of her current political apparition not only from that of her father but also from her own as a member of the *Front national* since 1986 and as Jean-Marie Le Pen's campaign director in the 2007 presidential elections. More importantly, it allows a French political elite to present antisemitism as confined to 'a long-past period of French history, identifiable with the Vichy regime and its residues within the extreme right'.[11]

This mystification of the actual history of French fascism and Nazi collaboration is necessary to ensure that it is the state, and not civil society, that directs and controls anti-antisemitism which, we can recall from Chapter 3, is best conceived as what Anna Younes designates a 'war', in line with the war on drugs and the war on terror.[12] Controlling this war allows the location of antisemitism uniquely on the (pro-Palestinian) left where, the 'new antisemitism' thesis asserts, the true threat to Jewish lives and culture lies. This serves to justify the ever-closer symmetry between the centre-right and what used to be considered the extreme fringes on matters of policing and migration particularly, seen in the overt militarisation of both the border and the street. Crucially, it also

---

9   Yves-Marie Robin, 'Présence du RN, absence de LFI ... Polémique autour de la marche contre l'antisémitisme', *Ouest-France*, 2023, https://tinyurl.com/3dj8yu5u (last accessed January 2025).
10 MD avec AFP, '"Nous Sommes Là Où Nous Devons Être": Le Pen Défend Sa Présence à La Marche Contre l'antisémitisme', *BFMTV*, 2024, https://tinyurl.com/3rdh4edk (last accessed August 2024).
11 Ugo Palheta, 'L'antisémitisme tourne toujours à droite', *Contretemps*, 2023, www.contretemps.eu/antisemitisme-droite-extreme-le-pen-rn-darmanin/ (last accessed August 2024). The translation from French is my own.
12 Anna-Esther Younes, 'Fighting Anti-Semitism in Contemporary Germany', *Islamophobia Studies Journal* 5, no. 2 (1 October 2020).

recruits Jews as partners in a war whose ends are the securing of western civilisation and the allied shoring up of white supremacy to which the Zionist project is an integral part. While this recruitment is successful among Zionists, Jews who refuse to be coopted into white supremacism thinly disguised as antiracism find themselves accused of antisemitism or of being a '*Kostümjude:* a costume Jew'.[13]

While the political landscape in diverse western states is locally specific, to understand the current contours of the politics of antisemitism we need to move beyond each locality and consider the wider effort to recapitulate western dominance in the face of global realignments and non-western challenges from below to the dominant western order. The blurring of the boundaries of the acceptable, on blatant display with the near universal western endorsement of Israel's genocide in Gaza, also serves to legitimate the erosion of the line superficially maintained between the extreme and the centre. This can be witnessed in the tacit convergence of European governments, who may differ in tone but who generally stand united in substance when it comes to reaffirming a commitment to 'strong borders' with all they entail; borders that have always been internally as well as externally constructed against Europe's negatively racialised others. Hence, outrage with the antisemitic rhetoric of Hungary's Victor Orbán or Italy's Fratelli d'Italia party[14] fades in the face of the more pressing imperative to effectively uphold the slogan Orbán used to announce Hungary's 2024 European Union presidency: 'Let's make Europe great again'.[15]

In this final chapter, I reiterate a crucial dynamic of the racial regime in Cedric Robinson's terms, namely, that it is incompatible with a 'discoverable history' as are 'its social relations'.[16] While

---

13 Alex Cocotas, 'How German Isn't It', *The Baffler*, 2024, https://thebaffler.com/latest/how-german-isnt-it-cocotas (last accessed January 2025).
14 Laura Gozzi, 'Italy's Meloni Rejects Fascist Nostalgia after Youth Wing Scandal', *BBC*, 2024, www.bbc.com/news/articles/cv2g62qz36lo (last accessed January 2025).
15 Jennifer Rankin, '"Make Europe Great Again": Hungary Sets Scene for Its EU Presidency', *Guardian*, 2024, https://tinyurl.com/yfex22md (last accessed January 2025).
16 Cedric James Robinson, *Forgeries of Memory and Meaning: Blacks and the Regimes of Race in American Theater and Film before World War II* (Chapel Hill, NC: University of North Carolina Press, 2007), p. xii.

this has always been the case for all forms of racialism, nowhere is this more visible than in the recent and present politics of antisemitism. I contend that all sides have misconstrued its function for the racial regime, perhaps because it has not been thought about by many in these terms, in other words, as essential for a complete understanding of Robinson's conceptualisation of racial capitalism.[17] While many, Marxists and liberals alike, have contended with the relationship between antisemitism and capitalism, few among them have given any great consideration to the role of the west's relationship to the Jews, not as Jews per se, but as a *question* in Marx's terms. Such a perspective foregrounds how 'racialism would inevitably permeate the social structures emergent from capitalism'; what Robinson calls racial capitalism.[18] In other words, the 'Jewish question' has not been subjected to analysis using racial capitalism. Doing so would place it within the 'historical agency' of racial capitalism, a structure inaugurated in Europe and put in place globally over the centuries from 'the emergence of Western Europeans from the shadow of Muslim domination and paternalism' to today.[19]

This chapter cannot do wholesale justice to this provocation, not least because it entails an historical project far beyond the remit of this book. However, I want to use it as a framework for thinking beyond the ways in which antisemitism *appears* today. In particular, I wish to suggest ways out of the cul-de-sac I earlier pointed to in *Why Race Still Matters*,[20] represented by the maxim that antisemitism is 'weaponised' by Zionists in an effort to shut down speech and action on Palestine specifically and de- and anticolonial movements more broadly. As the last two chapters showed in various ways, the widespread and insidious nature of this repres-

---

17 Yousuf Al-Bulushi, 'Thinking Racial Capitalism and Black Radicalism from Africa: An Intellectual Geography of Cedric Robinson's World-System', *Geoforum* 132 (2022): 252–62.
18 Cedric J. Robinson, *Black Marxism: The Making of the Black Radical Tradition*, Second edition (Chapel Hill, NC: University of North Carolina Press, 2000), p. 2.
19 Ibid., p. 3.
20 Alana Lentin, *Why Race Still Matters* (Cambridge, UK; Medford, MA: Polity Press, 2020).

sion is real and well organised. However, the tendency to propose that there are 'real' forms of antisemitism that are obscured by 'false' forms wielded in bad faith is unsatisfactory. This is not least because we never get a sense of what 'real antisemitism' is. It plays into the liberal Zionist notion that *some* criticisms of Israel are admissible, but not those that cross the line into antisemitism (a line which necessarily slips beyond the boundaries of the definable). My earlier suggestion was that speaking of antisemitism as a weapon is unhelpful for building relational theorisations of race that provide better frameworks for collective resistance, proposing that we need to 'decolonise antisemitism'. Here I further propose that the framing of antisemitism as weaponised obscures its function as always already in service of the European state, and by extension, the west and white supremacy.

This has taken different forms in different eras. However, the constant is the imperative to construe antisemitism as central to how 'the rationale and cultural mechanisms of domination' are assembled with race as 'its epistemology, its ordering principle, its moral authority, its economy of justice, commerce and power'.[21] This cannot be separated from the operations of race with regards to all of the populations who serve as a constitutive foil for Europe's self-constitution: Africans, Muslims, Jews, Roma and Sinti predominantly, both historically and today. The proposition that antisemitism must be theorised as a central feature of racial capitalism thus goes beyond construing it as another form of racism.[22] It adds to the crucial effort to de-exceptionalise antisemitism, long made to be the exemplar par excellence of racism to which all other forms are endlessly compared.[23] Further, it considers antisemitism as working dialectically within the racial regime for the advancement of racial capitalism. Its particular function is in the concealment of its own history as it was co-constitutively constructed with pre-colonial and colonial antiblack racism,

---

21 Robinson, *Black Marxism*, p. xxxi.
22 Abigail B. Bakan and Yasmeen Abu-Laban, 'Antisemitism as Anti-Jewish Racism: Reflections on an Anti-Racist Analytic', *Historical Materialism* 32, no. 1 (2024): 1–42.
23 Alana Lentin, 'The Lure of "Frozen" Racism', *The Occupied Times*, 2016, https://theoccupiedtimes.org/?p=14225 (last accessed January 2025).

Islamophobia and Orientalism. This concealment, per Robinson, plays a vital role in protecting the racial regime from the threats to its authority and vitality.[24] Today, particularly, there is much currency in separating and elevating antisemitism from other forms of racism. More than serving purely to displace antisemitism onto non-European populations, the distinction of antisemitism as a singular and incomparable form of racism 'made in Europe' serves to paradoxically task Europeans, and by extension the west, as uniquely capable of expunging it 'by any means necessary'. This purview permits and propels carcerality and violence targeting so-called 'new antisemites' in the name of saving Jews.

In what follows, I argue that the protection offered to Israel by the west is compelled not by the oft-touted guilt, which might be felt individually, but by the preservation of the structures of western dominance established by racial capitalism. The overbearing rationale is a one-for-one identification of the west with Israel as representative both of the highest achievement of western civilisation and as a portent of what can befall it. Palestinians, through their resistance and steadfastness, rather than their victimhood, represent a threat to Europe's future. This future is vulnerable economically and militarily on the global level, and domestically due to the failure to build societal cohesion and peace; the superficial promise of European integration. The attempt to manifest these promises of integration, peace and security occurred at the same time as a rush headlong into neoliberalism which evacuated much of what remained of the social state,[25] albeit unevenly. This hastened the identification of the proposed failure of integration with the figure of the migrant, the asylum seeker; the 'racialized outsider'.[26] As the UK riots and the success of the far right in the 2024 European elections[27] demonstrate within the more overt

---

24 Robinson, *Forgeries of Memory and Meaning*.
25 Christoph Hermann, 'Neoliberalism in the European Union', *Studies in Political Economy*, 79, no. 1 (2007): 61–90.
26 Satnam Virdee, *Racism, Class and the Racialized Outsider* (Basingstoke: Palgrave Macmillan, 2014).
27 Gilles Ivaldi, 'EU Elections: Far-Right Parties Surge, but Less than Had Been Expected', *The Conversation*, 2024, https://tinyurl.com/57hzrp3j (last accessed January 2025).

manifestation of fascism globally – only the most recent examples of a mounting crisis spanning a quarter of a century at least, beginning with the first shots of the war on terror – this figure is inextricably bound up with that of the Muslim.[28] In such a landscape, Israel's 'war of revenge' on Gaza[29] as a war to 'save western civilization, to save the values of western civilization', to recall again the words of the Israeli president,[30] is seen as what Europe needs to do to save itself. Understood in this way, Europe cannot take any other position with regard to Israel's genocide, for to do so would be to admit to its failure, on its own terms, to secure itself.

To elaborate the contours of this argument, I first develop the case that the predominance of the institutional language of safety vis-à-vis antisemitism indicates the objective of western civilisational self-preservation. In *Why Race Still Matters* I argued that anti-antisemitism is a proxy for antiracism which allows western states and institutions to claim they are taking action against racism by engaging in acts of commemoration and memorialisation that both place antisemitism at the top of a hierarchy of racisms and reduce it to an event 'frozen' in aspic. Here I go beyond this to assert that Jews themselves become a proxy for the western subject – *homo europaeus* – in need of saving from the marauding other. The presence of Jews and the need to defend them from harm become a means to enact punitive policies and violent action while protecting the state and institutions from criticism.

Second, I demonstrate how a politics of definition is instrumentalised towards this end.

The International Holocaust Remembrance Alliance working definition of antisemitism (IHRA-WDA) has been widely condemned from a liberal standpoint for chilling free speech and academic freedom with regards to Palestine. However, it is better understood as a carceral tool which must be countered with abo-

---

28 Arun Kundnani, *The Muslims Are Coming!: Islamophobia, Extremism, and the Domestic War on Terror* (London: Verso, 2015).
29 Gina Abercrombie-Winstanley, 'For Israel's War in Gaza, Vengeance Is a Downward Spiral', *Atlantic Council*, 2024, https://tinyurl.com/bdfcckde (last accessed January 2025).
30 Al Mayadeen English, 'Herzog Claims War in Palestine Would Save "Western Civilization"'.

litionist strategies. Alternative definitions of antisemitism, such as the Jerusalem Declaration on Antisemitism,[31] but also the attempts to institutionalise the recognition of anti-Palestinian racism, task the institutions responsible for reproducing racism with reforming it rather than radically challenging 'the terms of order' they impose.[32] The result is an obscuring of the co-constitutive histories of racial rule over all negatively racialised subjects despite their occupation of different structural locations under the same racial regime. I conclude that to begin to effectively mount a defence against fascism, we must refuse the structures within which we are constantly confined, starting with what Robinson called 'the first attack',[33] an attack on the dominant meanings of things.

ALL THOSE IN OUR COUNTRY

The democratic ethos of the Federal Republic of Germany, which is orientated towards the obligation to respect human dignity, is linked to a political culture for which Jewish life and Israel's right to exist are central elements worthy of special protection in light of the mass crimes of the Nazi era. The commitment to this is fundamental to our political life. The elementary rights to freedom and physical integrity as well as to protection from racist defamation are indivisible and apply equally to all. *All those in our country* who have cultivated anti-Semitic sentiments and convictions behind all kinds of pretexts and now see a welcome opportunity to express them uninhibitedly must also abide by this.[34]

In public discourse in the west today, antisemitism is presented as being everywhere and growing. In May 2024, *Time Magazine*

---

31 Other alternative antisemitism definitions include the 2020 Nexus Document produced by the Knight Program on Media and Religion affiliated with the Center for the Study of Hate at Bard, https://nexusproject.us/nexus-resources/the-nexus-document/ (last accessed January 2025).
32 Cedric J. Robinson, *The Terms of Order: Political Science and the Myth of Leadership* (Chapel Hill, NC: University of North Carolina Press, 2016).
33 Robinson, 'The First Attack Is an Attack on Culture'.
34 Nicole Deitelhoff, Rainer Forst, Klaus Günther, and Jürgen Habermas, 'Principles of Solidarity. A Statement', *Normative Orders*, 2023, www.normativeorders.net/2023/grundsatze-der-solidaritat/ (last accessed November 2023).

asked 'why won't antisemitism die, or at least die down?' It used statistics generated by the Anti-Defamation League, stating that 'from 2019 to 2022, the amount of people with highly antisemitic attitudes in the U.S. had nearly doubled'.[35] In Germany, where so-called *Staatsräson*, the 'special, unique relationship' to Israel forged through 'the Shoah [which] fills us Germans with shame',[36] motivates the blanket repression applied to pro-Palestine politics across the board, numbers tell a story. In 2017, for example, there were 28 antisemitic attacks, 95 per cent of which were committed by individuals associated with the far right. In contrast, 'there were almost 2000 attacks on refugees in 2017 alone, around 900 attacks on German Muslims, along with more than 100 attacks on refugee aid workers in Germany'.[37] These contrasting numbers, the omnipresence of antisemitism discourse, and the dominant conflation of anti-Zionist views with attacks on Jews qua Jews incite the widespread cynicism that antisemitism is a mere 'weapon' to be brandished to quell any protest against Israel's murderousness.

In the German case, Younes details the impact of a succession of parliamentary reports on antisemitism that identified what they named 'Israel-oriented Anti-Semitism'.[38] In the context of the war on terror dovetailing with the second Intifada in Palestine, these reports spurred a new policy outlook centred on *Sozialraum* (social space) zoning in on the Berlin 'migrant quarters of Kreuzberg and Neukölln',[39] today gentrified with co-work spaces for digital

---

35   Noah Feldman, 'The New Antisemitism', *Time*, 2024, https://time.com/6763293/antisemitism/ (last accessed January 2025). In her review of his book *Critical Theories of Antisemitism*, Safa Khatib rightly criticises Jonathan Judaken for also relying on *The ADL Global 100: An Index of Antisemitism* as a source in his book *Critical Theories of Anti-Semitism* (New York: Columbia University Press); Safa Khatib, 'Antisemitism Studies and the War against the Imagination', *Los Angeles Review of Books*, 2024, https://lareviewofbooks.org/article/antisemitism-studies-and-the-war-against-the-imagination (last accessed September 2024).
36   Die Bundesregierung informiert, 'Rede von Bundeskanzlerin Dr. Angela Merkel', *Die Bundesregierung informiert*, 2008, https://tinyurl.com/y2pjta9d (last accessed January 2025).
37   Younes, 'Fighting Anti-Semitism in Contemporary Germany', p. 257.
38   Ibid., p. 254.
39   Ibid., p. 255.

nomads tripping over discarded electric scooters. *Sozialraum* is a discourse used in youth work and education which designates the neighbourhoods inhabited by people of colour as flashpoints for 'Islamism, or sexism and homophobia'.[40] Adding the assumptions of the 'new antisemitism' as a predominantly Arab and Muslim problem into the mix served to further racialise the spaces in which already demonised populations lived precariously vis-à-vis citizenship, employment and criminalisation. The outcome was the implementation of a gamut of antisemitism training programmes targeting 'youths with a "Muslim background"' including those that specifically link antisemitism with the 'Israeli-Palestinian conflict'. Their remit is to target the 'common interpretation' that 'Jews stole the land of Palestine from Arabs'.[41] This is complemented by the mass repression of pro-Palestine speech and action, indeed the simple existence of Palestinians in public life, justified by a stated commitment to fighting antisemitism and safeguarding Jews.[42]

---

40   Ibid.
41   Esra Özyürek, *Subcontractors of Guilt: Holocaust Memory and Muslim Belonging in Postwar Germany* (Stanford, CA: Stanford University Press, 2023), p. 95.
42   A small sample of the content of this repression includes the early adoption of the IHRA working definition by the state in 2017, and the 2019 resolution of the German Bundestag that the Boycott, Divestment and Sanctions campaign is antisemitic. A whole series of bans have been enacted, for example, on Nakba Day demonstrations in 2022 and on Hamas and the Palestinian prisoner solidarity network Samidoun in November 2023. Attacks on the reputation and livelihoods of Palestinians and Muslims and their supporters have followed suit, ramping up exponentially during Israel's genocide of Gaza. In 2022, the 15th Documenta art festival was the subject of widespread allegations of antisemitism, including government inquiry. Pro-ceasefire protests have been met with arrests of children as young as seven as well as widespread police brutality. Coming on the back of the entrenched censorship of artists, academics and others for any expression of solidarity with Palestine over many years, in April 2024, the German authorities interrupted and cancelled the Palestine Congress in Berlin, cutting off the electricity to ensure the live-streamed appearance by Palestinian researcher and Nakba survivor, Salman Abu Sitta was disabled, following the refusal to permit the entry of Doctor Ghassan Abu Sittah to attend the Congress. In June 2024, an overhaul of the criteria for naturalisation in Germany led to the addition of twelve new questions on Jewish life and Israel in the citizenship test including 'What are the reasons that Germany has a special responsibility for Israel?' Al

The anthropologist Damani Partridge describes this in his ethnographic work in 'postmigrant/Black/POC Berlin theatres' in Germany which reveals how non-citizen actors struggle with the demands made on them to become combatants in the war on antisemitism under threat of the withdrawal of state support.[43] The 'everyday, mundane, repeatable qualities of racialised exclusion' faced by people of colour in Germany are counterposed to the 'monumental display' of 'moral superiority' which constitutes German Holocaust memorialisation.[44] 'Racialised youths who cannot see themselves' in what has been made the only acceptable frame within which to discuss racism[45] find themselves at risk, not only of losing funding, but with increasing regularity in the context of the Gaza genocide, of violence, arrest, incarceration, the removal of residency rights and deportation.[46]

Linking the repression of Palestinians and pro-Palestine action to the safety of Jewish people does three things. First, it tacitly recognises Jews only as outgrowths of the Zionist colony; the protection and celebration of Jewish life inseparable from the imperative to state, as the German foreign minister, Annalena Baerbock, did after 7 October, that 'these days we are all Israelis'.[47] Second, it

---

Jazeera, 'Germany Cancels Pro-Palestine Event, Bars Entry to Gaza War Witness', *Al Jazeera*, https://tinyurl.com/4pbhuamf (last accessed September 2024); Sal Ahmed, 'Meet the Jewish Activist Germany Arrested for Being Pro-Palestinian', *Middle East Eye*, https://tinyurl.com/2mywwt2m (last accessed September 2024); Germany Visa, 'Germany Will Include 12 New Questions Related to Judaism & Israel on Its Citizenship Test', *Germany Visa*, https://tinyurl.com/2xnjahcy (last accessed September 2024); Alex Greenberger, 'Documenta's Anti-Semitism Controversy, Explained: How a German Art Show Became the Year's Most Contentious Exhibition', *ARTnews*, 2022, https://tinyurl.com/mv52xsd4 (last accessed September 2024).
43   Damani J. Partridge, *Blackness as a Universal Claim: Holocaust Heritage, Noncitizen Futures, and Black Power in Berlin* (Oakland, CA: University of California Press, 2022), p. 119.
44   Ibid., p. 63.
45   Ibid.
46   James Jackson, 'Germany's Immigration Authorities Accused of "Anti-Palestinian Repression"', *Al Jazeera*, 2023, https://tinyurl.com/3zp3hufz (last accessed September 2024).
47   Lena Obermaier, '"We Are All Israelis": The Consequences of Germany's Staatsräson', *Carnegie Endowment*, 2024, https://tinyurl.com/3ep3ymmp (last accessed January 2025). This was further compounded by Germany's third-party

recruits Jews as subjects in need of safeguarding, to the project of racial rule over the racialised outsider. The consequence of this is to continue a process immanent to European colonialism and state building[48] that came to require Jews for the maintenance of the racial regime. Third, it leads to the demand to listen to the 'lived experience of antisemitism' becoming a legitimation for repressive action by the state and its institutions in the name of ensuring 'Jewish safety'.

Due to their self-assigned role as the primary perpetrators of historical antisemitism, Germans accord themselves a special place as those uniquely able to understand the significance of the Nazi genocide. As Emily Dische-Becker pointedly puts it, 'you have to have at least one serious Nazi criminal grandpa in order to be able to have the expertise it takes to talk about antisemitism in Germany'.[49] The extent to which this translates into a refusal to listen to dissenting Jewish voices over non-Jewish Zionists is made clear by the hounding of the Jewish author Deborah Feldman for saying during the genocide in Gaza that Germans were 'using the Holocaust as justification for the abandonment of moral clarity'.[50] In an attempt to make sense of the extent to which states go to repress and criminalise support for Palestine as antisemitic – Germany at the helm – there is a tendency to stress 'a guilt complex based on the Holocaust (Shoah) nurtured by most Western states towards the Jewish state'.[51] However, this has become a recited truth; there is often little

---

intervention in South Africa's case against Israel for genocide in the International Court of Justice (Application of the Convention on the Prevention and Punishment of the Crime of Genocide in the Gaza Strip – South Africa v. Israel). Khaled El Mahmoud, 'Measuring with Double Legal Standards', *Verfassungsblog*, 2024, https://doi.org/10.59704/1c5ec794a420161f (last accessed January 2025).
48   Enzo Traverso, *Pour Une Critique de La Barbarie Moderne: Ecrits sur l'histoire des Juifs et de l'antisémitisme* (Lausanne: Editions Page Deux, 1996).
49   Emily Dische-Becker, Sami Khatib, and Jumana Manna, 'Palestine, Antisemitism, and Germany's "Peaceful Crusade"', *Protocols*, 2020, https://prtcls.com/article/berlin-art-and-palestine-conversation/ (last accessed September 2024).
50   Jason Farago, 'A Conversation with Deborah Feldman, an Unorthodox Voice in Germany', *New York Times*, 2024, https://tinyurl.com/y66b9v67 (last accessed January 2025).
51   Tessa Talebi, 'Europe and the Abused "Shoah Guilt Complex" after October 7', *Project on Middle East Political Science*, 2024, https://tinyurl.com/39zfu29t (last accessed January 2025).

attempt to excavate why guilt, rather than the performance of guilt in service of western self-protection, is claimed as a motivator.

West Germany under Konrad Adenauer, whose 'German-Jewish treaty' did not lead Germans 'to confront the extent of their guilt for Nazi crimes',[52] became 'the most important supplier of military hardware to Israel in addition to being the main enabler of its economic modernisation'.[53] Adenauer viewed this as essential to 'restoring Germany's "international standing", adding that "the power of the Jews even today, especially in America, should not be underestimated"'.[54] Thus while some Germans' 'guilt is real and understandable',[55] it comes with a distinct antisemitic tinge. It is also a mode of advancing a compartmentalised approach to German racism past and present in which Germans are cast as perpetrators, and Jews – and Jews alone – are cast as victims; victims whose side the world now takes, and whom the German state required to be able to re-enter the international order. The polarity established between Germans and Jews diminishes the genocide of the Roma and Sinti and negates that of the Ovaherero and Nama peoples (1904–07) for whom concentration camps were implemented half a century before the Nazi genocide,[56] not to mention contemporary racism against migrants, Muslims, Black and Roma people. It also erases the anti-Nazi resistance of German communists who were presented by the victorious west 'as not or not-really German fully in accordance with the national ontology of the Nazis'.[57] Carrying

---

52   Frank M. Buscher, 'Kurt Schumacher, German Social Democracy and the Punishment of Nazi Crimes', *Holocaust and Genocide Studies* 5, no. 3 (1990), p. 261.
53   Pankaj Mishra, 'Review of *Memory Failure*, by Esra Özyürek and Andrew Port', *London Review of Books*, 2024, www.lrb.co.uk/the-paper/v46/no1/pankaj-mishra/memory-failure (last accessed September 2024).
54   Ibid.
55   Leandros Fischer, 'For Israel and Communism? Making Sense of Germany's Anti-Deutsch', *Historical Materialism* 32, no. 1 (2024), p. 2.
56   Zoe Samudzi, 'Reparative Futurities: Thinking from the Ovaherero and Nama Colonial Genocide', *The Funambulist Magazine*, 2020, https://tinyurl.com/3wys6v73 (last accessed January 2025).
57   Bue Rübner Hansen, 'The New German Chauvinism – Part II', *Lefteast*, 2024, https://lefteast.org/the-new-german-chauvinism-part-ii/ (last accessed January 2025).

the burden of being perpetrators of genocide outweighs being its victims, today or in the past.

Building on Younes' theorisation, the war on antisemitism appearing within the context of white supremacy, and built upon the war on terror, does not assuage German guilt. Rather, it is a proxy war against the west's racialised outsiders, embodied by the figure of the Palestinian against whom Jews, through our purposeful amalgamation with Zionists, can be easily counterposed. Selective attention to a singled-out form of racism is mobilised to justify the increased control over negatively racialised lives which is necessary for the restoration of white order. Younes' linking of the war on antisemitism to the wars on drugs and terror locate it within a wider geopolitical logic core to neoliberalism which disciplines populations who are always already racialised as posing a threat to 'our' safety. Each locates 'the origin of Europe's or American social ailments in the non-Western world, as well as in the migrant and people of color communities within the West'.[58] Making this link presses home the fact that state prioritisation of antisemitism across the west has little to do with care for Jews. An article in the *New York Times* on 'The New German Antisemitism' curiously pinpoints this fact. Recounting the experiences of a Jewish child at a German school whose Muslim classmates called him antisemitic names, one father observed that Germany's claim to have dealt with its past to the extent that the philosopher Susan Neiman proposes that the US can 'learn from the Germans'[59] is patently false: 'German society never truly reckoned with anti-Semitism after the war.' German politicians point the finger at Muslims 'importing their anti-Semitism to our wonderful, anti-anti-Semitic culture [but] that's bull. They're trying to politicize this.'[60]

At stake in the mission to ostensibly save Jews is the west's attempt to save itself.

---

58 Younes, 'Fighting Anti-Semitism in Contemporary Germany', p. 260.
59 Susan Neiman, *Learning from the Germans: Confronting Race and the Memory of Evil* (London: Penguin Books, 2020).
60 James Angelos, 'The New German Anti-Semitism', *New York Times*, 2019, www.nytimes.com/2019/05/21/magazine/anti-semitism-germany.html (last accessed May 2024).

A letter signed by the German philosopher Jürgen Habermas in November 2023 makes this clear. Its authors addressed 'all those who are in our country' who refuse to accept that 'Jewish life and Israel's right to exist' are 'fundamental to our political life'.[61] The words 'those who are in our country' recalls Stuart Hall's citation of C.L.R. James' reply to the question regarding his attitude to Europe. He was, he said, 'in but not of it'.[62] I was present in 2001 when Hall made these remarks. He had been invited to the European University Institute, a bastion of Eurocentric knowledge production, to speak at a colloquium on 'Images and Myths of Europe', and he subtly but brilliantly destabilised its precepts. The problem, Hall noted, is that attempting to 'examine Europe from the point of view of its imaginary' may lead to 'the production of yet another version of Europe's foundational story', one which 'license[s] Europe, once again, to disavow its historic instability and its deep interconnections with other histories'.[63] The point, Hall proposed, echoing Robinson's description of racial regimes as concealing their 'mechanisms of assembly',[64] is that the role of foundational myths is to obscure as much as they claim to reveal. Myths of origin, particularly those undergirding Europe as an idea and political formation, bind 'the disconcerting discontinuities, brutal ruptures, grim inequalities and unforeseen contingencies of Europe's real history into the telos of a consoling circular narrative whose end is already foreshadowed by its beginning'.[65] Using words that would risk punishment today, Hall asked was there a myth that could explain how 'the destruction of European Jewry ... came to be a burden expiated by the native inhabitants of the West Bank?'.[66]

Habermas et al.'s claim that '*despite* all the concern for the fate of the Palestinian population, however, the standards of judgement slip completely when genocidal intentions are attributed to Israel's

---

61 Deitelhoff et al., 'Principles of Solidarity'.
62 Stuart Hall, 'In But Not of Europe: Europe and Its Myths', in *Selected Writings on Race and Difference*, ed. Paul Gilroy and Ruth Wilson Gilmore (Durham, NC: Duke University Press, 2021), p. 375.
63 Ibid., p. 377.
64 Robinson, *Forgeries of Memory and Meaning*, p. xii.
65 Hall, 'In But Not of Europe', p. 377.
66 Ibid., p. 377.

actions' signals that no such myth is available to us today.'[67] The waving away of 'the Palestinian population' signalled by the word 'despite' obviously demonstrates the extent to which 'Jewish life is "more important than [Palestinian] freedom"',[68] or Palestinian existence tout court. However, the centrepiece of their statement, that antisemitism is especially unacceptable *in Germany* where the 'special protection' of 'Israel's right' is 'fundamental to our political life' presses home Younes' point that 'whoever attacks Jews, also attacks German national ethics – not the other way around … German democracy comes to stand in for Jews and Jews come to stand in for German democracy; meaning, if the Jews vanish, Germany vanishes.'[69]

In 'The First Attack Is an Attack on Culture', the essay from which this chapter's first epigraph is taken, Robinson engages Marx's essay, 'On the Jewish Question', in a passage of great importance for my discussion here. Contra the common misunderstanding of Marx's meaning, when he wrote that 'it was necessary for human emancipation that the Jews be destroyed', he was not talking about world Jewry, but about German society and Jews' function for it, and by extension for European civilisation.[70]

> The Jew has become the symbol of the society, a symbol that it cannot deal with directly, which it must project on to something, which must – in Marx's term alienate from itself. The society had developed a symbol for itself, but outside of itself. And it called that symbol the Jew. Marx was saying, it is no longer possible to understand German society unless you recognize it in the Jew, in its Jew.[71]

---

67 Deitelhoff et al., 'Principles of Solidarity'. My emphasis.
68 Mohammed El-Kurd paraphrasing the words of Israel's National Security Minister Itamar Ben Gvir in 2023. Mohammed El-Kurd, 'Jewish Settlers Stole My House. It's Not My Fault They're Jewish', *WRMEA*, 2023, https://tinyurl.com/4tjz6j3n (last accessed September 2024).
69 Younes, 'Fighting Anti-Semitism in Contemporary Germany', p. 258.
70 Robinson, 'The First Attack Is an Attack on Culture', p. 70.
71 Ibid., p. 71.

Marx was 'involved in the first attack, the attack on culture'.[72] I shall return to this.

BEFORE THE ENCOUNTER

Why, as Marx contends in 'On the Jewish Question', does European Jewry come to be equated with the nation-state. What does this equation permit under the racial regime? Why does the west require the phantasmic figuration of Jewishness to save itself? Or put another way, how is 'Jewish safety' a proxy for western preservation today? Deepening our purview beyond the present, why does the construction of western civilisation appear to require a Jew (who is not always Jewish)? Answering these questions by foregrounding the European origins and unfolding of racial capitalism undergirded by racial regimes permits us to go beyond the frames of 'hypocrisy', 'weaponisation' or 'the lobby' most often reached for when trying to make sense of the obsessional attention given to antisemitism in western discourse today.

Contra decolonial theory's proposition that 'slavery and racism occurred at the point of encounter between Europeans with non-Europeans',[73] it is necessary to pay attention to the 'unique logics and historical specificities' of race in Europe itself before 1492.[74] This is the argument made by Satnam Virdee and Dušan Bjelić in their respective work on the European origins of racial capitalism. Bjelić follows Robinson in viewing slavery as 'racialised labour, not as an anomaly but, rather, as an organising instrument of European – read Western – civilisation and foundational to it in its development through history'.[75] The practice of slavery under colonialism is thus continuous, and not a break, with its practice within Europe and this is what grounds racial capitalism as a global system. As Bjelić puts it, Robinson's assessment is forged

---

72 Ibid., p. 70.
73 Dušan Bjelić, 'Cedric J. Robinson, Black Radicalism and the Abolition of Europe', *Race & Class* 64, no. 4 (2023), p. 70.
74 Satnam Virdee, 'Racism and State Formation in the Age of Absolutism', *Historical Materialism* 31, no. 2 (2023): 104–35.
75 Bjelić, 'Cedric J. Robinson, Black Radicalism and the Abolition of Europe', p. 68.

by his 'militant critique of "Europe" as a civilisation founded in, grounded in, racism'.[76]

For Virdee, decolonial theory's 'encounter thesis'[77] has led to one of its more prominent exponents, Walter Mignolo, being able to conceive of the Nazi genocide only as 'a sort of one-off racist blowback into Europe', the result of 'the racialised logic of coloniality'.[78] According to Virdee, Aimé Césaire's argument that Europeans 'tolerated that Nazism before it was inflicted on them ... because, until then, it had been applied only to non-European peoples'[79] is submitted to a 'one-dimensional reading' by Mignolo.[80] Césaire's point, very similarly to Robinson's, is that Hitler 'is at the end of the blind alley that is Europe' and 'at the end of capitalism, which is eager to outlive its day, there is Hitler'.[81] Europe and capitalism conjoined produce racial fascism. The 'them' invoked by Césaire are not the Jews or the Roma and Sinti, the dissidents or the disabled, but the white Europeans who very quickly came to believe, much like the progressive Germans whose role as perpetrators is soon internalised as trauma, who *as perpetrators* were also the victims of Nazism; a reverse logic that continues to this day. After all, Césaire was the philosophy teacher who taught Fanon 'that the anti-Semite is inevitably a negrophobe'.[82] He thus deeply understood the futility of detaching colonial racism from the reverberations of its boomerang effect within Europe.

Taking these critiques of the limitations of decolonial theory's establishment of a sharp temporal and spatial boundary between Europe and the colonised world before and after 1492 supports Robinson's position. Racism for Robinson 'was not simply a convention for ordering the relations of European to non-European peoples but has its genesis in the "internal" relations of European

---

76 Ibid., p. 68.
77 Ibid., p. 69.
78 Virdee, 'Racism and State Formation in the Age of Absolutism', p. 107.
79 Aime Césaire, *Discourse on Colonialism* (New York: Monthly Review Press, 2000), p. 36.
80 Virdee, 'Racism and State Formation in the Age of Absolutism', p. 107.
81 Césaire, *Discourse on Colonialism*, p. 37.
82 Frantz Fanon, *Black Skin, White Masks* (New York: Grove, 1967), p. 122.

peoples'.[83] The dominant tendency to neglect this is not confined to decolonial theorists who at least foreground race as functioning 'as a modern/colonial technology of control and management [that] serves as an axis around which other structures of domination and exploitation revolve' after 1492.[84] In more mainstream and western Marxist accounts, in contrast, race is presented as 'a concomitant to slavery', 'racial discourses' having no presence 'before the advent of the Atlantic or African slave trade'.[85] Virdee criticises some western Marxist thinkers for operating with a purely functionalist view of race that narrowly identifies it in the relations of exploitation required by capitalism. Race is confined to the purely taxonomical and scientific from this viewpoint. It is assumed only to be possible after Enlightenment epistemologies enabled it to be thought up and is seen as confined to the realm of fictive ideas that can be manipulated for exploitative purposes at the whim of capitalists and rulers. Robinson, Virdee and Bjelić are asking a direct question, one also asked by Geraldine Heng, as discussed in this book's Introduction: How is it possible to assume that a phenomenon of such great historical force as race hatches fully formed at specific moments? Why would there be little curiosity, as Virdee puts it, to conduct the 'empirical investigation' to corroborate the thesis that race appears in pre-modernity, rather than dismiss it out of hand?[86]

The reason for stressing the differences between accounts of race that set its origins in 'deep time'[87] and those more common to a western Marxist tradition that are ill-equipped to explain the foundations and evolution of racialism is that it helps establish the bases for building an approach to antisemitism that conjoins it with prototypical Islamophobia, antiblackness and colonial racism and grounds it in racial capitalism. The long history of

---

83 Robinson, *Black Marxism*, p. 2.
84 Jairo I. Fúnez-Flores, 'Anibal Quijano: (Dis)Entangling the Geopolitics and Coloniality of Curriculum', *Curriculum Journal (London, England)* 35, no. 2 (2024): 288–306, p. 293.
85 Robinson, *Forgeries of Memory and Meaning*, p. 4.
86 Virdee, 'Racism and State Formation in the Age of Absolutism', p. 113.
87 Geraldine Heng, *The Invention of Race in the European Middle Ages* (New York: Cambridge University Press, 2018).

intra-European slavery is key, but so are the 'processes of racialisation that had already stained elite Western European cultures prior to the Spanish and English settlers' setting off on their so-called voyages of discovery'.[88] Virdee emphasises the Spanish absolutist regime's *Reconquista* which overthrew Muslim rule on the Peninsula and from which sprang forth the conquests of the Americas, setting in motion a 500-year history of colonisation, land conquest, population exchange and genocide. The need to bring to heel an 'increasingly multi-ethnic, multireligious, and multicultural population of Muslims, Jews, and Christians'[89] spurred the institutionalisation of practices of racial rule, for example, the punishment of social and sexual relations between Christians, and Muslims and Jews under this regime, women first and foremost. At an earlier time still, in one example of the mediaeval roots of race in Europe, Heng details how during the period leading up to the expulsion of the Jews from England 'Jews were marked off as racial subjects' in what she calls 'the first racial state known to Europe'.[90] Jews in the Middle Ages were established 'as the benchmark by which racial others were defined, measured, scaled, and assessed', leading to a 'near monomaniacal attention to congeal Jews as figures of absolute difference'.[91]

In a parallel scenario in the eighteenth and nineteenth centuries, 'the development of racist systems' in France and Germany drew upon 'colonial knowledge' which 'influenced the construction of the Jewish minority there'. Colonial travelogues and Caribbean slaveholding and plantation-owning eyewitnesses informed a comparable racist rendering of 'Blacks, Sinti and Roma, as well as Jews and indigenous populations outside of Europe'.[92] The earlier treatment of minoritised populations within Europe shaped colonial rule and returned to Europe, not in a linear or sequential manner but in a circulating movement that followed those of developing global racial rule within the world histor-

---

88 Virdee, 'Racism and State Formation in the Age of Absolutism', p. 117.
89 Ibid., p. 119.
90 Heng, *The Invention of Race in the European Middle Ages*, pp. 57–8.
91 Ibid., p. 55.
92 Bruns, 'Antisemitism and Colonial Racism', p. 103.

ical parameters established by the epistemologies underwriting racial capitalism. To consider these histories as wholly separate is to negate the multiple articulations on which race has depended then and now.

THE PRIMITIVE ACCUMULATION OF SAFETY (IN WHITENESS)

As our Palestinian people face the genocidal unmasking of the colonial world, we know that when colonizers talk about 'security,' they are in fact talking about 'violence.' In the colonial exchange – or the 'columbial' exchange, as Colón is Spanish for Columbus – security becomes violence, and violence becomes security. They merge and become the same word.[93]

A thesis that builds on both Robinson's and Heng's readings and complements those of Virdee and Bjelić helps us to construct a bridge between the deep history of intra-European racialism to which the racialisation of all minoritised peoples including Jews was key and the political utility of antisemitism in the current conjuncture. Siddhant Issar, Rachel Brown and John McMahon read Rosa Luxemburg's conceptualisation of primitive accumulation as crucial for understanding the violence of imperialism and as 'an organic and continuous part of capitalism'[94] alongside Heng and Robinson. They propose that 'the forging of a white, Christian, European subject (*homo europaeus*)' is fundamental to the primitive accumulation of capital, calling this the 'primitive accumulation of whiteness'. The primitive accumulation of whiteness is the first step, that which 'constitutes and structures racial capital-

---

[93] Devin G. Atallah, 'Beyond Grief: To Love and Stay with Those Who Die in Our Arms', *Institute for Palestine Studies*, 2023, https://tinyurl.com/2xj2uc7b (last accessed September 2024).

[94] Siddhant Issar, John McMahon, and Rachel H. Brown, 'Rosa Luxemburg and the Primitive Accumulation of Whiteness', in *Creolizing Rosa Luxemburg*, ed. Jane Anna Gordon and Drusilla Cornell (Lanham, MD: Rowman & Littlefield Publishers, 2021), p. 343.

ism'.[95] *Homo europaeus* is under constant, violent reconstruction both 'within and without Europe'.[96]

Whiteness, which is not 'a transhistorical category divorced from material social relations', must be continually (re)produced and accumulated in tandem with capital to bring about 'the bifurcation of human populations and their respective territories'.[97] Bifurcation, a concept also used by Said, complements the differentiation Robinson marks as the essential 'tendency of European civilization through capitalism'.[98] The primitive accumulation of whiteness helps explain how 'racial capitalism operates'.[99] It focalises the violence of this bifurcation noted by Houria Bouteldja when she addresses the Jews of North Africa whom France made 'French to tear you away from us, from your land, from your Arab-Berber identity. If I dare say so, from your Islamic identity', thus dispossessing her people of their Jewish neighbours.[100] Bouteldja is referring to the declaration of colonised Algerian Jews as French citizens in 1870 which initiated 'a process of deracination' of Jews 'from the people among whom they lived and with whom they shared language, cosmologies, beliefs, experiences, traditions, landscapes, histories, and memories'.[101]

Elaborating on the foundational significance of the primitive accumulation of whiteness within Europe, which is another way of casting Robinson's emphasis on intra-European differentiation as the seedbed of racial capitalism, Issar et al. turn to Geraldine Heng's discussion of 'Jewish racialisation'. Jews in Middle Ages England were both '"the engine of economic modernity" ... and subject to disproportionate taxation, land expropriation, stigma,

---

95 Ibid., p. 347.
96 Ibid., p. 350.
97 Ibid., p. 344.
98 Robinson, *Black Marxism*, p. 26.
99 Issar et al., 'Rosa Luxemburg and the Primitive Accumulation of Whiteness', p. 344.
100 Houria Bouteldja, *Whites, Jews, and Us: Toward a Politics of Revolutionary Love*, Semiotext(e) Intervention Series 22 (South Pasadena, CA: Semiotext(e), 2016), p. 60.
101 Ariella Aïsha Azoulay, 'Algerian Jews Have Not Forgotten France's Colonial Crimes', *Boston Review*, 2021, https://tinyurl.com/yyat4rck (last accessed January 2025).

and finally violence and expulsion underwritten by their racialization as not-white and not-English'. It is the coexistence of these two racialist practices towards the same population that connects 'race and proto-capitalism'.[102] The oppression of Jews cannot thus be reasoned in terms of class alone. The violence against Jews in twelfth- and thirteenth-century England, both physical and in the form of the power of the racial state, effectively turned them into property of the Crown.[103] This is exemplary of Hall's description of race as 'the modality in which class is lived'.[104] Hence, the participation of some Jews 'in commercializing processes is weaponized against them *through race*' whether or not individuals among them were involved in commerce'.[105] Fundamental to racial capitalism, the myriad practices enacted against them up to and including the expulsion of the Jews from England in 1290 made of them a 'racialized other against which a white subject coheres and accumulates'.[106] These operations were more than representational; Jews' property could be seized and repurposed to 'finance crusades against Muslims', the profits from which could be 're-circulated back through Europe'.[107] Jews and Muslims – here, the internal and external enemies – represented both the source of Europe's gathering wealth and the threat legitimating the violence essential to further accumulation.

The utility of the concept of primitive accumulation as introduced by Luxemburg is its continual nature. The 'primitive accumulation of whiteness and of capital constantly take new forms as the social relations undergirding them shift across time and space'.[108] This conceptualisation echoes how we speak of the recalibrating racial regime. It is now necessary to stitch the histories of Mediaeval

---

102   Issar et al., 'Rosa Luxemburg and the Primitive Accumulation of Whiteness', p. 351.
103   Heng, *The Invention of Race in the European Middle Ages*.
104   Stuart Hall, 'Race, Articulation and Societies Structured in Dominance', in *Sociological Theories: Race and Colonialism* (Paris: UNESCO, 1980), p. 239.
105   Issar et al., 'Rosa Luxemburg and the Primitive Accumulation of Whiteness', p. 352.
106   Ibid., p. 352.
107   Ibid., p. 353.
108   Ibid., p. 360.

Judeophobia, the racial rule of the Spanish absolutist state over Jews and Muslims, and the tendency to think of these, with slavery, as *prior* to race and capitalism to the contemporary politics of anti-antisemitism presented as the guarantee of Jewish safety.

Issar et al.'s discussion of the primitive accumulation of whiteness under neoliberalism reconnects these historical dimensions to the war on antisemitism. Homing in on the war on terror, they show how 'the resignification of *homo europaeus* ... works in tandem with the expansion of financial markets and for-profit security companies, ensuring the reproduction of racial capitalism', a process predicated on defining Muslims culturally as 'uncivilised, pre-modern, and terroristic'.[109] The ideological figuring of Muslims as a threat to the west drove the war on terror. The fruits borne by these ideological productions can be directly witnessed in Palestine where Zionists justify rape and massacre by calling Palestinians 'human animals' and 'rats or snakes'.[110] All the while, during the anti-migrant, Islamophobic and far-right riots that engulfed the UK, a British Tory leadership hopeful said it was '"wrong" to chant Allahu Akbar "without being arrested"'.[111]

The racial regime today functions to sever Jews from the 'Orientalist characterisations' that similarly target Arabs and Muslims and recruits us for the primitive accumulation of whiteness.[112] Jewish Zionists readily participate in this by using Jewish signifiers to install hegemony, literally slicing 'the Star of David into the cheek of 22-year-old Orwa Sheikh Ali, a young man they arrested from the Shu'fat refugee camp', one of innumerable similar incidents.[113] Over the course of two decades, the war on terror became

---

109 Ibid., p. 361.
110 Halil Ibrahim Medet, 'Israel Paints Palestinians as "Animals" to Legitimize War Crimes: Israeli Scholar', *AA*, 2023, https://tinyurl.com/89kvd7rz (last accessed January 2025).
111 Wilfred Frost, 'Tory Leader Hopeful Told Sky It Is "Wrong" to Chant Allahu Akbar "without Being Arrested"', *Sky News*, 2024, https://tinyurl.com/3apmmwjy (last accessed January 2025).
112 Issar et al., 'Rosa Luxemburg and the Primitive Accumulation of Whiteness', p. 362.
113 El-Kurd, 'Jewish Settlers Stole My House'.

the centrepiece of 'militaristic interventions for profit',[114] reciting racial scripts on the necessity of securing 'our' borders from those whose racialised status as primitive is said to prime 'them' to harm 'us'. The narrative in many ways was shaped by Zionists for whom, Edward Said wrote in 1979, the 'Palestinian struggle is essentially a terrorist attack on a Western democracy'.[115] But it did not originate with Zionism, a project of racial rule whose roots are grounded in western civilisation's will for destruction, dispossession and domination and whose foundational and continuing hegemony is propelled by the fact that it is 'an essentially Western ideology'.[116]

The extent of the west's need for Israel as 'the spearhead of imperialism in the region'[117] flows through a posture of defence of Jews who are resignified, not as *homo europaeus*, but as his (*sic*) proxy. The whole edifice of the west, through the conjoined wars on terror and antisemitism, via the myths of *Eurabia* and the 'Great Replacement', uniting elites clamouring to 'Stop the Boats' and street fighters brandishing Israeli flags while chanting 'Get them Out' in front of hotels housing asylum seekers, is on brazen display.

Whiteness today is perversely accumulated through the putative and performative securing of Jewish safety, the language in which the war on antisemitism is couched. University administrators calling police to violently halt protests do so in the name of Jewish students' safety even as Zionists threaten the lives of Palestinians and their supporters, as the stabbing to death of six-year old Wadea Al-Fayoume in Chicago in October 2023, among many other incidents, attests.[118] An example of how the signifier 'Jewish safety' functions to secure *homo europaeus* can be seen in

---

114 Issar et al., 'Rosa Luxemburg and the Primitive Accumulation of Whiteness', p. 361.
115 Edward W. Said, 'Zionism from the Standpoint of Its Victims', *Social Text*, no. 1 (1979), p. 54.
116 Ibid., p. 12.
117 Hassan Harb, 'Al-Aqsa Flood: Imperialism, Zionism and Reactionism in the 21st Century', *MR Online*, 2023, https://mronline.org/2023/11/09/al-aqsa-flood/ (last accessed January 2025).
118 Holly Langmaid, 'A 6-Year-Old Palestinian-American Was Stabbed 26 Times for Being Muslim, Police Say. His Mom Couldn't Go to His Funeral Because She Was Stabbed, Too', *CNN*, 2023, https://tinyurl.com/4cph9mhy (last accessed January 2025).

the French National Assembly's passage of the so-called 'Samuel Paty' article of the Anti-Separatism law in February 2021, which drew on the association of antisemitism with Muslims' purported separatism from French society and its values. The law allows for anyone who disrespects the 'values of the French republic', naming 'radical Islamism' in particular, to be imprisoned for three years or face a fine of 45,000 Euros. The Anti-Separatism law is necessary due to the insufficiencies of integration and of 'our fight against discrimination, and racism, such as antisemitism' which have bred 'our enemy'.[119] Here, Emmanuel Macron singles antisemitism out among racisms, and claims that it was the failure to act against it which created the conditions for the murder of Samuel Paty, who himself was not Jewish. The direct effect of the Anti-Separatism law can be seen in the dissolution of antiracist organisations, most notably the Collective against Islamophobia in France (CCIF) which was forced to cease operations in 2021. Despite no member of the association having ever been 'suspected or incriminated' of terrorism-related offences, 'the Minister of the Interior justified the dissolution of the CCIF by implicating it in the terrorist assassination' of Samuel Paty.[120] This is part of a more generalised crackdown on Muslim public life endemic in France but which has been more recently propelled by an anti-separatism agenda located within the logic of the war on antisemitism. The forced closure of the Pessac Mosque in Bordeaux in 2022, for example, followed 'vague accusations [of] "separatism" and "inciting hatred" against France and Israel'[121] here cemented in a united front against Muslims and the spectre of 'Islamoleftism'.

Ugo Palheta notes the thinness of the appeal to Jewish safety which was mobilised to pass the Anti-Separatism law, a 'new

---

119 Emmanuel Macron, 'La République en actes: discours du Président de la République sur le thème de la lutte contre les séparatismes', *Elysee.fr*, 2020, https://tinyurl.com/yhx7rkee (last accessed January 2025).
120 Abdellali Hajjat, 'Le Grand Retournement Du Droit Antiraciste: La Dissolution Paradoxale du Collectif Contre l'islamophobie en France', *Revue des Droits de l'homme* 25 (2024), p. 12. The translation from French is my own.
121 Ali Abunimah, 'Emmanuel Macron Wages War on France's Muslims', *Electronic Intifada*, 2022, https://electronicintifada.net/blogs/ali-abunimah/emmanuel-macron-wages-war-frances-muslims (last accessed September 2024).

demonstration of the coloniality of power' whose true purpose is to discipline Muslim cultural difference, not to deter the violence that befell Paty.[122] The same French minister of the interior, Gérard Darmanin, recalled Napoleon's aim to manage the Jews in France, 'some of whom practice usury and create unrest', citing the emperor 'delightedly' when he wrote, 'our aim is to reconcile the faith of the Jews with the duties of the French and to make of them useful citizens, remaining resolute to remedy the evil that many among them foment to the detriment of our subjects'.[123] State antisemitism is thus repurposed for ostensibly fighting it in the present, making Jews less, not more safe. The primitive accumulation of whiteness requires the persistence, and indeed the deepening of this insecurity. The war on antisemitism, hence, is meant to fail on its own terms.

PALESTINE IS THE PROBLEM TO WHICH DEFINITIONS ARE (NOT) THE SOLUTION (AFTER GILMORE AND GILMORE)

I have suggested that the survival of western civilisation is being outsourced to a Jewish proxy standing in for a *homo europaeus* battling an oriental threat that, like the Jew historically, is located within the western citadel, usurping him (*sic*) on his home turf. The Christians for Israel Australia website puts it directly: 'the canary is Israel, and the coalmine is Western Civilisation, based on its Judeo-Christian foundations'.[124] The west including Israel cannot, however, keep Jews safe, Joe Biden infamously admitting that 'if there weren't an Israel, every Jew in the world would be at risk'. It is clear then that western political interests are much more truth-

---

122   Fondation Frantz Fanon, 'Séparatisme: un pas de plus dans l'indignité', *Fondation Frantz Fanon*, 2021, https://fondation-frantzfanon.com/separatisme-un-pas-de-plus-dans-lindignite/(last accessed September 2024). The translation from French is my own.
123   Palheta, 'L'antisémitisme tourne toujours à droite.' The translation from French is my own.
124   Barry Rodgers, 'Israel Is Far More than the "Canary in the Coalmine"', *Christians for Israel Australia*, 2024, https://tinyurl.com/2juvpscm (last accessed September 2024).

fully reflected by Biden's words at an earlier time, 1986: 'Were there not an Israel, the United States of America would have to invent an Israel to protect her interests in the region.'[125] The war on antisemitism uses a discourse of Jewish safety to legitimise measures that subject Palestinians, as well as Black, Indigenous, anticolonial and by extension all radicals, to more and more repression and criminalisation. This should obviate the fact that appealing to institutions such as universities to apply non-selective, universal safety measures, while perhaps effective for exposing the patent hypocrisy at play, serves to divert resistance efforts.

One of the principal mechanisms used to accumulate whiteness in the perverse guise of 'safeguarding Jews' is the imposition of the IHRA working definition of antisemitism (IHRA-WDA), which in Germany[126] is treated effectively as a 'quasi-law'[127] despite its evolution in an atmosphere of mystification of its intent and function.[128] Antony Lerman provides an exhaustive account of the development of the working definition of antisemitism from its origins within the 'Israeli academic antisemitism industry',[129] via its publication by the European Union Monitoring Centre on Racism and Xenophobia in 2002. He moves on to its use by the US Department of State since 2010,[130] the reference to it in legal instruments such as the 2012 bill 'passed at the California state legislature' to condemn antisemitism on campuses, and to its adoption by the

---

125 Nur Ibrahim, 'Did Biden Say If Israel Didn't Exist, the US "Would Have to Invent an Israel"?' *Snopes*, 2024, www.snopes.com//fact-check/joe-biden-1986-israel/ (last accessed September 2024); Ali Harb, 'Biden Faces Ridicule for Saying He's Been "Very Supportive" of Palestinians', *Al Jazeera*, 2024, https://tinyurl.com/yp3vk4xs (last accessed September 2024).
126 Anna Younes and Hanna Al-Taher, 'Erasing Palestine in Germany's Educational System: The Racial Frontiers of Liberal Freedom', *Middle East Critique* 33, no. 3 (2024): 397–417.
127 Hanna Al-Taher and Anna-Esther Younes, 'Lebensraum, Geopolitics and Race – Palestine as a Feminist Issue in German-Speaking Academia', *Ethnography* 25, no. 2 (2024), p. 147.
128 Antony Lerman, *Whatever Happened to Antisemitism? Redefinition and the Myth of the 'Collective Jew'* (London: Pluto Press, 2022).
129 Ibid., p. 124.
130 'Defining Antisemitism', *United States Department of State*, 2024, www.state.gov/defining-antisemitism/ (last accessed August 2024).

International Holocaust Remembrance Alliance in 2016.[131] Since then, the IHRA-WDA has underpinned a proliferation of legalistic, rather than always strictly legal, institutional initiatives to embed a definition that presents 'Israel-related antisemitism'[132] as the predominant threat posed to a 'collective Jew' inextricable from Israel,[133] whose religion has been blasphemously commandeered by Zionism.[134]

The working definition has been widely criticised for being 'bewilderingly imprecise',[135] its focus on 'a certain perception of Jews' making it incumbent on those charging antisemitism to prove the intentions of those charged; 'notoriously difficult' to do.[136] Beyond the definition itself, the examples of antisemitism provided, seven out of eleven of which relate to criticisms of Israel, are used 'to police and censor the Palestinian critique of Israel'.[137] In April 2024, the US House of Representatives passed the Antisemitism Awareness Act, a bill that would expand the federal definition of antisemitism, effectively codifying the IHRA-WDA in the Civil Rights Act. The act is the 'federal anti-discrimination law that bars discrimination based on shared ancestry, ethnic characteristics or national origin'.[138] The passage into law would make Zionist a protected category akin to race, ethnicity, nationality or

---

131 Lerman, *Whatever Happened to Antisemitism?* p. 130.
132 Dina Porat, Giovanni Quer, and Talia Naamat, 'The IHRA Working Definition of Antisemitism: Criticism, Implementation, and Importance', *INSS*, 2021, www.inss.org.il/publication/ihra/ (last accessed September 2024).
133 Anna-Esther Younes, 'Islamophobia in Germany National Report', *European Islamophobia Report* (Türkiye, 2018), p. 390.
134 Lerman, *Whatever Happened to Antisemitism?* p. 5.
135 David Feldman, 'Will Britain's New Definition of Antisemitism Help Jewish People? I'm Sceptical', *Guardian*, 2016, https://tinyurl.com/2huv63km (last accessed January 2025).
136 Jonathan Judaken, *Critical Theories of Anti-Semitism*, New Directions in Critical Theory (New York: Columbia University Press, 2024), p. 10.
137 Muhannad Ayyash, 'The IHRA Definition Will Not Help Fight Anti-Semitism', *Al Jazeera*, 2020, https://tinyurl.com/cnh3et9w (last accessed September 2024).
138 Al Jazeera, 'US House Passes Controversial Bill That Expands Definition of Anti-Semitism', *Al Jazeera*, 2024, www.aljazeera.com/news/2024/5/1/us-house-passes-controversial-bill-that-expands-definition-of-anti-semitism (last accessed August 2024).

religion, a codification of the 'new antisemitism' thesis that already exists in institutional practice. However, as the proponents of the IHRA-WDA at the Kantor Center for the Study of Contemporary European Jewry at Tel Aviv University write tellingly, it is actually unnecessary for the definition to be integrated into law because it works with already existing legal instruments 'relating to racism, hate speech, and discrimination by clarifying what anti-Jewish hatred is and how it manifests itself in today's context'.[139]

In fact, the IHRA-WDA does not mention the aspects 'which have for the most part defined anti-Semitism for more than 500 years', preferring to dwell in the realm of 'feelings'.[140] Its amorphousness and polyvalence are by design. They make the IHRA-WDA the perfect instrument for establishing anti-antisemitism as the mechanism for rhetorically enclosing *homo europaeus* in a gated community shielded from 'outside agitators' understood as anyone protesting colonial violence and genocide, far beyond solely Palestinians. Settler colonialism comes home to roost in Europe via its 'features of capturing, conquering, surveilling, and securing *land* and *people* …, the very techniques developed by Europeans to control populations in the colonies' and used against Palestin-

---

139 The use of hate speech legislation against antiracists is a well-established practice. For example, the closure of the Collective against Islamophobia in France (CCIF) was partially justified by accusing it of 'provoking racist hatred'. The first time Western Australia's new racial vilification laws were applied in 2006 was in the case of an Indigenous teenager who called a woman a 'white slut'. According to the Anti-Defamation League, the popular chant 'from the river to the sea, Palestine will be free' is a 'hateful phrase'. In April 2024, the chant was deemed antisemitic by a resolution passed by the United States House of Representatives. Increasingly, as noted in Chapter 3, 'hate speech', defined by groups such as the ADL, serves to drive a Zionist agenda to discipline and punish any and all speech in favour of Palestine. Porat et al., 'The IHRA Working Definition of Antisemitism'; ADL, 'Slogan: "From the River to the Sea Palestine Will Be Free"', *Anti-Defamation League*, 26 October 2023, www.adl.org/resources/backgrounder/slogan-river-sea-palestine-will-be-free (last accessed February 2025); TOI Staff, 'US House Resolution Condemns Chant "From the River to the Sea, Palestine Will Be Free"', *Times of Israel*, 17 April 2024, www.timesofisrael.com/us-house-resolution-condemns-chant-from-the-river-to-the-sea-palestine-will-be-free/ (last accessed February 2025); Emmaia Gelman, 'The Anti-Defamation League Is Not What It Seems', *Boston Review*, 2019, www.bostonreview.net/articles/emmaia-gelman-anti-defamation-league/ (last accessed February 2025).
140 Younes, 'Fighting Anti-Semitism in Contemporary Germany', p. 260.

ian and other 'populations' who are 'surplus' to the west's economic requirements.[141] Their existence as 'intruder-figures'[142] justifies the increasingly militarised policing of public and domestic spaces and the building of more fortified borders employing surveillance and death-making materiel often 'field tested' and 'field proven' on Palestinians.[143]

The IHRA-WDA's role is to generate the antisemite the west requires for its own reproduction.[144]

Given this use of the IHRA-WDA, we should ask whether there is a definition of antisemitism that can have any other function. As Lerman notes, there is enough available scholarship to 'undermine fatally the credibility' of the IHRA-WDA.[145] This has not happened because of an acceptance that antisemitism had to undergo redefinition given the purportedly widespread nature of the 'new antisemitism', another way of saying that the antisemite of post-1967 was no longer a white Christian. That this contradicts the facts is irrelevant. As Younes and Al-Taher show, after a white supremacist in the East German town of Halle, intending to attack a synagogue on the eve of Yom Kippur, killed two passersby, German university leaders, citing the IHRA-WDA, moved to ban the boycott, divestment and sanctions campaign, branded 'Israel-related anti-Semitism'. This conflation of white supremacist terrorism and 'a grassroots human-rights movement (BDS,

---

141 Anna-Esther Younes, 'Palestinian Zombie: Settler-Colonial Erasure and Paradigms of the Living Dead', *Janus Unbound: Journal of Critical Studies* 2, no. 1 (2022): 27–46.
142 Ibid.
143 Visualizing Palestine, 'Field Tested: Elbit Systems', *Visualizing Palestine*, n.d., https://visualizingpalestine.org/visual/field-tested-elbit-systems/ (last accessed August 2024).
144 That this is true can be observed in the widespread mandating of antisemitism training across the US in schools and universities at the start of the 2024–25 school year in direct response to the protests in solidarity with Palestine that mushroomed earlier in that year. Cf. Troy Closson, 'New York City Schools Will Teach about Antisemitism and Islamophobia', *New York Times*, 2024, https://tinyurl.com/5n8ra43r (last accessed January 2025).
145 Lerman, *Whatever Happened to Antisemitism?* p. 172.

Boycott Divest Sanctions) initiated by Palestinians'[146] further indicates that the move to define antisemitism can do nothing to counter actually existing antisemitism. That is not its purpose.

The purpose of defining antisemitism anew to equate it with anti-Zionism and effectively obscure its westernness is first and foremost to 'clarify the targets of the struggle against it',[147] not to stop violence against Jews.

Recognising the intellectual weaknesses of the IHRA-WDA and understanding the extent of its politicisation, a group of academics developed and signed the alternative Jerusalem Declaration on Antisemitism (JDA). For its Jewish proponents, the JDA is 'far from perfect',[148] and 'subject to important criticisms',[149] but ultimately necessary to curb the political force of the IHRA-WDA. Palestinian critics such as Muhannad Ayyash and Samer Abdelnour pointed out the JDA's Orientalism, expressed in the 'silencing and erasure of Palestine and Palestinians',[150] and its ultimate failure to sever criticisms of Israel from antisemitism.[151] Today, these debates and counterpoints appear quaint. The JDA was and remains an elite project of liberal Zionism as can be seen in one of its principal proponents, the Israel studies academic Yair Wallach, who spuriously claims that even if those on the Jewish left 'reject Zionism as an ideology, they are still tied to Israeli society'.[152] Practically, its failure to constitute a 'decisive challenge to the IHRA'

---

146 Al-Taher and Younes, 'Lebensraum, Geopolitics and Race', p. 146.
147 Lerman, *Whatever Happened to Antisemitism?* p. 162.
148 Brian Klug, 'The Jerusalem Declaration on Antisemitism', *The Nation*, 2021, www.thenation.com/article/society/jerusalem-declaration-antisemitism-ihra/ (last accessed January 2025).
149 Barry Trachtenberg, 'Why I Signed the Jerusalem Declaration on Antisemitism', *Jewish Currents*, 2021, https://tinyurl.com/2vym56aw (last accessed January 2025).
150 Muhannad Ayyash, 'The Jerusalem Declaration on Antisemitism Is an Orientalist Text', *Al Jazeera*, 2021, https://tinyurl.com/y2cfuaas (last accessed January 2025).
151 Samer Abdelnour, 'The Jerusalem Declaration's Fatal Flaw', *Jewish Currents*, 2021, https://jewishcurrents.org/the-jerusalem-declarations-fatal-flaw (last accessed January 2025).
152 Yair Wallach, 'Jewish Progressives Are Deeply Critical of Israel, Yet Inextricably Tied to It', *New Statesman*, 2023, https://tinyurl.com/rkvdzkxa (last accessed January 2025).

is because it fights on 'the IHRA's ground – matching one prolix definition with another'.[153] While understanding the evolution of antisemitism is important, setting a definition in stone is beside the point of defeating it.

The JDA's obsolescence is grounded in its failure to situate antisemitism as a western project that requires the wholesale dismantlement of western supremacy for it to be overcome. Ayyash's critique goes in this direction by exposing the infeasibility of considering antisemitism as an 'internal Jewish question' severed from the fact that 'the destruction of Jewish life in Europe was dealt with by destroying Palestinian life in Palestine'.[154] However, as Younes claims in her conversation with self-named 'universalist Jew', Susan Neiman,[155] it is more correct to think of Palestinian displacement as being the result of 'an already (European-wide) existing settler colonial project' to solve demographic problems rather than being a consequence of the Nazi genocide.[156] Ayyash concludes that 'to properly name and tackle antisemitism means properly naming and tackling colonial modernity and the settler colonisation of Palestine'.[157] However, there is a glossing over of antisemitism's place in such a colonial modernity conjointly with other racialisms, and the function instruments such as the IHRA-WDA and the JDA play in perpetuating the role assigned to Jews therein. The fact that this role is readily taken on by liberal (Zionist) Jews does not negate the fact that any form of participation in Zionism functions not to free Jews from antisemitism, but to further entrench our subordinate role within western civilisation by literally trapping us within its logics and shutting the door on solidarity with other negatively racialised peoples.

If the search for the 'gold standard' definition of antisemitism fails as a measure to tackle actually existing antisemitism, because the remit of both the IHRA-WDA and the JDA, despite claims

---

153 Lerman, *Whatever Happened to Antisemitism?* p. 173.
154 Ayyash, 'The Jerusalem Declaration on Antisemitism Is an Orientalist Text'.
155 Susan Neiman and Anna-Esther Younes, 'Antisemitism, Anti-Racism, and the Holocaust in Germany: A Discussion between Susan Neiman and Anna-Esther Younes', *Journal of Genocide Research* 23, no. 3 (2021): 420–1, p. 423.
156 Ibid., p. 427.
157 Ayyash, 'The Jerusalem Declaration on Antisemitism Is an Orientalist Text'.

made by the latter's signatories, is to provide justification for Zionism and to symbolically (in the west) and materially (in Palestine) erase Palestinians, either overtly or more insidiously, then is there a scenario in which a definition can escape these pitfalls? Is one way to counter the hegemony of antisemitism definitions to institutionalise counterposed definitions of anti-Palestinian racism?

Racism, as the founder of the Palestine Research Center Fayez Sayegh made clear, is 'inherent in the very ideology of Zionism and in the basic motivation for Zionist colonization and statehood'.[158] Thus, 'wanting to create a purely Jewish, or predominantly Jewish, state in an Arab Palestine in the twentieth century could not help but lead to a colonial-type situation and to the development (completely normal, sociologically speaking) of a racist state of mind'.[159] The state built on the dispossession of Palestinian land and life is a 'racial state'.[160] It is specifically, often violently, antisemitic against non- and anti-Zionist religious Jews. It is also ideologically antisemitic in that its foundations exist in the embrace of the antisemitic interpretation of Jews as a problem for Europe. Theodor Herzl famously wrote in his treatise *The Jewish State*,

> The Jewish question persists wherever Jews live in appreciable numbers. Wherever it does not exist, it is brought in together with Jewish immigrants. We are naturally drawn into those places where we are not persecuted, and our appearance there gives rise to persecution. This is the case, and will inevitably be so, everywhere, even in highly civilised countries – see, for instance, France – so long as the Jewish question is not solved on the political level.[161]

---

158 Fayez Sayegh, *Zionist Colonialism in Palestine* (Beirut: Palestine Liberation Organization Research Centre, 1965), p. 21.
159 Maxime Rodinson, *Israel: A Colonial-Settler State?* (New York: Pathfinder, 1973), p. 77.
160 Ronit Lentin, *Traces of Racial Exception: Racializing Israeli Settler Colonialism* (London: Bloomsbury, 2018).
161 Theodor Herzl, *The Jewish State: An Attempt at a Modern Solution of the Jewish Question*, The Internet Archive, 1904, https://tinyurl.com/bdvatj3t (last accessed January 2025).

Applying 'two different standards of judging and evaluating' the 'reactions of the colonised peoples' based on belonging to a given group, in this case Jews, 'using both anti-Semitic and Zionist criteria', 'is called racism'.[162] It is racist to apply a different standard to Jews and to Palestinians; to assume that Jewish suffering, now or in the past, trumps Palestinian suffering. It is on this basis that advocates of the naming of anti-Palestinian racism as a form of racism, allied to but distinct from anti-Arab racism,[163] Orientalism and Islamophobia, which also affect Palestinians,[164] have made their case.[165]

Monitoring of repression against Palestinians and their supporters in Europe since 7 October 2023, reveals that 'anti-Palestinian racism coalesces around exclusion and punishment of anything visibly Palestinian'. The mere 'displaying of Palestinian symbols, including wearing the keffiyeh scarf or colours of the Palestinian flag' can lead to arrest across the capitals of Europe.[166] In addition to this intense policing of Palestinians and the criminalisation of Palestine in the public spaces of the west tout court, anti-Palestinian racism is defined by the Palestinian and Jewish scholars Yasmeen Abu-Laban and Abigail Bakan as constituting a form of 'racial gaslighting' which has three components: denial, operating through power inequities and victim blaming. As they themselves highlight, 'it is not a new insight to analyse the actions of Israel's defenders as racist toward Palestinians';[167] neither is it new to note the ways those targeted by racism are denied their experience and blamed for their own predicament. These are standard features of racism. Nonetheless, their paper draws out the specific ways in which they operate in

---

162   Rodinson, *Israel*, p. 78.
163   Steven Salaita, 'Beyond Orientalism and Islamophobia: 9/11, Anti-Arab Racism, and the Mythos of National Pride', *CR: The New Centennial Review* 6, no. 2: 245–66.
164   Yasmin Abu-Laban and Abigail Bakan, 'Anti-Palestinian Racism and Racial Gaslighting', *The Political Quarterly* 93, no. 3.
165   Ibid.; Ayyash, 'The IHRA Definition Will Not Help Fight Anti-Semitism'; Liz Fekete, 'Anti-Palestinian Racism and the Criminalisation of International Solidarity in Europe', *Race & Class* 66, no. 1 (2024): 99–120.
166   Fekete, 'Anti-Palestinian Racism', p. 106.
167   Abu-Laban and Bakan, 'Anti-Palestinian Racism and Racial Gaslighting', p. 509.

the case of Palestinians, noting that the IHRA-WDA is an example of a form of racial gaslighting that operates to 'legitimise censorship and repression of Palestinian voices'.[168] The key form this takes is through what Ayyash calls the 'toxification of the Palestinian as a racialized being who can only bring toxicity to the struggles of other racialized minorities'.[169] Hence, not only does anti-Palestinian racism involve intense disciplining, repression and, as we have seen, state and popular violence, both in Palestine and in the west (albeit at different scales), it also couches Palestinians and the issue of Palestine as having a negative impact on antiracism.

Palestinian critique, 'developed and advanced from the lived experiences of Palestinians for the purpose of liberating Palestinians',[170] is construed as inherently antisemitic by anti-Palestinian racists. Ayyash emphasises the epistemic racism that not only denies the Palestinian experience, but diminishes its significance in relation to antisemitism whose magnitude is presented as far outweighing it. The idea that 'the Palestinian is constituted as the manifestation of an epistemology that is inherently bigoted and racist towards Jews' is not unique to anti-Palestinian racism; 'Black scholars who are situated within Black studies, for example, are constantly attacked for an alleged anti-White racism.'[171] Moreover, it is vital to note the extent of the recrimination of Black protest in the US specifically. Of the 300 federal cases emanating from the 2020 'George Floyd protests', 70 were jailed for an average of 27 months and ten for over five years.[172] Therefore, it is not entirely evident that 'the specific denial of Palestinian racialization: the idea that only racism against Palestinians is not really racism' is unique to anti-Palestinian racism.[173]

---

168 Ibid., p. 514.
169 M. Muhannad Ayyash, 'The Toxic Other: The Palestinian Critique and Debates about Race and Racism', *Critical Sociology* 49, no. 6 (1 September 2023): 953–66.
170 Ibid., p. 954.
171 Ibid., p. 955.
172 Alanna Durkin Richer, Michael Kunzelman, and Jacques Billeaud, 'Records Rebut Claims of Unequal Treatment of Jan. 6 Rioters', *AP News*, 2021, https://tinyurl.com/3bs2xrmr (last accessed January 2025).
173 Ayyash, 'The Toxic Other', p. 958.

As I argued in *Why Race Still Matters*, a major dynamic of racism is not only its denial but its rescripting as 'not racism',[174] a dynamic that could be noted acutely in the racist responses to Black-led mobilisations against state violence. 'All lives matter' is the same discursive tactic as *Jews Don't Count*, the book by the British Jewish comedian, David Baddiel.[175] Baddiel's specious argument that 'Jews don't count as a proper minority'[176] is a clear projection of Ayyash's 'only racism against Palestinians is not really racism'.[177] Jews like David Baddiel are only writing books about Jews 'not counting' because Zionism works overtime to present Palestinians as an existential threat to the 'collective Jew', making them blameable for an antisemitism invented and promulgated in Europe by Europeans.[178] This recalibration of the racial regime hides and denies the conjoined Orientalism that structured the lives of Arabs, Roma and Sinti, Jews, African and colonised Indigenous people starting in pre-modern times and constructs a primordial, perennial and ordained enmity between us. In contradistinction, Palestinian scholars have generally been scrupulous in their recognition that, as Said put it, 'Jewish and Palestinian suffering exist and belong to the same history.'[179] Ayyash confirms, anti-Palestinian racism exists 'within larger structures of racism, orientalism and colonialism'.[180]

---

174 Lentin, *Why Race Still Matters*.
175 David Baddiel, *Jews Don't Count: How Identity Politics Failed One Particular Identity* (London: TLS Books, 2021). Indeed, in 2020 Baddiel posted on his X account that 'The need to constantly follow the phrase "anti-Semitism" with "and all forms of racism" is the Left's All Lives Matter.' Baddiel, X, 2020, https://x.com/Baddiel/status/1321815707970084864?mx=2 (last accessed January 2025).
176 Rebecca Nicholson, 'David Baddiel: Jews Don't Count Review – a Doc so Shocking It Sounds Like a Siren', *Guardian*, 2022, https://tinyurl.com/4h2uxzan (last accessed January 2025).
177 Ayyash, 'The Toxic Other', p. 958.
178 The platforms extended to Baddiel to complain about the lack of attention to antisemitism, which include a spin-off documentary, a podcast, multiple international appearances, and translations of his book to German and Portuguese, negate his thesis and expose it for being the racist-inflected (specifically antiblack) rant against antiracism that it is.
179 Edward W. Said, 'Nationalism, Human Rights, and Interpretation', in *Reflections on Exile and Other Essays* (Cambridge, MA: Harvard University Press, 2002), p. 435.
180 Ayyash, 'The Toxic Other', p. 959.

A lesson can be extracted from the evolution of antisemitism, the term coined by the self-named 'patriarch of antisemitism', the German 'radical left-winger', Willem Marr.[181] Marr's opposition to Jewish emancipation from an antiliberal perspective transformed into an espousal of a 'racist conception of difference' following the decade he spent in Central America.[182] Marr's description of Indigenous and African peoples in a racistly bestial language informed his 'transition from expounding anti-Judaism using religious arguments to antisemitism based on race' and declaring Judaism completely incompatibile with Germany due to its 'racial particularity'.[183] Developing on this, Marr came to see the 'Jewish body' as imbued with 'Negro blood', complementing a tradition going back to the Middle Ages which characterised Jews as Black.[184] Notable is the recursivity of the move from Jewishness to blackness and back again, thus infusing the foundational definition of antisemitism – a racist endeavour with a clear political aim of denying rights to Jews – with the abject imprimatur of blackness, ubiquitous in all forms of negative racialisation.

What is notable is the convergence of racialising practices, not so much their divergence. Moving then to the urgent questions of the present, but with these historical lessons in mind, what purpose does distinguishing anti-Palestinian racism serve when, per the Palestinian prisoner network Samidoun, 'Gaza Is a Strategy, Not Just a Place'?[185] Today, 'Palestinian critique' is not 'made by Palestinians only'.[186] What we thus have is a wholesale counterinsurgent attack on Palestine and what it symbolises, a fight brought to bear by the west against all that challenges its continued hegemony. As the last two chapters have shown, while Zionists make considerable effort to appropriate Indigeneity and colonise the Black civil rights struggle, both the Palestinian plight and most crucially the

---

181 Bruns, 'Antisemitism and Colonial Racism', p. 109.
182 Ibid., p. 111.
183 Ibid.
184 Ibid., p. 112.
185 Samidoun, 'Gaza Is a Strategy, Not Just a Place', *Samidoun: Palestinian Prisoner Solidarity Network*, 2023, https://samidoun.net/2023/11/gaza-is-a-strategy-not-just-a-place/ (last accessed January 2025).
186 Ayyash, 'The Toxic Other', p. 954.

resistance resonates deeply with both the experiences of racism and colonisation, and the fight to overthrow them by Black and Indigenous peoples, and all those in the sights of the racial state.

Academic inquiries into anti-Palestinian racism do much to illuminate the particularities of the phenomenon, and to my mind, sharpen our collective understanding of the racial regime and Palestine's place within it as an object of intense state repression. However, should that translate into a call for institutions to recognise the existence of anti-Palestinian racism as a response to the wholesale adoption of the IHRA-WDA? One example of this is the demand for anti-Palestinian racism to be included in the redraft of the Canadian government's Anti-Racism Strategy. Jasmin Zine argues that such a recognition would 'provide a groundwork for developing policies and practices so institutions can identify and challenge anti-Palestinian racism through their equity, diversity and inclusion initiatives'.[187] However, Chapter 3 has shown how such initiatives exist to control antiracism and to contain more radical elements by promoting a counterinsurgent narrative of 'good' versus 'bad' antiracism. In the current conjuncture, all solidarity with the Palestinian resistance movement is disciplined and criminalised because it is seen, correctly, as posing a threat to the normative order. Any desire to be granted space within these counterinsurgent apparatuses should be looked upon with suspicion.[188]

We can think about the problem I pose through an analogy with Gilmore and Gilmore's discussion of the anti-state state whose working can be seen in the 'expanded use of cages as catch-all

---

[187] Jasmin Zine, 'Anti-Palestinian Racism Needs to Be Included in Canada's Anti-Racism Strategy', *The Conversation*, 2024, https://tinyurl.com/ybxpf5eu (last accessed January 2025).

[188] The Arab Canadian Lawyers Association's report into anti-Palestinian racism suggests it is a tool to 'identify, articulate and address' it. However, its note that 'naming APR is not to be weaponized or be used to impede good faith discussions on Palestine/Israel' reveals its acceptance of the established terms; that speaking about or taking action for Palestine is always already construed as potentially antisemitic. We should thus be wary of these liberal demands. Arab Canadian Lawyers Association and Dania Majid, 'Anti-Palestinian Racism: Naming, Framing and Manifestations', *Arab Canadian Lawyers Association*, 2022, https://tinyurl.com/2sus3swr (last accessed January 2025).

solutions to social and political problems'.[189] 'Crime', under neoliberalism, they write, is portrayed as 'the problem for which prisons are the solution'.[190] To posit that crime is an out-of-control problem does not have to be coherent or demonstrable; it is only required that it makes sense to enough people 'whose opinions count'.[191] 'The term "crime" has become a code word for "Black and other people of color"', as the New Afrikan former political prisoner Sundiata Acoli remarks.[192] In the white supremacist settler colony of the US, this makes it clear in whose interest crime is posed as a problem. Similarly, in Palestine, the Israeli regime's prisons are sites of torture, rape,[193] and state killing as countless cases such as that of the political prisoner Walid Daqqa, left to die of cancer after 38 years of imprisonment on 7 April 2024, attests.[194] As Basil Farraj writes, 'a popular saying in Palestine goes, "In every Palestinian home, you would find a prisoner or a former prisoner." This is not far from reality.'[195] The 2018 Great March of Return, in which Gazans marched to the military boundary enclosing them only to be met with brutal Israeli force, was conceived as an attempt to break out of the prison of Gaza of which 'its prisoners had enough'.[196] Prisons are both a technology of colonial containment and of state investment. Israeli prisons, like those in other

---

189   Ruth Wilson Gilmore and Craig Gilmore, 'Restating the Obvious', in *Indefensible Space: The Architecture of the National Insecurity State*, ed. Michael Sorkin (New York: Routledge, 2008), p. 260.
190   Ibid., p. 266.
191   Ibid., p. 266.
192   Sundiata Acoli, 'An Updated History of the New Afrikan Struggle', in *Look for Me in the Worldwind: From the Panther 21 to 21st-Century Revolutions*, ed. Matt Meyer and dqui kioni-sadiki (Oakland, CA: PM Press, 2017).
193   Lisa Hajjar and Basil Farraj, 'State Secrets and Crimes – Rape at Israel's Sde Teiman Prison', *MERIP*, 2024, https://merip.org/2024/08/state-secrets-and-crimes-rape-at-israels-sde-teiman-prison/ (last accessed January 2025).
194   Basil Farraj, 'In Memory of Walid Daqqa', *Jadaliyya*, 2024, www.jadaliyya.com/Details/45912 (last accessed January 2025).
195   Basil Farraj, 'How Israeli Prisons Terrorize Palestinians – Inside and Outside Their Walls', *SAPIENS*, 2024, https://tinyurl.com/3zwjzsw5 (last accessed January 2025).
196   Hamza Abu Eltarabesh, 'Was Great March of Return the Best Way to Confront Israel?' *Electronic Intifada*, 2022, https://tinyurl.com/npmtkmve (last accessed January 2025).

settler colonies and racial states, are equally sites of economic exploitation as they are sites of brutality.[197]

Just as prisons are justified to an Israeli public through the mass characterisation of Palestinians as a terrorist threat, in the US, as Gilmore and Gilmore make clear, the explosion in prison building which could be seen acutely in the California Valley in the two decades from 1982 to 2002 had to be justified by the invocation of an explosion in crime that did not stand up to statistical scrutiny. Rather, prison-building was one way for both capitalism and the state to reinvent themselves under the new economic conditions imposed by globalisation.[198] What is posed to the public as a problem changes over time based on political requirements and most people accept the propaganda they are served.[199] The racial regime provides the requisite narrative of threat, not least via mass 'copaganda', to smooth this acceptance.

Gilmore and Gilmore situate the problematisation of crime in the late twentieth century with the anti-communism of earlier decades, reproduced in the 'red scare tactics used in the 20th century ... making a come-back to scare people from publicly supporting Palestine or participating in anti-imperialist resistance movements'.[200] Gilmore and Gilmore replace 'crime' with 'Communism' and 'prison' with 'War', writing, 'crime (Communism) is a problem that can only be solved by prison (War)'.[201] How can we

---

197 'Crucially, economic exploitation is key to entrenching Israel's military occupation and administering its colonial regime to control, exploit and quell rebellion. Palestinians are made to finance the cost of their subjugation by paying the occupiers to demolish their homes or have an executed relative's body returned for burial, and by paying the heavy fines imposed by the military courts on Palestinian prisoners. In 2016 alone, fines averaged half a million shekels ($145,000) per prisoner (Euro Med Human Rights Monitor 2017). Thus Israel's colonial judicial system is a central building block in the systematic racialisation and economic exploitation of the Palestinians.' Ronit Lentin, 'Racial Regimes and White European Jewish Supremacy as Property', *Journal of Holy Land and Palestine Studies* 23, no. 2 (2024), pp. 232–3.
198 Ruth Wilson Gilmore, 'The Other California (with Craig Gilmore)', in *Abolition Geography: Essays towards Liberation*, ed. Brenna Bhandar and Alberto Toscano (London: Verso, 2022), pp. 242–58.
199 Ibid.
200 Samidoun, 'Gaza Is a Strategy, Not Just a Place'.
201 Gilmore, 'The Other California (with Craig Gilmore)', p. 252.

transpose this to the question of definitions? Following Gilmore and Gilmore, we might write this as an equation.

'x is a problem to which y is the solution.'

'Palestine is a problem to which definitions are the solution' can be replaced by 'Jews were the problem (read: question) to which Zionism was the solution.' Zionism was the favoured solution for antisemitic imperialists[202] and continues to be 'a condensation of Western colonial and imperial power'.[203] Thus, the institutionalisation of definitions of antisemitism, even if one can be drafted that is successful in avoiding a tethering to Zionism, is a mechanism for managing a manufactured problem, like the problem of communism or the problem of crime: *the problem of Palestine*.

Here is where we return to Cedric Robinson's 'The First Attack Is an Attack on Culture'. It is not coincidental that Robinson chose to illustrate the issue he wished to communicate with Marx's essay 'On the Jewish Question'. Marx was drawing attention to the fact that the Jew of antisemitism did not exist but was created 'from the entrails of civil society' which 'ceaselessly engenders the Jew'.[204] Thus, the problem was not the Jews but the society that required them. We cannot expose the real meaning of that which is posed as the problem by recapitulating the terms that pose it as a problem in the first place. More bluntly, we cannot resist colonialism, racism and fascism with concepts elaborated by colonisers, racists and fascists. It is incumbent on us to refuse the terms,[205] like Marx who

---

202   Faris Yahya Glubb, *Zionist Relations with Nazi Germany* (Beirut: Palestine Research Center, 1978).
203   As Ajl writes, 'the harder and stronger Palestinians fight for liberation, the more, like lightning bolts of ever-increasing luminosity, they bring the relief of the world system into clearer view'. Max Ajl, 'Palestine's Great Flood: Part I', *Agrarian South: Journal of Political Economy* 13, no. 1 (2024): 62–88, p. 63. See also Joseph Massad, 'Why Blaming the Israel Lobby for Western Middle East Policies Is Misguided', *Middle East Eye*, 2024, https://tinyurl.com/57zy6nhs (last accessed January 2025).
204   Robinson, 'The First Attack Is an Attack on Culture', p. 70.
205   On this, I am drawn to Fred Moten's ambivalence regarding the call for universities to issue statements of solidarity with the Palestinians. In a conversation with Jared Ware on *Millennials Are Killing Capitalism Live!* he recalled his earlier

refused the terms established by German society. 'He could not accept them because he understood them to be distortions, because he understood them to be very pointed, very clearly related to distortions, to the oppression of a people.'[206] The only revolutionary solution, Robinson suggests Marx is advocating, is to reverse these terms and to 'transform the culture which it is opposed to in order to emerge a very different culture than existed before'.[207] The attack on culture is an attack on 'the meanings of things'.[208] In Gilmore and Gilmore's terms, this is the abolitionist demand, one which refuses the terms that prisons are necessary and militates not to reform them but to end their use.

The 'leadership', Robinson writes, 'always emerges after the mass'.[209] Definitions are an elite demand, not a popular one. If our aim is the dismantlement of the systems of oppression (imperialism, racial capitalism) which require *problems* (the Jew, Palestine), our aim should not be to replicate the solutions (Zionism, definitions) but to destroy them.

The recalibration of the racial regime restitches old cloth; our task is to painstakingly unstitch it, not to thread the needle on its behalf.

---

comment on statements of support for Black people after the murder of George Floyd in 2020. They were 'like the bad breath of the white world, you know, all up in our face'. On 11 November 2023, Moten told Ware, 'as far as the statement thing is concerned, look, I mean, you reminded me of something that we said, you know, years ago about this statement, being what, the bad breath of whiteness or something like that'. Jared Ware and Fred Moten, '"A Dam against the Motion of History" – Fred Moten on Palestine & the Nation-State of Israel', *Millennials Are Killing Capitalism Live!* 2023, https://tinyurl.com/resjm9yv (last accessed January 2025).
206 Robinson, 'The First Attack Is an Attack on Culture', p. 71.
207 Ibid., p. 73.
208 Ibid., p. 70.
209 Ibid., p. 74.

Index

1619 98, 101
1619 Project, the 92, 93-110
1776 63, 96, 98, 100, 104
1776 Report, the 97, 99
1776 Unites 96

Abdelnour, Samer 251
abolitionism 167, 262
abolitionism (slavery) 64, 74, 79
Aboriginal Passport Ceremony 181
Aboriginal Tent Embassy 120
Abu-Amer, Majd 199
Abu Eltarabesh, Hamza 259
Abu-Jamal, Mumia 166
Abu-Laban, Yasmeen 254
Abu-Lughod, Lila 198, 200-1
Abunimah, Ali 245
Abu-Saad, Ismael 210
Academy for Science and Freedom 67
   see also Hillsdale College
Accoli, Sundiata 259
Ackman, Bill A. 138
Adi, Hakim 157
Advanced Placement African American History 85
   see also history
Affirmative Action 39, 52, 59, 60, 66, 165
African American Policy Forum, the 165
   see also Crenshaw, Kimberlé W.
African people(s) 20, 21, 73, 75, 91, 95, 257
Agbetu, Toyin 78
Ahmed, Sara 93
AIATSIS 182
Aitlhadj, Layla 53, 55
Ajl, Max 125, 149, 217-18, 261
Alahmed, Nadia 137, 168
Al-Aqsa Flood 174

Alareer, Refaat 30
Alawi, Najma Sharif 175
Al-Bulushi, Yousuf 7, 17, 223
Alexander, Neville et al. 155
Al-Fayoume, Wadea 244
Alkalimat, Abdul 156
Allam, Lorena 37, 110
Allday, Louis 169
'All Lives Matter' 256
Al-Taher, Hannah 247, 250-1
Altman, Jon 206
AMCHA Initiative, the 144-5
American Civil War, the 15, 109
American Indian Movement, the 192, 199
American Revolution, the 104
Amrov, Sabrien 195
Anderson, Pat 185, 186
Angelos, James 233
Anike, Bola 57
antiblackness 94, 109, 161, 238
anticolonialism 131, 140, 156, 158, 168, 218
   Zionist misuses of 214
   see also Penslar, Derek
Anti-Defamation League, the (ADL) 136, 139-40
   anti-terrorism laws 142
   effect on antiracism 142
   hate speech 249
   liberal antiracism 140-1, 142
   statistics 228
   use of DEI 142
anti-Palestinian racism 227, 254-8
   see also Abu-Laban, Yasmin; Ayyash, M. Muhannad; Bakan, Abigail
antiracism 5, 25, 39, 44, 71
   and the *Anti-Defamation League* 142

appropriation of 150
attacks on 50, 60
counterinsurgent use of 28, 132, 197, 258
institutional 51
liberal 140
liberal cooptation of 64
training 44–5, 57, 126
state 129
universalist 108
Zionist involvement in 193
antiracist
consciousness 21
ideas 8
pedagogy 42
antisemitism
and colonial modernity 252
definitions of 196, 226, 227, 250–3
as European 134, 144, 256
as exceptionalised 224–5, 233
guilt and 225
'Israel-oriented'/'related' 228, 248, 250
as lived experience 231
medieval practices of 21
'new' 143, 144, 221, 229, 249, 250
politics of, the 222, 223
racial capitalism and 223, 224, 238
state 246
against US Jews 144
as 'weaponised' 223–4, 228, 236
as western 252
anti-antisemitism 26, 147, 221, 226, 249
see also war on antisemitism
Antisemitism Awareness Act 248
Aotearoa 180
Apartheid
South Africa 21, 155–6
Israel 155
Arab-Canadian Lawyers Association 258
Attal, Gabriel 85
Attalah, Devin G. 240
Australia 36–8, 92, 113–122
Australian national curriculum 88
ANZACs 121

see also history wars, the; Indigenous Voice to Parliament
Ayyash, M. Muhannad 251–2, 255–6
Azoulay, Ariella Aïsha 241

Baddiel, David 256
Badenoch, Kemi 56
Baerbock, Annalena 230
Bakan, Abigail 254
Balibar, Étienne 26–7
Ballas, Anthony 102, 104, 107
Bandung Conference, the 203
Bannerji, Himani 64
Barakat, Rana 195
Bargallie, Debbie 153, 154, 202
Barker, Joanne 183, 190
Barrows-Friedman 145
Bastani, Aaron 175
Beaman, Jean 40
Behrendt, Larissa 114
Bell, Derrick 45, 153, 163
Ben Gurion University 210, 211
Benjamin, Ruha 152
Berkon, Michelle 182
Bernstein, David L. 133, 136, 147
Bhabha, Homi 215–16
Bhandar, Brenna 7, 201
Biden, Joe 246–7
bifurcation 241
Biggar, Nigel 80
bin-Wahad, Dhoruba 4, 9, 28, 29
Birch Tony 77, 93, 110, 115–19
see also history wars, the
Bjelić, Dušan 236, 238, 240
Black
'analytics' 10
humanity 73
male body 15
scholars 91, 105, 162, 214, 255
solidarity with Jews 137
students 53
blackness 81–2, 94, 158, 257
Black Liberation Army 132
Black Lives Matter 43, 55
Black Panther Party 136

//
INDEX

Black people 1, 10, 46, 52, 86, 91, 93, 96, 100, 103, 105, 106, 109, 162, 192
  accused of antisemitism 133–4, 136
  critical race theory and 163, 164
    see also Bell, Derrick; Crenshaw, Kimberlé; Curry, Tommy
  identification with Palestinians 136, 137
  Jewish allyship with 137
  state killing of 9
Black Peoples Union 189
Black Power 192
Black Radical Tradition xvi, 4, 7, 17, 120
  imprisoned 167
Black radical scholarship 22
  as resistance 18
Black radical thinkers/intellectuals 5, 14, 76, 91, 107
Black Studies 156, 162, 164, 167, 255
  attacks on 157
  Third World Strike for 157
  see also Rojas, Fabio; Rabaka, Reiland; Wynter, Sylvia
Black Study 162
  see also Myers, Joshua; Wynter, Sylvia
Black thought 162
Blain, Keisha 127, 214
Blainey, Geoffrey 116–17
Blake, Felicia 150
Blanquer, Jean-Michel 40, 54
Bogues, Anthony 90
borders 222, 250
Bouteldja, Houria 56
  Algerian Jews 241
  imperialism 160
  class collaboration 56
  'state philosemitism' 129
Brager, Solomon 197
Bragman, Walker 67–8
Braverman, Suella 26, 77–9
Brayboy, Bryan 154
Brown, Michael 3, 137

Bringing Them Home report, the 113, 118
  see also Australia; Stolen Generations
Britain 83
  colonialism 81
  colonial alliance with Arab leaders 75
  slavery 78, 79, 83
  support for abolition 63, 74
  support for Zionism 125
Briond, Joshua 193
Bruns, Claudia 239, 257
Burden-Stelly, Charisse 46, 107, 110, 134, 169
Burris, Greg 161, 170
Burton, Orisanmi 81–2, 114, 119
  'institutionalisation of dissent' 151
Buscher, Frank M. 232
Business Council of Australia, the 189
Bynum, Victoria et al. 97–8

Cabral, Amílcar, 91, 100
  'The Weapon of Theory' 4, 167
Callai, Adi 27
capital 5, 8, 20
  finance 10, 15, 16, 56
  settler 202
capitalism 10, 15, 17, 19, 72–4, 78, 192, 193, 202
  anti- 58
  antisemitism and 223
  colonial 61, 206
  dispossession as a permanent feature of 24
  Europe and 237, 241
    see also Césaire, Aimé; racial capitalism; Robinson, Cedric J.
  exploitation 52, 238
  film and 10
    see also Forgeries of Memory and Meaning
  history of 17, 23–4
  primitive accumulation 240
  and race 22
  Zionism as the last phase of 189
    see also Leon, Abram

Capitol Hill riot 126
carcerality 37, 51, 54, 225
Caribbean 63, 73, 90
Carlson, Bronwyn 81
Carlson, Tucker 44
   'Tucker Carlson left' 107
Carson, Ben 94
Castan, Ron 182–3
Center for Constitutional Rights 142
Centre for Contemporary Cultural Studies 151
Césaire, Aimé 173, 174, 237
Charnley, Alex 110, 200
Chatterjee, Partha 215
Child Q 54
Christians for Israel Australia 246
Chumley, Cheryl K. 11
Christian missionaries 75
cinema 10
   see also film
Citizens for Renewing America 95
Civil Rights Act 59
civil rights movement, the 137
civilisation 74, 75
   European 20, 22, 74, 76, 235, 237
     see also Robinson, Cedric; Du Bois, W.E.B.
   'war to save western' 27
     see also Herzog, Isaac
   western 128, 150, 184, 194, 222, 226
   role of Jews for 236, 246
   and Zionist ideology 215, 225, 244, 252
civilising mission 14, 61, 66
Clark, Anna 115–17
class 103, 106, 159
   collaboration 105, 108
     see also Horne, Gerald; Bouteldja, Houria; Sakai J.
   exploitation 62
   solidarity 103
   struggle 101
   unity 102
Coalition for Liberated Ethnic Studies 163
Cohen-Hunter, Jasper 195
COINTELPRO 57

colonial
   expansion 74, 75
   exploitation 216, 260
colonialism 9, 15, 19, 38, 65–6, 73, 75, 78–80 113, 181, 236
   attempted destruction of culture under 191
   in *Black Marxism* 178
   capitalist 191
   Critical Race Theory's neglect of 132, 159, 166
   European 203, 231
   Fanon, Frantz and 173, 191
   racial 39, 87
   racial capitalism and 62
   resistance to 42
   and scholasticide 30
   teaching about 25, 41, 147
   Zionist 27
coloniality 42, 43, 49, 121, 161, 204, 205, 237
   of power, the 246
colonisation 111, 121
   of Africa 73
colonised people 16, 23, 87, 91, 100, 177, 254
   descendants of 54
   idea of Jews as a 194
colonised thinkers, scholars 91, 107
colourblindness 36, 58, 61
colour-blindness 57
Combrink, Tamira 79
Comrade Motopu 107
communism 168, 260–1
   anti-communism 52, 110, 260
   anti-red 92
   red-baiting 46
Communist Party, the 13
conjunctural
   analysis 25–6
   crisis 43
     see also Gramsci, Antonio; Hall, Stuart
Cop City 129
Coulthard, Glen 176–7, 202, 206
counterinsurgency
   and attacks on Palestine 140, 257

INDEX

against Black radicalism 46
and control of antiracism 258
counterinsurgent tactics and strategy 132, 137, 169, 177
'critical' 176
   see also Sinanan, Kerry
and diversity, equity and inclusion 142
and prisons 114
as a response to anticolonialism 177
and the use of critical race theory 123
the war on critical race theory as a technique of 70
and Zionism 136, 138, 150
   see also Rodríguez, Dylan
Counterinsurgency Field Manual, the 128
Covid-19 23, 67, 68, 81
   lockdown 54, 220
CPAC Conference 108
Crenshaw, Kimberlé W. 45
   and critical race theory 161, 164–5
   silence on Palestine 165–6
Crenshaw, Kimberlé W. et al. 61, 134, 159–60
Critical Race Theory: The Key Moments Writings that Formed the Movement 159
crime 260
   and neoliberalism 259
   see also Gilmore, Ruth Wilson; Gilmore, Craig
Critical Ethnic Studies Editorial Collective, the 157–8, 163
critical race
   application to Indigenous issues 154
      see also Kauanui, J. Kēhaulani
   ideology 35, 44, 45, 51
   scholars 49
   scholarship 154
   studies 131
   theorists 61
critical race theory 9, 18, 35, 46–7, 49, 55, 68, 97, 127, 152
   bans on 38, 44
   and book bans 83

campaigns against 165
defence of 127
Department of Defence approach to 125–6, 128, 214
   see also Milley, Mark
founders of 159, 164
and methodological nationalism 156
   see also Goldberg, David Theo; Meghji, Ali
synergy with decolonial approaches 153
   see also Meghji, Ali
teaching of 60, 71
CROTOAN 148
CRT 42, 47, 50, 56, 59–60, 64–71, 95, 101, 123, 161
   anti- activists 60
   as antisemitic 129, 142
   and analysis of whiteness as privilege 154
      see also Kauanui, J. Kēhaulani
   and critique of liberalism 127
   and globalisation 159
   and higher education institutions 166
   anti- ideologies 61
   anti- lobby 57, 136
   anti- rhetoric 9, 82
   common misreading of 101
   conflations with postcolonialism 158
      see also Curry, Tommy
   contrast with Black Studies 159
   counterinsurgent instrumentalisations of 123
      see also counterinsurgency
   epistemological limitations of 132
   defence of 164
   deployment in education 163–4
      see also Curry, Tommy
   institutional legitimacy of 151
   legal origins of 151, 156
   'nationalist and revolutionary fervour' of 158
      see also Curry, Tommy

neglect of anti-colonialism and anti-imperialism 153–61
scholars 45
 silence of in the face of Zionist attacks 163
 and US democracy 164–5
 see also Crenshaw, Kimberlé W.
 rhetorical themes of 147
 Zionist counterinsurgency and 138, 150
Cruse, Harold 159, 167
culture war(s) 56, 65, 116, 122
current conjuncture, the 6, 25, 65, 240, 258
curriculum
 Australian national 85, 87, 88–9, 92
 Third World 163
 indigenising the 202
 and the war on critical race theory 36, 38, 42, 48, 50, 95
Curry, Tommy 158, 161, 163–4
Curthoys, Ann 81

Dahomey 78
Dan David Prize 213–4
Dana, Tariq 194
Darmanin, Gérard 246
Daqqa, Walid 259
Davis, Megan 186
decoloniality 158, 214
decolonial theory 236–8
decolonisation 118, 121, 122, 155, 175–77, 190, 191
 domestication of 212, 214, 218
 non-performative 177
dehumanisation 51, 73, 74, 161
DEI 131, 138, 148
Deitelhoff, Nicole et al. 227, 234–5
definitions 246–62
Deloria, Philip J. 82, 84
denial
 of anti-Palestinian racism 254, 255
 of history 88
 Holocaust 220
 of racism 38, 73, 256
 of truth 111
 violence of 112

Democratic Party, the 102, 165
Delgado, Richard 60, 66, 159–60
De Santis, Rick 45, 48, 67, 85
 Don't Say Gay Act 48
 Stop W.O.K.E Act 45, 48, 95
De Vos, Betsy 69
developmentalism 24
differentiation 20, 21, 72
 intra-European 241
 see also racial capitalism
Discovery Institute, the 44
Dische-Becker, Emily 231
Disney 11–13
 De Santis' attack on 45, 48
 and 'race discourse' 12
 workers at 11
Disney, Abigail 11
dispossession 87, 124, 142
 of the Bedouin 211
 of land 24, 62, 121
 Indigenous 18, 49, 100, 121, 159, 183, 190
 myth of settler 187
 of Palestinians 253
 and recursivity 18, 115
 see also Nichols, Robert
 Zionist 244
diversity 26, 41
 as compatible with racial capitalism 9
 'hire' 45
 racialised 9
 social 55
 see also Forgeries of Memory and Meaning
 training 44, 45
 'viewpoint' 78
diversity, equity and inclusion 44, 131, 258
 and the ADL 142
 office of 143, 169–70
 mechanisms to punish pro-Palestine speech and action 143
 programmes 127
 and racial regime recalibration 142
 and Zionism 142, 163
Don't Divide Us 35, 36, 58, 69

INDEX

Dubois, Laurent 63
Du Bois, W.E.B. 5, 76, 104, 105, 110
   Black Reconstruction in America 91, 109
   'The Propaganda of History' 95, 99, 109
   and truth 103
   colonial capitalism 66
   Darkwater 111
   double consciousness 164
   liberalism 61–2
   Nasserism 168
   The World and Africa 73–5, 79
   history and truth 102–3
   Zionism 137, 168
Dunning, William 108–9

Elias, Hannah 90
Elhalaby, Esmat 213–16
elites 216–17
El-Kurd, Mohammed 235, 243
Elsana, Morad 211
empire 62, 99
   British 75, 81
   US 58, 162
enslaved people 72, 86, 97, 100
   see also slaves
Erakat, Noura 137, 161
Ethnic and Racial Studies 146
ethnic studies 123
   anticolonial stance of 148
   as an attack on Jews 129, 146–8
   attacks on 50
   California Assembly Bill 101 145
   institutionalisation of 158
   origins of 157
   Zionist attacks on 144–48, 197
      see also Anti-Defamation League, the; AMCHA; StandWithUs
epistemology 84, 104
   critical race
   race as 224
      see also Black Marxism
   and Palestinian critique 255
      see also Ayyash, M. Muhannad
   western 85

   of 'white time' 89
   see also Mills, Charles W.
eugenics 66, 108
Europe 72, 73, 76, 106, 162, 222, 224, 226, 234, 239, 241, 249, 254
   advancement due to 76
   and decolonial theory 236–7
      see also Bjelić, Dušan; Virdee, Satnam
   destruction of Jewish life in 252
   dominance of 73, 79
   Euro-Americans 106
   mercantilism in 72
   and Nazism 237
      see also Césaire, Aimé
   Robinson's 'militant critique' of 237
      see also Bjelić, Dušan
   securing of 226
   and Zionism 197, 215
eurocentric 17, 183, 234
   conception of racism 86
   Marxist accounts of slavery 22
European 80
   colonial benevolence 61
   elections 225
   Enlightenment 173
   fascist movements 5
   feudalism 17, 19, 20
   integration 225
   invaders 75, 105
   Jewry 234, 236
   modernity 81
   need for order 91
      see also Robinson, Cedric J.
   origins of racial capitalism 19
   wealth 62, 72, 73, 79, 80, 242
      see also Fanon, Frantz
   white 237
   white supremacist 129
Europeans 225, 249
European Union Monitoring Centre on Racism and Xenophobia 247
Evans, Raymond 112
exploitation 14, 18, 19, 20, 22, 62, 72, 73, 78, 87, 91, 195
   super- 16

FAIRStory curriculum, the 136–7
Falkof, Nicky 82
Fanon, Frantz 106, 154, 173–5, 216–17
   and Césaire on antisemitism 237
   First Congress of Negro Writers and Artists 102
   'Racism and Culture' 102
   Wretched of the Earth, The 61, 80, 191
Farraj, Basil 259
Farrelly, Terri 81
fascism xii, 5, 13, 15, 21, 23, 25, 26, 28, 100, 108, 226, 227, 261
   'democratic' 4
      see also bin-Wahad, Dhoruba
   French 221
   'more secure' 53
      see also Gilmore, Ruth Wilson
   racial 10, 29, 237
   and racial capitalism 52
      see also Robinson, Cedric J.
   reconstruction of 58
   as reform 4
      see also Jackson, George
   and Zionism 218
FBI, the 57, 60, 140
Fekete, Liz 254
Feldman, Deborah 231
Feldman, Noah 228
Ferguson, Missouri 3
Fernando, Nilmini 202
film 10
   US industry 9, 14
   Hollywood 11, 13, 191
   jungle 13–14, 192
   plantation 13, 192
      see also Robinson, Cedric J.; Horne, Gerald
Fischbach, Michael R. 142
Fischer, Leandros 232
Floyd, George 1, 35, 36, 45, 50–1, 80–1, 255, 262
Foley, Gary 183, 185
   history 120
   self-determination 208
Fondation Frantz Fanon 246
Foucault, Michel 170

France 39, 54, 56, 61, 239
   anti-Separatism law 245
   Collective Against Islamophobia in 245, 249
   extreme-right in 221
      see also Palheta, Ugo
   Islamophobia in 245
   and North African Jews 241
      see also Bouteldja, Houria; Azoulay, Ariella A.
   Jews in 246, 253
      see also Herzl, Theodor
   La France Insoumise 220
Fratelli d'Italia 25, 222
Freedom of Speech 71, 226
FreedomWorks 68
Friedland, Naomi 146
Friends of Zion Museum 178–9
Frontier Wars, the 121
Fúnez-Flores, Jairo 42, 238
Furedi, Frank 108

Gaetz, Matt 125–6
Gannon, Kevin 99
Garcia, J.L.A. 141
Gawenda, Michael 183–5
Gay, Claudine 45, 138–9, 144
Gelman, Emmaia 142, 144, 147, 249
Gelman, Emmaia et al. 142
'gender ideology' 45
genocide 42, 43, 78, 88, 249
   CRT and 154
   cultural 121
   Gaza 2, 27, 30, 55, 128–130, 132, 138, 169, 175, 204, 213, 222, 226, 229–31
   of Indigenous people 100, 112, 183
   Israel's in Palestine 27, 28, 143, 172
   justifications of 193
   Nazi, the 21, 231, 232, 237, 252
   of the Ovaherero and Nama 232
   of the Roma and Sinti 232
   scholars' silence about 151–2, 161, 201
   universities 210
   and the war on CRT 149
George, Murray, 186

INDEX

Germany 227–236, 250
  attacks on Muslims in 228
  guilt for the Holocaust 232–3
  Sozialraum 228–9
  Staatsräson 228
Giannacopoulos, Maria 118
Gilley, Bruce 80
Gilmore, Craig 258–62
Gilmore, Ruth Wilson 53
  abolition 43
  anti-state state, the 258–62
  'organised abandonment' 6, 66
  'vulnerability to premature death' 121
  see also Gilmore, Craig
Glissant, Édouard 89–90
Glubb, Faris Yahya 261
global Intifada, the 170, 172
Goldberg, David Theo 74
  relational and interactive approach to race 132, 152, 158
  methodological nationalism of CRT 154–6
  racial progressivism 74
Gouldhawke, Mike 191
Gove, Michael 85
Graham, Mary 84–5
Gramsci, Antonio 25
Great Barrington Declaration, the 67
Great March of Return 259
Great Replacement, the 28, 200, 244
Griffiths, Billy 209
guerrilla tactics (history) 110, 115
  see also Birch, Tony
Guinier, Lani 60, 65
Guyatt, Nicholas 98
  see also 1619 Project, the

Haaretz 134, 135
Habermas, Jürgen 234
Hage, Ghassan 118
Hall, Stuart 5, 23, 24, 26, 43, 242
  and the current conjuncture 24–5
  'Encoding/Decoding' 47
  Europe 234
  Palestine 234
  Policing the Crisis 50

Haiti 14, 62–4
Haitian Revolution, the 63, 105
  see also Horne, Gerald
Hajar, Lisa 259
Hajjat, Abdellali 245
Hamas 124–5, 126, 133, 145, 165, 175, 212, 220
Hames, Richard 220
Hannah-Jones, Nikole 93, 94, 96, 97–8, 100, 102–5
  see also 1619 Project, the
Hannan, Daniel 78–9
Hansen, Bue Rübner 232
Hanson, Pauline 38
Harari, Noah Yuval 82
Harb, Hassan 244
Harney, Stefano 210
Hartman, Saidiya 104
Hassan-Nahoum, Fleur 179
hate 140–1, 172
  see also Anti-Defamation League, the
Healey, Kieran 79, 175
Heng, Geraldine 238, 240
  deep time 238
  medieval roots of race 21, 239, 241–2
  multiple temporalities 21
  taxonomy of human difference 22
Heritage Foundation, the
  Project 2025 48, 70
  Project Esther 140
Hermann, Christoph 225
Herzl, Theodor 215, 253
Herzog, Isaac 27, 219, 226
Hesse, Barnor 10, 86
heterodox thinking 80
Heterodox Academy, the 144
Hickey, TJ 117, 199
Hill, Marc Lamont 50, 135, 137, 161
Hillsdale College 67
history 18, 20, 76, 77–123
  American 101
  Australian 121
  Black 144, 156, 162
  Black radical perspectives on 92
  'black armband view of' 116

colonial 116, 117
of colonialism 216
French 221
heterochronic approach to 90
   see also Elias, Hannah
of power 171
Indigenous 115, 119-20, 180
   see also Australia; Birch, Tony;
   Foley, Gary
Indigenous perspectives on 92
of invasion and dispossession 88, 121
Marxist analysis of 92
new 77, 90-3, 122
   see also Robinson, Cedric J.
presentist reading of 92
   see also presentism
of racial colonialism 87
reclaim 2, 82
retelling of 76
teaching of 86, 88
theories of 91
theory of 109
   see also Robinson, Cedric J.
'the tide of' 183-4
and truth-telling 39
US 14, 64, 98, 107, 109
world 72
history wars, the 76, 92, 110, 112-17, 119-21
   see also Australia; Howard, John
historians 2, 99, 109, 119
   Australian 116-17, 121
   liberal 93, 116
   settler 121, 122
      see also Birch, Tony
   white 93, 116
historiography 85, 100
   Black 107
   Black radical 104
   European 80, 234, 236
      see also Hall, Stuart; Robinson, Cedric J.
   new 116
   western 20
History Reclaimed 2, 82-3
Hochuli, Alex 108

Holmwood, John 53, 55
Holocaust, the 82, 124
   German memorialisation of 230-1
Homo europaeus 19, 226, 240-1, 243, 244, 246, 249
Horne, Gerald 64, 104, 105, 107, 108
   class collaboration 56, 105
   Euro-Americans 100
   Haitian Revolution, the 63
   Hollywood 13
   'our friends on the left' 107
   Texas 49
   The Counterrevolution of 1776 64, 104
   'unpaid workers' 102, 105
Howard, John 38, 81, 113, 116, 184-5
   see also Australia; History wars, the
human 62, 63
   anti- 84
   difference 21-2
      see also Heng, Geraldine
   management 170
   racialised vision of the 7, 15
      see also Wynter, Sylvia
human rights 63, 74
humanity 84, 102, 138, 170
   'indivisible from the collective relation' 34, 170
      see also Robinson, Cedric J.
   inhumanity 90
   lack of 161
      see also Wynter, Silvia
humanities, the 90, 161
   see also Robinson, Cedric J.; Wynter, Sylvia
hypocrisy 60, 121, 127, 236, 247

identity politics 107, 200
ideology 56, 72
   Herrenvolk 204
   liberal 64, 65
   modernist 61
   racial 60, 71
Ignatiev, Noel 106
imperialism 8, 52, 62, 123, 127, 136, 168, 262

INDEX

Black Panther Party position against 136
centrality of race for 28
Israel's role for 149, 172, 244
liberal 215
US capitalist 190
violence of 240
Ince, Onur 62
Indigeneity 113
　authentication of 183
　Bedouin 210–11
　blood quantum 204–5
　and colonialism 195, 206, 216–17
　DNA 204–5
　Jewish claims to 178, 187, 190, 198, 200, 204
　　see also Jews
　Palestinian 199, 200
　uses of for the racial regime 180, 181
　Zionist appropriation of 132, 190, 193, 195, 196, 199, 200, 218
Indigenisme 1
Indigenising initiatives 178, 201, 207, 208, 209, 212
　see also universities
Indigenous 7, 22, 53, 92
　acknowledgements of country 200–1
　anticolonial nationalism
　　see also Coulthard, Glen
　blockades 202
　child removal 111, 112, 113–14
　children 37, 111, 112, 119
　critique 24, 116
　flag 181
　land rights 212
　recognition 177, 178, 189
　scholars 107, 118
　soldiers 180
　sovereignty 200, 205, 208
　studies 117
　workers 20
　youth 54, 93, 115, 118
Indigenous Coalition for Israel 179, 180
Indigenous dispossession 49, 100
　as central to racial capitalism 190
　and recursivity 18
　see also Nichols, Robert
Indigenous Embassy Jerusalem 179, 181
Indigenous people 82, 91, 93, 105, 113–15, 118, 119, 120, 121, 205–6
　attempted assimilation of 187
　massacres of 111, 121
　relationship to land 190–1
　treaty with 184
Indigenous Voice to Parliament 178, 186–7
　'Black No' campaign 187
　racist No campaign 189
　Yes23 187, 190
Institute for the Critical Study of Zionism, the 147
International Holocaust Remembrance Alliance working definition of antisemitism (IHRA-WDA) 148, 247-52
　and anti-Palestinian racism 255, 258
　as a carceral tool 226
　codification in the Civil Rights Act 248
intersectionality 165, 197
Islamic identity 241
Ioanide, Paula 150
Islamogauchisme 40
Islamoleftism 1, 39, 245
Islamophobia 40, 225, 238, 245, 248, 249, 254
Islamophobic 130, 220, 243
Israel 28, 30, 125, 126, 130, 136, 137, 146–7, 149, 155, 173–6, 178–82, 185, 188, 194, 197–9, 204, 210–12
　far-right support for 220, 244
　German support for 227–32, 234–5
　lobby 149, 261
　as a racial state 253
　studies 214
　and the west 225, 246–7
　US backing of 149
　see also Zionism

Israeli 133–5, 138, 193, 201
   'academic antisemitism industry' 247
     see also Lerman, Antony
   antisemitism 253
   economic exploitation of Palestinians 260
   scholars 215
Issar, Siddhant et al. 240–44

Jackson, George xii, 4, 174
Jackson, James 130, 230
Jackson, Lauren Michelle 98
James, C.L.R. 154, 234
James, Joy 166–8, 171
Jarrett, Uncle Roger 111–12
Jerusalem Definition of Antisemitism, the (JDA) 227, 251–2
Jew, the collective 248, 256
Jews 82, 198, 203, 233
   amalgamated with Zionism 144, 233
   Kostümjude 222
   in Germany 233, 257
   in France 246
   in Middle Ages England 241–2
     see also Heng, Geraldine
   as a proxy for the western subject 226
   racial capitalism and 242
   and racial regimes 231
   relationship to blackness 257
   subordinate role within western civilisation 252
   the west's relationship to 223
   and whiteness 147
   as woke 135
'Jewish safety' 148, 230–1, 243, 244–5, 247
   and western preservation 236
Jews Indigenous to the Middle East and North Africa (JIMENA) 197, 204
Jimmy, Elwood et al.
   Towards Braiding 201–2
Johnson, Walter 139
Joint Chiefs of Staff 125, 128
Judaken, Jonathan 228, 248

Judeophobia
   Medieval 242–3

Kamola, Isaac A. 68, 71, 83
Kanafani, Ghassan 198
Kantor Center for the Study of Contemporary European Jewry 249
Kaplan, Elina 135
Kauanui, J. Kēhaulani 153–4, 205
   see also Indigeneity
Kaufmann, Eric 41, 53, 68
Kedar, Alexandre et al. 212
Kelley, Robin D.G. xiv, 124
   anti-wokeness 1, 2, 5, 35, 43, 50
   Black-Palestine solidarity 137
   Martin Luther King 57–8
   settler colonialism 155–6
Kendi, Ibram X 45, 127
Kennedy, Randall L. 163
Khatib, Safa 228
Kinchela Aboriginal Boys' Training Home 110
   KBHAC 111
King, Martin Luther Jr. 57–60, 134, 137
   see also Kelley, Robin D.G.
Kirk, Gabi 197
Klug, Brian 251
Koch Brothers, the 67–8, 71, 107–8
Konishi, Shino 117
Koshy, Susan et al. 24, 190
Kotch, Alex 67–8
Kundnani, Arun 64, 127, 226
Kunoth-Monks, Ngarla 186, 187
Kunoth-Monks, Rosalie 186
Kwaymullina, Ambelin 84

labour 16, 73–4
   'aristocracy' 106
   see also Sakai, J.
land back 51, 122, 189
Langton, Marcia 187, 196
la paperson 209
Lawrence, Peter D. 147
Leibler, Arnold Bloch 207
   Indigenous Solidarity Network 188
Leibler, Mark 182–5, 187–9, 213

INDEX

Lenin, Vladimir Ilyich 203–4
Lentin, Alana 9, 23, 52, 153, 154, 224
   Why Race Still Matters 26, 223, 226, 256
Lentin, Ronit 188, 260
Leon, Abram 189
Leonardo, Zeus 29
Le Pen, Marine 221
Lerman, Antony 247–8, 250–2
Lest We For/Get Over It 92–3, 119, 121
Levin, Sarah 197–8, 199, 204
   See also JIMENA
Levine, Mark 173–4
Levy, Daniel 174
liberalism 10, 62, 64, 71
Liddle, Catherine 115
Lindsay, James 46, 49, 95–6, 135
Lipsitz, George 87
Litvin, Yoav 140
Liu, Catherine 103, 107–8
Lorber, Ben 179
Losurdo, Domenico 64
Lowe, Kevin 89
Lowenthal, David 121
Luxemburg, Rosa 240, 242

Mabo decision, the 182, 183, 184
   see also Australia; Indigenous
Mabo, Eddie 182
Macintyre, Stuart 115–17
Mackaman, Thomas 101
Macron, Emmanuel 40, 85–6, 245
Magennis, Franck 170
Malloy, Sean 142
Manjapra, Kris 105
Mansell, Michael 186
Mansour, Noura 180
Marr, Wilhelm 257
Marx, Karl 19, 24, 109, 219
   'On the Jewish Question' 223, 235–6, 261–2
   see also Robinson, Cedric J.
Marxist 99
   antiracists 106
   Black 23
   vulgar 19
   Eurocentric accounts of slavery 22
   western 238
Massad, Joseph 203–6
   see also self-determination
Matsuda, Mari 164
Maynard, Robyn 43
Mazzig, Hen 197
McKinnon, Crystal 181
McQuire, Amy 114, 115, 187
McWhorter, John 71–2
Mearsheimer, John 150
Meghji, Ali 153, 156
Mélenchon, Jean-Luc 220
Mignolo, Walter 237
migration 181
   intra-European 20, 129
Millennials are Killing Capitalism xiv, 5, 82, 261–2
Miller, Taylor 201
Milley, Mark 124–8, 214
Mills, Charles W. 86-88
   antiracist liberalism 64
   aracial 86
   racial liberalism 64
   postraciality 86
   preraciality 86
   The Racial Contract 59
   'white time' 87–8, 89
Mishra, Pankaj 232
Moms for Liberty 36
Mondon, Aurelien 40
Moore, Roxanne 186
moral panic 17, 82
Moreton-Robinson, Aileen 182, 185, 213, 216
   cultural authentication 183
   Indigenous sovereignty 118, 208
   Indigenous Studies 117
   'the possessive investment in whiteness' 41–2, 55
   white possession 184
   whiteness studies 158–9
Morris, Aldon 109
Morris, Aldon et al. 62
Morrison, Aaryan 139
Moten, Fred 177–8, 210, 261–2
Moufawad-Paul, Joshua 106

multicultural narrative 89
  see also Robinson, Cedric J.
multiculturalism xii-iii, 28, 52
  liberal 35, 200, 213
  and remaking of Black Studies 162
    see also Wynter, Sylvia
  state 184
  white supremacist use of 150
    see also Rodríguez, Dylan
Munro, Lorna 185-9
Murray, Douglas 28, 41
  Holocaust denial 220
Muslim 219, 239, 245
  association with antisemitism 143, 229, 245
  association with terrorism 226
  children 53
Muslims 233, 242-3
  violence against 228
Myers, Joshua xiv, 10, 51-3, 91, 109
  Black study 157, 162
  'conceptual incarceration' 93, 171
  racial regimes 6, 17

Nabulsi, Jamal 28, 198-9
Nabulsi, Karma 30
Nakata, Sana 205, 212
Napoleon 85-6, 246
nationalism
  American 56, 94
  anticolonial 203
  Herrenvolk 198, 204
  'patriotic left' embrace of 107
  racism and 20
  white supremacist 28
national apology, the 113
  see also Stolen Generations
National Conservatism Conference 77, 82, 101, 108
national liberation 91
Native Title Act, the 182, 183
  see also Australia; Indigenous; terra nullius
Ndlovu, Morgan 215-6
Neiman, Susan 233, 252
neoliberal 83, 163
  elites 5
  university 218

neoliberalism 66, 225, 233
  and 'primitive accumulation of whiteness' 243
Netanyahu, Binyamin 138
New Antisemitism, The 144
Newsom, Gavin 145
  see also ethnic studies
Newton, Huey P. 136
New York Times, the 47, 92, 94, 98, 103, 233
  see also *1619 Project*, the
Nexus Document, the 227
Ngata, Tina 179
Nichols, Robert 18, 115
  see also Indigenous dispossession; recursivity
Niemuth, Niles et al. 101-2, 107
Nolan, Lindy 189, 190
North, David 101, 102
Northern Territory Emergency Response 113, 114
  see also Australia
nuance 78, 79, 174, 176, 216
  see also Healey, Kieran; Shatz, Adam

Obermaier, Lena 230
October 7, 2023 125, 127, 133
Okihiro, Gary 163
  see also ethnic studies
Omar, Abdaljawad 169, 174, 176
ontological position 84, 89
'Open Letter from Black Faculty' 214
Orbán, Viktor 108, 222
Orientalism 168, 225, 251, 254, 256
Orly, Aidan 179
Özyürek, Esra 229, 232

Page, Susan 207-8
Painter, Nell Irvin 98
Palestine 3, 199, 204, 218, 220, 243, 259
  academic silence about 165
    see also Crenshaw, Kimberlé W.
  Anti-Defamation League's role in restricting aid to 142
  attacks on education about 146-8

attempted erasure of 251
Black solidarity with 135
Du Bois and 168
Indigenous solidarity with 178
problem of, the 246, 261–2
question of, the 216
solidarity with 201
Palestine Action 28
Palestine Legal 142
Palestine Research Centre 30, 253
  see also Sayegh, Fayez
Palestinian(s) 28, 140, 173, 199, 214, 216–17, 243, 249, 250, 251
  authors 176
  Bedouin 210–11, 212
  erasure of 253
  repression of 129, 230, 247, 254, 255
  scholars 256
  violence against 244
Palestinian critique 257
  see also Ayyash, M. Muhannad
Palheta, Ugo 221, 245–6
Palma, Nuno 80
Parents Defending Education 36
Paresky, Pamela 144
Partridge, Damani 230
'patriotic socialism' 107, 108
Paty, Samuel 40, 245–6
Pearson, Luke 120
Pearson, Noel 185, 188
Peller, Gary 159
Penslar, Derek 194, 214–16
Peris, Nova 178–9, 181–2
Pioneer Fund, the 66
police 35, 53
  beating of Rodney King 161
  killing 117
  Israeli 3
  violence against pro-Palestine action 129–30, 144, 165
policing 250
  schools 53–5
Policy Exchange 53
Porat, Dina et al. 248, 249
Porter, Ronald K. 29
postcolonialism 40, 215
  Zionist misuses of 195, 216
  see also Penslar, Derek

postcolonial studies 215
  see also Robinson, Cedric J.
postracial 3, 86
  see also Mills, Charles W.
Povey, Rhonda et al. 206
Povinelli, Elizabeth 213
Prasad, Madhava 216
presentism 99, 102
  see also history
Prevent 54, 55
primitive accumulation 'of whiteness' 240–6
prisons 114, 259, 262
  and capitalism 260
  Gaza as 125
  Israeli 259–60
  see also Burton, Orisanmi; Daqqa, Walid; Farraj, Basil; Gilmore, Ruth Wilson; Gilmore, Craig
progress 55, 61, 72, 74, 84, 87, 89, 96, 99
pro-Palestine speech/action 129, 130–1, 152
  conflation of with threats to Jewish safety 148, 230
  counterinsurgency against 136, 140, 176, 257
  in educational settings 131
  Germany 130
  Harvard 45, 138–9
  see also Gay, Claudine
  positioning of Indigenous politics against 181, 188, 193, 196
  repression of 223, 228–230
  student encampments 28, 144, 209
  use of the war on CRT against 150
  'woke threat' of 2
public education, attacks on 69, 70, 76
Pugliese, Joseph 181
Pulitzer 94, 95, 103
  see also 1619 Project, the

Quadrant 112
Quan, H.L.T. xiii, 50, 123
Quillette Magazine 108

Rabaka, Reiland 81, 166

race
　American problem of 65
　British sociology of 151
　chaotic nature of 3, 120
　and class 23, 103, 106, 242
　comparative approach to 154
　debate on 50
　in decolonial theory 238
　euphemisms for 205
　and European civilisation 20
　　see also Robinson, Cedric J.
　evolving discursive expression of 74
　French rejection of 61
　history of 18–19, 87, 88
　and identity 73, 148
　instability of 18
　and liberalism 64
　litheness of 26, 76
　　see also Hall, Stuart
　Marxist approaches to 238
　materiality of 74
　as modern 20, 21
　and moralism 101
　movies 10
　multiple articulations of 240
　origins of 17, 21
　polarisation around 66
　pre-modern roots of 21–2, 238–9
　　see also Heng, Geraldine
　proto-capitalism and 242
　recursivity of 18, 23, 50
　　see also recursivity
　relational theorisations of 224
　and representation 5
　science 16, 204, 238
　as a social construct 19
　sociology of 156
　structural account of 72
　studies of 158
　subjectification of Indigenous
　　people through 216
　as a system of global rule 9
　in *Tarzan* 14
　Taxonomies of 61
　teaching on 41
　theories of 153
　and time 80–93

'Race Marxist' 43, 60, 68
　see also Lindsay, James
racialisation 239, 240
　of Black people 9
　Jewish 241
　　see also Heng, Geraldine
　negative 257
　neoliberalism 23, 71, 188
　self- 216
racial capitalism 76
　Australian 190
　Cedric Robinson's conception of
　　17–20, 22, 71, 178, 223
　　see also Black Marxism
　European origins of 223, 236,
　　238–9, 241
　　see also Bjelić, Dušan; Robinson,
　　Cedric J.; Virdee, Satnam
　ideology of 72, 89
　racial liberalism and 65
　recursivity and 17–24
　slavery 79, 238–9
　US 103
　war on CRT and 43
　war on terror and 243
　western civilisation and 194
　western dominance and 225
　western Marxism's misunderstand-
　　ing of 238
　Zionism as apotheosis of 193–4
Racial Discrimination Act, suspension
　of 113, 114
　see also Australia
racial gaslighting 254, 255
　see also anti-Palestinian racism
racial liberalism 60–66, 76, 88, 166
racial reckoning 1, 12
racial regime(s) 1, 7, 15, 25, 28, 30,
　46, 65
　analytic 6–9
　concealment of the history of 224–5
　'constant trembles in' 124, 169
　contradictory capacities of the 169
　as constructed social systems 6
　'covering conceit of' 6, 27
　early twentieth century 14
　framework of 17

INDEX

history and 88, 120
Hollywood 10–11
idea of 15
'mechanisms of assembly' of 47, 169, 234
methodology 9–15
motion pictures 10
new 10
nineteenth century 10
racial capitalism and 17–18, 24, 76, 236
  see also racial capitalism
recalibration 4, 31, 50, 129, 142, 160, 171, 176, 191, 193, 195, 256, 262
recursivity of the 55, 56
repair 55
representation 5
resistance to 29, 120, 170, 191
and transformation of capital 10
undiscoverability of 120, 170, 222
war on CRT and 65, 71, 82, 91
weak points of the 9, 169, 172
Zionism and 28, 215
and Zionist use of the war on CRT 150
  see also Robinson, Cedric J.
racial rule 239–40, 243
racialised outsider, the 231, 233
'racialized outsider', the 19, 225
  see also Virdee, Satnam
racism
  America's history of 49
  as 'individualistic failure' 200
    see also Salaita, Steven
  anti-Arab 254
  antiblack 224
  anti-Irish 21
  Australian 118
  crisis 26
    see also Balibar, Étienne
  co-constitutive 21
  colonial 237, 238
  as endemic to the US 101
    see also critical race theory
  epistemic 202
  Eurocentric conception of 86
  and Europe 76, 225
  experiences of 51, 70
  German 232
  as isolated events 85
  nationalism and 20
  naturalisation of 7
  as opposed to antiracism 25
  as past 86
  as a 'plague' 102
    see also Fanon, Frantz
  'reverse' 38, 138
  state 141, 155
  studies 154–5
  systemic 11, 36, 42, 60, 89, 193
  and time 75, 83, 86
  universalist vision of 59
  as volitional 141
  white 56, 96
  Zionism and 253, 254
racist
  Britain as least 83
  calling Black people 134
  'conception of difference' 257
    see also Bruns, Claudia
  representations 10, 12, 13
    see also Disney
  responses to Black-led mobilisation 256
  states 155
  stereotypes of Indigenous people 113
  systems in France and Germany 239
Rademaker, Laura 206, 212
Rao, Aditi 143, 169–70
Reagan, Ronald 59, 76
Recognise campaign, the 187, 190
  see also Australia; Indigenous
reconciliation 122, 189
  Action Plan 188
    see also Australia; Indigenous
Reconciliation Australia 184
  see also Leibler, Mark
Reconquista 239
Reconstruction Era 16, 109
  see also Du Bois, W.E.B.
recursivity 18, 24, 50, 55, 257

see also Indigenous dispossession; Nichols, Robert; race; racial capitalism; racial regimes
Reed, Adolph 101, 103
Reed, Alison
  'gentrifying disciplines' 132
Rees, Yves 119
reformism 4, 105, 151
resistance 51, 171, 193
  anticolonial 24, 125
  inhabitation of 193
  Black 50-1, 81
  Black radical thought as 18
  of the enslaved 105
  Indigenous 31, 51, 115, 118, 120, 195, 202
  Palestinian 4, 136, 169, 174, 194, 216, 217, 225, 258
  to racial regimes 170, 191
Revolutionary Communist Party 69
  see also Spiked
Richmond, Michael 110, 133-4, 200
Ritter, David 183, 184
Roberts-Smith, Ben 37-8
Robinson, Cedric J. 13, 16, 20, 71, 105, 120
  'Appropriation of Frantz Fanon, The' 173, 216-17
    see also Fanon, Frantz
  Black Marxism xii, xvi, 17-20, 22, 77, 90, 103, 108, 178
  Black radical scholarship 22
  Black radical time 81, 92
  Black Radical Tradition, the 4, 5, 7, 17, 120
  Blaxploitation 192-3
  cinema 10, 55, 192
    see also film
  critique of Marxist historiography 103
  Davis, Angela 192-3
  Du Bois, W.E.B. 107-109, 168
  Europe 72, 162, 236-238, 240
  'First Attack is an Attack on Culture, The' 219, 227, 261-2
  Forgeries of Memory and Meaning 4-5, 6, 9-11, 12, 15-18, 192

'Invention of the Negro, the' 15-16, 73
multiculturalism 52
new history 90-91, 108, 122
new theory of history 91
  see also history
new theory 77, 90, 108
'Notes Toward a Native Theory of History' 9
'ontological totality' 177
order 17, 91, 173, 192
  terms of, the 227
  of things, the 35, 50, 81, 90, 93, 171
'Ota Benga's Flight Through Geronimo's Eyes' xii, xiii, 52, 89
political correctness 51-2
postcolonialism 215-17
race 2, 3, 20, 224, 238
racialism 17, 19, 20, 72-3, 173, 223, 237, 238, 240
racial capitalism 17, 19, 223, 236, 241
racial regimes 2, 6, 169, 222, 225, 234
revolutionary consciousness 178
Robinson, Elizabeth P. 3
Robinson, Tommy 220
Rodinson, Maxime 253
Rodríguez, César "Che" 7
Rodríguez, Dylan 133
  counterinsurgency 128, 169, 172
  hate 140-1
  multicultural white supremacy 8
  'white reconstruction' 128, 150
Rojas, Fabio 157-8
Rolfe, Zachary 37
Rosenfeld, Arno 133, 136, 140
Rowse, Tim 185, 206, 212
Royal Commission into Aboriginal Deaths in Custody 37
Rubin, Daniel Ian 146
Rufo, Christopher 13, 44-5, 47, 50, 59, 66, 67, 127, 138
  see also war on critical race theory or CRT, the

Sahhar, Micaela 181

INDEX

Said, Edward 170, 199–200, 215, 217, 244, 256
Sakai, J. 105–6
Salaita, Steven 193, 198, 200, 254
Samidoun 229, 257, 260
Samudzi, Zoe 232
Sand, Shlomo 198
Satia, Priya 81, 99–100
Saunders, Grant Leigh 186
Sayed, Hamza 53
Sayegh, Fayez 125, 253
Sayigh, Yezid 176
Schleger, Fred 104
scholasticide 30
   see also Palestine
Scottsboro Boys, the 191
Sela, Rona 30
self-determination 178, 196, 203–5, 212
   Indigenous 190, 202–3, 205–8
   in Indigenous education 210, 213
   language of 196, 197, 200
   Lenin's conception of 203–4
   South Africa 203
   Wilsonian deployment of 203
   Zionist assertions of 195, 203
   see also Foley, Gary; Massad, Joseph
settler colonialism 7, 178, 189, 202
   Australian 122
   brown-washing of 197
   common experiences of 199
   Europe 249, 252
   see also Younes, Anna
   Indigenous dispossession under 18
   Israeli 155, 160, 172
   rejection of the interpretive framework of 177
   South African 156
   US 154, 160
settler societies 194
Serwer, Adam 97
Seymour, Richard 70
Sharansky, Natan 133, 134
Sharma, Nandita Rani 181
Shatz, Adam 174–6, 216

Simpson, Leanne Betasamosake 43, 195, 206
Sinanan, Kerry 176
slavery 64, 65, 72, 73, 77–80, 82, 83, 97–8, 107
   abolition of 63, 74, 75, 78
   see also abolitionism
   end of 16, 62, 76, 104, 105
   as foundational to the US 96, 99–100, 101, 103, 107
   see also 1619 Project, the; Du Bois, W.E.B.; Hannah-Jones, Nikole; Horne, Gerald
   intra-European 238–9
   'racialised labour' 236
   reinstatement of 86
   teaching the history of 25, 32, 42, 43, 78
   attacks on 88, 99
slaves 16, 20, 80
   freed 15, 102
   insurgent 64
   mass uprising of 177
   see also enslaved people
slave trade, the 80, 90, 238
   African involvement in 79
   ivory- 75–6
   transatlantic 78
   transformation of 75
Smith, Evan 36
Smith, Shelda Jane et al. 107
socialist(s) 109, 203
Sojoyner, Damien M. 54, 83, 92, 171
solidarity 199
   cross-racial worker 92
   Indigenous 188
   of Indigenous people with migrants 181
   interracial 105
   of Jews with other negatively racialised peoples 252
   transnational 213
   see also Palestine; Black-Jewish; class
Spiked 36, 69, 82, 108
Sriprakash, Arathi et al. 39, 122
StandWithUs 144

Stasiulis, Daiva 194
Stefancic, Jean 66
Stefanic, Elise 139
    see also Harvard
Starkey, David 82
Stewart-Assheton, Keiran 189, 195
    see also Black Peoples Union
Stokes, Doug 81
Stolen Generations, the 112, 113, 114
    see also Australia; Indigenous
Stop Cop City 28
Stovall, Tyler 61
Strakosch, Elizabeth 206
Student Nonviolent Coordinating Committee 141–2
Sweet, James 78, 79, 92, 98–9, 102
    see also American Historical Association; *1619 Project*, the; presentism
Sydney Morning Herald, the 38
Synot, Eddie 185

Taal, Momodou xiv, 165
Taguieff, Pierre-André 143
Talebi, Tessa 231
Tatour, Lana 155, 210
Taylor, Keeanga-Yamahtta 139, 142
Temin, David Myer 206
terra nullius 183
Tévanien, Pierre 86
Third World Liberation Front, 163
Thomas, Kendall 134
Thorpe, Bill 112
time 75, 80–93
    historical events as being of their 99
    linearity of 84, 89
    passage of 99
    and racial capitalism 83
    western 90
    see also Black radical time; deep time; history; race; white time
Titley, Gavan 23, 42, 52, 71
Tombs, Robert 82–3
Too Black 1, 171–2
Toscano, Alberto xii

Trachtenberg, Barry 251
Traverso, Enzo 231
Troen, Ilan 194, 198
Troen, Carol 194, 198
Trojan Horse Affair, the 53
Trouillot, Michel-Rolph 104
Trump, Donald J. xiii, 3, 44, 58, 69, 70, 94, 96–97, 100
Trudgett, Michelle 207–8
truth-telling 39, 88, 111, 115, 165, 186, 213
Tuck, Eve 175
Turner, Kieron 20

UC Ethnic Studies Faculty Council 145–7
UCLA Forward Tracking Project 48
UK riots 2024 219–20, 225, 243
Uluru 186
    Dialogue 185
    process 186
    regional consultation 185, 186
    Statement from the Heart, the 185
Unconscious bias 56, 231
    training 1
United Nations Declaration of the Rights of Indigenous People (UNDRIP) 207, 208, 212
United States of America or US, the 15, 48, 63, 64, 95, 92, 96, 99, 101, 106, 159
    Constitution of 126
    Department of State 247
    interests of 134
    founders of 97
    military 126, 128
    post-revolutionary 14
    support for Israel/Zionism 125, 247
UN Sustainable Development Goals 211
universalism 61, 89
universities 28, 142, 175, 209–10, 247
    built on occupied Indigenous land 210
    as colonial institutions 195
    land grab 208–9
USians 101

INDEX

van Rossum, Matthias 79
Vaughn-Roberson, Clayton 135, 137
Vidal, Frédérique 40
violence 112, 240
   against Jews in the Middle Ages 242
   as essential to accumulation 242
   of imperialism 240
   of racial segregation 58
   schools as a site of 54
   state 28, 256
   white mob 86, 115
Virdee, Satnam 19, 21, 236–40
Visualising Palestine 250

Wallach, Yair 251
Walt, Stephen 150
war on antisemitism, the 128–9, 135, 221, 228
   see also Younes, Anna
war on critical race theory 1, 24, 28, 39, 41, 44, 46, 49, 72, 76
   and book bans 83
   and war on antisemitism, the 128, 147, 156
   see also war on CRT
war on CRT, the 50, 51, 83, 85, 88, 91, 92, 98, 110, 125, 147
   anti-CRT warriors 75, 100–1, 144
   Zionist use of 150
   see also war on critical race theory
war on drugs 3, 135, 221
war on terror 221, 226, 228, 233, 243
Watson, Irene 184, 187, 190
Welsh, James Michael 'Widdy' 111
west, the 82, 90, 108
   leftists in 174
   liberal or leftist structures in 178
West, Cornel 59
white
   ignorance 74
   see also Mills, Charles W.
   innocence 18
   left 65, 105, 110
   lies 111
   mythologies 192

   nationalist 147
   people 87, 106, 111
   possessive power
      see also Moreton-Robinson, Aileen
   privilege 36
   rage 126, 128
   settlers 111
   settlerism 132
'white genocide' 41
whiteness 55, 100, 108, 113
   new 8, 14
   see also Forgeries of Memory and Meaning
   studies 158
   US American 105
'whitelash' 54
white supremacy 51, 61, 100, 137, 139, 142, 150, 224, 233
   global 128
   global imperialist 160
   recalibration of, the 8, 43, 81, 218
   US 43
   Zionism and 150, 222
white supremacist 2, 26, 28
   Europe 129
   mobilisation for Zionism 150
   settler colony
   terrorism 250
white supremacists 16
Wilentz, Sean 109
Williams, Eric Eustace 72, 79
Willoughby-Herard, Tiffany 148, 151–2
Wilson, Ralph 68, 71, 83
Wind, Maya 210
Windschuttle, 112–3, 116
woke 47
   anti- 89, 82, 89
   capital 45
   educators 41
   ideology 133, 135
   racism 71
   threat 2
   war on 1, 43
Woke Antisemitism 133
wokeisme, le 1

wokeness
  anti- 1, 2, 49, 50
    see also Kelley, Robin D.G.
  rejection of 107
Wolfe, Patrick 19, 155, 204
Woman King, the 78, 99
Woodson Center, the 96
world fairs 16
  see also Forgeries of Memory and Meaning
Wright, Michelle M. 98
Wynter, Sylvia 104
  classificatory logic 161
  culture 84
  homo economicus 62
  'No Humans Involved' 161–2, 214
  order of knowledge 152

X, Malcolm 59–60

Yiftachel, Oren 210–11
Yifatchel, Oren et al. 211
Yorta Yorta, the 183
  see also Australia; Indigenous; terra nullius
Younes, Anna 128–9, 135, 160, 221, 228, 233, 235, 247–52
  see also Germany; war on antisemitism
Younge, Gary 59–60
Yunkaporta, Tyson 89
Yuval-Davis, Nira 194

Zine, Jasmin 258

Zionism 28, 125, 128, 129, 132, 189, 193–4, 248, 252, 253, 256, 261, 262
  and the *Anti-Defamation League* 147
  Afro- 135
  anti- 251, 142, 147, 251
  as an 'anticolonial movement' 194, 215
    see also Penslar, Derek
  exceptionalisation of 194
  and fascism 218
  and Indigenous people 179–80, 187, 190, 193
  liberal 224, 251
  and postcolonialism 214
    see also Penslar, Derek
  as racial rule 244
  as 'self-determination' 198
  'from the standpoint of its victims' 170, 215
    see also Said, Edward
  as western ideology 244
  and western imperialism 172
  and white supremacy 150, 160
Zionist
  Christian 180
  colony in Palestine 3
  involvement in Indigenous politics 213
  as a protected category/identity 142, 248
Zreik, Raef 211
Zuckerman, Phil 62

The Pluto Press Newsletter

Hello friend of Pluto!

Want to stay on top of the best radical books we publish?

Then sign up to be the first to hear about our new books, as well as special events, podcasts and videos.

You'll also get 50% off your first order with us when you sign up.

Come and join us!

Go to bit.ly/PlutoNewsletter